www.wadsworth.com

www.wadsworth.com is the World Wide Web site for
Thomson Wadsworth and is your direct source to dozens
of online resources.

At *www.wadsworth.com* you can find out about supplements, demonstration software, and student resources.
You can also send e-mail to many of our authors and pre-
view new publications and exciting new technologies.

www.wadsworth.com
Changing the way the world learns[®]

Contemporary
Political Ideologies

A Comparative Analysis

Thirteenth Edition

LYMAN TOWER SARGENT
University of Missouri—St. Louis

THOMSON
™
WADSWORTH

Australia • Brazil • Canada • Mexico • Singapore • Spain
United Kingdom • United States

THOMSON
™
WADSWORTH

*Contemporary Political Ideologies: A Comparative
Analysis,* Thirteenth Edition
Lyman Tower Sargent

Publisher: Clark Baxter
Executive Editor: David Tatom
Associate Development Editor:
  Rebecca F. Green
Editorial Assistants: Cheryl C. Lee and
  Eva Dickerson
Technology Project Manager:
  Michelle Vardeman
Marketing Manager: Janise Fry
Marketing Assistant: Teresa Jessen
Marketing Communications Manager:
  Kelley McAllister
Project Manager, Editorial Production:
  Christine Sosa

Creative Director: Rob Hugel
Art Director: Maria Epes
Print Buyer: Barbara Britton
Permissions Editor: Sarah Harkrader
Production Service: International
  Typesetting and Composition
Photo Researcher: Stephen Forsling
Cover Designer: Jeanette Barber
Cover Image: Collier Campbell
  Lifeworks/CORBIS
Cover Printer: Webcom
Compositor: International Typesetting
  and Composition
Printer: Webcom

Thomson Higher Education
10 Davis Drive
Belmont, CA 94002-3098
USA

For more information about our products,
contact us at:
**Thomson Learning Academic
Resource Center
1-800-423-0563**

For permission to use material from this
text or product, submit a request online at
http://www.thomsonrights.com.

Any additional questions about permissions
can be submitted by e-mail to
thomsonrights@thomson.com.

Library of Congress Control Number:
  2005925745

ISBN 0-534-60241-X

To Evan

Contents

II NATIONALISM

About the Author

Lyman Tower Sargent is professor of political science at the University of Missouri–St. Louis and honorary research fellow at the University of London. He has been a fellow at the Institute for Advanced Study, Princeton; a visiting professor at the University of Exeter, England, the University of East Anglia, England, and Victoria University of Wellington, New Zealand; an academic visitor at the London School of Economics and Political Science; and an associate of the Stout Research Centre for New Zealand, Victoria University of Wellington, New Zealand.

Sargent is the author of *New Left Thought: An Introduction* (Dorsey, 1972); *Techniques of Political Analysis* (with Thomas A. Zant, Wadsworth, 1970); *British and American Utopian Literature, 1516–1985: An Annotated, Chronological Bibliography* (Garland, 1988); *New Zealand Utopian Literature: An Annotated Bibliography* (Stout Research Centre, 1997); *New Zealand Intentional Communities: A Research Guide* (Stout Research Centre, 1997); *Living in Utopia: Intentional Communities in New Zealand* (with Lucy Sargisson, Ashgate, 2004); and numerous articles in political theory. He is the editor of *Consent: Concept, Capacity, Conditions, Constraints* (Franz Steiner Verlag, 1979); *Extremism in America: A Reader* (New York University Press, 1995); *Political Thought in the United States: A Documentary History* (New York University Press, 1997); *The Utopia Reader* (with Gregory Claeys, New York University Press, 1999); and *Utopia: The Quest for the Ideal Society in the Western World* (with Roland Schaer and Gregory Claeys, Oxford University Press, 2000).

Preface

According to Feliks Gross, political ideologies have replaced religion as the focus of both human liberation and human fanaticism,[1] and in this book the essential features of a wide range of ideologies, such as *nationalism, democracy,* and *feminism,* are presented so they can be easily understood. To the extent possible, they are described as they are understood by their believers, together with some of the criticism by their opponents. In addition, each ideology is shown in the context of contemporary political and social issues and institutions. My goal is to help readers draw their own conclusions about each ideology based on a reasonably balanced presentation of that ideology and how it functions today.

This book was first published in the period known as the Sixties (in the United States, roughly 1965–75), when Americans were first becoming aware of ideological debate in the United States. Americans had taken pride in being free of ideological conflicts, and compromise was thought to be the essential component of U.S. politics. Many outside the United States saw this very belief as identifying a dominant U.S. ideology, and few Americans would today argue that political debate in this country is free from ideology. And, as I write in 2005, the United States is more deeply divided ideologically than at any time in its history.

Therefore, to understand what is happening both in the United States and the rest of the world, it is important to understand the ideologies that inform

---

[1]Feliks Gross, *Ideologies, Goals, and Values* (Westport, CT: Greenwood Press, 1985), xxiii.

the thought and actions of both politicians and average citizens. Today it is clearly essential that we understand how others think, and this book is designed to help that process.

Understanding ideologies can also help us understand ourselves and what we believe. Self-identity—who we are and how we came to be who we are—is a question that most of us face at various times in our lives. When we are students we are finding out who we are or creating ourselves, and part of that process of identity building is achieved through identification with like-minded others. Along with that identification often comes a set of beliefs, which sometimes constitutes an ideology. Later in life, we may reaffirm or change whom we identify with, and that change may bring a change in beliefs.

At the same time, many people are unaware of what different groups of people believe. I have heard many women say, "I am not a feminist, but . . . ," finishing the sentence with a statement that comes straight from feminism. The person is rejecting the stereotype of feminism, but not understanding the actual beliefs. When I have asked women who have used the phrase "I am not a feminist" about specific positions taken by most feminists, they have most often agreed with the feminist position. Because stereotypes are used as part of political debate to distort the position of an opponent, it is important to know the actual positions.

Ideologies are reflected in political institutions and policies and are often used as tools, both consciously and unconsciously, by political actors. Ideologies change over time, reflecting both reconsideration of the principles or core beliefs found in the ideologies and how practical political issues influence these beliefs. Thus the reader will find here much discussion of current political debates throughout the world to illustrate how ideologies affect politics and are affected by it.

Since the first edition of *Contemporary Political Ideologies: A Comparative Analysis* was published over thirty-five years ago, it has been the leading text in the field. The book has undergone dramatic changes over the years. In this latest incarnation, the structure of the book is very similar to that of the previous edition, but the content has changed because the lived experience of ideologies has changed. Most ideologies have become constellations of beliefs, with core beliefs and values but also with huge disagreements over how those beliefs and values fit together and how peripheral beliefs and values fit with the core.

This edition adds a substantial discussion of globalization, which, although it is too early to be certain, may be an emerging ideology. It also has an expanded discussion of political Islam to reflect both the continuing growth in importance of this constellation of beliefs and the strengthening of disagreements among its adherents. Even though there is disagreement over whether it should be considered an ideology, nationalism continues to be so important that it not only cannot be excluded but has even been expanded slightly. Also, because of its role in the antiglobalization movement, anarchism has become more important, and a brief section on that role has been added.

The most extensive revisions have been brought about by the responses of the ideologies to the threat of terrorism, particularly the responses within contemporary democracies. The disagreements over the appropriate way to respond to the possibility of terrorism have led to both the reconsideration and rein-forcement of essential characteristics of democracy, and these are considered at some length. Also, although terrorism is a tactic not an ideology, the "Note on Terrorism" introduced in the last edition has been expanded slightly. Through-out the book, I have added material to give a better understanding of the his-torical context in which ideas developed and changed, but the focus remains on the current situation.

I have maintained the essential character of the book as a comparative intro-duction to the dominant and some minor ideologies found in the world today. As always, I have included extensive lists of suggested reading so that readers can explore further questions that interest them. I have appended brief notes to some of the items indicating the subject or argument. I have expanded the list of websites in the suggested reading, but anyone familiar with the Web will know that some of these addresses will not be valid throughout the life of the book (as was true with the previous edition); however, I have tried to choose ones that seem likely to have a substantial life. As with the lists of suggested reading, these sites include both those designed to present information and those designed to advocate a position.

ACKNOWLEDGMENTS

Obviously I have accumulated an infinite number of debts in writing thirteen editions, debts much too numerous to mention. But I am also indebted to people who have helped me on this edition, so I want to thank Leesa Althen, who has learned the delights of fact checking and updating information and scoured the WWW for new sites while checking all the old ones; Chrystalla Ellina of Cyprus College, Nicosia, Cyprus, who provided information on the proce-dures the new countries have gone through in joining the European Union; Peter Fitting for information on the Zapatistas; and Deirdre Ni Chuanacháin and Jennifer Horan for pointing out needed changes.

Wadsworth and I would also like to thank the reviewers for the thirteenth edition: Earl Sheridan, University of North Carolina at Wilmington; Raymond B. Wrabley, Jr., University of Pittsburgh at Johnstown; and Louis C. Zuccarello, Marist College.

Contemporary Political Ideologies

1

Ideologies

What Are They and Why Study Them?

On September 11, 2001, terrorists attacked the World Trade Center in New York and the Pentagon in Washington, D.C., killing thousands of people. How could anyone justify such an act? In July 2001 a young man was killed in Genoa, Italy, while protesting at the so-called G-8 (Group of 8) meeting.[1] Although only a few hundred of the protestors used violence, thousands more opposed the actions of these world leaders. The leaders are certain that they are right and the protestors wrong; the protestors are certain that they are right and the leaders wrong. Why? Today the same group that attacked New York and Washington regularly threatens to attack other sites in the United States and has attacked many U.S. sites overseas. Why?

The answer to these questions is *ideology*. The attacks on the World Trade Center and the Pentagon and the threats that continue today reflect conflicts in the Middle East, all of which have strong ideological components. The protestors in Genoa came from many different groups, with varying agendas, but they all agreed that the assembled world leaders were damaging or destroying something they held dear (the environment, poor countries, poor people, and so forth).

---

[1] The G-7, or Group of Seven, is composed of the seven leading industrialized nations in the world: Canada, France, Germany, Italy, Japan, the United Kingdom, and the United States. The heads of state or government of these countries first met in 1975 as the G-6 (Canada joined in 1976) and have met annually since, with regular meetings of lower-level officials between the annual meetings. The G-8 is composed of those countries plus Russia. *Industrialized* is defined as having the resources and the ability to guide the world. In late 2004, the G-7 met with and in China as a probable first step toward China joining.

Most of the leaders believed that their actions were actually good for the environment, poor countries, poor people, and so forth. Because it is unlikely that both groups are right, it is necessary to look further at these beliefs. The purpose of this book is to provide some understanding of the beliefs that lie behind these actions and other issues and conflicts that flare up and die down repeatedly in all parts of the world.

Of course ideology is not the only thing that divides or unites people; race, ethnicity, religion, gender, class, national and regional identification, and many other things both pull people together and push people apart. But ideology is one of those things, and understanding how ideology works and the content of various significant ideologies is important if we are to understand what happens in the world. In addition, because we are influenced by ideology whether we are aware of it or not, understanding these ideologies will help us understand our own beliefs as well as those of our friends and associates.

We are surrounded by expressions of ideology. Our parents try to influence our thinking, as do our friends, teachers, religious leaders, and politicians. When we read newspapers or magazines, listen to the radio, or watch TV, we are getting partial views that are consciously or unconsciously distorted. Because these sources of information often disagree, we are exposed to a range of ideologies, and, in the development of our own set of beliefs, we may be influenced by a variety of ideologies.

As we grow older, we also make conscious choices among beliefs and attitudes, either because we weigh one position against another and conclude that one is preferable according some standard, or because we simply respect or dislike someone who holds that belief. Through this process of influence and choice, we gradually come to the set of beliefs and attitudes with which we live. This set of beliefs may change, but it changes less as we age. This happens because the experiences of a lifetime have led us to these views, and it is extraordinarily difficult to set aside what we have come to believe to be the truth and accept that we have been wrong. Some people do reach such conclusions, usually because they encounter someone whose life experiences have led to different conclusions, thus forcing a reevaluation of their beliefs.

How do we identify an ideology? The most obvious way is through particular words that are associated with the ideology. For example, someone influenced by capitalism will usually speak favorably of the free market, and someone influenced by Marxism will use the word *class* in specific ways.

IDEOLOGY DEFINED

Scholars disagree over the meaning and importance of ideology. One has even written, "ideology is the most elusive concept in the whole of social science."[2] As a result, today ideology is itself what we have come to call an *essentially contested*

---

[2] David McLellan, *Ideology*, 2nd ed. (Minneapolis: University of Minnesota Press, 1995), 1.

concept, or a concept about which there is truly fundamental disagreement.[3] (One study of ideology from the early 1990s listed sixteen definitions as currently in use, some of which are mutually exclusive.[4]) Most political debate swirls around such contested concepts, and all the ideologies discussed here contain one or more of them.

This section constructs a definition of *ideology,* distinguishes political ideologies from other ideologies, and shows how political ideology relates to political theory and political philosophy. Finally, a few of the most important theorists of ideology are presented, and some current controversies among theorists are described.

An ideology is a system of values and beliefs regarding the various institutions and processes of society that is accepted as fact or truth by a group of people. An ideology provides the believer with a picture of the world both as it is and as it should be, and, in doing so, organizes the tremendous complexity of the world into something fairly simple and understandable. Ideologies are organized or patterned beliefs. The degree of organization and the simplicity of the resulting picture vary considerably from ideology to ideology, and the ever-increasing complexity of the world tends to blur the pictures. At the same time, however, the fundamental pattern of each ideology remains fairly constant.

Ideologies are stories about the world we live in and our place in it. When we tell a story, we structure information to communicate our understanding of something to someone else. Stories can, of course, be "tall tales" or lies, but they are still trying to present a pattern that can be accepted as true. An obvious "tall tale" depends on our recognizing it as such; a lie works only if the hearer believes it to be true.

As in traditional stories, ideologies present a coherent, understandable picture of that world. Believers, telling the story of their beliefs, are, they think, telling the truth; it is up to the reader, viewer, or listener to sort truth from falsehood. When we read a story, we often suspend our disbelief in it, and at least while we are still reading, watching the film or video, or playing the computer game, the story becomes real. Some people so want a story to be real that they lose themselves in it and try to change their world to be like the story rather than to accept its untruth. Although the best-known cases of this are connected with sophisticated computer games, the political stories we are taught that become ideologies have the same effect on many people.

A *political ideology* is, in its simplest formulation, an ideology that focuses on the political. The political system is the way that societies make decisions about their most important values; one scholar defines the political system as "the

[3] See W. B. Gallie, "Essentially Contested Concepts," *Proceedings of the Aristotelian Society,* n.s., 56 (1955–56): 167–98; and William E. Connolly, *The Terms of Political Discourse,* 3rd ed. (Princeton, NJ: Princeton University Press, 1993). Discussions of the problems connected with this idea can be found in Terence Ball, "Political Theory and Conceptual Change," *Political Theory: Tradition and Diversity,* ed. Andrew Vincent (Cambridge: Cambridge University Press, 1997), 34–36; and Andrew Vincent, *The Nature of Political Theory* (Oxford: Oxford University Press, 2004), 98–104.

[4] Terry Eagleton, *Ideology: An Introduction* (London: Verso, 1991), 10–30.

authoritative allocation of values" for a society.[5] Another scholar titled a famous book *Politics: Who Gets What, When, How* (1936);[6] the definitions are much the same. Thus it would be possible simply to insert the word *political* in front of the word *ideology* in the definition three paragraphs earlier, and the result would be a perfectly acceptable definition of *political ideology.*

This book discusses only *political* ideologies. There are two partial exceptions, two cases where the political aspects of religious belief have become important enough to require treatment: what is generally now called political Islam and Liberation Theology, which started as a political movement within the Roman Catholic church and has now spread to Protestantism and throughout the Christian world.

Political Philosophy, Political Theory, and Political Ideology

The terms *political ideology, political theory,* and *political philosophy* are frequently used to refer to different ways of thinking about political ideas. The first term, *political ideology,* relates, as we have seen, to the beliefs of a group. That term should never be used in place of either of the other two. The other two terms are often used interchangeably, with nothing lost. But at other times, it is important to distinguish between them.

When narrowly defined, *political theory* refers to theories or generalizations about politics and society that are based on data, just like any generalization in any science. *Political philosophy,* on the other hand, is explicitly evaluative or normative. It is a set of ideas about how governments and people should behave.

All three terms are connected. Every political philosophy is based in part on a political theory. In other words, every statement about how people and governments should behave contains a statement about how they do behave. In addition, every political ideology contains both political theory and political philosophy—or generalizations about how people and governments do behave and how they should behave. But in a political ideology, these generalizations become belief systems rather than empirical or normative analyses of behavior.

Whatever words are used, the important thing to remember is that there are both differences and connections between generalizations about how social and political institutions and the people making them up behave, how they should behave, and the various belief systems that emerge from such generalizations.

SOCIAL MOVEMENTS AND IDEOLOGIES

Most ideologies initially developed in association with the growth and maturation of a social movement. This is obviously the case with the initial development of democracy in the seventeenth century, Marxism and anarchism in the nineteenth

[5] David Easton, *The Political System: An Inquiry into the State of Political Science,* 2nd ed. (New York: Alfred A. Knopf, 1971), 129.

[6] Harold Lasswell, *Politics: Who Gets What, When, How* (New York: McGraw-Hill, 1936). Rpt. *With Postscript (1958)* (New York: Meridian Books, 1958).

century, and fascism and National Socialism, feminism, Liberation Theology, and environmentalism in the twentieth century. But in all cases both scholars and believers have looked back before the emergence of a movement and found precedents and precursors. In the case of nationalism, there is a fundamental dispute over whether it has been around for many centuries or just a few; and as we shall see in the next chapter, the answers lead to very different interpretations of nationalism. At present, a new ideology may be emerging that is generally called *globalization*. It has strong supporters and fierce opponents and is already affecting all the other ideologies. The opponents of globalization clearly see themselves as forming a new social movement against the powerful supporters of globalization, and it has become important to understand the positions of both.

Today, when no social movement is completely unified, one of the most hotly contested areas is the ideology of the movement. Every faction vying for power says that it has the truth. Thus, in addition to conflicts between ideologies, there are deep divisions within ideologies. Probably only an ideology that has lost its vitality could be free from such differences, and if it were, it would no longer be included in this book.

IDEOLOGY AND PRACTICE

A central concern of all students of ideology is the extent to which and the ways in which ideology affects practice. Political leaders use the language of the dominant ideology of their country to justify their actions. But are their actions based on ideology or expediency? In addition, contradictions are often apparent between the actions of out-of-power adherents of some ideologies and their actions when in power. At the same time, ideological languages came to permeate politics in the last quarter of the twentieth century; it is not all facade with no reality behind it.

The most likely effect of ideology is in limiting options. Except in extraordinary circumstances, political leaders will not perceive as options policies that fall outside their ideology. In this way ideology limits but does not determine practice. However, we have had the opportunity to witness just such an extraordinary break from ideology in Eastern Europe and the former Soviet Union. Both political leaders and ordinary citizens have struggled to free themselves from the preconceptions of communism. Some have simply accepted an alternative ideology, while others have not changed significantly.

Some people may not even notice the differences between the various sets of beliefs that influence them, but others will be so torn apart by the conflict that they develop serious mental problems. Most of us muddle through, aware that we are not completely consistent in our beliefs and behavior but not terribly bothered by that fact.

Similar situations occur within countries. In most open societies where many ideologies are recognized and accepted, conflict within the individual is unlikely to become important. But conflicts among ideologies may become obvious, and, if the numbers of adherents of conflicting ideologies are large enough and close enough in size, a country's stability can be affected. On the other hand, in a closed system with only one official ideology, an individual who holds beliefs counter to that ideology will probably be intensely aware of the difference and be affected by it. The same thing is true for the country as a whole. Ideological differences, particularly differences *within* the official ideology, become more important and can cause serious conflict.

In any society, different segments of the population will hold different ideologies. For example, within the United States today, the overwhelming majority, if asked, would call themselves believers in democracy. But some would call themselves anarchists, National Socialists, and so forth. Every society exhibits a variety of ideologies. In no case will a given society be so completely dominated by a single ideology as to have no ideological alternatives available within the system, even though alternatives may be actively suppressed by the regime.

Many of those willing to label themselves as democrats or as adherents of some other ideology do not act as the ideology predicts. But most people build up a pattern of behavior, some aspects of which come directly from the dominant political ideology of the country in which they live. For example, it is a bit surprising that people accept the outcome of elections rather than fighting for their side when they lose. But most people in countries with established democracies are so conditioned to accept loss in elections that they do so without ever thinking about revolt. Just think about the reaction to the 2000 U.S. presidential election. Even though the person who won the most votes lost the election and many people remain convinced that electoral procedures in a number of states were somewhere between inefficient and corrupt, the result was accepted with little dissent.

This acceptance is not always the rule, though. In many countries elections produce violent, sometimes successful, attempts to change the results. Such violence occurs even in democratic countries.

THEORIES OF IDEOLOGY

The word *ideology* was first used in the early 1800s by a group of French thinkers called the Ideologues to describe an approach to understanding how ideas are formed. The word was picked up by others and used mostly as a label for ways in which people block out messages that threaten them. For all these thinkers, ideologies keep people from understanding the truth about their situations. Only recently have theories of ideology generally ceased to treat ideology negatively, as an escape from or a way to hide reality. In some cases this has meant abandoning the word *ideology* for terms that carry less historical baggage. Today both social scientists and political theorists are searching for neutral definitions. The following section briefly discusses how some theorists have discussed ideology and a debate over the end of ideology in the West.

Karl Marx

Karl Marx (1818–83) argued that ideologies blind people to facts about their place in society. He described as ideological any set of political *illusions* produced by the social experiences of a *class* (that is, a social group defined by its economic role—for example, owners or workers). Marx called ideology *false consciousness*. For Marx, a person's membership in a particular class produced a picture of the world shaped by the experiences of that class. Thus it would be almost impossible for an individual class member to form an accurate conception of the world. Marx argued that *socialization* (that is, the process by which an individual comes to learn about and accept the values of the society) is strongly shaped by that person's place in the class system of that society. In other words, he contended that the social setting in which each of us lives determines the broad outlines of the way we think. The members of different classes are both directly and indirectly taught to think and behave in ways "appropriate" for their own class. This pattern is often called the *social construction of reality*. What we perceive as reality is created by the social world we inhabit; living in a different society, we would perceive a different reality. Other Marxists, like Louis Althusser (1918–90) and Antonio Gramsci (1891–1937), refined Marx's analysis and are also discussed here.

Georges Sorel

Georges Sorel (1847–1922) proposed a different approach to ideology, using the word *myth* rather than *ideology*. Sorel argued that mass movements develop visions of the future in which their members don't quite believe, but that are an essential part of what motivates them. He called these visions *myths*. Sorel focused on fairly specific myths, like the belief in the general strike prevalent among syndicalists, rather than the broader belief systems that this text calls *ideologies*. Also, as the word *myth* implies, the depth of belief in a myth is not the same as for an ideology. But myths can galvanize people and are clearly part of all ideologies.

Sigmund Freud

Sigmund Freud (1856–1939) made one point that must be noted about beliefs such as ideologies. Freud was specifically concerned with religious belief, but his comments apply equally well to political ideologies. Freud argued that although belief systems are illusions based on the distortion or repression of our psychological needs, they still provide an organized framework for explaining the world and its ills. An accepted explanation, even one that is wrong, can be comforting. Thus Freud, like Marx, saw ideologies as illusions that keep us deluded and content with a difficult, if not intolerable, condition. Freud prescribed psychoanalysis if the illusion becomes sufficiently pathological; Marx prescribed revolution.

Antonio Gramsci

A political activist and social theorist influenced by Marx and Sorel, Antonio Gramsci (1891–1937) developed most of his contributions while imprisoned by the Italian Fascists during the last eleven years of his life. Gramsci argued that the ruling classes did not need to dominate the lower classes by force because they used the institutions of socialization (schools, churches, families, and so on) to create a social *hegemony*. This means that people are socialized into viewing the world in the same way that those in the ruling class view it. Being socialized to view the world this way means that the view is accepted subconsciously, as common sense or normal, as part of everyday life.[7]

Karl Mannheim

Karl Mannheim (1893–1947), who is generally considered the foremost theorist of ideology, gave a description of ideology close to Marx's, except Mannheim attempted to avoid the negative connotations that Marx intended in his definition. For Marx, ideologies were illusions that kept members of a class from understanding their true place in society. Mannheim attempted to address the same phenomenon scientifically. He argued that ideology should be treated from two perspectives, which he labeled the "total conception" and the "particular conception" of ideology.[8]

The "total conception" is a general description of the beliefs held in common by a group, such as a social class or an age group. These beliefs are similar to the blinders on a horse, limiting the believer's view of the world to what is acceptable to the ideology. A person whose mind has been sufficiently formed by his or her membership in a group either simply does not perceive information that conflicts with the belief system or is provided by that belief system with a convenient explanation that allows the contradiction to be set aside without being recognized as a threat. For Mannheim, an ideology is produced by a failing ruling class to protect itself from the realization of its coming extinction.

The "particular conception" is a description of the situation in which people recognize the beliefs of opponents as "more or less conscious disguises of the real nature of a situation, a true recognition of which would not be in accord with his interest."[9] This is the belief that the other person's ideas, but not our own, are false representations of the world, illusions or masks that hide the truth from the believer.

Mannheim believed that intellectuals who were not frozen into a class would be capable of recognizing ideologies and of providing a synthesis of perspectives that would help to overcome ideology. For individual believers he recommended education and psychoanalysis.

Louis Althusser

Louis Althusser (1918–90) revised Marx's approach to ideology by arguing that ideology did not simply obscure or hide reality but created a new reality. One's belief system becomes part of one's life; there is no reality outside of it. The workers accept their position as the natural order, which obviously reinforces the position of the ruling class.

---

[7] See, for example, Michel De Certeau, *The Practice of Everyday Life,* trans. Steven Rendall (Berkeley: University of California Press, 1984).

[8] Karl Mannheim, *Ideology and Utopia: An Introduction to the Sociology of Knowledge,* trans. Louis Wirth and Edward Shils (1936; London: Routledge, 1991), 50.

[9] Mannheim, *Ideology and Utopia,* 49.

Clifford Geertz

In 1964 the anthropologist and social theorist Clifford Geertz (b. 1926) published an article on "Ideology as a Cultural System"[10] in which he outlined a definition of ideology as a system of symbols. Geertz, like Mannheim, was searching for a relatively neutral definition of the term that would be useful to social scientists. As an anthropologist, Geertz sees ideology deriving from culture, which produces a set of psychologically satisfying symbols that bring order to the world by providing a mechanism through which it can be understood.

Charles Taylor

The philosopher Charles Taylor (b. 1931) has recently published a book, *Modern Social Imaginaries* (2004), which uses the phrase *social imaginary* in much the way that other writers use *ideology*. Taylor says that "the social imaginary is that common understanding that makes possible common practices and a widely shared sense of legitimacy,"[11] and he says that such understandings are expressed most often in stories and myths.

Michael Freeden

The most influential scholar writing on ideology today is Michael Freeden (b. 1944), author of *Ideologies and Political Theory* (1996) and editor of the *Journal of Political Ideologies* (founded 1996). Freeden argues that ideologies are "a distinguishable and unique genre of employing and combining political concepts."[12] They are "distinctive configurations of political concepts."[13]

Each ideology has a set of core concepts, some varying over time and others remaining unchanged. Through ideologies we come to know the right meaning of justice, liberty, equality, and so forth, and we "know" that other meanings given to these concepts are wrong.

The "End of Ideology" Debate

In the 1950s and 1960s a debate started, particularly in the United States, about whether ideological politics had ended in the West.[14] In a few cases this argument went so far as to suggest that ideological politics never existed in the United States. However, even if this were once true, it no longer is, and the roots of the

---

[10] See Clifford Geertz, "Ideology as a Cultural System," in *Ideology and Discontent,* ed. David E. Apter (New York: Free Press of Glencoe, 1964), 46–76.

[11] Charles Taylor, *Modern Social Imaginaries* (Durham, NC: Duke University Press, 2004), 23.

[12] Michael Freeden, *Ideologies and Political Theory: A Conceptual Approach* (Oxford: Clarendon Press, 1996), 48. See also his more recent statement, "Editorial: What Is Special about Ideologies?" *Journal of Political Ideologies* 6, no. 1 (2001): 5–12.

[13] Freeden, *Ideologies and Political Theory,* 4.

[14] For the debate, see Mostafa Rejai, ed., *Decline of Ideology?* (Chicago: Aldine-Atherton, 1971); and Chaim I. Waxman, ed., *The End of Ideology Debate* (New York: Funk & Wagnalls, 1968). The book that gave rise to the debate in the United States was Daniel Bell, *The End of Ideology: On the Exhaustion of Political Ideas in the Fifties* (Glencoe, IL: Free Press, 1960).

contemporary situation, in which ideological politics is common, go back precisely to the time when the debate over the end of ideology was raging.

Some writers argued that not only had ideology ended in the West, but that its demise was a good thing because ideology was a bad thing. Ideological politics was seen as divisive politics—politics that made compromise impossible, that drove people apart. Ideology also hindered Western progress toward the "good society." Had ideology not gotten in the way, a better society might have been possible in the near future through the usual practices of compromise politics.

The end of ideology, to the extent it existed at all, is better labeled the *exhaustion with ideology*. By the late 1950s, the twentieth century had seen two world wars; numerous minor wars; the full development of two major new ideologies, communism and fascism; and, in the United States, two major antileft campaigns (in the 1920s and 1950s) and a major antifascist campaign during World War II. One response to all this was an attempt to escape from ideology into objectivity. Particularly in the social sciences, attempts were made to eliminate value judgments from research. Although the social sciences are more objective than they were before World War II, scholars rapidly discovered that there are limits to objectivity where human beings are concerned. Also, the development of important political movements—such as the civil rights movement in the United States, which demanded that people take a stand—taught us that understanding a situation as objectively and thoroughly as possible and taking a position about it can be complementary actions rather than contradictory ones. And then came the conflict over the war in Vietnam, and the need to take a position shattered whatever remained of objectivity.[15]

The participants in the debate differed both over what they were talking about and to some extent over whether the end of ideology was a good thing. Some people suggested ideology was ending in communist as well as Western countries. Again, this was generally seen as favorable. The single point on which the debaters came closest to agreeing was that ideology is bad for us and if it hadn't ended, it should.

A redevelopment of the end of ideology theory greeted the publication in 1989 of "Have We Reached the End of History?" by Francis Fukuyama (b. 1952).[16] In this essay, Fukuyama argued that liberalism—his name for democratic capitalism—had obviously won the day and that no other ideology was a serious contender for dominance. For Fukuyama, fundamental contradictions no longer exist in the world, either in ideology or practice.

In his most recent reflections on his 1960 book *The End of Ideology,* Daniel Bell argues that he was right to say that ideology had ended, but says, "I conclude: the 'end of ideology,' as the great historic crossover of beliefs, has run its course,

---

[15] For an argument regarding the relationship between "facts" and "values," see Hilary Putnam, *The Collapse of the Fact/Value Dichotomy and Other Essays* (Cambridge, MA: Harvard University Press, 2002). Putnam's argument is specifically concerned with economic analysis but reflects broader debates within the social sciences.

[16] Francis Fukuyama, *The End of History and the Last Man* (New York: Free Press, 1992). The essay was originally published as "Have We Reached the End of History?" (Santa Monica, CA: RAND Corporation, February 1989).

I think. It is now the resumption of history that has begun," by which he appears to mean that the nations or "ethnies" of the world are clamoring for recognition of their unique identities.[17] Even the title of this essay is a direct challenge to Fukuyama's analysis.

The Situation Today

The overwhelming tradition has been that ideology hides truth. Thus it has been considered dangerous by most commentators. Today, influenced by post-modernism, scholars focus on competing ideologies and their "truths" without worrying too much about whether these ideologies are hiding a truth. To each set of believers, the other ideologies are hiding the truth.

In the recent past we have witnessed the emergence of numerous new or, more accurately, newly labeled views of the world that are sometimes called ideologies. We have also seen the advocates of certain well-established ideologies, such as capitalism, gain an intellectual self-confidence that was not apparent earlier, while adherents of other ideologies, most notably communism, have lost confidence. In addition, as groups have become aware of their ideological ties, they seem also to have become more aware of the roots of their beliefs, and forerunners who were not considered important have become more significant.

The competition among ideologies has become more clearly both political and intellectual.[18] The battle is for the hearts and the minds of adherents and for political converts, and within ideologies there is a quest for coherence and grounding that contradicts many of the theories we use to understand ideology, which suggest that any coherence is necessarily false. The ideological map is more complex than ever, and it is even more necessary to understand the theoretical roots of ideologies than it was in the past.

DO I (YOU) HAVE AN IDEOLOGY?

While I like to think that I select my beliefs, I am also aware of how I am influenced by different ideologies. Of course, as the author of this book I am likely to be particularly aware of such influences. And I have always thought that one purpose of this book should be to encourage readers to examine their own beliefs, and perhaps even critically evaluate them.

As a teacher I have had relatively few students who saw the world wholly through the viewpoint of an ideology, but I have had students who take the position of each of the ideologies in this book: Marxists, fundamentalist Muslims, anarchists, fascists, capitalists, socialists, feminists, quite a few nationalists, and a growing number of environmentalists, all of whom knew the answers to certain

[17] Daniel Bell, "The Resumption of History in the New Century," in Bell, *The End of Ideology: On the Exhaustion of Political Ideas in the Fifties with "The Resumption of History in the New Century"* (Cambridge, MA: Harvard University Press, 2000), xxviii.

[18] A controversial statement regarding these conflicts in the contemporary world can be found in Samuel F. Huntington, *The Clash of Civilizations and the Remaking of World Order* (New York: Simon & Schuster, 1996).

questions without needing to think about them. Thus it is clear that some of the people that we meet throughout life will have an ideology in the most complete sense of that term—they will be ideologues. Most of us, though, hold beliefs that are influenced by more than one ideology. One person is influenced by feminism, environmentalism, and Liberation Theology; another is influenced by Marxism and environmentalism; and so on.

In this sense, it is more accurate to say that we have beliefs rather than ideologies while recognizing that those beliefs come, in part, from ideologies. Because these beliefs are often drawn from more than one ideology, there is a potential for conflict among beliefs.

POSTMODERNISM

A new approach to thinking about the world, which some call an ideology, is *postmodernism,* a term coined by Jean-François Lyotard (1924–98). Postmodernism is not primarily political, so it will not be discussed here as a separate ideology; but because it both influences most of the ideologies under discussion and challenges the way we think about ideologies, it needs to be considered briefly. Although postmodernism is not generally thought of as an ideology, let alone a *political* ideology, it can lead to a position that asserts with absolute certainty that there is no truth. This crude form of postmodernism can sometimes look a lot like an ideology, but most postmodernists take a different position, arguing that truth depends on where you stand.

In this form, postmodernism has potential for undermining belief in any ideology because ideologies have traditionally claimed to have the singular truth, to be universal. Today, influenced by postmodernism, we in the twenty-first century are much more aware of the local and contingent, and if the standpoint is ideological, postmodernism can be seen as actually reinforcing ideologies rather than undermining them. Also, as noted earlier, each ideology is now probably best thought of as composed of subsets of closely related ways of viewing the world.

A complication for most of us is that we stand in more than one place. We view the world through lenses provided by ideology, gender, race, nationality, ethnicity, religion, and so forth. For many people, one of these will dominate, but others look through different glasses at different times regarding different issues. Most of us manage these shifts in perspective without conflict, often without even being aware that we are doing so. We see ourselves as a whole rather than as multiple selves.

IDEOLOGIES TO BE CONSIDERED

The ideologies considered in this book have been chosen for two main criteria: their importance in the world today and the author's desire to present a broad range of political beliefs. Nationalism; democracy and its two major forms, democratic capitalism and democratic socialism; and political Islam clearly fall into the first category. Each must be understood before the news of the day can be intelligently grasped. Anarchism clearly belongs in the second category. Although anarchism has never been dominant in any area for long, it still has many adherents and a continuing popularity, and a survey of political ideology would be incomplete without it. The other ideologies included fall somewhere between these two categories. Each is important for an understanding of recent history and current events but not to the same degree as nationalism, democracy, and political Islam. In addition, each represents a point on the spectrum of political beliefs that is not clearly occupied by any of the others.

One belief system, nationalism, is different from all the others because it is part of the other ideologies. Therefore, it will be discussed first to clarify its effects on the other ideologies. The placement and order of the other ideologies are not arbitrary, but other arrangements are possible. Feminism is placed in its own section, between democracy and Marxism, because it has developed so much internationally that it no longer fits anywhere else.

METHODS OF ANALYSIS

The wide variety of ideologies raises a problem for the analyst. Because each ideology differs significantly from the others, no single approach is appropriate to all of them. Each ideology emphasizes different aspects of society and ignores other aspects that are stressed by another ideology. Therefore, it is not possible to treat each ideology in exactly the same way. It is necessary to present ideologies as they exist in the world rather than on the basis of a formal model. Thus each one will be analyzed as its nature dictates.

Reasons for Comparing Ideologies

It is nevertheless desirable to compare ideologies. Why compare? Political scientists compare political systems and political ideologies for a number of reasons. At the simplest level, we compare to remind ourselves and others that there are different ways of doing things; in the context of ideologies, differing beliefs exist in the world. It is important to realize that people who hold these beliefs are as sure that they are right as we are that we are right. On a more complicated level, we compare things because it helps us better understand other people and ourselves—to see what both they and we do and believe. Understanding is important because we can't change anything unless we understand it and because we need to recognize that there are other ways of doing things and of believing that might be useful to us.

Through comparison we discover both great differences and great similarities; we discover that differences often hide similarities. We find, for example, that most belief systems rank people in some sort of hierarchy, but we also find that the bases for those rankings differ. Thus we conclude that there is disagreement over what is most important about the differences among people, but that there is agreement that some basis for making distinctions exists. In other words, we find that a difference is the result of a similarity.

Questions

Any analysis of any part of society, including the value system, is an attempt to answer a series of questions regarding the various institutions and processes already mentioned. This series of questions can be divided into two parts: (1) How should society function? and (2) How does society actually function? The answers to the first question describe the value system. The answers to the second question show us the social system in operation.

The following questions provide a fairly complete analysis of the assumptions of an ideology. Using questions like these, it is possible to compare ideologies.

1. Human nature
   a. What are the basic characteristics of human beings as human beings?
   b. What effect does human nature have on the political system?

2. The origin of society and government or the state
   a. What is the origin of society? Why does it develop?
   b. What is the origin of government or the state? Why does it develop?

3. Political obligation (duty, responsibility, law)
   a. Why do people obey the government?
   b. Why should people obey the government, or should they obey it at all?
   c. Is disobedience ever justifiable?
   d. Is revolution ever justifiable?

4. Law
   a. What are the nature and function(s) of law?
   b. Should the regulation of society depend on the immediate decisions of individuals or on sets of rules and regulations that place limitations on all members of society, including political leaders—in other words, the rule of law?
   c. Should there be sets of fundamental laws or constitutions that cannot be changed by the ordinary processes of legislation?

5. Freedom and liberty (rights—substantive and procedural)
   a. Are men and women free in any way vis-à-vis the government?
   b. Should they be free vis-à-vis the government?
   c. Assuming that some type or types of freedom are both possible and desirable, what should these be? Should they be limited or unlimited? Who places the limits?

6. Equality
   a. Are individuals in any way "naturally" equal?
   b. Should they be in any way equal?
   c. Assuming that some type or types of equality are both possible and desirable, what should these be? Should they be absolute or relative? If relative, what criteria should be used to establish them? Who establishes the criteria? Who enforces the criteria?

7. Community (fraternity)
   a. Should ties among individuals composing a group form a bond that takes precedence over the needs and wishes of the individual members of the group?

   b. If this is desirable, how can it be encouraged? If this is undesirable, how can it be discouraged? Who decides?

8. Power (authority)
   a. Should any individual or group of individuals be able to control, determine, or direct the actions of others?
   b. If this is desirable, what form or forms should it take? Should it be limited or unlimited? Who limits it and how?

9. Justice
   a. It is usually assumed that justice is desirable, but what is it? Is it individual or social?
   b. Who decides the characteristics of justice? Who enforces these characteristics?

10. The end of society or government
    a. For what purpose or purposes does society or government exist?
    b. Who decides what these purposes are, or are they consciously chosen?

11. Structural characteristics of government
    a. What is the best or best possible form of government? Why?
    b. Are alternative forms of government equally good?

The Social System

To compare differing ideologies, similar information must be made available for each ideology. In order to achieve some sort of comparability, the complex of interactions among individuals, groups, and institutions that we call society has been divided into five segments:

1. Value system
2. Socialization system
3. Social stratification and social mobility systems
4. Economic system
5. Political system

This breakdown is simply a loose set of categories designed to provide some minimal order to the analysis. These categories allow the attitudes found in the various ideologies to be described.

Is there, as Mannheim thought, some way of standing completely outside all ideologies, thus making it possible to evaluate them from something at least approaching objectivity? There is a growing consensus that this may not be possible or, at the minimum, is extremely difficult. At the same time it is essential that we evaluate ideologies and differentiate among them, and that evaluation needs to be based on something reliable. Evaluation cannot be based simply on belief or the lack of belief, although some people find that sufficient. For other people the answer is found in trying, as objectively as possible, to measure the effects of ideologies on human beings or, to include the most radical environmentalists, on the natural order as a whole.

Each chapter of this book attempts to explain the attitudes found in each ideology toward the various institutions and processes of society. As a result, we will see what questions are important within each ideology and therefore establish a basis for comparing them. Before this can be done, it is necessary to understand a bit more about each of these institutions and processes.

Values   The value system is determined by the answers given to the questions listed earlier, which show the hierarchy of values in each society and each ideology. The value system gives us a basis for evaluating each ideology from within itself. To what extent are the expressed values of the ideology compatible with one another? Do the adherents of the ideology live up to the values expressed in the ideology or at least try to? Do followers of the ideology adhere to its values when in power?

Socialization   The socialization system is the process by which individuals accept the values of a society as their own. The most important institutions affecting how and the degree to which individuals gain these values are (1) the family system, (2) the educational system, (3) the religious system, and (4) a variety of other influences, such as the mass media and the peer group. We are not always sure how the various institutions of socialization operate. It is obvious that a child is strongly influenced in her or his whole outlook on life by family environment and by early school years. It is, perhaps, less clear how the other institutions of socialization influence an individual's outlook on life. We can assume that the same messages repeated in institutions that the individual has been taught to respect, such as the religious and educational systems, have a cumulative effect and thereby become part of the individual's value system. The mass media operate in the same way.

Social Stratification   The social stratification system is the way in which a society ranks groups within it. This ranking may be a clearly defined class system or it may be loose, with hazy lines between classes or status groups. Social stratification is usually summed up within a political ideology by the question of equality. Some ideologies contain the idea that everyone within the society should be equal in specified ways. For example, some people talk about equality of opportunity and political equality; others believe in economic and social equality. Only if there were no economic, social, political, or any other inequalities would there be no social stratification system. Almost no one has ever suggested such complete equality, but each of these more limited types of equality has been suggested or tried at various times.

Social Mobility   One type of equality—equality of opportunity—is particularly important in any society. Equality of opportunity means that no artificial obstacles or barriers keep any individual or group from moving from one class to another. Equality of opportunity defines certain parts of the social mobility system within a society. Every society has a social mobility system determining the ease or difficulty with which an individual can move among classes or other strata in the society. The system also determines the basis for such movement. For example, in traditional China an individual could move into the upper classes of society by successfully completing a series of examinations. Many contemporary societies have no such formal system but base mobility on standards such as wealth.

The Economic System The economic system is concerned with the production, distribution, and consumption of wealth. The major parts of the economic system that interest us here relate to (1) production, (2) distribution and consumption, and (3) the relationship of the economic system to the political system. We will particularly examine the desired degree of economic equality and the means for achieving this goal. Most ideologies reject extremes of wealth and poverty; therefore, each contains means of correcting the imbalance, such as a graduated income tax or nationalization of industries. But each ideology also differs from others as to what constitute extremes of wealth and poverty.

These days it is generally accepted that the economic and political systems are closely intertwined. This has not always been the case, and some ideologies still stress the separation of the two systems. Therefore, it is particularly important to understand each ideology's position on the appropriate relationship between the economic system and the political system.

The Political System The political system is that segment of society that draws together or integrates all the others. Within the political system decisions are made that bind the whole society; thus the political system holds the key to understanding the whole ideological and social system. A political ideology does not concern itself only with narrowly defined governmental activity, but rather touches on all aspects of the social system; therefore, a political ideology provides answers, in one form or another, to all of the questions outlined earlier.

A NOTE ON TERRORISM

On September 11, 2001, the reality of world terrorism was brought home to the United States in the destruction of the World Trade Center and the attack on the Pentagon. Although there had been a prior attack on the World Trade Center on February 26, 1993, numerous attacks on American individuals and institutions abroad, and the destruction of the Alfred P. Murrah Federal Office Building in Oklahoma City in 1995, the impact of the September 2001 attacks on people in the United States has been of a much greater magnitude than any of the earlier cases.[19] Today there are over four thousand terrorist websites, many of which move continuously, often more than once a day. In general, terrorists

---

[19] On contemporary terrorism, see Mark Juergensmeyer, *Terror in the Mind of God: The Global Rise of Religious Violence*, 3rd ed. (Berkeley: University of California Press, 2003); and Yoram Schweitzer and Shaul Shay, *The Globalization of Terror: The Challenge of Al-Qaida and the Response of the International Community* (New Brunswick, NJ: Transaction, 2003).

do not see themselves as terrorists; the language they use refers to themselves as militants and paramilitaries. They justify their acts as necessary to protect their own communities, which they believe are under attack.[20]

Terrorism is not an ideology, and it should not be tied to a single ideology because it has been used by many ideologies.[21] Terrorism is a form of killing for political ends. It differs from assassination in that it is frequently directed at non-political targets and groups of people rather than individuals. Its purpose, as implied by the word, is to terrorize.

Advocates of political murder can be traced far back in history, and in the Middle Ages there was a debate over the justification of tyrannicide (the murder of a tyrant). But these actions were aimed at individuals perceived to have earned attack by their personal actions and do not constitute terrorism as we now know it.[22]

Since the nineteenth century, adherents of various ideologies have resorted to terrorism to attack their opponents and publicize their beliefs. Anarchists in the second half of the nineteenth century called these actions "propaganda by the deed." Around the same time a group of Russian terrorists earned the name "nihilist," which indicated that their aim was the destruction of current social institutions with no concern for what might replace them. The best-known statement of this position is *Catechism of the Revolutionist* (1869), usually attributed to Sergei Nechaev (1847–82) and Mikhail Bakunin (1814–76), although Bakunin's role was limited.[23] In this pamphlet, Nechaev uses the word *revolutionist* where we would use the word *terrorist;* even most supporters of violent revolution have rejected Nechaev. Typical of the statements in the *Catechism,* and one in which the connection to contemporary terrorism is obvious, is "He [the terrorist] despises public opinion. He despises and hates the present day code of morals with all its motivations and manifestations. To him whatever aids the triumph of the revolution is ethical; all that which hinders it is unethical and criminal."[24]

During the antiwar movement, there were a small number of bombings in the United States. Most of these were directed at institutions like banks and did not target individuals. Later the so-called Unabomber, on the other hand, targeted individuals, sending them mail bombs, some of which seriously injured their recipients.

---

[20] See Juergensmeyer, *Terror in the Mind of God,* 9, 12.

[21] But see Luciano Pellicani, *Revolutionary Apocalypse: Ideological Roots of Terrorism* (Westport, CT: Westport, 2003).

[22] On the history of terrorism, see Walter Laqueur, *A History of Terrorism* (New Brunswick, NJ: Transaction Books, 2001). Originally published as *Terrorism* (Boston: Little, Brown, 1977). The new edition has a new introduction by the author. See also Walter Laqueur and Yohan Alexander, eds., *The Terrorism Reader: An Historical Anthology,* rev. ed. (New York: NAL Penguin, 1987). On the motivations of terrorists, see Walter Reich, ed., *Origins of Terrorism: Psychologies, Ideologies, Theologies, States of Mind* (Cambridge: Woodrow Wilson International Center for Scholars and Cambridge University Press, 1990); and Christoph Reuter, *My Life Is a Weapon: A Modern History of Suicide Bombing,* trans. Helena Ragg-Kirkby (Princeton, NJ: Princeton University Press, 2004).

[23] On the relationship, see Paul Avrich, *Bakunin & Nechaev* (London: Freedom Press, 1974).

[24] The text of the *Catechism* can be found in Max Nomad, *Apostles of Revolution,* rev. ed. (New York: Collier Books, 1961), 230–35, with the quoted passage on 230.

Today terrorism is obviously most closely connected with the events of September 11, 2001, Osama bin Laden (b. 1957), and his particular brand of Islam. But terrorism is also connected with ethnic nationalism (certain Basques in Spain, for example), the American right wing (Timothy McVeigh and various militia groups, for example), and religious conflict (the continuing conflicts between the Protestants and Roman Catholics in Northern Ireland, for example).

We tend to identify terrorism with the acts of individuals and small groups, but *state terrorism* describes a state using terrorist acts against its enemies (Iraq and Libya have been identified as doing this) or against its own citizens (Argentina and Peru did this in the recent past).[25] Thus terrorism is a complex phenomenon driven by many motives and ideologies. It has existed in isolated, irregular acts since the mid-nineteenth century, but has occurred with increasing frequency in the past twenty-five years.

Terrorism continues as a tool of contemporary politics and warfare, and the responses to it from within the countries affected have raised important issues for many ideologies, particularly democracy and political Islam. Therefore, the effects of terrorism will also be discussed in a number of the following chapters.

SUGGESTED READING

Some Classic Works

Bell, Daniel. *The End of Ideology: On the Exhaustion of Political Ideas in the Fifties.* Glencoe, IL: Free Press, 1960. Republished as *The End of Ideology: On the Exhaustion of Political Ideas in the Fifties with "The Resumption of History in the New Century."* Cambridge, MA: Harvard University Press, 2000.

Geertz, Clifford. "Ideology as a Cultural System." In *Ideology and Discontent,* edited by David E. Apter, 47–76. New York: Free Press of Glencoe, 1964.

Mannheim, Karl. *Ideology and Utopia: An Introduction to the Sociology of Knowledge.* Translated by Louis Wirth and Edward Shils. New York: Harcourt, Brace & Co.,

1936; London: Routledge, 1991. The English edition brings together *Ideologie und Utopie* (Bonn, Germany: Cohen, 1929) and other essays by Mannheim.

Marx, Karl, and Friedrich Engels. *The German Ideology.* Vol. 5 of Karl Marx and Frederick Engels, *Collected Works.* 50 vols. New York: International Publishers, 1976.

Books and Articles

Althusser, Louis. "Ideology and Ideological State Apparatuses (Notes towards an Investigation)." In Althusser, *Lenin and Philosophy and Other Essays,* translated by Ben Brewster, 121–73. London: NLB, 1971.

---

[25] There has been a flood of books on all aspects of terrorism in the last three years. The Suggested Reading includes a representative sample. William T. Vollmann has produced a remarkable seven-volume reflection on violence in fiction, journalism, and photography that serves as an introduction to terrorism and state terrorism; see his *Rising Up and Rising Down,* 7 vols. (San Francisco: McSweeney's Books, 2003). On contemporary terrorism in general, see Barry Cooper, *New Political Religions, or an Analysis of Modern Terrorism* (Columbia: University of Missouri Press, 2004); Walter Laqueur, *The New Terrorism: Fanaticism and the Arms of Mass Destruction* (New York: Oxford University Press, 1999); and Charles Selengut, *Sacred Fury: Understanding Religious Violence* (Walnut Creek, CA: AltaMira Press, 2003). On state terrorism, see Jeffrey A. Sluka, ed., *Death Squad: The Anthropology of State Terror* (Philadelphia: University of Pennsylvania Press, 2000).

20PART I INTRODUCTION

Crick, Bernard. *In Defense of Politics*. 5th ed. London: Continuum, 2000.

De Certeau, Michel. *The Practice of Everyday Life*. Translated by Steven Rendall. Berkeley: University of California Press, 1984.

Donskis, Leonidas. *The End of Ideology & Utopia: Moral Imagination and Cultural Criticism in the Twentieth Century*. New York: Peter Lang, 2000.

Eagleton, Terry. *Ideology: An Introduction*. London: Verso, 1991.

———, ed. *Ideology*. London: Longman, 1994.

Freeden, Michael. "Editorial: What Is Special about Ideologies?" *Journal of Political Ideologies* 6:1 (2001): 5–12.

———. *Ideologies and Political Theory: A Conceptual Approach*. Oxford: Clarendon Press, 1996.

———. *Ideology: A Very Short Introduction*. Oxford: Oxford University Press, 2003.

———, ed. *Reassessing Political Ideologies: The Durability of Dissent*. London: Routledge, 2001.

Gabel, Joseph. "Political Ideologies." In Gabel, *Ideologies and the Corruption of Thought,* edited by Alan Sica, 129–43. New Brunswick, NJ: Transaction, 1997.

Gerring, John. "Ideology: A Definitional Analysis." *Political Research Quarterly* 50:4 (December 1997): 957–94.

Goodwin, Jeff, James M. Jasper, and Francesca Poletta, eds. *Passionate Politics: Emotions and Social Movements*. Chicago: University of Chicago Press, 2001.

Gramsci, Antonio. *Pre-Prison Writings*. Edited by Richard Bellamy. Cambridge: Cambridge University Press, 1994.

Hamilton, Malcolm B. "The Elements of a Concept of Ideology." *Political Studies* 35:1 (March 1987): 18–38.

Journal of Political Ideologies 1:1–present (founded February 1996).

Lazarus, Neil, ed. *The Cambridge Companion to Postcolonial Literary Studies*. Cambridge: Cambridge University Press, 2004.

Mazrui, Ali A. "Ideology and African Political Culture." In *Explorations in African Political Thought: Identity, Community, Ethics,* edited by Teodros Kiros, 97–131. New York: Routledge, 2001.

McLellan, David. *Ideology*. 2nd ed. Minneapolis: University of Minnesota Press, 1995.

Mészáros, István. *The Power of Ideology*. New York: New York University Press, 1989.

Meyer, David S., Nancy Whittier, and Belinda Robnett, eds. *Social Movements: Identity, Culture, and the State*. New York: Oxford University Press, 2002.

Parenti, Michael. *Land of Idols: Political Mythology in America*. New York: St. Martin's Press, 1994.

Rejai, Mostafa. "Ideology." In *Dictionary of the History of Ideas,* edited by Philip P. Wiener. 5 vols. New York: Scribner's, 1973.

Schwartzmandel, John. *The Age of Ideology: Political Ideologies from the American Revolution to Postmodern Times*. New York: New York University Press, 1998.

Scott, Alan. *Ideology and the New Social Movements*. London: Unwin Hyman, 1990.

Sim, Stuart, ed. *The Routledge Critical Dictionary of Postmodern Thought*. New York: Routledge, 1999. Also published as *The Icon Critical Dictionary of Postmodern Thought*. Cambridge, England: Icon Books, 1998.

Spivak, Gayatri Chakravorty. *A Critique of Postcolonial Reason: Toward a History of the Vanishing Present*. Cambridge, MA: Harvard University Press, 1999.

Taylor, Charles. *Modern Social Imaginaries*. Durham, NC: Duke University Press, 2004.

Taylor, Victor E., and Charles E. Winquist, eds. *Encyclopedia of Postmodernism*. London: Routledge, 2001.

Thompson, Simon. "Postmodernism." In *New Political Thought: An Introduction,* edited by Adam Lent, 143–62. London: Lawrence & Wishart, 1998.

Tilly, Charles. *Social Movements, 1768–2004*. Boulder, CO: Paradigm Publishers, 2004.

Tourish, Dennis, and Tim Wohlforth. *On the Edge: Political Cults Right and Left*. New York: M.E. Sharpe, 2000.

Van Dijk, Teun A. *Ideology: A Multidisciplinary Approach*. London: Sage, 1998.

Williams, Raymond. *Keywords: A Vocabulary of Culture and Society*. Rev. ed. New York: Oxford University Press, 1983.

Žižek, Slavoj. *For They Know Not What They Do: Enjoyment as a Political Factor.* 2nd ed. London: Verso, 2002.

———. *The Sublime Object of Ideology.* London: Verso, 1989.

———, ed. *Mapping Ideology.* London: Verso, 1994.

Terrorism

AbuKhalil, As'ad. *Bin Laden, Islam and America's New "War on Terrorism."* New York: Seven Stories Press, 2002.

Ahmad, Eqbal. *Terrorism Theirs and Ours.* New York: Seven Stories Press, 2001.

Baudrillard, Jean. *The Spirit of Terrorism and Requiem for the Twin Towers.* Translated by Chris Turner. London: Verso, 2002.

Bovard, James. *Terrorism and Tyranny: Trampling Freedom, Justice, and Peace to Rid the World of Evil.* London: Palgrave Macmillan, 2003.

Cooper, Barry. *New Political Religions, or an Analysis of Modern Terrorism.* Columbia: University of Missouri Press, 2004.

Cronin, Audrey Kurth, and James M. Ludes, eds. *Attacking Terrorism: Elements of a Grand Strategy.* Washington, DC: Georgetown University Press, 2004.

Elshtain, Jean Bethke. *Just War against Terror: The Burden of American Power in a Violent World.* New York: Basic Books, 2003.

Gareau, Frederick H. *State Terrorism and the United States: From Counterinsurgency to the War on Terrorism.* Atlanta, GA: Clarity Press/London: Zed Books, 2004.

Gray, John. *Al Qaeda and What It Means to Be Modern.* New York: New Press, 2003.

Hershberg, Eric, and Kevin W. Moore, eds. *Critical Views of September 11: Analyses from around the World.* New York: The New Press, 2002.

Howard, Russell D., and Reid L. Sawyer. *Terrorism and Counterterrorism: Understanding the New Security Environment. Readings & Interpretations.* Rev. and updated ed. Guilford, CT: McGraw-Hill/Dushkin, 2004.

Howitt, Arnold M., and Robyn L. Pangi, eds. *Countering Terrorism: Dimensions of Preparedness.* Cambridge, MA: The MIT Press, 2003.

Juergensmeyer, Mark. *Terror in the Mind of God: The Global Rise of Religious Violence.* 3rd ed. Berkeley: University of California Press, 2003.

Laqueur, Walter. *A History of Terrorism.* New Brunswick, NJ: Transaction Books, 2001. Originally published as *Terrorism.* Boston: Little, Brown, 1977. (The new edition has a new introduction by the author.)

———. *No End to War: Terrorism in the Twenty-First Century.* New York: Continuum, 2004.

Laqueur, Walter, and Yohan Alexander, eds. *The Terrorism Reader: An Historical Anthology.* Rev. ed. New York: NAL Penguin, 1987.

National Commission on Terrorist Attacks upon the United States. *The 9/11 Commission Report: Final Report of the National Commission on Terrorist Attacks upon the United States. Thomas H. Kean, chair, Lee H. Hamilton, vice-chair.* Washington, DC: National Commission on Terrorist Attacks upon the United States, 2004.

Onwudiwe, Ihekwoaba D. *The Globalization of Terrorism.* Aldershot, England: Ashgate, 2001.

O'Sullivan, Meghan L. *Shrewd Sanctions: Statecraft and State Sponsors of Terrorism.* Washington, DC: Brookings Institution, 2003.

Parenti, Christian. *The Soft Cage: Surveillance in America from Slavery to the War on Terror.* New York: Basic Books, 2003.

Pellicani, Luciano. *Revolutionary Apocalypse: Ideological Roots of Terrorism.* Westport, CT: Westport, 2003.

Ratner, Michael, Jennie Green, and Barbara Olshansky of the Center for Constitutional Rights. *Against War in Iraq.* New York: Seven Stories Press, 2003.

Reuter, Christoph. *My Life Is a Weapon: A Modern History of Suicide Bombing.* Translated by Helena Ragg-Kirkby. Princeton, NJ: Princeton University Press, 2004.

Reich, Walter, ed. *Origins of Terrorism: Psychologies, Ideologies, Theologies, States of Mind.* Cambridge: Woodrow Wilson International Center for Scholars and Cambridge University Press, 1990.

Schweitzer, Yoram, and Shaul Shay. *The Globalization of Terror: The Challenge of Al-Qaida and the Response of the International Community*. New Brunswick, NJ: Transaction, 2003.

Selengut, Charles. *Sacred Fury: Understanding Religious Violence*. Walnut Creek, CA: AltaMira Press, 2003.

Sluka, Jeffrey A., ed. *Death Squad: The Anthropology of State Terror*. Philadelphia: University of Pennsylvania Press, 2000.

Tilly, Charles. *The Politics of Collective Violence*. Cambridge: Cambridge University Press, 2003.

Vollmann, William T. *Rising Up and Rising Down*. 7 vols. San Francisco: McSweeney's Books, 2003.

Wilkinson, Paul. *Terrorism versus Democracy: The Liberal State Response*. London: Frank Cass, 2001.

Wood, Neal. *Tyranny in America: Capitalism and National Decay*. London: Verso, 2004.

Zinn, Howard. *Terrorism and War*. New York: Seven Stories Press, 2002.

Žižek, Slavoj. *Welcome to the Desert of the Real! Five Essays on September 11 and Related Dates*. London: Verso, 2002.

Websites

Ideology

Systematic ideology: http://www.gwiep.net

Terrorism

CIA: http://www.cia.gov/terrorism/

Department of Homeland Security: http://www.dhs.gov

FBI: http://www.fbi.gov/terrorinfo/terrorism.htm

UK Home Office: http://www.homeoffice.gov.uk/terrorism/

UN: http://www.un.org/terrorism/

2

Nationalism

I s nationalism an ideology? Scholars flatly disagree. On the one hand, Michael
Freeden writes that nationalism is not a distinct ideology.[1] On the other
hand, one of the most common topics of the *Journal of Political Ideologies,*
which Freeden edits, is nationalism. And many articles there explicitly refer to
nationalism as an ideology. Both positions can be defended. Each actual nationalism differs, and nationalism can be found affecting (some would say infecting)
other ideologies. Thus many, like Freeden, say that nationalism cannot be called
an ideology. But nationalism also has a set of core attributes that parallel the
core attributes of other ideologies. Thus, many, like the authors of the articles
in the *Journal of Political Ideologies,* say that nationalism clearly is an ideology.
Some even use Freeden's definition of ideology in doing so. My position is
simply that it is impossible to understand the world of the twenty-first century
without understanding nationalism, and its similarities to other ideologies mean
that we can plausibly treat nationalism as an ideology.

The importance of nationalism is underscored by this statement of Robert
Coles (b. 1929), an authority on the political beliefs of children: "Nowhere on
the five continents I've visited in this study has nationalism failed to become an

---

[1] Michael Freeden, "Is Nationalism a Distinct Ideology?" *Political Studies* 46 (1998): 748–65.
Another recent argument that nationalism is not an ideology can be found in Mark N.
Hagopian, "Ideology," in *Encyclopedia of Nationalism,* ed. Alexander J. Motyl (San Diego:
Academic Press, 2001), 1:385–403.

important element in the developing conscience of young people."[2] A recent scholar has argued, "No single political doctrine has played a more prominent role in shaping the face of the modern world than nationalism."[3] Or as the editors of an anthology put it, "It is incontestable that the resurgence of nationalist sentiment in many areas of the world is one of the most important and least anticipated phenomena of contemporary international politics. People are increasingly conscious of their national identities; they are rediscovering their national histories, pressing for recognition of their distinctness, and making various demands under the banner of national self-determination."[4]

Because nationalism has such impact on other ideologies, it must be discussed first. Of course, as will be clear throughout this text, ideologies also affect nationalism. This interchange is a clue to one of the greatest difficulties in dealing with nationalism. For many, there are "good" and "bad" forms of nationalism, often meaning "ours" and "theirs" but equally often reflecting a considered analysis of the types of nationalism or the differential impacts of nationalism. The tradition, both popular and scholarly, has been to view nationalism as mostly bad; but a number of recent scholars have pointed out that nationalism has many positive factors. In the United States we have always had this dual position without recognizing it because we use *patriotism* for a "good" nationalism and reserve *nationalism* for a "bad" nationalism.

This chapter presents nationalism as a coherent set of beliefs that produces a wildly divergent set of actually existing nationalisms. It illustrates how important nationalism is today, for good and ill, and addresses a number of countervailing forces that may, in time, diminish the importance of nationalism. These forces include globalization, internationalism or cosmopolitanism, and regionalism. None of these are, at present, ideologies, but it is possible to visualize a future in which one or more of them have become ideologies, perhaps even important ones. Today some thinkers argue that globalization has already emerged as such a new ideology, but I don't find the case quite strong enough yet.

The root of the word *nationalism* is *nation;* it means a people with a common culture and history that produce an identity. Nations can have the same geographical boundaries as countries; can occur as small, identifiable units within the political boundaries of a country; or can, at times, cross those boundaries. Most countries, often called *nation-states,* are examples of the first sort. The French Canadians in Canada are an example of the second sort. The Romany, or Gypsies, are an example of the third sort. They exist in many countries while having certain traditions in common, and many of them share a common language. A fourth type might be represented by Black Nationalism within the United States because, while Black Nationalists perceive themselves as a people

---

[2] Robert Coles, *The Political Life of Children* (Boston: Atlantic Monthly Press, 1986), 66.

[3] Umut Özkirimli, *Theories of Nationalism: A Critical Introduction* (New York: St. Martin's Press, 2000), 1.

[4] Robert McKim and Jeff McMahon, introduction to *The Morality of Nationalism,* ed. Robert McKim and Jeff McMahon (Oxford: Oxford University Press, 1997), 3.

with a common culture and history and call for some form of cultural, economic, or political separation from the United States, they live in many places
throughout the country rather than as a small, identifiable unit.[5] Immigration is
producing a fifth type: identifiable groups within one country with ties to
another country that may or may not over time become integrated within the
new country.

DEFINING NATIONALISM

Most definitions of *nationalism* include the following:

1. National consciousness or awareness of oneself as part of a group
2. National identity or identification with the group
3. Geographical identification or identification with a place (there are exceptions, such as the Romany, or Gypsies)
4. Patriotism or love of the group
5. Demands for action to enhance the group

The neutral term *group* is used because commentators disagree about who or
what constitutes a national group.

There is a difference between consciousness and identity. I can be aware of
my membership in a group without identifying myself with it. In fact, there
may well be groups that I am aware I belong to, such as by birth or upbringing,
but that I do not identify with—that I actually reject.

Most of us are born in a nation, but we are not aware of that until later. We
have to be taught about all the communities of which we are members. In the
language of Benedict Anderson (b. 1936), nations are "imagined communities"
because they, like most other communities, are created by the actions of those
who, over time, come to believe in or accept certain myths and symbols that
powerfully affect those who identify with the community.[6] Symbols of nationality such as the flag and the national anthem evoke such feelings of identification, even, at times, in those who do not think of themselves as having a strong
identification with the country. But, as already noted, identification is also an
active process in which the various symbols are molded into something that
affects how we live and interact with others—both those who are members of
our nation and those who exist legally or physically outside its boundaries.

---

[5] See, for example, Wilson Jeremiah Moses, ed., *Classical Black Nationalism: From the
American Revolution to Marcus Garvey* (New York: New York University Press, 1996);
William L. Van Deburg, ed., *Modern Black Nationalism: From Marcus Garvey to Louis
Farrakhan* (New York: New York University Press, 1997); Eddie S. Glaude Jr., ed., *Is It
Nation Time? Contemporary Essays on Black Power and Black Nationalism* (Chicago: Univer-
sity of Chicago Press, 2002); and Dean E. Robinson, *Black Nationalism in American Politics
and Thought* (Cambridge: Cambridge University Press, 2001).

[6] Benedict Anderson, *Imagined Communities: Reflections on the Origin and Spread of
Nationalism,* rev. and ext. ed. (London: Verso, 1991).

One of the most common identifying characteristics of a nation is language. In the United States, Native American children were once punished for speaking their national languages (some of which have been lost altogether or are now endangered), and some states have passed laws mandating the use of English. Language is immensely important as a marker of national identity. Those who watched the closing of the 2004 Olympics in Athens, Greece, will have heard some of the closing ceremony in Greek, which relatively few of the people watching the ceremony around the world would have understood; but to the Greeks, having part of the ceremony in Greek was an important symbol of their nationality.

When people in a country speak different languages, it usually means that different groups of people existed or still exist who have separate identities. For example, the country that was known as Czechoslovakia was formed after World War I from two ethnic groups, the Czechs and the Slovaks. After the overthrow of communism, Czechoslovakia became the Czech and Slovak Federative Republic, which, in 1993, became two separate countries, the Czech Republic and Slovakia. Likewise, Yugoslavia was formed after World War I from five ethnic groups and has fragmented into at least that number of countries—and the process of fragmentation may not have ended yet.

I become most conscious of being an American when I am out of the country. Partially this is because others identify me as American, but mostly it is the contrast between what I am used to and what I am surrounded by elsewhere. But before I ever left the country, I was aware of my membership in this group because I grew up surrounded by the symbols of group identity like the flag, the national anthem, July 4th, and Thanksgiving. And my parents and others made the connection between the symbols and the nation explicit. For most of us, this is how national consciousness develops.

National identity is a choice, a conscious act. It means that I identify myself as an American both to myself and to others. For those of us born in this country, there is no universal rite of passage in which we become officially American like the naturalization (note the word meaning to become natural) process in which someone born in another country becomes a citizen of this one; so identification either takes place gradually or occurs during some rite of passage such as joining the military.

Most of us tend to think of ourselves as having multiple identities based on our "unique" combination of class (a term Americans avoid), ethnicity, gender, and race. When we leave the United States, we are certain to add national identity. Think about how you answer the question asked by yourself or others, Who or what are you? This is usually answered in terms of occupation or ethnicity. But outside one's country, national identity is likely to be part of the answer. Sometimes Canadians seem obsessed with what it means to be a Canadian, which is often defined as being different from the United States. Over the past few years, the British have become more concerned with what it means to be British or, alternatively, English, Scottish, or Welsh, with a number of books published or still being written on these subjects.

One of the earliest theorists of nationalism, Johann Gottfried von Herder (1744–1803), argued that a basic human need is to belong to a group, and that being part of a nation gives us part of our identity. We have a history, ancestors—"roots"—that place us in a tradition. We are born in a "stream of tradition" that helps define us as individuals.[7]

In a small country, the geographical dimension of one's nationalism is clear. In the United States, it is not as clear, except, perhaps, when we leave the country. I have visited forty-six of the fifty states, but even though I have a picture of the United States in my head, I cannot say that I have a real sense of the country as a unit, a whole.

For most Americans, geographic identification is with a region, but with the awareness that this region is part of a whole. In smaller countries there may also be a regional identification, but the national boundaries are much clearer. And boundaries and their maintenance are central to the nation and nationalism. Of course, boundaries are clearer the closer you are to them. I was much more aware of the boundary between the United States and Canada when I lived in Minnesota than now when I live in Missouri.

Patriotism, or love of the nation, like most of our loves, depicts the loved one as better than it actually is because we have created an image of the loved one for ourselves. Remember Benedict Anderson's idea of the nation as an imagined community. We create an image of the nation in a form that fits our needs. This image will have certain core elements like symbols of nationhood (flag, anthem, Statue of Liberty), fundamental documents (the Declaration of Independence, the Constitution), institutions (democracy, electing our leaders), and events (the American Revolution). But other things will be added to this list, such as the Civil War/War between the States, World War II, or the civil rights movement. It is how we create our image of the nation through the mix of images that characterizes the nation we love.[8]

Demands for action are what generally provoke opposition to nationalism. These range from the demand for self-government, to a demand for recognition of a nation within the borders of an existing country (often a request of indigenous populations), to the demand to change borders to enlarge the nation. Such demands may include dismembering an existing country to create one or more new political entities. For example, at the time of independence from Great Britain in 1947, India included what is now Pakistan and Bangladesh, which was part of Pakistan (called East Pakistan) until 1971. Thus, in this case, three countries were created from one, and India and Pakistan have been at war over Kashmir, a region claimed by both, since 1948. Recently the two sides have come close to nuclear war (both sides have nuclear weapons), but in 2004 they began to slowly move toward negotiating the future of Kashmir.

As this last example indicates, nationalist demands often lead to conflict, and this has given nationalism a bad name. The current list of examples where nationalism has produced violence includes the Basques in Spain; Israel and the

---

[7] Isaiah Berlin, "The Bent Twig: A Note on Nationalism," *Foreign Affairs* 51, no. 1 (October 1972): 16.

[8] For a discussion of patriotism in the United States, see John Bodnar, ed., *Bonds of Affection: Americans Define Their Patriotism* (Princeton, NJ: Princeton University Press, 1996).

Palestinians; the Albanians in Macedonia; Bosnia; Northern Ireland; Chechnya; the Kurds in Iran, Iraq, and Turkey; and the Hutu and Tutsi in central Africa— and this list could be much longer.

Nationalism: Ancient or Modern?

One current debate over the nature of nationalism is whether it is an ancient or modern phenomenon. This dispute has connections with the two ways most scholars categorize nationalism today: ethnic or cultural and civic or liberal. Clearly some ethnicities have ancient roots, although the awareness of that ethnicity may be more recent. Thus whether nationalism is ancient or recent has no simple answer. One of the classic statements regarding the nation, Ernest Renan's (1823–92) "What Is a Nation?" says that "Nations . . . are fairly new in history,"[9] and Homi K. Bhabha (b. 1949) writes, "The nation's claim to modernity, as an autonomous or sovereign form of political rationality, is particularly questionable."[10]

Until recently, most scholars treated nations and nationalism as a modern phenomenon and argued that a coherent *doctrine* of nationalism came into existence only in the eighteenth century, first in Germany and later in France. The major parts of the mix of ideas that came together to become nationalism were seen as originating in the fourteenth through the sixteenth centuries.[11] As Isaiah Berlin (1909–97) wrote, "consciousness of national identity may be as old as consciousness itself. But nationalism, unlike tribal feeling or xenophobia, to which it is related but with which it is not identical, seems scarcely to have existed in ancient or classical times."[12]

Those arguing for ancient roots to nationalism contend that the argument for modernity rests entirely on the experience of western Europe and ignores, for example, China, which existed as a nation centuries before any western European nation. Also, and more important to the current debate over nationalism, those arguing for ancient roots are saying that the source of the nation is the ethnic group and that those arguing for a modern nationalism are confusing nation and state, which is why I have carefully avoided using the word *state*.

John J. Breuilly says that nationalism "is intimately linked to the development of the modern state [defined in terms of legitimacy, sovereignty, and territoriality], which both shapes nationalism and which nationalists claim for themselves."[13] But Margaret Moore says, as I noted earlier, that nations and

---

[9] Ernest Renan, "What Is a Nation?" trans. Martin Thom, in *Nation and Narration*, ed. Homi K. Bhabha (London: Routledge, 1990), 9. Originally given as a lecture titled "Qu'est-ce qu'une nation?" March 11, 1882.

[10] Homi K. Bhabha, "DissemiNation: Time, Narrative, and the Margins of the Modern Nation," in Bhabha, *Nation and Narration*, 293.

[11] The best discussion is by Quentin Skinner, *The Foundations of Modern Political Thought* (Cambridge: Cambridge University Press, 1978).

[12] Berlin, "Bent Twig," 15.

[13] John J. Breuilly, "The State," in Motyl, *Encyclopedia of Nationalism*, 1:796.

states are not identical. My example was the Romany, or Gypsies, as a nation with no state; she notes the Kurds and the Palestinians as nations with no states.[14] And, of course, the desire for a state by both the Kurds and the Palestinians has caused years of bloodshed in the Middle East. The Kurds in Iraq have been effectively independent since 1991. Kurdistan has built three thousand schools, held democratic elections, opened two universities, and has a free press, and it is concerned about the form that a future Iraq will take. It is also well-armed with a well-trained military. In mid-2005 it is impossible to tell how the relations between the Kurds and the other groups in Iraq will work out. The Kurds did well in the January election, but no group won enough votes to dominate and negotiations have proved to be very difficult.

Nationalism: Ethnic and Civic

The division between ancient and modern versions of nationalism is reflected in the other current conflict between scholars of nationalism: that between cultural or ethnic nationalism and civic or liberal nationalism. Roughly speaking, the former is based on ancient roots and the latter on modern ones, and for most people the distinction is between "bad" (ethnic) and "good" (civic) nationalism.

Civic nationalism reflects positive versions of nationalism or patriotism; having shared identity and purpose counteracts apathy and atomization, currently considered major problems in the United States.[15] One scholar argues, "Civic nationalism maintains that the nation should be composed of all those—regardless of race, color, creed, gender, language, or ethnicity—who subscribe to the nation's political creed. This nationalism is called civic because it envisages the nation as a community of equal, rights-bearing citizens, united in patriotic attachment to a shared set of political practices and values."[16] And another scholar says, "To make sense, democracy requires a 'people,' and social justice a political community within which redistribution can take place, while the liberal discourse of rights and the rule of law demands a strong and impartial polity."[17] To her this means that nations and people identifying with nations are necessary for democracy.

One author has noted, "Nations have called forth heroism and sacrifice as well as murder and torture. People have risked their lives to restore democracy and civil rights in their own country, when they could easily have chosen comfortable exile elsewhere. Programmes of health reform, social welfare and environmental repair have gained political support because they appeal to a sense of national identity."[18]

[14] Margaret Moore, *The Ethics of Nationalism* (Oxford: Oxford University Press, 2001), 6.

[15] See Robert D. Putnam, *Bowling Alone: The Collapse and Revival of American Community* (New York: Simon & Schuster, 2000).

[16] Michael Ignatieff, *Blood and Belonging: Journeys into the New Nationalism* (New York: Farrar, Straus & Giroux, 1993), 261.

[17] Margaret Canovan, *Nationhood and Political Theory* (Cheltenham, England: Edward Elgar, 1996), 2.

[18] Ross Poole, *Nation and Identity* (London: Routledge, 1999), 1.

On September 11, 2001, and the days following, Americans could readily see these two faces of nationalism. The terrorists were ethnic nationalists, and much of the response within the United States reflected civic nationalism. The fact that there were many attacks (from verbal to violent) on Arab Americans, anyone wearing a turban, Muslims, and others thought to be from the Arab world demonstrates that ethnic nationalism is not just a phenomenon found outside U.S. borders.

COUNTERVAILING TENDENCIES

Regionalism

At various times two or more countries have established ties that have raised questions about the continuing identity of the parts, but turning such agreements into long-term successes has proved difficult. For example, in 1964 Tanganyika and Zanzibar established a new country, the United Republic of Tanzania. And while Tanzania still exists, many Zanzibaris have never been entirely happy with the arrangement; even after almost forty years, there is a strong movement for greater autonomy.

The single most successful effort at regionalism is among developed nations. The European Union, or EU, originated as the European Coal and Steel Community (ECSC); became the European Economic Community (EEC), popularly known as the Common Market; and then became the European Community (EC). In 1993 the name was changed again to the European Union. The ECSC began with six countries; as of June 2004 the EU had twenty-five members, with four countries considered candidates. In October 2004 a new EU constitution was signed; but this now must be ratified by all the countries involved, some of which have proposed holding national elections on the issue.

As the EU has grown, it has changed from an almost purely economic union to an economic and political one. The European Court of Justice acts as an appeals court for cases brought against national laws. The European Parliament, composed of directly elected members, has begun to act as an independent political body and has even managed to force the EU bureaucracy to become more responsive to it.

The European Parliament has 732 members chosen by proportional representation, which ensures that a wide range of parties across the political spectrum will win seats. The largest groups are the political center with 268 seats and the socialists with 200 seats; thus no group has anywhere near a majority. In the 2004 election only 45.7 percent of eligible voters cast votes, indicating that this parliament has not convinced voters of its importance.[19]

---

[19] On the European Parliament, see Bernard Steunenberg and Jacques Thomassen, eds., *The European Parliament: Moving toward Democracy in the EU* (Lanham, MD: Rowman & Littlefield, 2002).

The EU is a powerful economic bloc, and its expansion into Central Europe will make it even stronger. Officially all interior barriers to trade were dropped in 1992. In 1998 a European Central Bank was established to set monetary policy for the EU. And in 2001 a single currency, the euro, was instituted and became the only legal currency for most EU countries during the first months of 2002.[20] The euro zone countries are aiming for convergence of inflation rates, convergence of interest rates, stability of exchange rates, budget deficits of less than 3 percent GDP (gross domestic product), and national debt levels of less than 60 percent GDP. The last two are proving to be the most difficult to achieve.

The ten countries that joined the EU in 2004 must bring their economic, political, and social systems in line with the EU on thirty-one issues. During the discussions leading to membership, individual countries negotiated transitional periods relating to specific issues, but on the whole, the systems were harmonized with the EU before the countries joined. The potential problem after a nation joins is whether the new laws are implemented; if they are not, the EU can take a member state to the European Court of Justice, and individuals and companies can take their own state to court. Candidate countries must harmonize their systems with the EU before they will be considered for membership. For example, Turkey abolished its death penalty to be considered for candidacy.

Africa may be beginning to form a union similar to the European Union. The Organization of African Unity voted to disband, and an African Union, modeled on the European Union, is being established. The African Union is modeled on the European Union, although it is much larger in that it includes all fifty-three countries of Africa, some of which are at war with each other. The Constitutive Act of the African Union includes all the institutions that it took the EU years to develop, such as a Pan-African Parliament and a Court of Justice. In addition, the African Union has developed a detailed program for economic development in Africa called The New Partnership for African Development (NEPAD), which is designed to initiate a program of sustainable development throughout Africa.[21]

It is too early to do more than note this attempt, but the attempt is important in that it is explicitly designed to counteract the nationalism that has divided African countries against themselves. The size of the African Union suggests that it will not achieve its far-reaching goals, but some members of the AU are aware of the problems and hope to move slowly in implementing the proposed institutions. Meanwhile, the AU provides a mechanism through which African leaders can meet and discuss common problems. Also, the African Union has managed to assist in conflicts in Africa by providing some peacekeeping troops that operate under the auspices of the AU rather than individual countries.

---

[20] Three countries in the European Union—Denmark, Sweden, and the United Kingdom—chose not to adopt the euro.

[21] On the African Union, see http://www.africa-union.org/; http://www.africa-union.org/About_AU/AbConstitutive_Act.htm; and http://www.nepad.org/en.html

In addition, a variety of primarily economic regional agreements, such as NAFTA (the North American Free Trade Agreement), FTAA (the Free Trade Association of the Americas), and APEC (Asia-Pacific Economic Cooperation), are slowly encouraging greater regional economic cooperation. CAFTA or the Central American Free Trade Agreement is currently being discussed as an additional economic agreement. There are also security-based organizations like NATO (the North Atlantic Treaty Organization) and SEATO (the South East Asia Treaty Organization), through which governments come together to discuss security issues and, in the case of NATO, sometimes act on them.

Cosmopolitanism

The emphasis on a whole within which differing peoples and cultures can be accepted is the heart of internationalism or cosmopolitanism. In Western thought this goes back to ancient Greek and Roman philosophers who saw themselves as "citizens of the world." During the same period that gave rise to the nation-state, Dante (1265–1321) wrote *Monarchia* (1310–11?), arguing for a worldwide monarchy. But despite significant areas of world cooperation like the Universal Postal Union (founded 1874), the International Civil Aviation Organization (founded 1944), and the Food and Agricultural Organization (founded 1945), a number of international organizations have either failed or been perceived as failures. Even the United Nations, extremely successful in many of its activities, is thought of by many, mostly in the United States, as both a failure and a serious threat to national sovereignty. How a failed organization can constitute a threat is rarely discussed.

Space exploration has produced pictures of earth hanging in space surrounded by absolutely nothing (see the example in Chapter 12). The realization that human beings live together with nowhere else to go has led many to believe that some way must be found for all of us to get along peacefully. Cosmopolitanism, or thinking of oneself as a citizen of the world, or at least as a member of the human race that together inhabits a fragile earth, is a growing phenomenon; many people see themselves as having much in common with others around the world. This usually comes about from contact with people from different backgrounds through travel, business or professional contacts, interaction with immigrants, or education.

Internationalists believe that the world should be united in some way. They do not all agree on what this way should be. Some, for example, argue for a world government with strong powers. Others argue for some sort of loose confederation. Still others argue for a federal system of government similar to that of the United States, with powers divided between a world government and the government of each country belonging to the federation. Others are unsure what form unity might take but believe strongly that unity is essential.

In a recent article, David Miller argued against cosmopolitanism, saying that what he called "weak" cosmopolitanism is simply a general statement about the need to treat all people as objects of ethical concern, whereas what he called "strong" cosmopolitanism requires a world government and is therefore unworkable.[22] On the other hand, many commentators refer to "The Cosmopolitan Manifesto," first published in 1998 and often reprinted, as providing guidelines for a workable cosmopolitanism.[23]

In a general sense, internationalism is similar to nationalism. It requires recognition of ties among all individuals in the world just as nationalism requires recognition of ties among those living in a country. We have noted the symbols that can help create feelings of nationalism. Internationalism does not have many such symbols, and it is likely that an individual will have less emotional identification with the world as a whole than with a nation or region, even though he or she may intellectually recognize ties to others around the world. Thus internationalism is not likely to be as strong a force as nationalism unless some crisis produces the emotional fervor that would bring about an identification of the individual with a world community. A science fiction cliché has an invasion from outer space acting as the crisis that produces the recognition that we are all human beings living together.

Today recognition that actions in one country affect the health and safety of people in another country—through pollution such as acid rain, the destruction of the ozone layer, changes in weather patterns, and other impacts on the global environment—has brought a new urgency and prominence to internationalism. Although there have been few specific policy changes, there is a growing sense that nations must find ways of cooperating on environmental issues.

In addition, the world now seems to recognize that conflict in one place is dangerous for other places, and the United Nations is involved in a number of "peacekeeping" missions. Part of the reason for internationalizing peacekeeping through the United Nations is that nationalism produces resentment at the involvement of powerful countries like the United States; the use of troops from small countries, particularly countries from the same general area of the world, helps reduce this resentment. Thus nationalism is helping to create at least one instance of internationalism.

But one author notes that "cosmopolitanism is the privilege of those who can take a secure nation-state for granted,"[24] which implies that cosmopolitanism is not in opposition to nationalism, but instead something that can be built on nationalism.

NATIONALISM IN THE THIRD WORLD

Until the breakup of the former Soviet Union, we were most aware of nationalism in the Third World. In the terminology in use then, the *First World* was the United States and those countries aligned with it, the *Second World* was the

---

[22] David Miller, "Cosmopolitanism: A Critique," *CRISPP: Critical Review of International Social and Political Philosophy* 5:3 (Autumn 2002): 80–85. Responses to Miller's article, published in the same issue, include Thomas Pogge, "Cosmopolitanism: A Defence" (86–91) and Thom Brooks, "Cosmopolitanism and Distributing Responsibilities" (92–97).

[23] Ulrich Beck, "The Cosmopolitan Manifesto," *New Statesman* 127 (March 20, 1998): 28–30.

[24] Ignatieff, *Blood and Belonging,* 13.

Soviet Union and those countries aligned with it, and the *Third World* was everything else but specifically the developing countries that tried to avoid being aligned with either. With the Second World conceptually gone, the Third World is now the most common term in use to describe the underdeveloped or developing countries of the world.[25] Other "worlds" have been added to the list. *Fourth World* is used by some to refer to the poorest of the poor countries and by others to refer to the indigenous or native peoples of the world. Recently others have begun to use *Fifth World* to refer to those who have lost status through immigration.

Movements for National Liberation

Most Third World countries have gone through a series of stages in the process of development from the colonial period to independence. The colonial experience was the first stage, followed, not necessarily in this order, by the development of a movement for independence, the revitalization of the indigenous culture, political independence, neocolonialism, one-party rule with internal conflict, and, often, a military takeover.

The Colonial Experience   The one experience that all Third World countries share is having been colonies. Although Western countries like the United States, Canada, Australia, and New Zealand were also colonies (of Britain) at one time, generally the experience is sufficiently past so there is little awareness of what it means politically, economically, and psychologically. For most countries of the Third World the colonial experience is still recent.

Being a colony meant that others made all decisions for their own benefit. Even major decisions were made not in the colony but in Europe; a colonial bureaucracy composed of people sent from Europe made other decisions. In political terms, a colony was just a minor concern in the overall policy of the European power.

Economically, the colony was there to provide raw materials for the "home" country, a market for its goods, and cheap labor. Most colonies were required to limit their economies to one or two cash crops or other raw materials and were not allowed to diversify. Little more than minimal processing was done in the colony; that would have required trained workers, and training workers might raise their expectations and pose problems. Ultimately, this happened; training workers for skilled jobs did raise expectations and produced leaders of the independence movements.

Even more dangerous was education. Most colonial powers did not educate the indigenous population, although Christian missionaries provided schools and, in fact, educated many leaders of the later independence movements. The fact that most education was provided by Christian missionaries illustrates another fact about the colonial experience—the attack on indigenous culture. This process of deculturation proved traumatic for many people,

---

[25] "Third World" was first used in 1952 by Albert Sauvy (1898–1990), a French demographer, to refer to those countries trying to find a "third" way between capitalism and communism.

but it also provided the tools that made independence possible. On the one hand, the imposition of an alien culture stripped many people of their sense of self. Their religions were suppressed; their languages were replaced; their customs were denigrated; even their clothes and hairstyles were replaced by Western styles. Everything indigenous was treated as inferior, and this attitude was taught in schools.

On the other hand, the acceptance, at least temporarily, of Western culture provided both the intellectual and physical tools needed for independence. The Western traditions of liberty and equality provided the vocabulary needed for an independence movement. Technical training provided the ability to replace the colonial rulers in running the government and the economy. And at least some colonial rulers found it more difficult to treat as inferior someone who dressed and spoke as they did and who had been educated at the same schools and universities.

The Independence Movement The most common scenario for an independence movement was years of covert and overt opposition. Most, if not all, independence leaders spent time in prison for their activities; in fact, in many countries some years in prison became a requirement for gaining acceptance, respect, and credibility.

In most cases independence was actually won through violent revolution or long years of a war for independence. India was the major exception: although there were violent incidents, its independence leaders, Mohandas K. Gandhi (1869–1948) and Jawaharlal Nehru (1889–1964), used nonviolent techniques to win independence.

The struggle for independence provided a focus for the development or redevelopment of a national identity. It also became the basis for a national culture. In almost all cases, independence movements attempted to ensure that their supporters worked solely for the benefit of the people as a whole rather than for their own benefit. A good example of this approach is found in the "Rules of Discipline" announced by Kwame Nkrumah (1909–72), the leader of the independence movement in what was the British colony of Gold Coast, which became Ghana on independence in 1957. In his "Rules of Discipline," Nkrumah says that those involved in the revolution should "not take a single needle or piece of thread from the masses," "not take liberties with women," "always guide and protect the children," and "always be the servant of the people."[26] Julius K. Nyerere (1922–99), the leader of the independence movement in Tanganyika (later Tanzania), went even further in the Arusha Declaration, declaring that no member of government or leader in a political party should "hold shares in any company," "hold directorships in any privately owned enterprise," "receive two or more salaries," or "own houses which he rents to others." He states explicitly that the prohibition extends to spouses.[27] Until independence and for a while

---

[26] Kwame Nkrumah, *Handbook of Revolutionary Warfare: A Guide to the Armed Phase of the African Revolution* (New York: International Publishers, 1969), vii.

[27] Julius K. Nyerere, *Ujamaa—Essays on Socialism* (Dar es Salaam, Tanzania: Oxford University Press, 1968), 36.

Julius K. Nyerere (1922–99) was president of the United Republic of Tanzania (formed by uniting Tanganyika and Zanzibar) from 1964 to 1985. He is one of the few leaders of an African independence movement not to be overthrown (a few attempts were made) and to retire from office. He was president of the Tanganyika African National Union (TANU), the political party active in bringing independence to Tanganyika, from 1954 on. He was known for his advocacy of African socialism and what he called *ujamaa* (a Swahili word that he translates as "familyhood") as the basis for developing Third World economies.

afterward, such programs usually worked, but after a time, many leaders of liberation movements used their new power to line their own pockets rather than to help develop the country as a whole. There were, of course, exceptions. Nyerere was one.

The Revitalization of Indigenous Cultures　Despite colonization, indigenous cultures were damaged but not destroyed, and national identity required that the culture be revived.[28] Language, literature, and the arts, together with religion and music, were all rediscovered, encouraged, and, with independence, taught in a refashioned educational system. In places where the traditional culture had been most nearly destroyed, notably sub-Saharan Africa, the process of revitalization has been slow, but it is still taking place and provides more and

---

[28] See, for example, Sékou Touré, "A Dialectical Approach to Culture," in *Pan-Africanism*, ed. Robert Chrisman and Nathan Hare (Indianapolis: Bobbs-Merrill, 1974), 52–73; Amilcar Cabral, "National Liberation and Culture," trans. Maureen Webster, in Cabral, *Return to the Source: Selected Speeches* (New York: Monthly Review Press, 1973), 39–56; and Cabral, "The Role of Culture in the Battle for Independence," *UNESCO Courier* (November 1973): 12–16, 20.

more people a recovered sense of self. Still, the continuing Westernization and urbanization that have followed independence have added to the difficulty of establishing a national culture. Independence is not the solution to all problems that it had seemed to many.

For most Third World countries, political independence, which had been the sole goal, suddenly became a step to the goals of economic independence, political stability, and decent lives for their citizens. The first action needed to achieve these goals was to take effective control of the economy, but this proved difficult.

Neocolonialism After formal independence has been achieved, economic ties with the former colonial power may resemble continued control. This is known as *neocolonialism*. Most new countries have developed some sort of agreement with the former colonists, usually to their mutual advantage. The problem of neocolonialism is a complex one. It is essential for rapid economic development that the new nation trade with older, more established nations. Often the only thing the new nation has to trade is raw materials. In return it gets manufactured goods or even industries. The problem stems from the fact that raw materials sell on the world market at a much lower price than do manufactured goods. Therefore, the new nation feels it is being exploited by selling a commodity that is relatively inexpensive in order to purchase one that is relatively expensive.

Such problems make neocolonialism an important and difficult issue for the new nation. It must deal with older, more developed countries, often including its previous colonial ruler, in order to survive, but it feels it is being exploited in virtually the same way it was while still a colony. Therefore, many new countries have insisted that processing of raw materials take place at home, thus producing an industry, employing people, and giving them some sense that they are not being exploited.

Political Instability After independence, usually one political party dominated, and it often allowed no significant opposition to develop. One-party rule, it was argued, was necessary to provide the unity and stability needed to forge a new nation. Frequently one-party rule resulted in military coups because the military was the only alternative center of power. This pattern has left many Third World countries struggling for political and economic survival and searching for an identity that allows them independence from the former colonial powers.

NEW NATIONS

Throughout the twentieth century new nations were created, but national consciousness and identity cannot be created overnight. In most new twentieth-century nations the experience of being a colony and the movement to overthrow the colonial power helped the citizens develop a sense of themselves as a people. But these experiences are not enough to maintain the identity for long.

The ancient/modern, ethnic/civic splits can be seen in the process of creating a nation or *nation-building,* as it used to be called.[29] Identification is easiest if it is based on a single ethnic group, which has to have a consciousness of itself that long precedes the creation of the new nation. It is relatively easy to proclaim a new nation with agreed-on boundaries and a government; it is much harder to imagine that nation into existence in the minds of its inhabitants. Flags, national anthems, and other symbols of nationhood must be accepted by the people and become part of their personal identities before more than an outer shell of a nation can be said to exist.

The first new nation that succeeded in developing a national consciousness and identity was the United States.[30] It was a difficult process even though some states that united had histories as lengthy as 150 years. These states had the initial advantage of an enemy, Britain, but they also had separate identities in the minds of many of their citizens, and the process of creating an identification with the new nation was long and arduous. The United States went through a civil war before it was clear that a nation had been established, and the United States reached its current geographic dimensions only in 1959, when Alaska and Hawaii were admitted as the 49th and 50th states.

CURRENT TRENDS

Contemporary scholarship indicates that past studies of nationalism neglected three subjects: minorities, women, and postcolonial societies. Postcolonialism has become a major theme of contemporary scholarship, but the other two, while attracting some attention, are still generally neglected.

These neglected subjects are important for different reasons. Minorities are important because they complicate the imagining of the nation. As previously noted, it is fairly easy to imagine a nation composed of one ethnic group but much harder if there are minorities. Assimilation or the belief in assimilation (the "melting pot") has been the traditional strategy to address the problem. This approach suggests that there are no important minorities, just people who are in the process of becoming part of the nation. But today we realize both that the process takes much longer than was previously thought and that assimilation is almost always partial. In other words, minorities remain who identify with both the nation they live in and the one they emigrated from.

Women play particularly important roles in both bearing the future citizens of the nation and in socializing those future citizens. In the latter case, they are likely to give their children the first sense of the nation to which they belong and their future role in it. Thus if women do not identify with the nation, their children are less likely to do so.

---

[29] See Karl Deutsch and William J. Foltz, eds., *Nation-Building* (New York: Atherton Press, 1963).

[30] See Seymour Martin Lipset, *First New Nation: The United States in Historical and Comparative Perspective* (New York: Basic Books, 1963).

In addition, in a world of multiple identities and as feminism becomes more global, with whom should women identify: other women wherever they reside, or just those men and women—or just other women—residing in the same country? In other words, which of their (and our) identities should take precedence? In a world half female, this is obviously an important question for each nation.[31]

Postmodernism/Postcolonialism

Nationalism, because it is based on "imagined" or "created" communities, can easily be read from the perspective of postmodernism. Specifically, as postmodernism undermines the idea of universalism, particularly a universalism seen through Western eyes, nationalism becomes extremely important, especially from the postcolonial perspective.[32] Although those of us who are born and stay within the bounds of a country are likely to see the nation as a given, it is not. In the United States we used to use the metaphor of the "melting pot" to suggest that in some way those who immigrated to the United States from other places melted together into one whole. (The term originated with a play of that name that was performed on Broadway in 1908.)[33] What we forgot was that each melting changed the whole, and today many people are more likely to use a metaphor like "tossed salad" to suggest that while a whole is created, the parts of that whole remain recognizable.

And this perspective shows how nationalism today reflects postcolonialism, although postcolonialism is itself a contested concept.[34] As Homi K. Bhabha put it, "the founding dictum of the political society of the modern nation" is *"out of many one."*[35] But it is clear that the multicultural, multiethnic modern state remains multiple.

Secession

Many ethnic groups argue for positions ranging from the recognition of some degree of autonomy for their group within the larger political unit to secession from that unit to establish a new unit. Today such movements exist among the Kurds in Iraq and Turkey, French Canadians in Québec, the Basques in Spain, Tibetans in China, and Aceh in Indonesia. Although not based on ethnicity, a secessionist movement occurred in the United States during the period of the

---

[31] For various perspectives on women and nationalism, see Cynthia Cockburn, *The Space Between Us: Negotiating Gender and National Identities in Conflict* (London: Zed Books, 1998); Caren Kaplan, Norma Alarcón, and Minoo Moallem, eds., *Between Woman and Nation: Nationalism, Transnational Feminisms, and the State* (Durham, NC: Duke University Press, 1999); and Tamar Mayer, ed., *Gender Ironies of Nationalism: Sexing the Nation* (New York: Routledge, 2000).

[32] See Rachel Walker, "Postmodernism," in *Encyclopedia of Nationalism,* 1:611–30.

[33] Israel Zangwill, *The Melting Pot: Drama in Four Acts* (New York: Macmillan, 1909).

[34] See Leela Gandhi, *Postcolonial Theory: A Critical Introduction* (New York: Columbia University Press, 1998), for a discussion of the conflicted nature of postcolonial studies.

[35] Bhabha, "DissemiNation," 294. Emphasis in the original.

Civil War (known in the South as the War between the States or the War of Northern Aggression). Abraham Lincoln (1809–65) is remembered as one of the greatest U.S. presidents because of his dedication to saving the Union, for which he was assassinated. Proponents of secession argue for it as national self-determination, asking, Shouldn't a people who want their own state be able to have it? Opponents, like Lincoln, argue that the maintenance of the current state takes precedence over the desires of a minority within it.[36]

Nationalist Conflicts

Many conflicts in the world today reflect nationalism. Some are of long standing, such as the Basque nationalist movement in northern Spain and southern France, the conflict in Northern Ireland, and the struggle between Israel and the Palestinians. The terrorist attacks on the United States led both the Basques and the Irish Republican Army (IRA) to make conciliatory gestures so as not to be targets of the world campaign against terrorism.

Although the Basques suggested they might be willing to enter negotiations with the Spanish government, the Basque movement is deeply divided and little actual progress has been made. However, in a major concession, the IRA began to make some of their weapons unusable. They had long declared that they would never allow themselves to be in a position where they could not defend themselves. But in the most recent election in Northern Ireland, the Democratic Unionist Party led by Ian Paisley (b. 1926) won the most votes, and it is the Protestant party most opposed to the peace process and the establishment of shared power arrangements. Both the Catholic IRA and the Protestant UDA (the Ulster Defense Association), the largest paramilitary organization in Northern Ireland, have made gestures toward peace, and in late 2004 Paisley visited the Republic of Ireland (Eire) for talks. Thus, while there are major roadblocks, there is at least some movement. In early 2005 the IRA and Sinn Fein, the largest Catholic party, were accused of involvement in or knowledge of a major bank robbery in Northern Ireland and men identifying themselves as members of the IRA threatened witnesses of a murder with IRA retaliation if they told what they saw. The IRA denied involvement in the robbery and disowned the men, but their cause was at least temporarily badly damaged, even within the Catholic community.

As of 2004, the situation between Israel and the Palestinians was much worse than it had been a few years ago. There are a number of reasons for this. The present Israeli government was less inclined to negotiate than were some previous governments, and a growing number of Palestinians used terror tactics within Israel. As a result, violence on both sides escalated and resulted in many deaths, mostly of Palestinians.

Israel is building a wall between Israeli and Palestinian areas, which Israel hopes will reduce violence in Israel; but the Palestinians see this wall both as a

---

[36] On secession movements, see Percy Lehning, ed., *Theories of Secession* (London: Routledge, 1998); and Margaret Moore, *The Ethics of Nationalism* (Oxford: Oxford University Press, 2001).

device to take back land ceded to them and, because many Palestinians work in Israel, as a means of destroying the already weak Palestinian economy.

Yasir Arafat (1929–2004), the leader of the Palestinian Authority, was unable to control the many factions into which Palestinians are divided, but he was the symbolic leader of all Palestinians, even those who rejected him. Relations between Israel and the Palestinian Authority have improved since the election of Mahmoud Abbas (b. 1935) as president of the Authority, known to Palestinians as the Palestinian National Authority. There has been a reduction but not elimination of violence by Palestinians and the Israeli government has indicated that it will abandon some settlements in areas claimed by the Palestinians, a decision opposed by those living in the settlements. Both sides are at least trying to give the impression that they want and can achieve a negotiated settlement.

In particular, Hamas (Harakat al-Muqawama al-Islamiyya, or the Islamic Resistance Movement), which opposed Arafat and has solidly established itself within the Palestinian territories by providing human services, is the source of most of the violent acts that take place within Israel. Hamas's goal is the establishment of an Islamic Palestinian state.[37] In the immediate aftermath of Arafat's death, Hamas appeared to be intending to continue its opposition to the Palestinian leadership, but in early 2005, it changed its policy and began to cooperate on a limited basis. It has indicated that it might participate in elections in the Palestinian territory, and, if it does, it will be expected to do well.

Other nationalist conflicts are more recent. One of these stands out in the Chiapas region of Mexico. Although it has deeper roots, the Zapatista rebellion began on the day that Mexico and the United States signed the North American Free Trade Agreement (NAFTA). Called "the first postmodern revolution,"[38] it represents an unusual coalition between the so-called two Mexicos, the indigenous people of the region and the white elite. Subcomandante Marcos (recently tentatively identified as Rafael Sebastián Guillén Vicente) and the others identified as "leaders" of the rebellion always appear masked and say they do so to stress that there are in fact no leaders, but only a collective of elected village representatives who are bound by the decision of each village they represent. Subcomandante Marcos is described as a university-educated poet, and his writings include stories and poems as well as manifestos and political tracts. In the January 1, 1996, "Fourth Declaration of the Lancandon Jungle," Marcos writes,

> Our fight has been to make ourselves heard, and the bad government creates arrogance and closes its ears with its cannons.
> Our fight is caused by hunger, and the gifts of the bad government are lead and paper for our children's stomachs.

---

[37] For different views of Hamas, see Shaul Mishal and Avraham Sela, *The Palestinian Hamas: Vision, Violence, and Coexistence* (New York: Columbia University Press, 2000); and Andrea Nüsse, *Muslim Palestine: The Ideology of Hamas* (Amsterdam: Harwood Academic Publishers, 1998).

[38] Ana Corrigan, "Afterword: Chiapas, The First Postmodern Revolution," in Subcomandante Marcos, *Our Word Is Our Weapon: Selected Writings,* ed. Juana Ponce de León (New York: Seven Stories, 2001), 417–43.

Our fight is for a worthy roof over our heads, and the bad government destroys our homes and our history.

Our fight is for knowledge, and the bad government distributes ignorance and disdain.

Our fight is for land, and the bad government gives us cemeteries.

Our fight is for a job that is just and dignified, and the bad government buys and sells our bodies and our shame.

Our fight is for life, and the bad government offers death as our future.

Our fight is for respect, for our right to sovereignty and self-government, and the bad government imposes the laws of the few on the majority of the people.

Our fight is for freedom of thought and movement, and the bad government builds jails and erects graves.

Our fight is for justice, and the bad government is made up of criminals and assassins.

Our fight is for history, and the bad government proposes to erase history.

Our fight is for the homeland, and the bad government dreams with a foreign flag and language.

Our fight is for peace, and the bad government announces war and destruction.[39]

Although there have been many setbacks, the rebellion in Chiapas temporarily forced the Mexican government to negotiate with representatives of local communities. These negotiations went well, but the Mexican congress rejected the negotiated settlement. While the Zapatistas still have widespread international support, the political situation seems to be a stalemate, and the Zapatistas have developed autonomous institutions within the Chiapas area. Their economy depends almost entirely on the international sale of organic coffee, and world coffee prices are weak, so there are economic as well as political problems.

Nationalism in the United States

Nationalism in the United States mirrors nationalism elsewhere. For the most part, Americans have responded to the attacks on the World Trade Center and the Pentagon with the sort of widespread patriotism—the positive support for and identification with country—that represents the best of civic nationalism. "Good" nationalism clearly predominates. On the other hand, a small minority has exhibited the "bad" nationalism, sometimes called *jingoism,* that we condemn as ethnic nationalism when we see it elsewhere. The murder of Muslims and Sikhs (a religion originating in India that is unrelated to Islam but requires its men to wear turbans and beards) illustrates that this sort of nationalism exists in the United States also. And the treatment during World War II of Japanese-American U.S. citizens, who were interned in prison camps, shows that this is not a new U.S. phenomenon. The Council on American-Islamic Relations

---

[39] "Fourth Declaration of the Lancandon Jungle," in Marcos, *Our Word Is Our Weapon,* 87.

(CAIR) reported 1,019 claims of verbal or physical abuse in the United States in 2003–04, up from 602 in the previous year.

Indigenous Peoples

In addition to the activities of Native Americans in the United States and the First Nations in Canada, which take place largely within the political realm, there are indigenous peoples' movements throughout the Americas. In the Amazon River basin in Brazil, native people are struggling for recognition and against the oil and other companies that have been given access to the natural resources in the area. Because few South American countries have strict environmental laws or choose not to enforce those that exist, a number of indigenous people have become involved with environmental activists in attempting to protect the environment that is central to their way of life. They have generally been ignored, have failed even when their efforts were recognized as just, or have been murdered.

Globalization

Undoubtedly the most widely discussed force working against nationalism today is globalization, which has grown so much that some scholars are beginning to label it a new ideology. But so far globalization is being defined through ideological spectacles, and it is too early to label it as a separate ideology. Is it a positive force bringing people together, creating jobs, saving the Third World from poverty, and diminishing the likelihood of war? Or is it a negative force shifting power from individuals and legislatures to unelected corporate leaders and bureaucrats; destroying the environment in the name of profit; shifting jobs from developed countries to Third World countries where wages are low, working conditions poor, and environmental regulations nonexistent; and reinforcing the dominance of the industrialized countries over the rest of the world? These differences are reflected in the different views of the demonstrators at various meetings of world economic leaders such as the World Trade Organization (WTO) meetings in Seattle, November 30 to December 3, 1999, and at the G-8 meeting in Genoa, Italy, in July 2001. In particular, the Seattle meeting and the demonstrations there have become a symbol of the antiglobalization movement's power.

From the point of view of its advocates, globalization will benefit everyone economically and will help spread democracy. It does this by opening up or liberalizing markets and integrating markets worldwide.

To the antiglobalization movement, globalization equals Americanization and is about power: it means a new colonization in which the Western countries support those who support them. From this point of view globalization suggests that it will produce inclusion in the world economy but in fact produces exclusion from the world economy. In the United States there are two antiglobalization movements, one from the left and one from the right. The left's argument is based on a worldwide perspective; the right's argument is based on patriotism.

One positive result of globalization, from the point of view of Third World workers, is that corporate codes of behavior developed within the First World have sometimes, usually because of protests within the First World, been applied in the

Third World to help oppressed workers there. The best known example is the international campaign against the wages and working conditions found in Third World suppliers to Nike. Protests and boycotts in North America and Europe helped change conditions in Third World factories. Protests by Third World workers alone, without First World support, generally have little effect.

Offshoring/Outsourcing   One issue in globalization is the movement of jobs from the developed countries to the developing world. An interesting case can be seen by following the U.S. textile industry from its origins in New England to new plants in the American Southeast, to Texas, to Mexico, and now to China. The argument in favor is that everyone benefits from higher wages in poor countries that still leave overall costs lower in the developing world. The argument against is that the loss of jobs and the lowering of wages in the developed countries outweigh the cost savings for displaced workers.

A related question currently being investigated is who gains and who loses: men or women. Many of the jobs lost by women in the developed world are gained by men in the developing world. But some jobs in the developing world go to women, and some writers argue that this will lead to greater freedom and independence for these women. The evidence is mixed. On the one hand, the real beneficiaries are the companies in the developed world; on the other hand, some women in the Third World are getting higher wages than they would have otherwise. It is also often women of color who are losing the low-paying jobs in industrialized countries and women of color in the Third World who are gaining from the new jobs.

The Tobin Tax   One effect of globalization is increased volatility in financial markets and loss of control over national currencies by national governments. As early as 1972 James Tobin (1918–2002) proposed a 0.5 percent (later lowered to 0.1–0.25 percent) tax on foreign exchange and bond trading to curb this volatility. This idea is now championed by some groups as a mechanism for funding international social programs. The primary organization promoting the idea, with branches in many countries, is ATTAC (Association for the Taxation of Financial Transactions for the Aid of Citizens).

Migration   The United States is a nation of immigrants, the only difference being when our ancestors arrived. Even the ancestors of the Native Americans appear to have immigrated here at a much earlier stage in history. Thus the famous poem "The New Colossus" by Emma Lazarus (1849–87) that appears on the Statue of Liberty:

> Give me your tired, your poor,
> Your huddled masses yearning to breathe free,
> The wretched refuse of your teeming shore.
> Send these, the homeless, tempest-tost to me,
> I lift my lamp beside the golden door.[40]

[40] http://www.libertystatepark.com/emma.htm

For various reasons, immigration is today a major issue throughout the developed world. Immigrants are being divided roughly into "political" immigrants, or those fleeing their homelands in fear for their lives, and "economic" immigrants, or those hoping to improve their lives. Of course, the categories overlap, but economic reasons have always propelled the vast majority of immigrants. Today countries are much more welcoming to political than economic immigrants.

One reason for the concern with immigration is that contemporary economies are less able to absorb large numbers of new workers than they once were. Countries are worried that the new immigrants will be unable to find work and will become an economic burden as well as providing a dissatisfied minority ripe for exploitation by extremist elements. This concern is related to the problem of ethnic nationalism because it reflects the worry that ethnic enclaves will develop within countries and resist integration into the national culture. It is related to civic nationalism because civic nationalism depends on a growing identification with the new nation by immigrant groups. While we now recognize that it can take years for a new immigrant to become fully identified with the new nation (the melting pot), civic nationalism depends on there being sufficient identification with the new nation to clearly become part of it (the tossed salad).

Many theorists of civic nationalism are aware of this problem. For example, in *Citizenship and National Identity* (2000), David Miller argues against multiculturalism and suggests positive steps to incorporate immigrants into their new country. Will Kymlicka, a major theorist of multiculturalism, argues, in his *Politics in the Vernacular* (2001), in favor of multiculturalism but also in favor of education for citizenship.

The entire question looks different from the point of view of the immigrant. Some people (as mentioned earlier) have begun to use the phrase *Fifth World* to refer to immigrants and those who lose status through immigration. For others the whole concept of immigration no longer applies, and they prefer the word *diaspora,* which suggests the scattering of a people. Homi K. Bhabha writes, "I have lived that moment of the scattering of the people that in other times and other places, in the nations of others, becomes a time of gathering."[41]

Globalization involves the mass movement of people around the world, legally and illegally. In most countries people are welcomed who are highly skilled. For example, the United States is not currently producing enough engineers and computer scientists to meet its needs and welcomes such immigrants. At the other end of the wage scale, many U.S. crops are picked by illegal migrants who are deported if discovered. Farmers say they can't get the seasonal labor they need to pick the crops, and before September 11, 2001, efforts were being made to provide legal status for many such workers.

Immigration among the poor is having a striking effect on the position of women. Most women immigrate with their husbands and families rather than on their own, although there is a growing tendency for single women to migrate

---

[41] Bhabha, "DissemiNation," 291.

to places where there is already an established community from their country. After immigration, women appear to integrate more quickly into the new country and learn the new language faster than men. This seems to be due to the fact that women, particularly those with children, have to deal with the wider community, whereas men tend to stay within the immigrant community. As a result, some scholars are seeing the empowerment of women through immigration.

A special subcategory of immigrants are refugees, who are defined as "[Any person who] . . . owing to well-founded fear of being persecuted for reasons of race, religion, nationality, membership of a particular social group or political opinion, is outside the country of his nationality and is unable to, or owing to such fear, is unwilling to avail himself of the protection of that country."[42] Today the definition has been informally extended to cover those forced to flee their homes but who remain within their country of nationality, such as the thousands living in refugee camps in the Darfur region of the Sudan. Such immigrants or potential immigrants often pose major problems in that they are often ill, extremely poor, and without marketable skills. On the other hand, I have recently had students who came to the United States as refugees from the former Yugoslavia, having experienced horrendous violence and the death of one or more of their parents, who have done extremely well in my classes, graduated with honors, and are now employed locally or are in graduate or law school.

To the antiglobalization forces, globalization amounts to exporting exploitation; to its advocates, globalization exports opportunity. The problem is that both arguments can be supported.[43]

Empire and *Empire*

There is much talk today about the creation of a new American empire, but if such an empire is coming into being, it will differ from past empires. Past empires, such as the Greek, Roman, Chinese, Spanish, Arab Muslim, Venetian, Dutch, and British, were all based on acquisition of territory, whereas the new American empire appears to be based primarily on economic dominance backed up by military might and the willingness to use it. Another way of looking at the situation is simply to note that at present the world is unipolar; there is only one very strong economic and military power. But such a situation may not last. The European Union is currently the second strongest economic area; and China, with its huge population, is rapidly becoming a strong economic force in the world and has nuclear weapons.

A recent book that quickly became influential, *Empire* (2000) by Michael Hardt and Antonio Negri, argues that "over the past several decades, as colonial regimes were overthrown and then precipitously after the Soviet barriers to the

---

[42] United Nations High Commission for Refugees, *The State of the World's Refugees: Fifty Years of Humanitarian Action* (Oxford: Oxford University Press, 2000), 23.

[43] For the differing positions, see the websites listed as Suggested Reading.

capitalist world market finally collapsed, we have witnessed an irresistible and irreversible globalization of economic and cultural exchanges."[44] They contend that a new form of socio-political-economic-cultural organization has emerged, which they label "Empire." It is "composed of a series of national and supranational organisms united under a single logic of rule"[45] and has neither spatial nor temporal boundaries. Thus nations, states, and nationalism are already outmoded and in the process of being supplanted. We are, to Hardt and Negri, already living in a postnational era dominated by institutions that are based in existing states but reach throughout the world.

Hardt and Negri followed *Empire* with *Multitude* (2004), which argues that what they have called *empire* has the potential of creating global democracy, not as a world government but through networks of interconnected communities and individuals. *Empire* clearly tapped into what many believed to be the next great social change, and there is limited evidence of the potential for the interconnected world suggested in *Multitude* in movements and organizations like the World Social Forum, which met in Brazil in 2005. The World Social Forum brings together thousands of individuals and groups under the slogan "Another World Is Possible" and in opposition to organizations like the World Bank, the IMF (International Monetary Fund), the World Trade Organization (WTO), and the World Economic Forum, which are seen as dominating the world economically and politically. Participants believe that the informal networks being created provide centers of opposition that have the potential for bringing about far-reaching change.

Humanitarian Intervention

Another important issue today is what is called *humanitarian intervention,* or intervention in a country by another country or group of countries either to alleviate extreme human suffering or to keep or restore peace. The two best known recent examples are in the former Yugoslavia in which whole populations were at risk and in the Darfur region of the Sudan, where its population has faced constant attacks from other regions of the country. The wars in Afghanistan and Iraq are seen by some or presented as examples of humanitarian intervention; others reject that label. The question involved is what happens to the idea of independent nations if one or more nations can invade another nation, arguing that it is for the good of the country invaded. Who should decide when and where intervention is appropriate? On what grounds and to whom can such intervention be justified? Thus humanitarian intervention raises, in only a slightly new form, the old debate over the nature of a just war.[46]

---

[44] Michael Hardt and Antonio Negri, *Empire* (Cambridge: Harvard University Press, 2000), xi.

[45] Ibid.

[46] For recent contributions, see Jean Bethke Elshtain, ed., *Just War Theory* (New York: New York University Press, 1992); Michael Walzer, *Just and Unjust Wars: A Moral Argument with Historical Illustrations*, 3rd ed. (New York: Basic Books, 2000); and Walzer, *Arguing about War* (New Haven: Yale University Press, 2004).

Universal Jurisdiction

A new legal theory that runs directly counter to nationalism is *universal jurisdiction*. This theory, most obviously applied in the case of the former Chilean dictator Augusto Pinochet (b. 1915), who was arrested in the United Kingdom on a Spanish warrant for crimes committed in Chile, says that any court can claim jurisdiction over crimes committed anywhere in the world. Although Pinochet was released on the grounds of ill health and no other actual case has arisen, the theory has attracted considerable attention.[47] A related issue is the establishment of the International Criminal Court under a 1998 agreement that has now been signed by over 100 countries; the United States has not signed. The idea behind the International Criminal Court is a court that could try individuals accused of crimes anywhere in the world for which no national or local court has or chooses to take jurisdiction. The Pinochet case might, for example, have been appropriate for such a court. Many people fear that charges could be brought against people who are unpopular for actions that were perfectly legal under the laws of their own country or for political acts that would not normally be considered criminal but that political opponents might see as criminal. Historically, the only international criminal trials have been for crimes committed during war, such as the Nuremberg trials after World War II and the trials currently in progress concerning the civil war in Rwanda and the conflicts in the former Yugoslavia. In these examples special tribunals were established just for those cases. There is a long-established International Court of Justice (its predecessor was established in 1922), but it only hears cases between states or gives advisory opinions.

The problem with nationalism is that it both unites and divides. Renan eloquently describes the nation as "a soul, a spiritual principle. Two things, which in truth are but one, constitute this soul or spiritual principle. One lies in the past, one in the present. One is the possession of a rich legacy of memories; the other is present-day consent, the desire to live together, the will to perpetuate the value of the heritage that one has received in an undivided form."[48] At the same time nationalism defines any nonnational as "other," "alien," with the implication of fundamental difference, often leading to fear. The alien may be "naturalized" and assimilated, but even these characteristics do not necessarily eliminate the fear of the outsiders, which often leads to violence against them.

Thus nationalism is both a positive and a negative force in the world today, pulling people together and pushing them apart. And in one aspect or another it is a force in all other ideologies.

---

[47] See Stephen Macedo, ed., *Universal Jurisdiction: National Courts and the Prosecution of Serious Crimes under International Law* (Philadelphia: University of Pennsylvania Press, 2004); and Luc Reydams, *Universal Jurisdiction: International and Municipal Jurisdictions* (Oxford: Oxford University Press, 2004).

[48] Renan, "What Is a Nation?" 19.

SUGGESTED READING

Some Classic Works

Anderson, Benedict. *Imagined Communities: Reflections on the Origin and Spread of Nationalism.* Rev. and ext. ed. London: Verso, 1991.

Berlin, Isaiah. "The Bent Twig: A Note on Nationalism." *Foreign Affairs* 51, no. 1 (October 1972): 11–30. Reprinted in his *The Crooked Timber of Humanity: Chapters in the History of Ideas,* edited by Henry Hardy, 238–61. London: John Murray, 1990.

———. "Nationalism: Past Neglect and Present Power." *Partisan Review* 46, no. 3 (1979): 337–58. Reprinted in his *Against the Current: Essays in the History of Ideas,* edited by Henry Hardy, 333–55. London: Hogarth Press, 1979.

Deutsch, Karl W. *Nationalism and Its Alternatives.* New York: Knopf, 1969.

———. *Nationalism and Social Communication: An Inquiry into the Foundations of Nationality.* 2nd ed. Cambridge: MIT Press, 1966.

Hayes, Carlton J. H. *The Historical Evolution of Modern Nationalism.* New York: Macmillan, 1931.

———. *Nationalism: A Religion.* New York: Macmillan, 1960.

Kohn, Hans. *The Age of Nationalism: The First Era of Global History.* New York: Harper & Row, 1962.

———. *American Nationalism: An Interpretive Essay.* New York: St. Martin's Press, 1957.

———. *The Idea of Nationalism: A Study in Its Origins and Background.* New York: Macmillan, 1944.

Smith, Anthony D. *Nationalism in the Twentieth Century.* Oxford, England: Martin Robertson, 1979.

Snyder, Louis L. *The Meaning of Nationalism.* New Brunswick, NJ: Rutgers University Press, 1954.

———. *New Nationalism.* Ithaca, NY: Cornell University Press, 1968.

Tagore, Sir Rabindranath. *Nationalism.* New York: Macmillan, 1917.

Books and Articles

Abdel-Nour, Farid. "National Responsibility." *Political Theory* 31:5 (October 2003): 693–719. What responsibility do we have as members of a national community?

Balibar, Etienne. *Politics and the Other Scene.* London: Verso, 2002.

Baum, Gregory. *Nationalism, Religion, and Ethics.* Montréal, Québec: McGill-Queen's University Press, 2001.

Bauman, Zygmunt. *Identity: Conversations with Benedetto Vecchi.* Cambridge, England: Polity, 2004.

Beck, Ulrich. "The Cosmopolitan Manifesto." *New Statesman* 127:4377 (March 20, 1998): 28–30.

Beiner, Ronald, ed. *Theorizing Nationalism.* Albany: State University of New York Press, 1999.

Berezin, Mabel, and Martin Schain, eds. *Europe without Borders: Remapping Territory, Citizenship and Identity in a Transnational Age.* Baltimore, MD: Johns Hopkins University Press, 2003.

Berlin, Isaiah. "The Bent Twig: A Note on Nationalism." *Foreign Affairs* 51, no. 1 (October 1972): 11–30.

———. "Nationalism: Past Neglect and Present Power." *Partisan Review* 46, no. 3 (1979): 337–58.

Bhabha, Homi K., ed. *Nation and Narration.* London: Routledge, 1990.

Breuilly, John. *Nationalism and the State.* 2nd ed. Chicago: University of Chicago Press, 1994.

Brown, David. *Contemporary Nationalism: Civic, Ethnocultural, and Multicultural Politics.* New York: Routledge, 2000.

Buchanan, Allen, and Margaret Moore, eds. *States, Nations and Borders: The Ethics of Making Boundaries.* Cambridge: Cambridge University Press, 2003.

Burton, Antoinette, ed. *After the Imperial Turn: Thinking With and Through the Nation.* Durham, NC: Duke University Press, 2003.

Canovan, Margaret. *Nationhood and Political Theory*. Cheltenham, England: Edward Elgar, 1996.

Carey, Roane, and Jonathan Shainin, eds. *The Other Israel: Voices of Refusal and Dissent*. New York: New Press, 2002.

Castle, Gregory, ed. *Postcolonial Discourses: An Anthology*. Oxford: Blackwell, 2001.

Chatterjee, Deen K., and Don E. Scheid, eds. *Ethics and Foreign Intervention*. Cambridge: Cambridge University Press, 2003. Humanitarian intervention.

Cheah, Pheng, and Jonathan Culler, ed. *Grounds of Comparison: Around the Work of Benedict Anderson*. New York: Routledge, 2003.

Cockburn, Cynthia. *The Space between Us: Negotiating Gender and National Identities in Conflict*. London: Zed Books, 1998.

Cocks, Joan. *Passion and Paradox: Intellectuals Confront the National Question*. Princeton, NJ: Princeton University Press, 2002.

Cohen, Joshua, ed. *For Love of Country: Debating the Limits of Patriotism*. Boston: Beacon Press, 1996.

Connor, Walker. *Ethnonationalism: The Quest for Understanding*. Princeton, NJ: Princeton University Press, 1994.

Dallmayr, Fred. *Alternative Visions: Paths in the Global Village*. Lanham, MD: Rowman & Littlefield, 1998.

———. *Beyond Orientalism: Essays on Cross-Cultural Encounter*. Albany: State University of New York Press, 1996.

Dawisha, Adeed. *Arab Nationalism in the Twentieth Century: From Triumph to Despair*. Princeton, NJ: Princeton University Press, 2003.

Delanty, Gerard, and Patrick O'Mahony, eds. *Nationalism and Social Theory: Modernity and the Recalcitrance of the Nation*. London: Sage, 2002.

Eley, Geoff, and Ronald Grigor Suny, eds. *Becoming National: A Reader*. New York: Oxford University Press, 1996.

Fanon, Frantz. *Black Skin, White Masks*. Translated by Charles Lam Markmann. New York: Grove Press, 1967. Originally published as *Peau noire, masques blancs*. Paris: Éditions du Seuil, 1952.

———. *The Wretched of the Earth*. Translated by Constance Farrington. New York: Grove Press, 1963. Originally published as *Les Damnés de la terre*. Paris: F. Maspero, 1961.

Farrell, Mary, Stefano Fella, and Michael Newman, eds. *European Integration in the 21st Century: Unity in Diversity*. London: Sage Publications, 2002.

Fawcett, Louise, and Yezid Sayigh. *The Third World beyond the Cold War: Continuity and Change*. Oxford: Oxford University Press, 1999.

Fischbach, Michael R. *Records of Dispossession: Palestinian Refugee Property and the Arab–Israeli Conflict*. New York: Columbia University Press, 2003.

Fukuyama, Francis. *State-Building: Governance and World Order in the 21st Century*. Ithaca, NY: Cornell University Press, 2004.

Gandhi, Leela. *Postcolonial Theory: A Critical Introduction*. New York: Columbia University Press, 1998.

Gandhi, M[ohandas] K[aramchand]. *Hind Swaraj and Other Writings*. Edited by Anthony J. Parel. Cambridge: Cambridge University Press, 1997.

Gillingham, John. *European Integration, 1950–2003: Superstate or New Market Economy?* Cambridge: Cambridge University Press, 2003. History of European integration.

Gould, Carol C., and Pasquale Pasquino, eds. *Cultural Identity and the Nation-State*. Lanham, MD: Rowman & Littlefield, 2001.

Greenfeld, Liah. *Nationalism: Five Roads to Modernity*. Cambridge: Harvard University Press, 1992.

Guibernau, Montserrat, and John Hutchinson, eds. *Understanding Nationalism*. Cambridge, England: Polity, 2001.

Haas, Ernst B. *Nationalism, Liberalism, and Progress*. 2 vols. Ithaca, NY: Cornell University Press, 1997–2000.

Hall, John A., ed. *The State of the Nation: Ernest Gellner and the Theory of Nationalism*. Cambridge: Cambridge University Press, 1998.

Hansen, Phillip. "Hannah Arendt and Bearing with Strangers." *Contemporary Political Theory* 3:1 (April 2004): 3–22.

Hardt, Michael, and Antonio Negri. *Empire.* Cambridge: Harvard University Press, 2000.

————. *Multitude: War and Democracy in the Age of Empire.* New York: Penguin Press, 2004.

Harvey, Neil. *The Chiapas Rebellion: The Struggle for Land and Democracy.* Durham, NC: Duke University Press, 1998.

Hastings, Adrian. *The Construction of Nationhood: Ethnicity, Religion, and Nationalism.* Cambridge: Cambridge University Press, 1997.

Hayden, Tom, ed. *The Zapatista Reader.* New York: Thunder's Mouth Press/Nations Books, 2002.

Hechter, Michael. *Containing Nationalism.* Oxford: Oxford University Press, 2000.

Ho, Fred, ed. *Legacy to Liberation: Politics and Culture of Revolutionary Asian Pacific America.* San Francisco: AK Press, 2000.

Hughey, Michael W., ed. *New Tribalisms: The Resurgence of Race and Ethnicity.* New York: New York University Press, 1998.

Huntington, Samuel P. *Who Are We? The Challenges to America's National Identity.* New York: Simon & Schuster, 2004.

Hutchinson, John, and Anthony D. Smith, eds. *Nationalism: Critical Concepts in Political Science.* 5 vols. New York: Routledge, 2000.

Ignatieff, Michael. *Blood and Belonging: Journeys into the New Nationalism.* New York: Farrar, Straus & Giroux, 1993.

International Commission on Intervention and State Sovereignty. *The Responsibility to Protect.* Ottawa, Canada: International Development Research Centre, 2001.

Isbister, John. *Promises Not Kept: The Betrayal of Social Change in the Third World.* 5th ed. Bloomfield, CT: Kumarian Press, 2001.

Johnston, Steven. "This Patriotism Which Is Not One." *Polity* 34:3 (Spring 2002): 285–312.

Kaplan, Caren, Norma Alarcón, and Minoo Moallem, eds. *Between Woman and Nation: Nationalism, Transnational Feminisms, and the State.* Durham, NC: Duke University Press, 1999.

Kumar, Krishan. *The Making of English National Identity.* Cambridge: Cambridge University Press, 2003.

Kushner, Tony, and Alisa Solomon, eds. *Wrestling with Zion: Progressive Jewish-American Responses to the Israeli–Palestinian Conflict.* New York: Grove Press, 2003.

Kymlicka, Will. *Politics in the Vernacular: Nationalism, Multiculturalism, and Citizenship.* New York: Oxford University Press, 2001.

Lazarus, Neil. *Nationalism and Cultural Practice in the Postcolonial World.* Cambridge: Cambridge University Press, 1999.

Lehning, Percy, ed. *Theories of Secession.* London: Routledge, 1998.

Levy, Jacob T. *The Multiculturalism of Fear.* Oxford: Oxford University Press, 2000.

Máiz, Ramón. "Framing the Nation: Three Rival Versions of Contemporary Nationalist Ideology." *Journal of Political Ideologies* 8, no. 3 (October 2003): 251–67.

Mandela, Nelson. *Long Walk to Freedom: The Autobiography of Nelson Mandela.* Boston: Little, Brown, 1994.

Manual, George, and Michael Posluns. *The Fourth World: An Indian Reality.* New York: Free Press, 1974. Use of the phrase *Fourth World* to refer to indigenous peoples.

Marcos, Subcomandante. *Our Word Is Our Weapon: Selected Writings.* Edited by Juana Ponce de León. New York: Seven Stories, 2001.

————. *Shadows of Tender Fury: The Letters and Communiqués of Subcomandante Marcos and the Zapatista Army of Liberation.* Translated by Frank Bardacke, Leslie López, and the Watsonville, California, Human Rights Committee. New York: Monthly Review Press, 1994.

Marx, Anthony W. *Faith in Nation: Exclusionary Origins of Nationalism.* New York: Oxford University Press, 2003.

Mayer, Tamar, ed. *Gender Ironies of Nationalism: Sexing the Nation.* New York: Routledge, 2000.

McCrone, David. *The Sociology of Nationalism.* New York: Routledge, 1998.

McGarry, John. "Explaining Ethnonationalism: The Flaws in Western Thinking." *Nationalism and Ethnic Politics* 1, no. 4 (Winter 1995): 121–42.

McKim, Robert, and Jeff McMahon, eds. *The Morality of Nationalism*. Oxford: Oxford University Press, 1997.

Miller, David [Leslie]. *Citizenship and National Identity*. Cambridge, England: Polity Press, 2000.

———. *On Nationality*. Oxford: Oxford University Press, 1995.

Mishal, Shaul, and Avraham Sela. *The Palestinian Hamas: Vision, Violence, and Coexistence*. New York: Columbia University Press, 2000.

Moore, Margaret. *The Ethics of Nationalism*. Oxford: Oxford University Press, 2001.

———, ed. *National Self-Determination and Secession*. Oxford: Oxford University Press, 1998.

Morris, Benny. *The Birth of the Palestinian Refugee Problem Revisited*. Cambridge: Cambridge University Press, 2004.

Motyl, Alexander J., ed. *Encyclopedia of Nationalism*. 2 vols. San Diego: Academic Press, 2001.

Nasser, Gamal Abdel. *The Philosophy of the Revolution*. Buffalo, NY: Smith, Keynes & Marshall, 1959.

Nkrumah, Kwame. *The Autobiography of Kwame Nkrumah*. Edinburgh: Thomas Nelson & Sons, 1957.

———. *I Speak of Freedom: A Statement of African Ideology*. New York: Praeger, 1970.

Nussbaum, Martha C., with respondents. *For Love of Country: Debating the Limits of Patriotism*. Edited by Joshua Cohen. Boston: Beacon Press, 1996. Reprint with no subtitle and revisions. Boston: Beacon Press, 2002.

Nüsse, Andrea. *Muslim Palestine: The Ideology of Hamas*. Amsterdam: Harwood Academic Publishers, 1998.

Nyerere, Julius K. *Freedom and Development: Uhuru na Maendelo. A Selection from Writings and Speeches 1968–1973*. Dar es Salaam, Tanzania: Oxford University Press, 1973.

———. *Freedom and Socialism: Uhuru na Ujamaa. A Selection from Writings and Speeches 1965–1970*. Dar es Salaam, Tanzania: Oxford University Press, 1968.

———. *Ujamaa—Essays on Socialism*. Dar es Salaam, Tanzania: Oxford University Press, 1968.

Özkirimli, Umut. *Theories of Nationalism: A Critical Introduction*. New York: St. Martin's Press, 2000.

Pappe, Ilan. *A History of Modern Palestine: One Land, Two Peoples*. Cambridge: Cambridge University Press, 2004.

Pecora, Vincent P., ed. *Nations and Identities: Classic Readings*. Oxford: Blackwell, 2001.

Poole, Ross. *Nation and Identity*. London: Routledge, 1999.

Punter, David. *Postcolonial Imaginings: Fictions of a New World Order*. Lanham, MD: Rowman & Littlefield, 2000.

Robinson, Dean E. *Black Nationalism in American Politics and Thought*. Cambridge: Cambridge University Press, 2001.

Rotberg, Robert I., ed. *When States Fail: Causes and Consequences*. Princeton, NJ: Princeton University Press, 2004.

Rubenberg, Cheryl A. *The Palestinians: In Search of a Just Peace*. Boulder, CO: Lynne Rienner, 2003.

Said, Edward W. *Orientalism*. New York: Pantheon Books, 1978. Reprint with a new afterword. Harmondsworth, England: Penguin, 1995.

Sandoval, Chela. *Methodology of the Oppressed*. Minneapolis: University of Minnesota Press, 2000.

San Juan, E[pifanio], Jr. *Beyond Postcolonial Theory*. New York: St. Martin's Press, 1998.

Schöpflin, George. *Nations, Identity, Power*. New York: New York University Press, 2000.

Schwarz, Henry, and Sangeeta Ray, eds. *A Companion to Postcolonial Studies*. Malden, MA: Blackwell, 2000.

Sen, Amartya. *Development as Freedom*. New York: Knopf, 1999.

Smith, Anthony D. *Myths and Memories of the Nation*. Oxford: Oxford University Press, 1999.

———. *Nationalism and Modernism: A Critical Survey of Recent Theories of Nations and Nationalism.* London: Routledge, 1998.

———. *Nationalism: Theory, Ideology, History.* Cambridge, England: Polity Press, 2001. Introductory survey of the current landscape of nationalism research.

Smith, Rogers M. *Stories of Peoplehood: The Politics and Morals of Political Memberships.* Cambridge: Cambridge University Press, 2003.

Spencer, Philip, and Howard Wollman. "Good and Bad Nationalisms: A Critique of Dualism." *Journal of Political Ideologies* 3, no. 3 (October 1998): 255–74.

Spivak, Gayatri Chakravorty. *A Critique of Postcolonial Reason: Toward a History of the Vanishing Present.* Cambridge: Harvard University Press, 1999.

Stephen, Lynn. *Zapata Lives! Histories and Cultural Politics in Southern Mexico.* Berkeley: University of California Press, 2002.

Tamir, Yael. *Liberal Nationalism.* 2nd ed. Princeton, NJ: Princeton University Press, 1995.

Todd, Emmanuel. *After the Empire: The Breakdown of the American Order.* Translated by C. Jon Delogu. New York: Columbia University Press, 2003.

Uvin, Peter. *Human Rights and Development.* Bloomfield, CT: Kumarian Press, 2004.

Vertovec, Steven, and Robin Cohen, eds. *Conceiving Cosmopolitanism: Theory, Context and Practice.* Oxford: Oxford University Press, 2002.

Vincent, Andrew. *Nationalism and Particularity.* Cambridge: Cambridge University Press, 2002.

Viroli, Maurizio. *For Love of Country: An Essay on Patriotism and Nationalism.* Oxford: Clarendon Press, 1995.

Wasserstein, Barnard. *Israelis and Palestinians: Why Do They Fight? Can They Stop?* New Haven, CT: Yale University Press, 2003.

Weitz, Eric D. *A Century of Genocide: Utopias of Race and Nation.* Princeton, NJ: Princeton University Press, 2003.

Wicker, Hans-Rudolf, ed. *Rethinking Nationalism and Ethnicity: The Struggle for Meaning and Order in Europe.* Oxford: Berg, 1997.

Wiebe, Robert H. *Who We Are: A History of Popular Nationalism.* Princeton, NJ: Princeton University Press, 2002.

Yack, Bernard. "The Myth of the Civic Nation." *Critical Review* 10:2 (Spring 1996): 193–211.

Zapatista Encuentro: Documents from the 1996 Encounter for Humanity and Against Neoliberalism. The Zapatistas. New York: Seven Stories Press, 1998.

¡Zapatistas! Documents of the New Mexican Revolution (December 31, 1993–June 12, 1994). Brooklyn: Autonomedia, 1994.

Globalization

Agosín, Marjorie, ed. *Women, Gender and Human Rights: A Global Perspective.* New Brunswick, NJ: Rutgers University Press, 2001.

Anderson, Sarah, ed. *Views from the South: The Effects of Globalization and the WTO on Third World Countries.* Oakland, CA: Food First Books and the International Forum on Globalization, 2000.

Archibugi, Daniele, and David Held, ed. *Cosmopolitan Democracy: An Agenda for a New World Order.* Cambridge, England: Polity Press, 1995.

Barker, Jonathan, with Anne-Marie Cwikowski, Christie Gombay, Katherine Isbester, Kole Shettima, and Aparna Sundar. *Street-Level Democracy: Political Settings at the Margins of Global Power.* Toronto: Between the Lines/West Hartford, CT: Kumarian Press, 1999.

Bello, Walden. *The Future in the Balance: Essays on Globalization and Resistance.* Edited by Anuradha Mittal. Oakland, CA: Food First Books; Focus on the Global South, 2001.

Brecher, Jeremy, Tim Costello, and Brendan Smith. *Globalization from Below: The Power of Solidarity.* Cambridge, MA: South End Press, 2000.

Broad, Robin, ed. *Global Backlash: Citizen Initiatives for a Just World Economy.* Lanham, MD: Rowman & Littlefield, 2002.

Chomsky, Noam. *Hegemony or Survival: America's Quest for Global Dominance.* New York: Metropolitan Books, 2003.

Clark, John D. *Worlds Apart: Civil Society and the Battle for Ethical Globalization.* Bloomfield, CT: Kumarian Press, 2003.

Cohen, David, Rosa de la Vega, and Gabrielle Watson. *Advocacy for Social Justice: A Global Action and Reflection Guide.* Bloomfield, CT: Kumarian Press, 2001.

Croucher, Sheila L. *Globalization and Belonging: The Politics of Identity in a Changing World.* Lanham, MD: Rowman & Littlefield, 2004.

Dallmayr, Fred. *Achieving Our World: Toward a Global and Plural Democracy.* Lanham, MD: Rowman and Littlefield, 2001.

Danaher, Kevin. *10 Reasons to Abolish the IMF & World Bank.* 2nd ed. New York: Seven Stories Press, 2004.

Dunning, John H., ed. *Making Globalization Good: The Moral Challenges of Global Capitalism.* Oxford: Oxford University Press, 2003. Generally favors global capitalism.

Eaton, Heather, and Lois Ann Lorentzen, eds. *Ecofeminism and Globalization: Exploring Culture, Context, and Religion.* Lanham, MD: Rowman & Littlefield, 2003.

Etzioni, Amitai. *From Empire to Community: A New Approach to International Relations.* London: Palgrave Macmillan, 2004.

Graeber, David. "For a New Anarchism." *New Left Review,* 2nd series 13 (January/February 2002): 61–73. Globalization.

Halper, Stefan, and Jonathan Clarke. *America Alone: The Neo-Conservatives and the Global Order.* Cambridge: Cambridge University Press, 2004.

Harvey, David. *The New Imperialism.* Oxford: Oxford University Press, 2003.

Hawthorne, Susan. *Wild Politics: Feminism Globalisation Bio/Diversity.* North Melbourne, Vic, Australia: Spinifex Press, 2002.

Held, David. *Global Covenant: The Social Democratic Alternative to the Washington Consensus.* Cambridge, England: Polity, 2004.

Jordan, Bill, and Franck Düvell. *Irregular Migration: The Dilemmas of Transnational Mobility.* Cheltenham, England: Edward Elgar, 2002.

———. *Migration: The Boundaries of Equality and Justice.* Oxford, England: Polity, 2003.

Kaldor, Mary. *Global Civil Society: An Answer to War.* Cambridge, England: Polity, 2003.

Keane, John. *Global Civil Society?* Cambridge: Cambridge University Press, 2003.

Klein, Naomi. *No Logo.* London: Flamingo, 2000.

Leadbeater, Charles. *Up the Down Escalator: Why the Global Pessimists Are Wrong.* London: Viking, 2002.

Mann, Michael. *Incoherent Empire.* London: Verso, 2003. Distinguishes between national liberationist terrorists, who are hard to defeat because embedded in the culture, and international terrorists, who can be defeated because exposed in another culture (too simple, given multiculturalism).

Mansbridge, Jane, and Aldon Morris, eds. *Oppositional Consciousness: The Subjective Roots of Social Protest.* Chicago: University of Chicago Press, 2001.

Monbiot, George. *Manifesto for a New World Order.* New York: New Press, 2004.

Naples, Nancy, and Manisha Desai, eds. *Women's Activism and Globalization: Linking Local Struggles and Transnational Politics.* New York: Routledge, 2002.

Norberg, Johan. *In Defense of Global Capitalism.* Washington, DC: The Cato Institute, 2003. From a libertarian perspective, capitalism as providing freedom and opportunity to even the poorest peasant.

Paehlke, Robert C. *Democracy's Dilemma: Environment, Social Equity and the Global Economy.* Cambridge, MA: MIT Press, 2003.

Patomäki, Heikki. *Democratizing Globalization: The Leverage of the Tobin Tax.* London: Zed Books, 2001.

Pieterse, Jan Nederveen. *Globalization and Culture: Global Mélange.* Lanham, MD: Rowman & Littlefield, 2004.

Rondinelli, Dennis A., and G. Shabbir, eds. *Reinventing Government for the Twenty-First Century: State Capacity in a Globalizing Society.* Bloomfield, CT: Kumarian Press, 2003.

Roy, Arundhati. *The Algebra of Infinite Injustice.* Rev. & updated ed. New Delhi, India: Penguin Books India, 2002.

Roy, Arundhati. *War Talk.* Cambridge, MA: South End Press, 2003.

Roy, Arundhati, and David Barsamian. *The Checkbook and the Cruise Missile. Conversations with Arundhati Roy. Interviews by David Barsamian.* Cambridge, MA: South End Press, 2004.

Rupert, Mark. *Ideologies of Globalization: Contending Visions of a New World Order.* London: Routledge, 2000.

Shapiro, Ian, and Lea Brilmayer, eds. *Global Justice.* New York: New York University Press, 1999.

Shepard, Benjamin, and Richard Hayduk, eds. *From ACT UP to the WTO: Urban Protest and Community Building in the Era of Globalization.* London: Verso, 2002.

Singer, Peter. *One World: The Ethics of Globalization.* 2nd ed. New Haven, CT: Yale University Press, 2004. Argues that ethically there is only one world; sections/chapters on one atmosphere, one law, one community.

Slaughter, Anne-Marie. *A New World Order.* Princeton, NJ: Princeton University Press, 2004.

Smith, Jackie, and Hank Johnston, eds. *Globalization and Resistance: Transnational Dimensions of Social Movements.* Lanham, MD: Rowman & Littlefield, 2002.

Starr, Amory. *Naming the Enemy: Anti-Corporate Movements Confront Globalization.* London: Zed Books, 2000.

Steger, Manfred B. *Globalism: The New Market Ideology.* Lanham, MD: Rowman & Littlefield, 2002.

———, ed. *Rethinking Globalism.* Lanham, MD: Rowman & Littlefield, 2004.

Thomas-Slayter, Barbara P. *Southern Exposure: International Development and the Global South in the Twenty-First Century.* Bloomfield, CT: Kumarian Press, 2003.

Welton, Neva, and Linda Wolf, eds. *Global Uprising: Confronting the Tyrannies of the 21st Century: Stories from a New Generation of Activists.* Gabriola Island, BC: New Society, 2001.

Went, Robert. *Globalization: Neoliberal Challenge, Radical Responses.* Translated by Peter Drucker. London: Pluto Press with the International Institute for Research and Education, 2000. Consideration of globalization from the "progressive" point of view. Proposes reregulation of the financial sector, cancellation of Third World debt, a break with export-led growth, redistribution of income, and democracy and planning as opposed to rule by the market.

Wolf, Martin. *Why Globalization Works.* New Haven, CT: Yale University Press, 2004.

Woodin, Michael, and Caroline Lucas. *Green Alternatives to Globalisation: A Manifesto.* London: Pluto Press, 2004. Economic localisation, LETS, local food.

Young, Iris Marion. "Responsibility and Global Labor Justice." *The Journal of Political Philosophy* 12:4 (2004): 365–88.

Websites

The Nationalism Project: http://www.nationalismproject.org/

Third World

Third World Network: http://www.twnside.org.sg/

Indigenous Peoples

Center for World Indigenous Studies: http://www.cwis.org/

Convention Concerning Indigenous and Tribal Peoples in Independent Countries: http://www.cwis.org/fwdp/treaties.html and http://www.cwis.org/fwdp/International/ilo_169.txt

Draft Declaration on the Rights of Indigenous Peoples:
http://www.cwis.org/drft9329.html

Fourth World Journal: http://www.cwis.org/fwj/

Indigenous Peoples Council on Biocolonialism: http://www.ipcb.org

Second Continental Congress of Indigenous Pueblos and Nationalities of Abya Yala:
http://www.cumbreindigenabyayala.org/index_en.html

Survival International: http://www.survival-international.org/

Globalization

Anti-Capitalist Convergence: http://www.abolishthebank.org/

Asia-Pacific Economic Cooperation (APEC): http://apec.org/

Association for the Taxation of Financial Transactions for the Aid of Citizens (ATTAC):
http://www.attac.org/

European Social Forum: http://www.fse-esf.org/

Free Trade Agreement of the Americas (FTAA): http://www.ftaa-alca.org/

International Monetary Fund: http://imf.org/

Landless Workers' Movement (Brazil): http://www.mstbrazil.org/

Midwest Unrest: http://www.midwestunrest.net/

Mobilization for Global Justice: http://sept.globalizethis.org/

North American Free Trade Agreement (NAFTA) Secretariat: http://www.nafta-sec-alena.
org/DefaultSite/index.html

Organisation for Economic Cooperation and Development: http://oecd.org/

Our World Is Not for Sale: http://www.ourworldisnotforsale.org/

Peoples' Global Action: http://www.nadir.org/nadir/initiativ/agp/

Stop the Free Trade Agreement of the Americas: http://www.stopftaa.org/

United for Peace and Justice: http://unitedforpeace.org/

World Bank: http://worldbank.org/

World Economic Forum: http://www.weforum.org/

World Social Forum: http://www.wsfindia.org/

World Trade Organization: http://wto.org

3

The Principles
of Democracy

The word *democracy* comes from two Greek words: *demos* = people and *kratos* = rule. Therefore, the word means "rule by the people," sometimes called "popular sovereignty," and can refer to direct, participatory, and representative forms of rule by the people. Today the word has a positive meaning throughout most of the world—so much so that, to connect themselves with this positive image, even some political systems with little or no rule by the people are called democratic.

The following analysis uses a simple model of the key elements of democracy as it exists today:

1. Citizen involvement in decision making
2. A system of representation
3. The rule of law
4. An electoral system—majority rule
5. Some degree of equality among citizens
6. Some degree of liberty or freedom granted to or retained by citizens
7. Education

CITIZEN INVOLVEMENT

The most fundamental characteristic of any democratic system, truly its defining characteristic, is the idea that citizens should be involved in making political decisions, either directly or through representatives of their choosing. These two approaches can be characterized as

1. *Direct democracy*—Citizens take part personally in deliberations and vote on issues. Citizens debate and vote on all laws.
2. *Representative democracy*—Citizens choose (elect) other citizens to debate and pass on laws.

Voting on issues personally is the defining activity of a citizen in a direct democracy. Direct democracy has only rarely been practiced as a means of governing a country, but most people have experienced such involvement at a lower level. Almost everyone in the West has, at some time, had a chance to discuss and vote on an issue. This may have taken place at a school or university; in a church, mosque, or synagogue; in a union or club meeting; or in one of the hundreds of other groups that allow voting members to decide at least some questions that concern the membership.

In addition, most people have voted in an election in some such organization, thereby taking part in one of the basic steps of choosing a representative; fewer people, but still a substantial number, have cast their votes to elect a public official. These are the defining activities of a citizen in a representative democracy.

Other forms of citizen involvement in a democratic system include actively participating in a political party or interest group, attending and participating in political meetings or public hearings, discussing politics with friends or colleagues, or contacting a public official about an issue. A growing area of involvement is for citizens to work for or against issues that will be voted on during an election. This area is growing because interest groups or groups of citizens are bringing more issues directly to the electorate through initiative petitions or referenda (see the definitions in the glossary and the discussion in Current Trends later in this chapter).

In a representative system, citizen involvement helps to ensure that public officials are accountable and responsive to the people. Candidates for public office must convince voters that there are good reasons to vote for them rather than their opponents. In particular, elected officials are expected to show that they respond to the changing needs and demands of their constituents. Of course, no system can guarantee responsive public officials, but having to run for reelection helps.

In addition, involvement is thought to be good for citizens. Defenders of democracy believe that being involved in decision making (even if this means simply voting in an election) expands the horizons of voters and makes them more aware of issues. Involvement encourages a feeling of responsibility, a sense of belonging to a community, and knowledge. Involved citizens become better, more complete people. Of course, this positive effect depends on citizens being informed about the issues involved and demonstrates why education is considered important in a democracy.

The positive effect is particularly true for those whose involvement goes beyond the vote to more active participation. Citizens who choose to get directly involved in the political life of their community will benefit more than more passive citizens who limit their participation to the vote.

Defenders of democracy ask a simple question: Who else should make political decisions? A monarch? A political boss? Bureaucrats? The rich? Who better knows the interests of the average citizen than the average citizen?

In some countries, including the United States, many people—sometimes even the majority—do not bother to vote. In the 2000 U.S. presidential election, just 51 percent of eligible voters participated. The 2004 turnout of 59.6% was the highest since 1968, when it was 60.84% and 1964 when it was 61.92%. The lowest turnouts in late-20th century presidential elections were 1986 with 36.40% and 1990 with 36.52%. Turnouts are counted in two ways, the percentage of people eligible to vote (VEP) and percentage of people of voting age (VAP). The former is much more accurate in that it excludes noncitizens and others who are for some reason not eligible.

Not voting does not mean that decisions won't be made; someone will still make them. Do high levels of nonvoting undermine democracy? Does this matter? These questions have produced a number of approaches to either justify the system that exists or propose changes in it. These approaches include elitism, pluralism, corporatism or neocorporatism, and participatory theories of democracy. The first three all assume that democracy is working fairly well with low levels of participation. In addition, these three approaches recognize and support differences in power within the political system. Participatory theories argue that democracy is not working and that ways must be found to increase participation. In addition, participatory theories claim that the differences in power supported by the other three approaches are part of the problem, not part of the solution.

Elitism

The elitist approach asserts that democracy is "a method of making decisions which ensures efficiency in administration and policy making and yet requires some measure of responsiveness to popular opinion on the part of the ruling elites."[1] In this view, citizen involvement primarily functions as a check on political leaders while maintaining competition among rival elites. The arguments for elitist theories center on efficiency and the perceived inability of voters to make informed decisions. The citizen casting his or her vote is, in this view, simply a mechanism for deciding among competing elites. Given the complexity of the modern world and the issues involved, the argument goes, it is impossible for the average citizen to know enough to participate intelligently in decision making. But competition is still thought desirable, so the vote is used to choose the group that will be given temporary power.

---

[1] Jack L. Walker, "A Critique of the Elitist Theory of Democracy," *American Political Science Review* 60 (June 1966): 286.

The classic response to elitist theories is to argue that (1) efficiency is not as important as the positive influence of participation on the citizen and (2) the average citizen is probably capable of understanding most issues. The elitist theorists say, in effect, that classical representative democracy does not—even cannot—work in the modern world. Their opponents argue that a truly informed citizenry is even more important than in the past and that representative democracy can work even though new problems make it more difficult to achieve. But they also argue that people need to be actively encouraged to participate and given the means of informing themselves regarding the issues.

Pluralism

Closely related to the elitist view is pluralism, in which the political system is composed of interest groups competing for power with none strong enough to dominate. As long as competition exists and is fair, no single interest can gain too much power; one interest will always be held in check by the other interests. Advocates contend that pluralism is the best system for a representative democracy, because pluralism protects citizens from too great a centralization of power and allows all the diverse interests within a society to be expressed. In the United States today, pluralism connects neatly to the growth of interest in multiculturalism (structuring society around competing and cooperating cultures). But it is important to note that pluralism is about distribution of power and multiculturalism is about toleration of difference.

Most modern societies are pluralistic in that they are composed of a variety of groups based on characteristics such as wealth, race, gender, ethnic or national origin, profession, and religion. Defenders of pluralism argue that this diversity should be recognized and protected. Thus pluralism includes both a positive awareness of the group basis of most contemporary societies and the belief that democracy needs to incorporate that awareness. Pluralists in the United States assert that pluralism supplements the system of checks and balances enshrined in the U.S. Constitution with additional checks on power. Outside the United States, pluralists argue that competition among groups is often the primary means of limiting centralized power.

Critics of pluralism make two major points. First, according to the antipluralists, the only thing of interest to the competing elites is staying in office; all values are secondary to this overriding goal. Thus the suggestion that pluralism protects freedom is false. Pluralism is a protection for freedom, or any other value, only as long as that value is to the political benefit of the competing groups. Second, antipluralists note that the supposedly competing groups cooperate to maintain the present system and their positions of power within it. As a result pluralism and the groups that compete within it are obstacles to change, particularly in trying to avoid the emergence of new groups that might successfully compete for power.

Corporatism

Corporatism (or neocorporatism, as some of its proponents prefer to call it to distinguish it from a similar idea found in fascism) contends that interest groups both compete and cooperate with each other and share power with government bureaucracies. Interest groups do not merely consult with government but are fully integrated into the process of policy making and implementation. As one writer put it, corporatism means the "negotiation of policy between state agencies and interest organisations arising from the division of labour in society, where policy agreements are implemented through the collaboration of the interest organisations and their willingness and ability to secure the compliance of their members."[2]

The theory of corporatism has had a great impact on how interest organizations perceive their relations with one another and with government. Although corporatism has not significantly reduced competition among interest groups, it has provided the theoretical basis for their taking a more active role in actually developing policy in cooperation with government bureaucracies.

Critics of corporatism argue that it simply justifies greater power on the part of unelected people, that the similarity of the concept in fascism is no accident, and that corporatism explicitly denies the power of citizens to control their own lives in a democracy. Critics of elitism, pluralism, and corporatism often suggest that more, not less, direct participation on the part of the citizens is the best approach to democracy.

Participatory Democracy

The most direct challenge to the previous approaches is found among those who say that the low level of citizen involvement is a problem that should not be rationalized away but solved. Advocates of participatory democracy see elitism, pluralism, and corporatism as disregarding the most fundamental principle of democracy, and they contend that shifting power away from elected officials to citizens can save the principle. In other words, they propose moving the system away from representative democracy in the direction of direct democracy.[3]

The participatory democrat argues that laws they did not help make or participate in making should not bind individuals. In other words, the individual—all individuals—must be consulted in the making of laws that will affect them. If they are not consulted, the laws should be considered invalid.

In addition to asserting that more participatory democracy can work, advocates of this position contend that only with greater participation can the other principles of democracy be fulfilled. According to this argument, people will never be politically equal or free unless they become active and involved citizens committed to making the system work by making representative democracy more like direct democracy. At the same time, contemporary defenders of participatory democracy do not oppose representation; they just believe that voters should keep their representatives on a shorter leash.

Opponents of participatory democracy argue that it simply goes too far and, as a result, is impractical. It would be fine if it was possible, but it cannot be

---

[2] Wyn Grant, introduction to *The Political Economy of Corporatism,* ed. Wyn Grant (London: Macmillan, 1985), 3–4.

[3] See, for example, Carole Pateman, *Participation and Democratic Theory* (Cambridge: Cambridge University Press, 1970); and Benjamin R. Barber, *Strong Democracy: Participatory Politics for a New Age* (Berkeley: University of California Press, 1984).

achieved in our complex world. Also, the fact that many choose not to vote raises questions about any participatory theory. These critics assert that contemporary political decisions require both expertise and time not available to the average citizen. As a result, they say, a system of representative democracy is necessary.

REPRESENTATION

If direct participation is difficult to achieve or not a good idea, then it is necessary to develop a way for people to participate indirectly. The primary means has been through representatives, or people chosen by citizens to act for them. In other words, citizens delegate to one of their number the responsibility for making certain decisions. The person chosen may be a delegate from a geographical area or of a certain number of people (representation by area or population). The citizens represented are called the *constituents,* or the representative's *constituency.*

The word *represent* is used in a number of different ways that help provide an understanding of the situation:

1. Something *represents* something else when it is a faithful reproduction or exact copy of the original.
2. Something that symbolizes something else is said to *represent* it.
3. A lawyer *represents* a client when he or she acts in place of or for the client.

Clearly, the third meaning is closest to the way we think of a representative in democracy, but it is not that simple because no constituency is composed of citizens whose interests are identical. As a result, there are two main approaches to the relationship between the representative and her or his constituency, with most actual representatives fitting somewhere between the two extremes.

Some representatives try to reflect the varied interests of their constituents as precisely as possible, while others take the position that they were elected to make the best decisions they can for the nation as a whole. The latter position was first put forth by Edmund Burke (1729–97), who said,

> To deliver an opinion is the right of all men; that of constituents is a weighty and respectable opinion, which a representative ought always rejoice to hear, and which he ought always most seriously to consider. But *authoritative* instructions, *mandates* issued, which the member is bound blindly and implicitly to obey, to vote for, and to argue for, though contrary to the dearest conviction of his judgment and conscience—these are things utterly unknown to the laws of this land, and which arise from a fundamental mistake of the whole order and tenor of our Constitution.
>
> Parliament is not a *congress* of ambassadors from different and hostile interests, which each must maintain, as an agent and advocate, against other agents and advocates; but Parliament is a *deliberative* assembly of *one* nation,

with one interest, that of the whole; where, not local purposes, not local prejudices, ought to guide, but the general good, resulting from the general reason of the whole. You choose a member, indeed; but when you have chosen him, he is not a member of Bristol, he is a member of *Parliament*. If the local constituent should form a hasty opinion evidently opposite to the real good of the rest of the community, the member for that place ought to be as far as any other from an endeavor to give it effect.[4]

Here Burke presents a case for the representative as an independent agent who is a representative solely in the sense that she or he is elected by the people in a particular area. In doing this, Burke specifically rejects representation in the third sense: the representative as agent for some individual or group.

Seldom, if ever, will an elected official fit exactly one and only one of the roles assigned by the theories of representation. Even the most Burkean representative will act as a constituency agent at times or on certain issues. The typical representative is likely to act as a constituency agent whenever constituents are actively concerned with a particular issue or to assist individuals or groups of constituents when they need help in dealing with a bureaucracy. At the same time, the typical representative is likely to act as a Burkean representative on issues that do not directly concern the constituency (and thus about which little or no pressure is received from the constituency).

As we have already seen in the discussion of participatory theories, an issue that concerns some theorists is how to give representative democracy some attributes of direct democracy. In the United States such practices as the initiative, referendum, and recall were developed to allow people to play a direct role in political decision making, and these devices are presently being used extensively.

This issue can be seen most clearly in the thinking of Jean-Jacques Rousseau (1712–78), who said, "Thus deputies of the people are not, and cannot be, its representatives; they are merely its agents, and can make no final decisions. Any law which the people have not ratified in person is null, it is not a law."[5] Here Rousseau has used two of our definitions of *represent*. For him a representative is not an independent agent but one who acts only with constituent approval. Rousseau realized that within a large country direct democracy was impractical, even impossible, and although he maintained the ideal of direct democracy, he did discuss representation in a more favorable light. He said,

> I have just shown that government weakens as the number of magistrates [elected officials] increases; and I have already shown that the more numerous the people [are], the more repressive force is needed. From which it follows that the ratio of magistrates to government should be in inverse proportions to the ratio of subjects to sovereign; which means that the more the state expands, the more the government ought to contract; and

---

[4] Speech to the Electors of Bristol (1774), in *The Works of the Right Honorable Edmund Burke,* 7th ed. (Boston: Little, Brown, 1881), 11:96 (emphasis in the original).

[5] Jean-Jacques Rousseau, *Du contrat social* (Paris: Le Renaissance de Livre, 1762), 86.

Library of Congress

Jean-Jacques Rousseau (1712–78) is best known as a political philosopher. His works *Discours sur les sciences et les arts* (*Discourse on the Arts and Sciences,* 1750), *Discours sur l'origine et les fondements de l'inégalité* (*Discourse on the Origin and Foundations of Inequality,* 1755), *Émile* (1762), a treatise on education, *Du contrat social* (*The Social Contract,* 1762), and others placed him in the forefront among critics of contemporary society. He argued that civilization was corrupting and that a return to a simpler society in which each individual could fully participate was the remedy for the current social ills. His arguments were used as justifications for the French Revolution. The meaning, intent, and effect of Rousseau's ideas are still widely debated; interpretations of his thought range from the belief that he was one of the founders of modern totalitarianism to the belief that he was an important defender of democracy.

thus that the number of rulers should diminish in proportion to the increases of the population.[6]

Rousseau would have liked to see a country small enough so every person could be his[7] own representative, but as population increases this becomes more and more difficult. Thus the number of rulers must of necessity diminish through the establishment of some type of representative system, and the larger the country the more powerful those representatives must be. Rousseau believed that the closer a system can come to a direct democracy through an increase in the number of magistrates, the better the system will be, but this is only possible in a very small country. Rousseau's approach to representation has gained favor in recent years in movements that support participatory democracy.

THE RULE OF LAW

In a democracy an elected representative participates in making laws but is still bound by the law. Once passed, the law is supreme, not those who made the law. Representatives can participate in changing a law, but until it is changed they, along with everyone else, must obey it.

---

[6] Rousseau, *Du contrat social,* 59.

[7] In Rousseau's case it is fairly clear that he would not extend direct political involvement to women. On Rousseau's treatment of women, see Susan Moller Okin, "Rousseau," in Okin, *Women in Western Political Thought* (Princeton, NJ: Princeton University Press, 1979), 99–194.

This apparently simple notion came about only after a long struggle. It was one of the basic principles demanded in the early conflicts that led to the establishment of democratic institutions. Before that, monarchs claimed that they had been appointed by God to rule (the divine right of kings) and were, therefore, above the law. The principle involved is that a society should be able to bind itself by the rules it collectively has chosen, and no individual or institution should be outside the rules so chosen.

Of course, the rule of law can be complex. For example, not all—perhaps even few—laws are so clear that everyone agrees on their meaning. Therefore, every country has procedures for interpreting the meaning of laws, and those interpretations can change over time. In the United States, for example, the Supreme Court ruled in *Plessy v. Ferguson* (163 US 537 [1896]) that racially segregated facilities were legal under the U.S. Constitution. In *Brown v. Board of Education of Topeka* (347 US 483 [1954]), it ruled that they were not.

Another way in which the rule of law is not so simple is that some laws conflict or at least appear to conflict with other laws. Countries have to rely on some mechanism for deciding which law takes precedence and must be obeyed. In the United States the Supreme Court has the role of deciding which laws conflict with the U.S. Constitution and is the ultimate arbiter of all disputes over conflicting laws. Other countries have a wide variety of institutions to make this determination, but some means is always available.

THE ELECTORAL SYSTEM

The means of choosing representatives is central to making democracy work, and there has been considerable conflict over procedures to do this. As we learned during the Florida vote count in the 2000 presidential election, the details of electoral procedures can be a significant part of determining the outcome of an election.[8] What might appear to be simple questions prove to raise serious issues. Consider the following examples:

1. For what period of time should someone be elected?

2. Should elected representatives be allowed to be reelected to the same office? If yes, how many times? If no, can they be elected again after not holding the office for a period? How long?

3. What percentage of the vote does a person need to be chosen? Fifty percent plus one (called a *simple majority*) works nicely if there are only two candidates, but poses problems if there are more than two.

4. If there are more than two candidates, should there be a second election (called a *runoff*) to choose between the two highest vote getters in the first election?

---

[8] The 2004 election was not close enough for major conflicts to develop, but thousands of lawyers were standing by to step in and raise procedural issues if it had been. If the election had been as close as the 2000 election, suits would have been brought in a number of states.

5. Are there any circumstances where more than a simple majority should be required?

6. How large should a representative assembly be?

7. How many representatives should be chosen from each area or for what population size?

All of these questions have been disputed at times, and most still are. Also, many countries are currently going through what is being called *democratization,* in which these questions *must* be answered in the process of establishing representative institutions where none had existed.

The electoral process begins with the selection of candidates. The means by which this takes place varies from country to country and even within countries. In some cases, the system is entirely under the control of political parties, and a citizen must become active in a party to influence the choice of candidates. In other cases, although the political party is still important, an election (in the United States this is called a *primary*) is held to reduce the number of candidates. In this situation citizens can influence the final list of candidates by voting, donating money to a candidate, or working actively for a candidate.

For a citizen who simply wants to vote intelligently, deciding whom to vote for will depend largely on the available information. For many offices a high percentage of voters vote on the basis of party identification alone; others depend on information provided by the candidate's campaign and the media. Reliable information is not always easy to come by, and voters often feel they are forced to choose without the information necessary to make a fully informed decision. This may be one reason for the low voter turnout in some countries. Getting adequate information can take more effort than some voters are willing to expend. And sometimes simply making a decision that reflects your own beliefs is hard. For example, recently there was a local election in my area. Both candidates took positions I liked and both took positions I disliked, and it was a fairly dirty campaign. In these circumstances, the temptation to not vote is strong, and it is hardly surprising that many people choose not to. But not voting is giving the decision on who holds power to others.

The normal rule of elections is that the side with the most votes wins, but it is always important to remember that this does not mean that those with the most votes are right; it just means that because more people voted for A rather than B, A must be accepted until the next election gives people the chance to change to B if they wish. Majority rule tends to be based on the assumption that any issue has only two sides. If, for example, there are three candidates in an election, majority rule becomes more complicated because it is harder to determine what the majority wants. In addition, in many elections relatively few potential voters actually cast their ballots; therefore, the majority may not be represented in the result. (Some countries, therefore, *require* their citizens to vote.) This objection can, of course, be answered by saying that those who do not vote do not care; but what if some of the people who do not vote do not feel that any candidate sufficiently reflects their position? This difficulty illustrates the advantage of having more than two candidates in an election, but we have already seen the disadvantage of such an arrangement—if no one receives a clear majority, does this constitute majority rule?

To avoid these problems, various governments have made it difficult or impossible for more than two sides to be represented on the ballot, and other governments have used a system called *proportional representation* (PR), which allocates seats in the legislature on the basis of the percentage of the votes cast for an individual or party. In a simple example of PR, using a 100-seat legislature like the U.S. Senate, if a minor party got 10 percent of the vote it would get 10 seats, whereas in the usual system where only the party that gets the majority of votes in a district is seated, the minor party would almost certainly get no seats.

Another way to make a representative system more representative is to change from single-member to multiple-member districts. In the usual system, one person is elected from each district, but some places elect two or more people from a district. In most, but not all, cases, this results in more women and minorities being elected.[9]

A final institutional arrangement designed to protect minorities is the common practice in the United States of requiring more than a simple majority on certain issues, such as money issues and amending basic sets of rules like constitutions. The purpose is to protect the rights of the minority, it being felt that at least on some issues a minority with strongly held opinions should not be dictated to by the majority.

The electoral system, although seemingly only a mechanism for determining the composition of the government over the next few years, actually provides the major and sometimes the sole means of political participation for individuals living in a large, complex, modern society. The electoral system, therefore, takes on peculiar importance for democratic theory. Because it often provides a significant or the only means of political participation, the electoral system is the key to whether the system is democratic. Individuals, when entering the voting booth, must be sure that their votes will be counted; that the election provides some choice; and that the choice is meaningful in that voters are actually free to vote for any of the options. It is also important to remember the most obvious point—that is, that an individual is allowed to vote in the first place. Finally, each vote should be equal to any other vote, although in the nineteenth century proposals for plural votes based on some criterion like education were fairly common.[10]

These questions of electoral procedure bring into focus other important problems. The electoral system, in addition to providing a means of political participation, is designed to guarantee the peaceful change of political power

---

[9] On the different systems and their relationship to democracy, see Douglas J. Amy, *Behind the Ballot Box: A Citizen's Guide to Voting Systems* (Westport, CT: Praeger, 2000); Richard S. Katz, *Democracy and Elections* (New York: Oxford University Press, 1997); and G. Bingham Powell, *Elections as Instruments of Democracy: Majoritarian and Proportional Visions* (New Haven, CT: Yale University Press, 2000).

[10] See, for example, John Stuart Mill, *Considerations on Representative Government*, ed. Currin V. Shields (New York: Liberal Arts Press, 1958), 136–43.

Library of Congress

James Madison (1751–1836) was secretary of state (1801–1809) during the presidency of Thomas Jefferson and then was the fourth president of the United States (1809–17). Madison is now remembered mostly as one of the authors of *The Federalist Papers* (1787–88) and as a major contributor to the drafting of the U.S. Constitution. Madison was concerned with the problem of minority rights and argued that the Constitution as written would provide adequate protection for minorities.

from one individual or group to another. This in turn raises the issue of leadership within a democracy, a question confronting democratic theorists since ancient Athens. The importance of leadership in democratic theory is particularly significant in representative democracy. Whatever theory of representation is accepted, the elected official is given some political power not directly held by constituents. This power can be removed through the electoral process, but in the meantime it is held by an individual who can directly participate in political decision making to the extent of the power vested in the office. In addition, the official may exercise political leadership by helping form or inform the opinions of constituents and others by defining the political issues he or she believes significant and by propagandizing for particular positions.[11]

Historically, most democratic theorists have been concerned with limiting the political power held by any individual or group within a society while at the same time providing intelligent and capable leadership. For example, James Madison (1751–1836), an important figure in the framing of the U.S. Constitution and the fourth president of the United States, was greatly worried about the possibility of some faction, including a "majority faction," gaining political power and exercising it in its own interest.

In the tenth number of *The Federalist Papers* (1787–88), Madison suggested that the best protectors of freedom are the division of powers between the states and the national government; the separation of powers among the executive, legislative, and judicial branches of government found in the U.S. Constitution;[12]

---

[11] On leadership, see Arnold M. Ludwig, *King of the Mountain: The Nature of Political Leadership* (Lexington: University Press of Kentucky, 2002).

[12] The idea of the separation of powers came mostly through the writings of the French political theorist Montesquieu (1689–1755), particularly his *De l'esprit des lois* (*The Spirit of the Laws*) (1748).

and the diversity of a large country. Others involved in the writing and defense of the Constitution advocated an enlightened aristocracy exercising political power but periodically checked through election, rather than rule by the people. In other words, they accepted Burke's theory of representation and made it the essence of their theory of government.

A central problem with majority rule and the purpose of all these proposals to limit it is the tendency of majorities to suppress minorities. Systems like proportional representation, requirements for a higher percentage than 50 percent of the vote, and Madison's proposals regarding the U.S. Constitution are attempts to ensure that minorities are protected from the majority.

EQUALITY

Although equality has been discussed for centuries, it became centrally important only in the twentieth century. Today equality is one of those concepts, called *essentially contested concepts,* that produce fundamental disagreement (see Chapter 1). For some people the achievement of some form of equality is absolutely essential; for others the achievement of any form of equality is impossible; for still others, even if some form of equality were possible, it would not be desirable. Part of this disagreement comes from lumping together very different types of equality in one concept. *Equality* as a general concept includes five separate types of equality: political equality, equality before the law, equality of opportunity, economic equality, and equality of respect or social equality.

If there is a strict sense of equality applicable to human beings, it is sameness in relevant aspects.[13] But the phrase "in relevant aspects" modifying "sameness" shows that we have to define carefully what is relevant in talking about equality; failure to do this is another source of disagreement over the meaning and importance of equality.

Political Equality

The importance of defining *relevant aspects* can be seen even in what would appear to be the simplest form of equality, political equality. If we assume the existence of some form of representative democracy, *political equality* refers to equality at the ballot box, equality in the ability to be elected to public office, and equality of political influence.

Voting Equality at the ballot box entails the following:

1. Each individual must have reasonably easy access to the place of voting.

2. Each person must be free to cast his or her own vote as he or she wishes.

3. Each vote must be given exactly the same weight when counted.

---

[13] See the discussion in *Nomos IX: Equality,* ed. J. Roland Pennock and John W. Chapman (New York: Atherton Press, 1967), particularly the article "Egalitarianism and the Idea of Equality" by Hugo Adam Bedau, 3–27.

These conditions constitute an ideal and are much harder to fulfill than they at first appear. There are a number of reasons for this difficulty.

First, there is the question of *citizenship.* To vote one must be a citizen. Each country has regulations defining who is a citizen and how citizenship is acquired. For example, in most countries, if you are born in that country you are a citizen. But if your parents are citizens of another country, you will probably have the right to be a citizen of their country. Some countries also allow their citizens to be simultaneously citizens of another country; others do not. Citizenship also can be gained by being *naturalized,* or granted citizenship by a country. Naturalization usually requires a formal process culminating in a ceremony in which allegiance is sworn to the new country.

Citizenship can also be lost. In many, though not all, countries, swearing allegiance to another country will result in the loss of citizenship. In the United States, serving in the military of another country is supposed to result in the loss of U.S. citizenship. Each country has its own rules on the loss of citizenship: in some countries it is virtually impossible to lose citizenship, whereas in others many different actions can result in such loss.

Second, there is an age requirement for voting. Each country establishes an age at which citizens are first allowed to vote. At present the most common voting age is eighteen, although there are exceptions (for example, the voting age in Indonesia is seventeen and in India, twenty-one). No one under that age can vote.

Third, various people may have had the right to vote taken away from them. In the United States, for example, people convicted of certain crimes lose the right to vote in some states. Also, at times various countries have formally limited the right to vote. Examples of such limitations are requirements that a voter own a specified amount of property or belong to a particular religion; race and gender have also served as limitations and in some places still do.

In addition, there are many informal avenues of inequality. First, and perhaps most obvious, are racial and sexual discrimination. Even with legal limitations on voting removed, women and minorities in many countries still vote at a much lower rate than males of the racial majority. Second, some older and many disabled voters may have difficulty getting to the polling place. For example, the polling place in my area requires voters to negotiate two sets of stairs, and although arrangements can be made to vote without having to use the stairs, some voters don't know this or feel that the effort required is too great and choose not to vote. This example illustrates that the right to vote can be taken away simply by not thinking through what is required to actually vote.

Also, a person who cannot influence what names are printed on the ballot— that is, choose the candidates—is not equal to those who can. There are two ways to influence the choice of who becomes a candidate: money and active participation in the political system. For many people the lack of money makes it difficult to participate actively, but most people who don't participate simply choose not to.

Finally, each voter votes in a district, which should be roughly equal in population to other districts. If one district has a much larger population than another district, each vote is diluted in that it does not have the same strength in determining the outcome as a vote in a smaller district. The closer the districts are in population size, the closer the votes will be in strength. For example, to take an extreme case, if voter A lives in a district of 50,000 voters and voter B lives in one with only 10,000, B's vote will be worth five of A's. Some countries, such as the United States, require that district boundaries be changed regularly (usually after each census) to achieve this form of equality. The process is called *reapportionment*.

Running for Office   Equality in the ability to be elected to public office means that everyone who has the vote can be elected to public office, although particular offices usually have age qualifications and other specific requirements, such as residence in a specified area. In many countries it has become very expensive to run for public office; hence equality in the ability to be elected to public office has been seriously eroded. Most countries have seen attempts to limit the effect of wealth by legally controlling campaign spending. Some countries, such as Great Britain, strictly limit the amount that candidates can spend. It has been estimated that an average recent U.S. Senate campaign cost $5.6–5.7 million. In the United Kingdom, by contrast, candidates spent well under $200,000 in a campaign for the British Parliament and under $90,000 in campaigns for the European Parliament.

In addition, there are social constraints on running for office. Traditionally in the United States, it has been difficult or even impossible for women and African Americans, Hispanics, and other ethnic minorities, to name just a few groups, to become serious candidates for office. Similar situations, although with different groups, exist in most countries. Although members of such groups may have the legal right to run for office, that right has frequently been meaningless because there was no chance they could be elected. To avoid this, many countries set aside seats based on ethnicity or gender. In the United States, while districts used to be drawn to guarantee white representation, some are now drawn to guarantee black representation. Also, Hispanics are now better represented because their numbers have grown substantially in recent years.

Political Influence   *Political equality* also refers to an equality of political influence among citizens. Such equality means that all who choose to participate can do so without any formal limitations based on their membership in any religious, racial, ethnic, gender, or economic category. The point is the lack of legal limitations prohibiting participation. Of course, all these categories have at times both formally affected political influence and informally affected people's ability to participate and the likelihood that they will choose to participate. In much of the world, most of these limitations still exist.

Equality before the Law

Equality before the law resembles the definition of equality as sameness in relevant aspects because it means that all people will be treated in the same way by the legal system, and it is not hedged about by so many formal definitions of relevant aspects. Depictions of justice usually show a blindfolded woman holding a scale. The scale is an indication that the issues will be weighed; the blindfold indicates that they will be weighed fairly, taking into account nothing beyond the issues of the case.

Because a major function of law and legal procedures is to establish general rules that all people are expected to accept, law, by its nature, is an equalizing force in society if it is enforced fairly. Clearly, equality before the law in practice is undermined by the socioeconomic inequalities that exist in all societies. But equality before the law is one of democracy's clearest goals.

Equality of Opportunity

The third type of equality is related to social stratification and mobility systems. *Equality of opportunity* means, first, that every individual in society can move up or down within the class or status system depending on that individual's ability and application of that ability. Second, it means that no artificial barrier keeps any person from achieving what she or he can through ability and hard work. The key problem in the definition of equality of opportunity is the word *artificial,* which refers to individual characteristics that do not affect inherent abilities. Race, gender, religion, ethnic or national origin, and sexual orientation are most often cited as such artificial barriers.

Social stratification and mobility systems vary greatly from society to society. We tend to think of social status and mobility as easy to measure because we link them to an easily quantifiable object—money. In most Western societies today, that measure is a fairly accurate guide to status (except at the level of the traditional aristocracy) and the major means of gaining or losing status. But even in the West it is not quite that simple because status depends on the respect a position in society is given as well as the income that goes with the position. For example, clergy are not generally well paid but are accorded a status higher than their income. In a society that accords status on the basis of some other value (such as education), money would not automatically bring status. Equality of opportunity depends on the value accorded status.

Economic Equality

The fourth aspect of equality, economic equality, is rarely used to refer to economic sameness, but a complete discussion of the subject cannot ignore this definition. *Economic equality* could mean that every individual within a society should have the same income, and Edward Bellamy (1850–98) in his popular novel *Looking Backward* (1888) proposed such a definition. This definition is normally avoided because most advocates of economic equality are more concerned with the political and legal aspects of equality and with equality of opportunity than with strict financial equality. In addition, complete equality of income could be unfair to everyone because it would not take into account the differing needs of different individuals. Of course, if income levels were sufficiently high, differences in need would be irrelevant, because all individuals would have enough no matter what their needs were. But few exponents of economic equality expect such high income levels; therefore, what constitutes basic or fundamental human needs is a matter of considerable concern.

The usual argument for economic equality is that every individual within society must be guaranteed a minimum level of economic *security*. The stress is on security, not equality. Such security would allow the individual to become a fully active citizen. The major contention, the key to the argument, is that without some degree of security citizens will not be in a position to participate effectively even in the limited role of voter.

Extreme levels of poverty effectively bar an individual from participation in the life of the community and can create continuing inequalities. This effect is particularly significant in education. A child in a typical middle-class or lower-middle-class home has had toys and other objects that help teach many skills essential to learning. A simple thing such as having a book read aloud a number of times shows the child the turning of the pages and indicates that the English language is read from left to right, thus setting up a pattern the eyes will follow. The child without this preparation will start out behind the child who has. There are also certain skills essential even for relatively unskilled jobs that a child learns by playing with toys. A child who has simple toys to play with is learning these skills; a child who does not have such toys will not gain these skills and will have to learn them later or be barred from even those unskilled jobs. The effect of such deprivation on a child's life can be profound, and we are unsure whether some of these effects can be reversed for children who are already in our school systems. Thus children at age five or six may already have handicaps they will never be able to overcome. There are exceptions: Some children brought up in families that have suffered generations of extreme poverty do make it. However, the overwhelming majority do not.

Does great inequality in income eliminate equality of opportunity? How great an inequality is permissible? How can the extremes be brought closer together? We will look at these problems in greater detail as we discuss the differences between democratic capitalism and democratic socialism in the next chapter.

Equality of Respect or Social Equality

The fifth type of equality, equality of respect or social equality, is in some ways the most difficult to define. At its base is the belief that all human beings are due equal respect just because they are human; we are all equal in our fundamental humanity. Social equality is derived from this belief. *Equality of respect* refers to a level of individual interpersonal relations not covered by any of the other aspects of equality. The civil rights movement in the United States once developed a slogan, "Black Is Beautiful," which illustrates the point. In Western society, the color black has long connoted evil, as in the black clothes of the villain in early movies about the Old West. Advertising on television and in magazines used to reinforce this stereotype by never using black models. The slogan "Black Is Beautiful" was directed particularly at African American children to teach them that it was good, not bad, to be black, and that they could be black and still respect themselves and be respected by others.

Library of Congress

Thomas Jefferson (1743–1826), the third president of the United States, was involved in almost all the issues that dominated American political life during his lifetime. Of all the things he accomplished, Jefferson thought his three most important actions were writing the Declaration of Independence, writing the Virginia Act for Establishing Religious Freedom, and founding the University of Virginia.

In a narrow sense, social equality means that no public or private association may erect artificial barriers to activity within the association. Again, there is the problem of defining *artificial,* but generally we use it in the same sense described earlier—that is, denoting characteristics, such as gender, sexual orientation, race, ethnic or national origin, or religion, that do not affect an individual's inherent abilities. Examples of this type of equality might be the lack of such barriers to membership in a country club or the use of a public park. Thus *social equality* refers to the absence of the class and status distinctions that raise such barriers. In this sense, it includes aspects of equality of opportunity.

Education is believed to be one of the main mechanisms for overcoming inequality, but in many countries education is also a means of preserving inequalities. For example, in Britain large numbers of students are educated privately in what are called public schools. These students then proceed to the best universities and generally into the best jobs. (The same process takes place in most countries but on a smaller scale.) Thus these students are cut off from the broader society, and privilege, antagonism, and ignorance establish the basis for significant social inequality. Some countries have tried to overcome such patterns by establishing schools that bring together people from a wide variety of backgrounds in an attempt to eliminate class or racial ignorance and animosity.

FREEDOM, LIBERTY, AND RIGHTS

Historically, the desire for equality has often been expressed as an aspect of liberty. When Thomas Jefferson (1743–1826), drafting the Declaration of Independence, spoke of equality, he meant that people were equal in the rights they had. Equality of opportunity is often thought of as a right. On the other hand, many people believe attempts to achieve a degree of economic equality conflict directly with attempts to maintain economic liberty.

The words *liberty, freedom,* and *right* are most often used interchangeably. Although some distinguish carefully among the meanings, it is not necessary to do so. All three refer to the ability to act without restrictions or with restrictions that are themselves limited in specified or specifiable ways. *Freedom* is the most general term. *Liberty* usually refers to social and political freedom. *Right* usually refers to specific legally guaranteed freedoms. Also, *right* has been broadened to include basic human or natural rights. Finally, rights have become the focus of those in the United States who wish to expand constitutional guarantees and protections. As a result such questions as "Does the U.S. Constitution provide for a right of privacy?" or, more recently, "Is there a right to die?" have become the center of legal, political, and philosophic debate.

There is no such thing as complete freedom. In the first place, one must maintain life and perform a number of essential bodily functions. It is possible to choose when one eats, drinks, sleeps, and so on, but one cannot choose not to eat, drink, or sleep for long. In the second place, there are other people. Although they are essential for a complete life, they are restricting. An old adage states, "Your freedom to swing your arm stops at my nose." Although superficial, it does point out that the existence of others must be taken into account and that other people can limit free action.

A democratic society should be fairly free and open rather than controlled. It is the general assumption of democratic theory that whatever does no damage to the society as a whole or to the individuals within it should be the concern of no one but the individual or individuals involved.

Natural Rights and Civil Rights

The most influential approach to liberty is found in the distinction between the rights a person has or should have as a human being and the rights derived from government. The former are often called *natural rights;* the latter are called *civil rights.* Although the trend today is either to reject the concept of natural rights altogether and call all rights civil rights or to replace the word *natural* with *human,* the traditional distinction is still useful.

Many democratic theorists, such as John Locke, have argued that human beings, separate from all government or society, have certain rights that should never be given up or taken away. People do not give up these rights on joining a society or government, and the society or government should not attempt to take these rights away. If a government does try to take them away, the people are justified in revolting to change the government. Not all theorists make this last argument, but the point is that natural rights establish limits. The Bill of Rights in the U.S. Constitution is a good example. Many of the amendments in the Bill of Rights begin, "Congress shall make no law regarding. . . ." The wording clearly indicates a limit on governmental activity. Isaiah Berlin calls this approach *negative liberty.* By this term he describes the area of life within which

John Locke (1632–1704) was an important British philosopher and political thinker of the seventeenth century. His most important works were *Essay Concerning Human Understanding* (1689) and, in political thought, *Two Treatises of Government* (published in 1690 but written earlier). The first of the two treatises attacks the divine right of kings as put forth by Robert Filmer (1588–1653). The second treatise is an argument for rule by consent of the governed, a defense of private property and majority rule, and a justification for revolution. The U.S. Declaration of Independence was based on the second treatise, and Locke was a major influence on a number of thinkers in the United States at the time of the revolution and the drafting of the U.S. Constitution.

one "is or should be left to do or be what he is able to do or be, without interference by other persons."[14]

In the United States, tradition emphasizes the danger of possible interference from government. Certain areas of life, such as speech, religion, press, and assembly, have been defined as areas of "negative liberty" where each person is left to do, on the whole, what she or he wants. Negative liberty as practiced illustrates the complexity of democracy. Government is seen as the most likely agent to attempt to restrict liberty. Government is also the major protector of liberty, and it must protect people even against itself. This is one reason many Western democracies have established what we call a system of checks and balances within the government. No segment of government should be able to rule unchecked by any other segment; as a result, the rights of citizens are protected.

Berlin also developed a concept that he called *positive liberty.* As used by Berlin, this refers to the possibility of individuals controlling their own destiny or their ability to choose among options. For Berlin, positive liberty is the area of rational self-control or "self-mastery." For others, positive liberty means that the government should ensure conditions in which the full development of each individual is possible.[15] On the whole, as will be seen in the next chapter, democratic capitalists stress negative liberty and democratic socialists stress positive liberty while trying to maintain most of the negative liberties.

---

[14] Isaiah Berlin, "Two Concepts of Liberty," in Berlin, *Four Essays on Liberty* (London: Oxford University Press, 1969), 121–22.

[15] See, for example, the argument in Christian Bay, *The Structure of Freedom* (Stanford, CA: Stanford University Press, 1958); and Bay, *Strategies of Political Emancipation* (Notre Dame, IN: University of Notre Dame Press, 1981).

The most important natural right—the right to self-preservation—is basic to this understanding of positive liberty. This right can be interpreted to mean that every person has a right to the necessary minimum of food, clothing, and shelter needed to live in a given society. Because standards vary considerably from society to society, the necessary minimum might vary a great deal.

From this perspective, positive liberty might include the right to an education equal to one's ability and the right to a job. This approach to positive liberty logically extends to establishing as a right anything that can be shown to be essential to the development, and perhaps even the expression, of each person's potential as a human being.

Thus positive liberty can include as rights a wide variety of economic and social practices in addition to the political rights that usually come to mind when speaking of rights. The Universal Declaration of Human Rights[16] adopted by the United Nations includes such rights in its definition of human rights. For example, Article 22 states that "everyone, as a member of society, has the right to social security and is entitled to realization, through national effort and in accordance with the organization and resources of each State, of the economic, social and cultural rights indispensable for his dignity and the free development of his personality." Positive liberty is not usually extended this far, but these examples illustrate the complexity of the questions involved.

Other so-called natural rights have also been widely debated. One of the most controversial is the right to property. Some contend that there must be a nearly absolute right to acquire and accumulate private property because ownership of property is an avenue to the full development and expression of the human personality. Others argue that private property must be limited because the control of such property gives additional power to those who own it. (Additional arguments for and against the institution of private property will be considered in Chapter 4.)

Although there is widespread disagreement on specific natural rights, it is generally agreed that after the formation of government, these rights must become civil rights or rights specifically guaranteed and protected by the government, even—or particularly—against itself. This formulation of liberty raises many difficulties. The most basic difficulty is the assumption that a government will be willing to guarantee rights against itself. Many thinkers have assumed that representative democracy with frequent elections will solve this problem. Any such government should recognize that an infringement of people's civil rights would ensure its defeat in the next election. Experience has shown this is not necessarily true, and the result has been apathy, civil disobedience, and revolution, with apathy currently the greatest concern in most developed democracies. At the same time, protecting liberties is still considered a primary duty of a democratic political system and a central part of democratic theory.

---

[16] "The Universal Declaration of Human Rights" was adopted by the United Nations in 1948. The text can be found at http://www.un.org/Overview/rights.html.

Types of Liberty

It is more difficult to define types of liberty than types of equality; but, loosely, civil rights include the following specific liberties or freedoms:

1. The right to vote
2. Freedom of speech
3. Freedom of the press
4. Freedom of assembly
5. Freedom of religion
6. Freedom of movement
7. Freedom from arbitrary treatment by the political and legal system

The first six of these are areas of life that the democratic argument says should be left, within broad limits, to the discretion of the individual. Of these six, freedom of movement is the least commonly discussed among theorists of democracy. The seventh item, freedom from arbitrary treatment, is simply a way of stating positively the belief that government must protect the citizen from government. The various freedoms—particularly those of speech, press, assembly, and religion—are closely related. Among the other means by which freedom has been expressed are toleration, the silence of the law, and unenforceability.

The Right to Vote The right to vote without interference is, of course, the key to the ability to change the system. It is the ultimate check on government and the true guarantor of any freedom.

Freedom of Speech With some minimal disagreement, most thinkers consider freedom of speech the most important freedom. Within democracy freedom of speech has a special place. The right to vote does not mean much if it is impossible to hear opposing points of view and to express one's opinion. The same reasoning is behind the freedoms of press and assembly. The rights to publish opinion and to meet to discuss political issues are fundamental if people are to vote intelligently. The right to vote implies, even requires, a right to information and the free expression of opinion both orally and in writing. Freedom of speech requires freedom of assembly; freedom to speak is meaningless without the possibility of an audience.

John Stuart Mill (1806–73) explained the importance of freedom of speech and press in a slightly different way in his classic *On Liberty* (1859):

> This, then, is the appropriate region of human liberty. It comprises, first, the inward domain of consciousness; demanding liberty of conscience in the most comprehensive sense; liberty of thought and feeling; absolute freedom of opinion and sentiment on all subjects, practical or speculative, scientific, moral, or theological. The liberty of expressing and publishing opinions may seem to fall under a different principle, since it belongs to that part of the conduct of an individual which concerns other people; but, being almost of as much importance as the liberty of thought itself

and resting in great part on the same reasons, is practically inseparable from it.[17]

For Mill, thought requires the freedom to express oneself orally and in writing. The search for truth requires that challenge, debate, and disagreement be possible. Mill argued this from four different perspectives:

> First, if any opinion is compelled to silence, that opinion may, for aught we can certainly know, be true. To deny this is to assume our own infallibility.
>
> Secondly, though the silenced opinion be an error, it may, and very commonly does, contain a portion of truth; and since the general or prevailing opinion on any subject is rarely or never the whole truth, it is only by the collision of adverse opinions that the remainder of the truth has any chance of being supplied.
>
> Thirdly, even if the received opinion be not only true, but the whole truth; unless it is suffered to be, and actually is, vigorously and earnestly contested, it will, by most of those who receive it, be held in the manner of a prejudice, with little comprehension or feeling of its rational grounds. And not only this, but, fourthly, the meaning of the doctrine itself will be in danger of being lost or enfeebled, and deprived of its vital effect on the character and conduct; the dogma becoming a mere formal profession, inefficacious for good, but cumbering the ground and preventing the growth of any real and heartfelt conviction, from reason or personal experience.[18]

Without freedom of expression truth is lost, is never found, becomes mere prejudice, or is enfeebled. Assuming that there is truth to be found, freedom of expression is essential; if there is no truth to be found, freedom of expression is even more important as the only device available to sort out the better opinion from the worse.

Speakers Corner on the northeast corner of Hyde Park in London, across from where people used to be executed for religious beliefs, is open every Sunday morning to anyone with the urge to speak. It was designed as a "safety valve" and appears to have functioned as such for some time. Today it is mostly viewed as entertainment.

Freedom of the Press   Mill joined speech and press closely together and, for political concerns, the argument that a generally free press is essential in a democracy is almost noncontroversial. But there are areas of concern outside the strictly political realm, most obviously related to the publication of pornography, and there are even concerns about some more narrowly political issues.

If freedom of the press is absolute, there should be no restrictions on the publication of pornography. With some exceptions, much pornography depicts individuals of one of two groups—women or children—as objects to be used, often violently, by another group—men. Viewed this way, pornography is an

---

[17] John Stuart Mill, *On Liberty*, 4th ed. (London: Longman, Reader & Dyer, 1869), 26.

[18] Mill, *On Liberty*, 95.

issue with strong political overtones and illustrates a central concern of contemporary students of democracy, the conflict of rights. Whose rights should be protected, the publishers and consumers of pornography or the women and children who are turned into consumer goods?

A more narrowly political issue involves the publication of material designed to incite the overthrow of government by violence. Absolute freedom of the press would require the government to ensure that those trying to overthrow it have the right to publish calls for its overthrow and even manuals on how to produce bombs and directions on where and how to place them. Many people find such a position ludicrous; many find it perfectly reasonable.

A third issue is governmental secrecy. Some, particularly those working for the press, contend that the press should have free access to the whole government decision-making process. Others, especially those working in government, argue that government should be free to choose what the press is allowed to know and publish. Most people fall somewhere in between, believing that some governmental actions must be secret and that other actions, ranging from a few to most, should not be secret. The problem is that governments decide what must be secret, and this leads to distrust. There is no way around this problem, and the press and government will inevitably be at odds about the extent of permissible secrecy.

A related issue is self-censorship by the press. Media that are privately owned (most of them in the developed world) must attract and keep readers/viewers/listeners to make a profit. Some media sensationalize material to attract a larger audience; others limit what they report or the language used to avoid upsetting their owners, corporate sponsors, or the audience they have already attracted. Both tendencies distort the information available and undermine the value of a free press.

In the United States, conservatives consistently argue that most journalists are liberals and bias their reporting to support the liberal position; liberals argue that most media outlets are owned by wealthy conservatives and that they require that reporting be slanted to support the conservative position. While it is impossible to be certain, on the whole journalists are more liberal than their bosses; but most media outlets and journalists strive for accuracy and balance. They do not always succeed, and it is not hard to find evidence for the arguments made by both conservatives and liberals.

Historically, newspapers and news magazines separated reporting and opinion, with pages devoted to opinion clearly marked. Today both print and electronic media are less careful in making such a separation, and getting accurate and balanced news is more difficult than it used to be. At the same time, electronic media provide a range of news sources never before available, and the Internet in particular is a source of serious investigative reporting, the expression of minority viewpoints, and bias presented as objectivity.

Tension between the press and government is unavoidable and probably healthy. Western democracies criticize countries with a controlled press while trying to keep their own press from publishing things they want kept secret. The degree of press freedom varies among democracies; there is no such thing as a completely free press, but a fairly high degree of such freedom is essential in a democracy because in the modern world the communication of political ideas requires the right to publish those ideas.

Freedom of Assembly The freedom to speak requires the freedom to have an audience. Although in broadcasting the audience need not be gathered in one place, the ability to meet together to discuss political issues, make decisions on those issues, and choose candidates is clearly still fundamental to a functioning democracy.

The political issues related to freedom of assembly are issues of public order. Should parades and demonstrations that may produce violence be allowed? What limitations on assembly are permissible to keep traffic moving or to prevent violence? All governments, from the local to the national, in all democracies constantly face the problem of how to regulate assembly without making it politically ineffective. Some governments clearly use the excuse of necessary regulation through the need for permits, for example, to limit the freedom of assembly, but on the whole such attempts have proved ineffective.

Freedom of Religion Freedom of religion is usually supported on precisely the same grounds Mill used to defend freedom of speech and press, and worshipping together requires the freedom of assembly. Even if we are certain that we have the whole truth—perhaps particularly if we are certain—we should always distrust our own presumed infallibility and welcome the continuation of the search. Freedom of religion has, particularly in North America, come to be identified with the separation of church and state. The search for religious truth, in this view, requires that government be a neutral bystander neither favoring nor suppressing any aspect of that search.

In many countries this issue takes a more complex form. Some countries have an established church or a church that is officially recognized by the government that may receive financial and other public support. In addition, many countries have political parties that are tied (directly or indirectly) to religious bodies. In Europe most of these parties are labeled Christian Democrats or some variant thereof. These parties are often conservative. In such circumstances the quest for freedom of religion becomes more problematic. But every religion has at some time faced the question of its relationship to political power. This issue is particularly important today in the Third World, and it deeply divides the Roman Catholic Church.

Freedom of Movement Freedom of movement is less commonly included among the basic freedoms, but it is as important as the others because the ability to move freely is a major protection for other freedoms. Some restrictions are already in effect. Many democratic countries, particularly in Europe, require their citizens to carry identity papers and, for example, require hotels to record the number on these papers when someone registers. All countries require passports for foreign travel. And the growth of government programs means that most countries have records of the location of and changes of permanent address for a growing number of citizens. But in no democracy is it necessary to get prior approval from a government to travel within its borders, and, most important, within a democracy people can freely move from place to place for political activity.

Freedom from Arbitrary Treatment Freedom from arbitrary treatment by the political and legal system also protects the other freedoms. All democratic societies have clearly established procedural rights designed to guarantee that every individual will be treated fairly by the system. Without these procedural rights, the substantive rights of freedom of speech, press, and so on would not be as secure. Basic guarantees include those found in the U.S. Bill of Rights, such as freedom from cruel and unusual punishment (designed to prohibit torture, now an issue in the debate over capital punishment); the right to a writ of habeas corpus (Latin meaning "[that] you have the body") or the right to demand that a prisoner be brought before an officer of the court so that the lawfulness of the imprisonment can be determined; and the right to a trial by a jury of one's peers.

Toleration Toleration means that one accepts another person believing or doing something that one believes to be wrong. Religious toleration is the most obvious case, and in some ways it is the most difficult. If I am certain that my way is the only one that leads to salvation, I am unlikely to tolerate an opposing belief that I am convinced is dangerous to my and your salvation. Religious tolerance is, in fact, a relatively recent phenomenon; as late as the seventeenth century the word *tolerance* had a negative meaning and *intolerance* a positive one. Within a relatively short time, though, the connotation of the words shifted: tolerance became a virtue and intolerance a vice, although even now many do not tolerate beliefs or behaviors they are convinced are wrong. Today most people accept toleration and extend it beyond religion to other beliefs and ways of life. In this way, freedom includes a large area in which we accept other people even though we disagree with them.

Politically, tolerance is basic to modern democracy because one key to democracy is the recognition and acceptance of basic disagreements among citizens. The diversity of the population and the protection of that diversity through tolerance are extremely important. Tolerance must exist or democracy cannot work.

The Silence of the Law and Unenforceability Two other areas of freedom should be noted briefly: the silence of the law and unenforceability. It is part of the Anglo-American tradition that if there is no law prohibiting an action, that action is within the area of individual discretion until such a law is written. In the United States, when the law is written, it cannot affect actions that preceded it. In many other countries, newly passed laws can be used to find past acts illegal. Also, the experience of Prohibition in the United States indicated that there are unenforceable laws, laws that people simply won't accept. Thus unenforceability can also be seen as an aspect of freedom.

Liberty is limited to some extent by all political systems. The democratic system has built-in safeguards that protect individuals from having their freedoms too severely restricted. Of course, these safeguards do not always work.

The most fundamental of these safeguards is the basic characteristic of a democracy—the people have some control over their government. Democratic theorists have never adequately addressed the problem of severe restrictions of rights that are desired or acquiesced in by the majority. Thus a problem for democracy is how to achieve sufficient tolerance of differences so that the majority is willing to protect the rights of the minority. For many the answer is education.

EDUCATION

Education as a fundamental principle of democracy may be mildly controversial, but it should not be. Democratic theorists such as John Locke, Jean-Jacques Rousseau, and John Stuart Mill wrote treatises on education that tied their political theories loosely or tightly to the need for an educated populace. In the United States the founders of the democracy believed education essential to making an effective democracy possible. In fact, the statement that an educated citizenry is necessary in a democracy is commonplace. The argument regarding the need for education is fairly simple. Citizens are required to choose among candidates and issues. To do so they must have the basic skills of reading, writing, and arithmetic (rather illiterately known as the three Rs) because the information provided is often communicated in print, because it may be necessary for citizens to communicate in writing, and because numbers are used extensively. Equally important, citizens must be able to evaluate the information, weigh pros and cons, and decide what positions best correspond to their interests. Of course, citizens must also be able to correctly identify those interests.

A democracy can operate without an educated populace. India is a functioning democracy with a high level of illiteracy. But a democracy of illiterates is limited unless the culture actively encourages oral dissemination of information and discussion of issues. The elitist model of democracy would have no trouble with a high level of illiteracy, but every other approach to democracy would find it an issue requiring solution. Thus it is fair to say that an educated populace is a prerequisite of a fully functioning democracy.

The principles of democracy all relate to one another, and all stem from the most fundamental democratic principle: citizen involvement. Politically, equality and freedom both characterize and protect citizen involvement. They characterize citizen involvement in that democracy demands the freedom to vote and equality of the vote; they protect citizen involvement because a free and equal electorate can insist on the maintenance of that freedom and equality. A free and equal electorate needs education to ensure that freedom and equality are meaningful and to make informed choices as citizens. Today the electoral system is the major avenue for the expression of citizen involvement, and of course the system of representation is the purpose and result of the electoral system and the way in which citizens are involved.

CURRENT TRENDS

The principles of democracy do not change, but their interpretation does. The most obvious current trend is that many countries are trying to reestablish democracy or establish it for the first time, but there are also other significant trends.

Democratization

If any ideology is dominant today, it is democracy. Most countries at least pretend to be democratic in the most minimal sense, holding elections. And many countries are going through a process called democratization. Thus it is particularly important today to understand what range of meanings can be applied to *democracy*. Does it mean merely holding elections, even though the electoral process is corrupt? If the elections are honestly run, is that enough? If more is required, what is necessary? What constitutes a full democracy, and do any exist?

Since 1989 and the fall of the Berlin Wall, *democratization*—the process by which countries establish democratic institutions and procedures and, even more important, a culture of democracy—has been a major topic of discussion. Putting such institutions and procedures in place is fairly easy; making them work is often difficult. But the success of South Africa under Nelson Mandela (b. 1918) reminds us that it is possible.

Democratization continues in the Third World, where elections are common but the development of a democratic culture lags far behind; and the countries of Central Europe and the former Soviet Union face similar problems. Some countries in Central Europe had democratic institutions before World War II, but few current citizens have any experience with democracy. Few of the countries that emerged from the former Soviet Union have ever experienced democracy. And in the Third World, democratic institutions borrowed from the previous colonial rulers were put in place, but again, citizens have little or no previous experience with these institutions. In a few cases, the Czech Republic and India for example, democracy has taken root; but in most of these countries it is fragile. As a result, dictators of various sorts exist throughout the Third World, in many countries of the former Soviet Union, and in a few Central European countries. Russia, for example, has established institutions that look democratic, but its president, Vladimir Putin (b. 1952), recently simply announced a change in governmental structure. The fact that the Russian parliament dutifully supported the change does not make the system democratic.

Myanmar (formerly Burma) is an interesting case that has gained publicity primarily though the house arrest since 1989 of its main democratic leader, Daw Aung San Suu Kyi (b. 1945), who won the Nobel Peace Prize in 1991 for her efforts to restore democracy to Myanmar. Myanmar has had brief periods of democracy since gaining independence from Britain in 1947, but most of the time it has been ruled by the military, a common phenomenon throughout the Third World. In its most recent free election in 1990, the National League

Louise Gubb/Corbis Saba

Nelson Rolihlahla Mandela (b. 1918) helped transform the African National
Congress (ANC) into a mass movement opposed to apartheid or racial separation
in South Africa. He helped lead a movement of mass civil disobedience, for which
he was arrested, tried, found guilty, and given a suspended jail sentence even
though the court found that he had always advocated peaceful action. A lawyer,
Mandela was active both in the courts and on the streets to fight against the
growing number of apartheid laws. He was charged with treason and arrested.
When the trial collapsed, he called for a new constitution for South Africa based
on democratic principles. After a new constitution was adopted that strengthened apartheid, Mandela accepted that violence was necessary and led the military wing of the ANC that attacked governmental and economic activities. He was
arrested for leaving the country illegally and incitement to strike, found guilty,
and sentenced to five years in prison. While in prison, he was charged with sabo-
tage and sentenced to life in prison. Having refused a number of offers of release
if he renounced his principles, he served his sentence from 1964 to 1990. After his
release, he was elected President of the now-legal ANC, and in 1994 he was the
first State President of South Africa elected under a system of racial equality. He
served until 1999.

for Democracy, led by Aung San Suu Kyi, who was already under house arrest,
won a large majority of seats in the legislative assembly, but the military simply
ruled the election invalid and has continued in power. Aung San Suu Kyi has
continued to agitate for the restoration of democracy, and, from time to time,
the military rulers have made gestures to conciliate her. So far, the military is
still in power.

   Myanmar is a good example of the central problem faced by countries struggling with democracy: the weakness or nonexistence of a culture that supports
democratic culture, procedures, and institutions. And given the extreme poverty
of many of these countries, particularly those in the Third World, many argue
that development must come first and then democracy will follow.

But Amartya Sen (b. 1933), who won the Nobel Prize in economics in 1998, has recently written that development and at least some features of democracy are inseparable:

> Development requires the removal of major sources of unfreedom: poverty as well as tyranny, poor economic opportunities as well as systematic social deprivation, neglect of public facilities as well as intolerance or overactivity of repressive states. Despite unprecedented increases in overall opulence, the contemporary world denies elementary freedoms to vast numbers—perhaps even a majority—of people.[19]

Sen contends that the establishment of such freedoms will spur economic development.

Civil Society

The culture that supports democracy includes a concept that has a long history but had largely been forgotten. *Civil society* refers to the largely voluntary associations and interactions found in the family, clubs, neighborhood associations, religious organizations, and so forth that operate outside the formal political system. In these social interactions, people learn tolerance, the process of winning and losing elections, living with rules determined by the group, and other key democratic values.

Civil society also includes economic relationships and institutions that are outside direct political control, such as private banking and the free market. Just as democratic values must be learned, so must the attitudes and behaviors appropriate to private economic life, such as profit and loss, the ability of enterprises to both succeed and fail, and the need to be responsible for one's own future economic health. Many argue that a healthy civil society is essential to the existence of both democracy and private economic institutions.

In Central Europe and the former Soviet Union the problem is how to create a civil society where most associations were controlled by the state. In the Third World the problem is how to create a specifically democratic civil society where private institutions have been based on hierarchical relationships of clans, ethnic groups, religions, tribes, and so forth.

The United States used to be described as a country based on voluntary associations, but recently, as popularly explained in *Bowling Alone: The Collapse and Revival of American Community* (2000) by Robert D. Putnam, Americans are much less likely to be members of such associations. For many, this suggests that even in the United States, civil society is less vital than it must be to support a vibrant democratic culture.

Group Rights

A focus of attention that relates to many other contemporary points of contention is the issue of group rights. When we think of legally enforceable rights, we tend to think solely in terms of individuals (although the fact that in the

---

[19] Amartya Sen, *Development as Freedom* (New York: Knopf, 1999), 3–4.

United States corporations are legally classified as individuals complicates the issue). Today many believe they are deprived of rights solely based on their membership in a group and that, therefore, the rights of groups should be protected. The argument goes, if I lose my rights or am discriminated against because of my membership in a group, shouldn't my rights be protected as a member of a group?

The assumption has been that individuals make up groups and, as a result, there is no need to have rights for groups. But the issue today is the belief that in practice only some individuals are in fact protected, and those whose rights are not protected are in that situation because they are members of a group.

Some of these claims are based on the American myth of the "melting pot" in which ethnic, religious, and other differences are supposed to disappear. But of course racial and gender differences have never disappeared. Many contend that without group rights the pressure to conform to the majority violates people's ability to practice their religion (particularly if that religion is not Christian), to maintain their ethnic identity, to speak their native language, to have a sexual orientation other than heterosexual, and so forth, putting them at risk of prosecution and persecution, or at least threatening their cultural identity.

Of course, the obvious problem is deciding what groups need their rights protected. Most of us are members of multiple groups. Some are more important to us than others, and most of us might easily say that we most identify with our ethnic group, our religious group, or some other identifiable group; but others might not find this as easy. Are all groups worthy of legal protection? And what if the culture of one group includes discrimination against members of another group? As a result of these problems, a number of approaches to groups have developed.

Multiculturalism One growing concern with democratic pluralism is multiculturalism, particularly in education. To what extent should a society with a dominant culture or cultures teach children about the dominant cultures rather than the minority cultures? Put another way, don't children have a right to learn about their heritage rather than being forced to learn about the dominant culture? These two ways of putting what is essentially the same question illustrate the problem. Those in the dominant culture have as much right to value their culture as those in the minority cultures, but do they have a right to impose it? In the past this practice was never questioned. Today people in minority cultures are demanding that their cultures be taught as well as the majority culture. Multiculturalism raises questions of majority versus minority rights and how to make a diverse society genuinely pluralistic.

As noted in the previous chapter, the issues raised by multiculturalism are also part of the current debate around immigration. In *Democracy and the Foreigner* (2001), Bonnie Honig (b. 1959) illustrates how immigration enriches a democratic society while raising issues of autonomy, citizenship, and rights, among others that the foreigner poses for democracy.

Difference How can individual and group differences be recognized and valued in a society that believes in equality? Or should they? In a development that has changed the focus of debate, a shift has occurred, stemming primarily from debates within feminism, from a concern with the *sameness* component of equality to the recognition that *difference* is important and valuable and should be protected, even fostered. The argument does not depend on whether the differences are based on biology or are socially constructed.

Although the definition of equality as "sameness in relevant aspects" does not prohibit a focus on difference, the emphasis since the beginning of the civil rights movement has been on sameness. The change is to move the focus to what is a *relevant* difference. Thirty years ago such an emphasis was used as an excuse to take rights from minorities; the assumption today is that such rights are so well established that it is safe to recognize relevant differences.

The issue comes back to one of the fundamental questions of democracy: How do we balance the interests of the majority and the minority? Or as may more accurately reflect the current situation in the United States: How do we balance the interests of various minorities given that there is no longer an over-all or general minority—only temporary majorities and minorities on specific issues?

For example, what does *equality* mean to someone who is disabled? Immediately after World War II various European countries tried to compensate for war injuries by giving those disabled in the war easier access to certain jobs and transportation, and they established other programs to integrate the physically disabled as much as possible into postwar society. The United States had much more limited programs. With time these programs gradually disappeared, but recently, and now beginning in the United States, people with disabilities have been gaining recognition by stressing that they must be compensated for their disabilities so they can fully participate in society. The establishment of legally protected rights moves in this direction. Again, note the connection between rights and equality.

Groups advocating for people with disabilities have also attempted to change the language used to describe them. The earlier usage was "handicapped." Later usage has included "disabled," "people with disabilities," and "differently abled."

I teach at a public university that happens to be located on hilly terrain. Some years ago, before there were advocacy groups for the disabled, some faculty and students decided to demonstrate the difficulties faced by students in wheelchairs by spending a few days trying to get around the campus in wheelchairs. In many places it was virtually impossible to get between buildings, into buildings, or from parking lots to buildings. On the whole, the university responded positively by removing certain barriers, replacing steps with ramps, and providing a parking area that was close to and on the same level as the center of the campus. But not until laws requiring access were passed did other barriers disappear, and problems still remain.

Most efforts to bring about equality of opportunity for the disabled have focused on those with observable physical disabilities; those with less obvious problems have had difficulty getting the help they need. For example, a student with heart problems that restricted the distance she could walk was regularly chastised by other disabled students for using handicapped parking because she had no outward signs of disability.[20]

Consociational Democracy An approach to all these issues that redefines some of the usual organizational structures is *consociational democracy,* which is, in essence, a system of formal power sharing. Each significant group in a country is guaranteed a place in the governing bodies and has a veto on some issues. In addition, representation is based on proportionality, and each group controls its own affairs.[21] The central problem in such a system is getting the groups to agree in the first place. Disagreements on who is to be included and what issues will be covered by the veto are other problems, but the system is designed to avoid the division of countries into separate nations and is working in countries like Lebanon.

Deliberative Democracy

A new approach to democratic participation is called *deliberative democracy*, a theory that has developed along somewhat different lines in Europe and the United States, with variants in each. One generally accepted definition calls it "a form of government in which free and equal citizens (and their representatives), justify decisions in a process in which they give one another reasons that are mutually acceptable and generally accessible, with the aim of reaching conclusions that are binding in the present on all citizens but open to challenge in the future."[22] Under this approach, the purpose is to provide communication between citizens and leaders, participation, and recognition of fundamental disagreements that need to be discussed. A basic problem in democracy is how it can function where differences are deep. How does democracy handle issues when those on one side are absolutely convinced that they are right and the other side is wrong? How does democracy address a situation where a temporary majority is willing to impose its version of the truth on a sizable minority? How does democracy deal with a situation in which "informing" voters becomes "manipulating" voters with half-truths and outright lies? Deliberation has the potential of avoiding the second and third problems, and mitigating the first by encouraging people to listen to each other.

A specific proposal is for a "Deliberation Day," a national holiday to be held two weeks before a national election. On Deliberation Day (actually

---

[20] For the Americans with Disabilities Act of 1990, see http://www.usdoj.gov/crt/ada/pubs/ada.txt. On disability issues, see Ruth O'Brien, ed., *Voices from the Edge: Narratives about the Americans with Disabilities Act* (New York: Oxford University Press, 2004); and Susan Stefan, *Unequal Rights: Discrimination against People with Mental Disabilities and the Americans with Disabilities Act* (Washington, DC: American Psychological Association, 2001).

[21] On consociational democracy, see Arend Lijphart, *Democracy in Plural Societies: A Comparative Exploration* (New Haven, CT: Yale University Press, 1977), 25–52.

[22] Amy Gutmann and Dennis F. Thompson, *Why Deliberative Democracy?* (Princeton, NJ: Princeton University Press, 2004), 7.

two days to encourage wider participation) registered voters would meet in neighborhood groups to discuss the issues raised by the election. Participants would be paid $150 so they could afford to attend (and to encourage them to attend).[23]

Deliberative democracy assumes a degree of trust in the system, something that many believe is lacking today. Deliberative democracy also assumes that citizens will have the ability to participate and evaluate; but there is concern that citizens in some democracies, including the United States, lack the information needed to do so. As a result, education is again a significant issue.

Education Today

Education has become a major debate in a number of democracies. The issues vary, but central to all of them are questions about what education is necessary for a democratic citizen in the twenty-first century, and who should decide the content of that education. Many Western democracies have national curricula, whereas in the United States such decisions are left up to either the states or local school boards.[24]

One central concern today is how to educate citizens. This applies both to children as they grow up and immigrants hoping to become citizens of their new country. Given the apparent level of apathy in the United States, many people feel that it has become essential to educate for citizenship, to help people realize the advantages of active, involved citizenship.

A number of studies have shown that people in many democracies, including the United States, know little about how their political systems work. For example, in a 1998 study of fourth-, eighth-, and twelfth-grade students in the United States, at least 30 percent of students scored below what was considered the basic level of information.[25] This lack of knowledge about how the system works, combined with a lack of knowledge regarding the issues, is considered dangerous to democracy, which has always been based on the assumption of an educated and informed populace. As a result of similar concerns in England, an Advisory Group on Citizenship was established and issued their report (popularly known as the Crick Report after its Chair Bernard Crick), titled "Education for Citizenship and the Teaching of

---

[23] Bruce Ackerman and James S. Fishkin, *Deliberation Day* (New Haven, CT: Yale University Press, 2004).

[24] For some comparisons among countries, see Derek Heater, "The History of Citizenship Education: A Comparative Outline," *Parliamentary Affairs* 55:3 (July 2002): 457–74; and Heather Marquette and Dale Mineshima, "Civic Education in the United States: Lessons for the UK," *Parliamentary Affairs* 55:3 (July 2002): 539–55.

[25] U.S. Department of Education, Office of Educational Research and Improvement, National Center for Education Statistics, *The NAEP 1998 Civics Report Card for the Nation*, NCES 2000-457, by A. D. Lutkus, A. R. Weiss, J. R. Campbell, J. Mazzeo, and S. Lazer (Washington, DC: 1999). For the specific information, see http://nces.ed.gov/nationalreportcard/civics/findings.asp/ or page x of the report. For a study, see Henry Milner, *Civic Literacy: How Informed Citizens Make Democracy Work* (Hanover, NH: Tufts University; published by the University Press of New England, 2002).

Democracy in Schools," in 1998; this report suggested adding material on citizenship to the curriculum.[26]

In the modern world the knowledge and evaluative skills necessary to judge the issues might appear to require considerable formal education, and that is where part of the current controversy lies. What constitutes an educated populace? On this question there are basic divisions. Some people believe that knowledge of how the government functions is sufficient. Others believe that formal education in the principles of democracy and how to evaluate arguments is necessary. Many positions between these are taken, with the only agreement in most democracies being that the educational system isn't doing what it should.

England, unlike the United States, has a national curriculum, so it was possible for the national government to require (after long negotiation with school authorities, teachers' groups, and the various bureaucracies involved) the addition of such materials. Thus, while much has been said and written about the need to do something to ensure that citizens can cast an informed vote, little has actually been achieved.

Also, in the United States, many people stress the right of parents to choose the sort of education they want their children to receive, including whether certain subjects are taught as part of the curriculum. In the United States the most famous legal case on this issue is *Wisconsin v. Yoder,* in which an Amish community in Wisconsin was exempted from sending their children to school beyond the elementary grades on the grounds that as members of their community they did not need further education.[27] Today the issues center more around alternatives to public education such as homeschooling (see the discussion in Chapter 8) and charter schools, in which parents choose significantly different educational patterns for their children. Charter schools originated in the 1980s and 1990s as a movement designed to improve elementary and secondary education by providing alternatives to public education as it currently existed; charter schools have had support from both major political parties. Since Minnesota established the first one in 1991, some 3,000 such schools have been established with mixed results. A number failed quickly; some have shown potential to produce educational innovation; and it is too early to judge most of them. The political issue, and the issue for democracy, that charter schools and homeschooling raise is who will determine what education is appropriate to produce the next generations of informed citizens.

The Revival of the Initiative, Recall, and Referendum

The initiative, recall, and referendum were developed in the late nineteenth and early twentieth centuries to bring direct citizen participation into state and local politics. Initially they were used sparingly and then generally fell out of use almost completely. But in the late twentieth century the initiative and referendum

---

[26] The report can be seen at the website of the Qualifications and Curriculum Authority: http://www.qca.org.uk/. In an e-mail message to me in October 2004, Professor Crick reported that Scotland is in the process of adopting similar provisions.

[27] *Wisconsin v. Yoder* 406 U.S. (1971): http://religiousfreedom.lib.virginia.edu/court/ wisc_v_yode.html or http://caselaw.lp.findlaw.com/cgi-bin/getcase.pl?court=US&vol= 406&invol=205

were revived, particularly on the West Coast, and used by both citizen groups and corporations to put issues on the ballot to force the legislature to act. Some states see dozens of such measures on a ballot with a great deal of money spent supporting and, less often, opposing the proposals. The recall is used less often, but the recent case in California where one governor was removed from office and another elected in his place shows its power.

It is difficult to judge the results of this revival. Citizens have been able to force legislatures to act when they had chosen not to; however, proposals are often presented in a deliberately misleading way, and the actual effects are difficult to determine. Also, the ability to fund a campaign may determine the result.[28]

National Security and Civil Liberties

A recurrent issue for democracy is the relationship between civil liberties and national security. Since the attacks on the United States in 2001, this issue has resurfaced, and Americans are deeply divided over how to balance the two or even whether a balance is desirable. Some people believe that national security should take priority, others that civil liberties should prevail.

It is essential to understand both sides of this issue. Security is essential for democracy to function, so the case for national security is also a case for the full functioning of the democratic system. Civil liberties are, of course, an absolutely fundamental aspect of democracy. The problem is one of balance. National security must not be an excuse for destroying democratic institutions, and civil liberties must not be an excuse for allowing them to be destroyed.[29]

The basic question is to what extent fundamental freedoms should be limited in the name of national security, and this is not the first time the United States has faced the issue. In fact, such concerns go back to 1798 and the "Alien and Seditions Acts," which Congress passed at the request of President John Adams (1735–1826) to give him the power to limit free speech, deport or imprison aliens, and make it harder to become a U.S. citizen. The real purpose of the acts was to limit the power of Adams's then political rival Thomas Jefferson (1743–1826), who had the support of most new citizens, which illustrates the potential misuse of such laws.

The issue arises most often in connection with war, and there are examples of the limitations on freedom in the name of security during the Civil War, World Wars I and II, the Korean War, the Vietnam War, and the first Gulf War. There were also two such periods where civil liberties were severely restricted in the name of national security, the Red Scare of the 1920s and the McCarthy era of the 1950s and 1960s, that were not directly connected to wars.

In addition to legal restrictions, there is the fear factor, in which people limit their activities out of fear of reprisals, real or imaginary. I recall being told

---

[28] On the initiative today, see Richard J. Ellis, *Democratic Delusions: The Initiative Process in America* (Lawrence: University Press of Kansas, 2002).

[29] See Helen Cothran, *National Security: Opposing Viewpoints* (Farmington Hills, MI: Greenhaven Press, 2004), for a collection of brief essays on both sides of the issue. In addition, the Suggested Reading includes texts arguing for each side.

as an undergraduate during the end of the McCarthy era to never sign a petition if I ever wanted a government job because my name would go on a list. It may or may not have been true, but it shows the way that fear can make people choose to limit the exercise of their freedoms even when they are perfectly legal. Such statements are being made again today, and again it is difficult to know if there is any truth to them.

A specific issue is how free a press can be in a crisis. The British press was critical of the British government over Iraq and other issues; the U.S. press generally chose not to be critical and was even criticized worldwide for its unquestioning presentation of the official position. The choice to limit what is generally considered a major protector of freedom—a press willing and able to criticize and question government—is now being debated within the media and among citizens.

Most importantly, the Uniting and Strengthening America by Providing Appropriate Tools Required to Intercept and Obstruct Terrorism Act, better known as the USA Patriot Act (passed in 2001 with little debate), has been used to ask bookstores and libraries for lists of the book purchases and borrowings of their patrons. In addition, under this act, many people, including both citizens and legal immigrants, are now in prison in the United States without having had due process of law such as access to a lawyer or even knowing the charges against them.[30] Various U.S. courts have begun to question the constitutionality of some provisions of the act and are suggesting the need to reassert a balance between national security and civil liberties. The same pattern took place in earlier periods in the United States; after a while limitations on civil liberties in the name of national security began to be questioned by citizens and the courts, and movements to rebalance took place. At present, though, the defenders of national security over civil liberties argue that terrorism presents the United States with a different situation than the previous cases and that restrictions must be continued or even expanded.

SUGGESTED READING

Classic Works

Bentham, Jeremy. *An Introduction to the Principles of Morals and Legislation* (printed 1780 but not published until 1789).

Burke, Edmund. *Reflections on the Revolution in France* (1790).

The Constitution of the United States of America (1787).

Declaration of Independence of the United States (1776).

Hamilton, Alexander, John Jay, and James Madison. *The Federalist Papers* (1787–88).

Locke, John. *Two Treatises of Government* (first edition dated 1690; probably written sometime between 1679 and 1682).

---

[30] See the Suggested Reading for the text of the act and criticisms of it by the American Civil Liberties Association and the American Library Association. For a reference guide to the act and its effects, see Howard Ball, *The USA Patriot Act of 2001: Balancing Civil Liberties and National Security: A Reference Handbook* (Santa Barbara, CA: ABC-CLIO, 2004).

Mill, John Stuart. *On Liberty* (1859).

Montesquieu, Charles-Louis de Secondat. *De l'esprit des lois (The Spirit of the Laws)* (1748).

Rousseau, Jean-Jacques. *Du contrat social (The Social Contract)* (1762).

Wollstonecraft, Mary. *A Vindication of the Rights of Woman* (1792).

Books and Articles

Ackerman, Bruce, and Anne Alstott. *The Stakeholder Society*. New Haven, CT: Yale University Press, 1999.

Ackerman, Bruce, and James S. Fishkin. *Deliberation Day*. New Haven, CT: Yale University Press, 2004.

Ackerman, Peter, and Jack DuVall. *A Force More Powerful: A Century of Nonviolent Conflict*. New York: St. Martin's Press, 2000.

Ake, Claude. *The Feasibility of Democracy in Africa*. Dakar, Senegal: Council for the Development of Social Science Research in Africa, 2000.

Allen, Anita L., and Milton C. Regan, Jr., eds. *Debating Democracy's Discontent: Essays on American Politics, Law, and Public Philosophy*. Oxford: Oxford University Press, 1998.

Amy, Douglas J. *Real Choices/New Voices: The Case for Proportional Representation Elections in the United States*. 2nd ed. New York: Columbia University Press, 2002.

An-Na'im, Abdullahi Ahmed, ed. *Human Rights under African Constitutions: Realizing the Promise for Ourselves*. Philadelphia: University of Pennsylvania Press, 2003.

Ankersmit, F. R. *Political Representation*. Stanford, CA: Stanford University Press, 2002.

Arato, Andrew. *Civil Society, Constitution, and Legitimacy*. Lanham, MD: Rowman & Littlefield, 2000. Democratization.

Balibar, Étienne. *We, the People of Europe? Reflections on Transnational Citizenship*. Translated by James Swenson. Princeton, NJ: Princeton University Press, 2004.

Barber, Benjamin R. *A Passion for Democracy: American Essays*. Princeton, NJ: Princeton University Press, 1998.

———. *Strong Democracy: Participatory Politics for a New Age*. 20th anniversary ed. Berkeley: University of California Press, 2003.

Barry, Brian. *Culture and Equality: An Egalitarian Critique of Multiculturalism*. Cambridge: Harvard University Press, 2001.

Barry, John, and Marcel Wissenburg, eds. *Sustaining Liberal Democracy: Ecological Challenges and Opportunities*. Basingstoke, England: Palgrave, 2001.

Batstone, David, and Eduardo Mendieta, eds. *The Good Citizen*. New York: Routledge, 1999.

Bauer, Joanne R., and Daniel A. Bell, eds. *The East Asian Challenge for Human Rights*. Cambridge: Cambridge University Press, 1999.

Bay, Christian. *The Structure of Freedom*. Stanford, CA: Stanford University Press, 1958.

Becker, Ted, and Crista Daryl Slaton. *The Future of Teledemocracy*. Westport, CT: Praeger, 2000.

Beiner, Ronald, ed. *Theorizing Citizenship*. Albany: State University of New York Press, 1995.

Berlin, Isaiah. *Liberty Incorporating "Four Essays on Liberty."* Edited by Henry Hardy. Oxford: Oxford University Press, 2002.

Bohman, James, and William Rehg, eds. *Deliberative Democracy: Essays on Reason and Politics*. Cambridge, MA: The MIT Press, 1997.

Bollinger, Lee C., and Geoffrey R. Stone, eds. *Eternally Vigilant: Free Speech in the Modern Era*. Chicago: University of Chicago Press, 2002.

Bowles, Samuel, and Herbert Gintis. *Recasting Egalitarianism: New Rules for Communities, States, and Markets*. Vol. 3 of *The Real Utopias Project,* edited by Erik Olin Wright. London: Verso, 1998.

Braithwaite, Valerie, and Margaret Levi, eds. *Trust and Governance*. New York: Russell Sage Foundation, 1998.

Brown, Cynthia, ed. *Lost Liberties: Ashcroft and the Assault on Personal Freedom*. New York: New Press, 2003.

Callan, Eamonn. *Creating Citizens: Political Education and Liberal Democracy*. Oxford, England: Clarendon Press, 1997.

Callinicos, Alex. *Equality*. Cambridge, England: Polity, 2000.

Carens, Joseph H. *Culture, Citizenship, and Community: A Contextual Exploration of Justice as Evenhandedness*. Oxford: Oxford University Press, 2000.

Carter, April. *The Political Theory of Global Citizenship*. London: Routledge, 2001.

Carter, April, and Geoffrey Stokes. *Liberal Democracy and Its Critics: Perspectives in Contemporary Political Thought*. Cambridge, England: Polity Press, 1998.

————, eds. *Democratic Theory Today: Challenges for the 21st Century*. Cambridge, England: Polity, 2002.

Carter, Ian. *A Measure of Freedom*. Oxford: Oxford University Press, 1999.

Cavanagh, Matt. *Against Equality of Opportunity*. Oxford, England: Clarendon Press, 2002.

Cohen, Jean L. *Regulating Intimacy: A New Legal Paradigm*. Princeton, NJ: Princeton University Press, 2002.

Cohen, Joshua, and Joel Rogers. *Associations and Democracy*. Vol. 1 of *The Real Utopias Project,* edited by Erik Olin Wright. London: Verso, 1995.

Cole, David. *Enemy Aliens: Double Standards and Constitutional Freedoms in the War on Terrorism*. New York: New Press, 2003.

Cook, Karen S., ed. *Trust in Society*. New York: Russell Sage Foundation, 2001.

Cothran, Helen. *National Security: Opposing Viewpoints*. Farmington Hills, MI: Greenhaven Press, 2004.

Crick, Bernard. *Democracy: A Very Short Introduction*. Oxford: Oxford University Press, 2002.

————. *Essays on Citizenship*. London: Continuum, 2000.

Cunningham, Frank. *Theories of Democracy: A Critical Introduction*. New York: Routledge, 2002.

Dahl, Robert A. *Democracy and Its Critics*. New Haven, CT: Yale University Press, 1989.

————. *How Democratic Is the American Constitution?* 2nd ed. New Haven, CT: Yale University Press, 2003.

————. *On Democracy*. New Haven, CT: Yale University Press, 1998.

Dalton, Russell J. *Democratic Challenges, Democratic Choices: The Erosion of Political Support in Advanced Industrial Democracies*. Oxford: Oxford University Press, 2004.

Dash, Samuel. *The Intruders: Unreasonable Searches and Seizures from King John to John Ashcroft*. New Brunswick, NJ: Rutgers University Press, 2004.

Delanty, Gerard. *Citizenship in a Global Age: Society, Culture, Politics*. Buckingham, England: Open University Press, 2000.

Donnelly, Jack. *Universal Human Rights in Theory and Practice*. 2nd ed. Ithaca, NY: Cornell University Press, 2003.

Dryzek, John S. *Deliberative Democracy and Beyond: Liberals, Critics, Contestations*. Oxford: Oxford University Press, 2000.

Dworkin, Ronald M. *Sovereign Virtue: The Theory and Practice of Equality*. Cambridge, MA: Harvard University Press, 2000. Equal concern for all citizens. Equality of resources. Argues there is no conflict between liberty and equality.

Edmundson, William A. *An Introduction to Rights*. Cambridge: Cambridge University Press, 2004.

Edwards, George C., III. *Why the Electoral College Is Bad for America*. New Haven, CT: Yale University Press, 2004.

Elkin, Stephen L., and Karol Edward Soltan, eds. *Citizen Competence and Democratic Institutions*. University Park: Pennsylvania State University Press, 1999.

Ellis, Richard J. *Democratic Delusions: The Initiative Process in America*. Lawrence: University Press of Kansas, 2002.

Elster, Jon, ed. *Deliberative Democracy*. Cambridge: Cambridge University Press, 1998.

Estlund, David, ed. *Democracy*. Malden, MA: Blackwell Publishers, 2002.

Faulks, Keith. *Citizenship*. London: Routledge, 2000.

Freeman, Michael. *Freedom of Security: The Consequences for Democracies Using Emergency Powers to Fight Terror.* Westport, CT: Praeger, 2003.

Fung, Archon, and Erik Olin Wright. *Deepening Democracy: Institutional Innovations in Empowered Participatory Governance.* Vol. 4 of *The Real Utopias Project,* edited by Erik Olin Wright. London: Verso, 2003.

Gagnon, Alain-G., and James Tully, eds. *Multinational Democracies.* Cambridge: Cambridge University Press, 2001.

Gibney, Matthew J. *The Ethics and Politics of Asylum: Liberal Democracy and the Response to Refugees.* Cambridge: Cambridge University Press, 2004.

Giddens, Anthony, ed. *The Progressive Manifesto: New Ideas for the Centre-Left.* Cambridge, England: Polity, 2003.

Goodin, Robert E. *Reflective Democracy.* Oxford: Oxford University Press, 2003.

Gould, Carol C., and Pasquale Pasquino, eds. *Cultural Identity and the Nation-State.* Lanham, MD: Rowman & Littlefield, 2001.

Green, Judith M. *Deep Democracy: Community, Diversity, and Transformation.* Lanham, MD: Rowman & Littlefield, 1999.

Green, Philip. *Equality and Democracy.* New York: New Press, 1998.

Gregg, Gary L II, ed. *Securing Democracy: Why We Have an Electoral College.* Wilmington, DE: ISI Books, 2001.

Guinier, Lani. *The Tyranny of the Majority: Fundamental Fairness in Representative Democracy.* New York: Free Press, 1994.

Gutmann, Amy. *Identity in Democracy.* Princeton, NJ: Princeton University Press, 2003.

————, ed. *Freedom of Association.* Princeton, NJ: Princeton University Press, 1998.

Gutmann, Amy, and Dennis F. Thompson. *Why Deliberative Democracy?* Princeton, NJ: Princeton University Press, 2004.

Hagopian, Elaine C., ed. *Civil Rights in Peril: The Targeting of Arabs and Muslims.* Chicago: Haymarket Books/London: Pluto Press, 2004.

Hardin, Russell. *Trust and Trustworthiness.* New York: Russell Sage Foundation, 2002.

Hénaff, Marcel, and Tracy B. Strong, eds. *Public Space and Democracy.* Minneapolis: University of Minnesota Press, 2001.

Hentoff, Nat. *The War on the Bill of Rights—and the Gathering Resistance.* New York: Seven Stories Press, 2003.

Honig, Bonnie. *Democracy and the Foreigner.* Princeton, NJ: Princeton University Press, 2001.

Katz, Richard S. *Democracy and Elections.* New York: Oxford University Press, 1997.

Keane, John. *Violence and Democracy.* Cambridge: Cambridge University Press, 2004.

Kekes, John. *The Illusions of Egalitarianism.* Ithaca, NY: Cornell University Press, 2003.

Kelly, David, and Anthony Reed, eds. *Asian Freedoms: The Idea of Freedom in East and Southeast Asia.* Cambridge: Cambridge University Press, 1998.

Keyssar, Alexander. *The Right to Vote: The Contested History of Democracy in the United States.* New York: Basic Books, 2000.

Kramer, Matthew H. *The Quality of Freedom.* New York: Oxford University Press, 2003.

Kymlicka, Will, and Wayne Norman, eds. *Citizenship in Diverse Societies.* New York: Oxford University Press, 2000.

Kymlicka, Will, and Magda Opalski, eds. *Can Liberal Pluralism Be Exported? Western Political Theory and Ethnic Relations in Eastern Europe.* Oxford: Oxford University Press, 2001.

Kymlicka, Will, and Alan Patten, eds. *Language Rights and Political Theory.* Oxford: Oxford University Press, 2003.

Lakoff, Sanford. *Democracy: History, Theory, Practice.* Boulder, CO: Westview Press, 1996.

Lauren, Paul Gordon. *The Evolution of International Human Rights.* 2nd ed. Philadelphia: University of Pennsylvania Press, 2003.

Leone, Richard C., and Greg Anrig, Jr., eds. *The War on Our Freedoms: Civil Liberties in an Age of Terrorism.* New York: Public Affairs, 2003.

Lijphart, Arend. *Democracy in Plural Societies: A Comparative Exploration*. New Haven, CT: Yale University Press, 1977.

———. *Patterns of Democracy: Government Forms and Performance in Thirty-Six Countries*. New Haven, CT: Yale University Press, 1999.

Lipset, Seymour Martin, ed. *The Encyclopedia of Democracy*. 4 vols. Washington, DC: Congressional Quarterly, 1995.

Loury, Glenn C. *The Anatomy of Racial Inequality*. Cambridge, MA: Harvard University Press, 2002.

Lummis, C. Douglas. *Radical Democracy*. Ithaca, NY: Cornell University Press, 1996.

Lyon, David. *Surveillance after September 11*. Cambridge, England: Polity, 2003.

Macedo, Stephen. *Diversity and Distrust: Civic Education in a Multicultural Democracy*. Cambridge, MA: Harvard University Press, 2000.

———, ed. *Deliberative Politics: Essays on Democracy and Disagreement*. New York: Oxford University Press, 1999.

Mack, Raneta Lawson, and Michael J. Kelly. *Equal Justice in the Balance: America's Legal Response to the Emerging Terrorist Threat*. Ann Arbor: University of Michigan Press, 2004.

Macpherson, C. B. *The Real World of Democracy*. Oxford, England: Clarendon Press, 1966.

Mansbridge, Jane J. *Beyond Adversary Democracy*. New York: Basic Books, 1980.

McKinnon, Catriona, and Iain Hampsher-Monk, eds. *The Demands of Citizenship*. London: Continuum, 2000.

Meijer, Martha, ed. *Dealing with Human Rights: Asian and Western Views on the Value of Human Rights*. Oxford, England: WorldView Publishing/Bloomfield, CT: Kumarian Press, in association with The Netherlands Humanist Committee on Human Rights (HOM), 2001.

Miller, David. *The Principles of Social Justice*. Cambridge, MA: Harvard University Press, 1999.

Miller, David, and Michael Walzer, eds. *Pluralism, Justice, and Equality*. Oxford: Oxford University Press, 1995.

Milner, Henry. *Civic Literacy: How Informed Citizens Make Democracy Work*. Hanover, NH: Tufts University, published by the University Press of New England, 2002.

Morsink, Johannes. *The Universal Declaration of Human Rights: Origins, Drafting, Intent*. Philadelphia: University of Pennsylvania Press, 1999.

Mouffe, Chantal. *The Democratic Paradox*. London: Verso, 2000.

Musch, Donald J. *Civil Liberties and the Foreign Intelligence Surveillance Act*. Dobbs Ferry, NY: Ocean Publications, 2003.

Niemi, Richard G., and Jane Junn. *Civic Education: What Makes Students Learn*. New Haven, CT: Yale University Press, 1998.

Norris, Pippa. *Democratic Phoenix: Reinventing Political Activism*. Cambridge: Cambridge University Press, 2002.

Olshansky, Barbara, and the Center for Constitutional Rights. *Secret Trials and Executions: Military Tribunals and the Threat to Democracy*. New York: Seven Stories Press, 2002.

O'Neill, Onora. *A Question of Trust. The BBC Reith Lectures 2002*. Cambridge: Cambridge University Press, 2002.

Paehlke, Robert C. *Democracy's Dilemma: Environment, Social Equity, and the Global Economy*. Cambridge, MA: MIT Press, 2003.

Patman, Robert G., ed. *Universal Human Rights?* New York: St. Martin's Press, 2000.

Phelan, Shane. *Sexual Strangers: Gays, Lesbians, and Dilemmas of Citizenship*. Philadelphia, PA: Temple University Press, 2001.

Powell, G. Bingham, Jr. *Elections as Instruments of Democracy: Majoritarian and Proportional Visions*. New Haven, CT: Yale University Press, 2000.

Putnam, Robert D. *Bowling Alone: The Collapse and Revival of American Community*. New York: Simon & Schuster, 2000.

Raphael, D[avid] D[aiches]. *Concepts of Justice*. Oxford, England: Clarendon Press, 2001.

Ravitch, Diane, and Joseph P. Viteritti, eds. *Making Good Citizens: Education and Civil*

Society. New Haven, CT: Yale University Press, 2001.

Robin, Corey. *Fear: The History of an Idea*. New York: Oxford University Press, 2004.

Roemer, John E. *Equality of Opportunity*. Cambridge, MA: Harvard University Press, 1998.

———. *Theories of Distributive Justice*. Cambridge, MA: Harvard University Press. 1996.

Rosenblum, Nancy L. *Membership and Morals: The Personal Uses of Pluralism in America*. Princeton, NJ: Princeton University Press, 1998.

———, ed. *Obligations of Citizenship and Demands of Faith: Religious Accommodation in Pluralist Democracies*. Princeton, NJ: Princeton University Press, 2000.

Rubio-Marín, Ruth. *Immigration and Democratic Challenge: Citizenship and Inclusion in Germany and the United States*. Cambridge: Cambridge University Press, 2000.

Savi_, Obrad, for the *Belgrade Circle Journal*, ed. *The Politics of Human Rights*. London: Verso, 1999.

Schuck, Peter H. *Diversity in America: Keeping Government at a Safe Distance*. Cambridge, MA: Harvard University Press, 2003.

Schulz, William F. *Tainted Legacy: 9-11 and the Ruin of Human Rights*. New York: Thunder's Mouth Press/Nation Books, 2003.

Sennett, Richard. *Respect in a World of Inequality*. New York: W.W. Norton, 2003. UK ed. as *Respect: The Formation of Character in a World of Inequality*. London: Allen Lane, 2003.

Shapiro, Ian. *The State of Democratic Theory*. Princeton, NJ: Princeton University Press, 2003.

Shapiro, Ian, and Stephen Macedo, ed. *Nomos XLII: Designing Democratic Institutions*. New York: New York University Press, 2000.

Shweder, Richard A., Martha Minow, and Hazel Rose Markus, eds. *Engaging Cultural Differences: The Multicultural Challenge in Liberal Democracies*. New York: Russell Sage Foundation, 2002.

Siedentop, Larry. *Democracy in Europe*. New York: Columbia University Press, 2001.

Singer, Peter. *The President of Good and Evil: The Ethics of George W. Bush*. New York: Dutton, 2004.

Skocpol, Theda. *Diminished Democracy: From Membership to Management in American Civic Life*. Norman: University of Oklahoma Press, 2003.

Skocpol, Theda, and Morris P. Fiorina, eds. *Civic Engagement in American Democracy*. Washington, DC: Brookings Institution Press/New York: Russell Sage Foundation, 1999.

Skrentny, John D. *The Minority Rights Revolution*. Cambridge, MA: Harvard University Press, 2002.

Smith, Rogers M. *Civic Ideals: Conflicting Visions of Citizenship in U.S. History*. New Haven, CT: Yale University Press, 1997.

Sunstein, Cass. *Republic.com*. Princeton, NJ: Princeton University Press, 2001.

———. *Why Societies Need Dissent*. Cambridge, MA: Harvard University Press, 2003.

United States Congress, Senate Committee on the Judiciary. *The War against Terrorism: Working Together to Protect America: Hearing before the Committee on the Judiciary, United States Senate. One Hundred Eighth Congress, First Session, March 4, 2003*. Washington, DC: GPO, 2003. Also available on the GPO (Government Printing Office) website.

Van Gunsteren, Herman. *A Theory of Citizenship*. Boulder, CO: Westview Press, 1998.

Verba, Sidney, Kay Lehman Schlozman, and Henry E. Brady. *Voice and Equality: Civic Voluntarism in American Politics*. Cambridge, MA: Harvard University Press, 1995.

Walzer, Michael. *On Toleration*. New Haven, CT: Yale University Press, 1997.

———. *Spheres of Justice*. New York: Basic Books, 1983.

Warren, Mark E. *Democracy and Association*. Princeton, NJ: Princeton University Press, 2001.

———, ed. *Democracy and Trust*. Cambridge: Cambridge University Press, 1999.

Weale, Albert. *Democracy*. New York: St. Martin's Press, 1999.

Weart, Spencer R. *The Discovery of Global Warming*. Cambridge, MA: Harvard University Press, 2003.

Weithman, Paul J. *Religion and the Obligations of Citizenship*. Cambridge: Cambridge University Press, 2002.

West, Cornel. *Democracy Matters: Winning the Fight against Imperialism*. New York: Penguin Press, 2004.

Whitehead, Laurence. *Democratization: Theory and Experience*. Oxford: Oxford University Press, 2002.

———. "The Vexed Issue of the Meaning of 'Democracy.'" *Journal of Political Ideologies* 2, no. 2 (June 1997): 121–35.

Young, Iris Marion. *Inclusion and Democracy*. Oxford: Oxford University Press, 2000.

Zagorin, Perez. *How the Idea of Religious Toleration Came to the West*. Princeton, NJ: Princeton University Press, 2003.

Zakaria, Fareed. *The Future of Freedom: Illiberal Democracy at Home and Abroad*. New York: W.W. Norton, 2003.

Zucker, Ross. *Democratic Distributive Justice*. Cambridge: Cambridge University Press, 2001.

Civil Society

Barber, Benjamin R. *A Place for Us: How to Make Society Civil and Democracy Strong*. New York: Hill & Wang, 1998.

Chambers, Simone, and Jeffrey Kopstein. "Bad Civil Society." *Political Theory* 29:6 (December 2001): 837–65.

Cohen, Jean L., and Andrew Arato. *Civil Society and Political Theory*. Cambridge, MA: MIT Press, 1992.

Deakin, Nicholas. *In Search of Civil Society*. New York: Palgrave, 2001.

Ehrenberg, John. *Civil Society: The Critical History of an Idea*. New York: New York University Press, 1999.

Gellner, Ernest. *Conditions of Liberty: Civil Society and Its Rivals*. New York: Allen Lane/Penguin Press, 1994.

Gibney, Matthew, ed. *Globalizing Rights: The Oxford Amnesty Lectures 1999*. Oxford: Oxford University Press, 2003.

Hall, John A., ed. *Civil Society: History, Comparison*. London: Polity Press, 1995.

Janoski, Thomas. *Citizenship and Civil Society: A Framework of Rights and Obligations in Liberal, Traditional, and Social Democratic Regimes*. Cambridge: Cambridge University Press, 1998.

Kaldor, Mary. *Global Civil Society: An Answer to War*. Cambridge, England: Polity, 2003.

Keane, John. *Civil Society: Old Images, New Visions*. Stanford, CA: Stanford University Press, 1998.

———. *Global Civil Society?* Cambridge: Cambridge University Press, 2003.

Kleinberg, Remonda Bensabat, and Janine A. Clark. *Economic Liberalization, Democratization, and Civil Society in the Developing World*. New York: St. Martin's Press, 2000.

Mohanty, Manoranjan, and Paratha Nath Mukherji, with Olle Törnquist, eds. *People's Rights: Social Movements and the State in the Third World*. New Delhi: Sage, 1998.

Norton, Augustus Richard, ed. *Civil Society in the Middle East*. 2 vols. Leiden: E. J. Brill, 1995–96.

Rosenblum, Nancy L., and Robert C. Post, eds. *Civil Society and Government*. Princeton, NJ: Princeton University Press, 2002.

Democracy in the Third World

Barker, Jonathan, with Anne-Marie Cwikowski, Christie Gombay, Katherine Isbester, Kole Shettima, and Aparna Sundar. *Street-Level Democracy: Political Settings at the Margins of Global Power*. Toronto: Between the Lines/West Hartford, CT: Kumarian Press, 1999.

Bauzon, Kenneth E., ed. *Development and Democratization in the Third World: Myths, Hopes, and Realities*. Washington, DC: Crane Russak, 1992.

Diamond, Larry, Juan J. Linz, and Seymour Martin Lipset, eds. *Democracy in Developing Countries*. 4 vols. Boulder, CO: Lynne Rienner, 1988.

Fawcett, Louise, and Yezid Sayigh. *The Third World beyond the Cold War: Continuity and Change*. Oxford: Oxford University Press, 1999.

Haynes, Jeff. *Democracy in the Developing World: Africa, Asia, Latin America and the Middle East.* Cambridge, England: Polity, 2001.

Mutua, Makau. *Human Rights: A Political and Cultural Critique.* Philadelphia: University of Pennsylvania Press, 2002. From an African perspective; sees human rights as a Western phenomenon.

Nyerere, Julius K. *Freedom and Development: Uhuru na Maendelo. A Selection from Writings and Speeches 1968–1973.* Dar es Salaam, Tanzania: Oxford University Press, 1973.

———. *Freedom and Unity: Uhuru na Umoja. A Selection from Writings and Speeches, 1952–1965.* Nairobi, Kenya: Oxford University Press, 1967.

Pinkey, Robert. *Democracy in the Third World.* 2nd ed. Boulder, CO: Lynne Rienner, 2003.

Websites

Core documents of U.S. democracy: http://www.gpoaccess.gov/coredocs.html

The Democracy Online Project: http://democracyonline.org/

International Human Rights Instruments: http://www.unhchr.ch/html/intlinst.htm

The Internet Democracy Project: http://www.internetdemocracyproject.org/

The International Institute for Democracy and Electoral Assistance: http://www.idea.int/

The National Endowment for Democracy: http://www.ned.org/

New York Public Library Utopia Exhibit (includes a discussion of the Internet as democratic space): http://www.nypl.org/utopia/I_meta.html

The Norwegian Study of Power and Democracy:
http://www.sv.uio.no/mutr/english/index.html

U.S. charter schools: http://www.uscharterschools.org/pub/uscs_docs/index.htm

USA Patriot Act (Uniting and Strengthening America by Providing Appropriate Tools Required to Intercept and Obstruct Terrorism Act) of 2001, H.R. 3162: http://frwebgate.access.gpo.gov/cgi-bin/getdoc.cgi?dbname=107_cong_public_laws&docid=f:publ056.107.pdf or http://thomas.loc.gov/cgi-bin/query/z?c107: H.R.3162.ENR:

Criticism of the USA Patriot Act:

American Civil Liberties Union: http://www.aclu.org/SafeandFree/SafeandFree.cfm?ID=12126&c=207

American Library Association: http://www.ala.org/ala/washoff/WOissues/civilliberties/theusapatriotact/alaresolution.htm and http://www.ala.org/ala/oif/ifissues/usapatriotact.htm

4

Capitalism, Socialism, and Democracy

To most citizens of North America, democracy and capitalism are so closely tied that the idea of an alternative seems foolish; to many citizens of some countries in other parts of the world, it is self-evident that democracy and socialism are the only possible partners. In the United States the word *socialist* is so negative that using this word produces rejection of an idea without further discussion; in many countries the word *capitalist* has the same effect. To put it mildly, there is a lot of disagreement and misunderstanding concerning these two economic systems.

The discussion that follows is intended to clarify the meaning of *capitalism* and *socialism* and show why adherents of each claim to be the only true democrats. Thus the emphasis is on the arguments for and against capitalism and socialism as supportive of democracy. Both positive and negative arguments are presented, because in each case much of the argument for one alternative is based on the argument against the other. Both capitalism and socialism can be found combined with democratic and authoritarian political systems;[1] therefore, it is particularly important to understand how both advocates and critics see their relationship to democracy.

---

[1] There have been many studies of authoritarianism, going back to Theodor W. Adorno et al., *The Authoritarian Personality* (New York: Harper & Row, 1950).

DEMOCRATIC CAPITALISM

Today democratic capitalism is perceived as having won the argument with socialism. With the collapse of the authoritarian socialism that we call *communism,* capitalists have a renewed confidence. Capitalism has returned to its roots in the free market, and many of its defenders contend that the problems capitalism encountered were due to a loss of faith in the free market rather than any inherent problem with the system. This resurrected belief in the free market makes the whole argument much simpler than it was when most capitalists supported what they called the *mixed economy;* but it also simplifies and focuses the attack on capitalism because the operations of the free market are the traditional point of attack.

The Principles of Democratic Capitalism

Traditional capitalism, often called *free market capitalism* or *laissez-faire capitalism,* is characterized by

- Private ownership of property
- No legal limit on the accumulation of property
- The free market—no government intervention in the economy
- The profit motive as the driving force
- Profit as the measure of efficiency

The fundamental position as stated by Adam Smith (1723–1790), the Scottish economist and moral philosopher who is generally thought of as the intellectual father of capitalism, is that human beings are most effectively motivated by self-interest.[2] In economic terms, this means that individuals should be free (the free market) to pursue their interests (profit). The result should be the most efficient economic system, and, therefore, everyone will benefit. Goods will be produced that sell as cheaply as possible because, if they aren't, someone else will step in and replace the current manufacturer. Jobs will be created by entrepreneurs searching for a way to make a profit. The entire economy will be stimulated and grow, thus producing a higher standard of living for everyone, as long as the entrepreneur is free to operate and can make a sufficient profit. Workers can choose to spend their money on consumer goods or, by saving, enter the competition by going into business for themselves. Some will fail, some will succeed, and some will succeed beyond all expectations. All commentators agree that capitalism tends to increase production; even Karl Marx (1818–83), the founder of communism, said this. But critics of capitalism like Marx argue that the costs are too high.

The Mixed Economy In the twentieth century some changes were made in capitalism. First, in the culmination of a trend that began in the late nineteenth

---

[2] For an extensive history of the development of capitalism, see Fernand Braudel, *Civilization and Capitalism, 15th–18th Century,* 3 vols. (New York: Harper & Row, 1982–1984).

Adam Smith (1723–90) is best known as the author of *An Inquiry into the Nature and Causes of the Wealth of Nations* (1776), better known under the short title *The Wealth of Nations*. In *The Wealth of Nations* he presented a history of economics in Europe, a description of manufacturing in his day, and, most important, a set of recommendations. The key argument is that individuals, each pursuing his or her own self-interest, will produce the greatest benefits for everyone. He applied this idea to the operations of the economic system and thereby became famous for providing the moral justification for and part of the intellectual foundation of capitalism.

century, government regulation of the economy was accepted. Regulation came about because the English economist John Maynard Keynes (1883–1946) had argued, and generally convinced other economists, that depressions could be avoided by regulating the economy, specifically by using public expenditure to pump money into the economy and soak up excess unemployment. By doing this, prosperity for all without serious fluctuations—the so-called boom-and-bust cycle—could be virtually guaranteed.

Second, during the Great Depression banks closed, causing the loss of people's life savings, and pensions disappeared along with the companies that had provided them. These events left many people without the financial support they had counted on for their old age. As a direct result, government-administered retirement systems were established in most Western countries. In the United States this was the beginning of the social security system, which was initially designed to be self-supporting (monies paid in by employees and employers would accumulate and be paid out on retirement). The expansion of the program to most of the population, the expansion of benefits, and the rapid increase in the number of people who not only lived long enough to retire but then lived a long time after retirement combined to undermine the financial base of the system.

On the same principle—that people should be protected from radical shifts in economic fortune—other programs were added. Countries varied in the speed and extent of expansion of such governmental intervention in the economy; the United States was probably the slowest economically developed democracy to add programs, and it added far fewer than most. In the United States most programs were established in the so-called War on Poverty during the presidency (1963–69) of Lyndon Johnson (1908–73). These programs were then greatly expanded during the presidency (1969–74) of Richard Nixon (1913–94).

The argument for regulation goes as follows:

- The amount of property and money held by individuals directly affects the amount of money they spend.
- The amount individuals spend directly affects the amount any industry can produce.
- The amount industry can produce affects the number of people it can hire.
- The number of people industry can hire again affects the amount of money available to be spent by individuals for the products of industry.
- The number of products industry can produce affects its profit.

In this way, some limitation on the amount of property or money that can be held by any individual helps rather than deters the entire capitalist system because it forces the money to circulate more widely. Thus even some strong supporters of capitalism argue for some regulation.

Democratic capitalism originated in the West, and that area has provided the model for many countries; but alternative models are available. The best-known alternative occurs in Asia. In Japan an attempt was made to avoid the continual conflict between owners or managers and workers that has character-ized the West and that still exists in some countries. The largest Japanese corpo-rations used to provide what were, in essence, lifetime contracts for workers. In return they expected the workers to have a real identification with the corpora-tion. Some such contracts still exist, but the practice is no longer standard. In other Asian countries, like Singapore, a free market was combined with an authoritarian political system that, although democratic, regulated many details of daily life. There was a period in which the economies of many Asian coun-tries grew rapidly; however, currently most of them are strong and stable but not growing.

A number of Western countries are trying to replace the conflict or adver-sary model of industrial relations that has dominated democratic capitalism with a model that sees management and labor as dependent on each other for success. Germany, the most successful Western industrial democratic capitalist country, has a system that gives a great deal of power to unions as a means of avoiding conflict. Continuing attempts to modify that relationship have so far had only limited success, but Germany is still experiencing difficulties integrating the former German Democratic Republic (East Germany) into the German econ-omy, and the expansion of the European Union means that lower-wage coun-tries are readily available as competition.

Avoiding conflict is also one goal of the corporatist or neocorporatist theory of democracy described in the previous chapter. Corporatists want workers and employers to join with government in ensuring the smooth running of the economy.

The Return to the Free Market As has already been mentioned, capitalists have turned against the mixed-economy model and reasserted the primacy of the free market. During the 1980s and 1990s, most Western countries dismantled at least some government regulation, cut back assistance and pension programs, and privatized parts of the economy that had been publicly owned or operated. But many programs have proved immensely popular with citizens and politically difficult or impossible to eliminate. Still, the extent of economic regulation has clearly dropped throughout the world of democratic capitalism.

Capitalism and Democracy

For capitalists, democracy requires capitalism because, they believe, it supports the central democratic value of freedom. Capitalists believe that freedom is based on private property, and capitalism, by stressing private property, makes economic freedom central. Capitalists also believe that economic freedom is a primary support for political liberty. Economic freedom means that everyone is free to enter the marketplace, accumulate property without limit, and use that property as they choose. Capitalists see two potential sources of control that must be blocked—monopolies and government. Monopolies, they believe, will always be temporary if the free market is allowed to operate; therefore, the real problem is government.

Free market capitalists argue that any government regulation destroys the basis for the capitalist system and, hence, individualism and liberty. The defenders of some government regulation (but not control) of the economy say that the absence of government regulation itself destroys the democratic capitalistic system because a few people can control the economy, and even the government, through monopolies. Other bad effects of a lack of government regulation are sometimes mentioned, but the development of monopolies is the most important politically.

Monopolies The problem of monopolies was illustrated in the United States during the first growth of industrialism and particularly the great expansion of the railroads. Such men as J. P. Morgan (1837–1913) virtually controlled the American economy and thereby the American government. This monopolistic tendency, some capitalists argue, destroys the capitalist system by radically limiting competition. The system is not competitive when only a few companies can set prices. Under such circumstances few people with new ideas or approaches are able to try them out; it is not talent that succeeds in such a system but the monopolist's will. This situation does not fit the traditional myth of the capitalist system in which the clerk becomes corporation president by hard work. The clerk of a monopolist might become a business president someday, but not necessarily by hard work. The key to success would be the whim of the monopolist.

The most important effect of monopoly, viewed from the perspective of democracy, is that the monopolist can control the government. Such control severely restricts the degree to which democracy can exist because it might even negate the effect of popular participation in political decision making.[3]

---

[3] For a different view, see Gabriel Kolko, *The Triumph of Conservatism: A Reinterpretation of American History, 1900–1916* (New York: Free Press, 1963).

President Dwight D. Eisenhower (1890–1969, president 1953–61), in his farewell address, warned the American people about a military–industrial complex that he contended was close to ruling the United States through informal channels. Eisenhower was concerned about the close relationship between the military and the large industries that produced military goods under contract to the Pentagon. He was also concerned with the fact that many high-ranking officers "retired" after twenty years in the military to take jobs in the industries with which they had negotiated contracts and with which their former colleagues would be negotiating future contracts. He believed that these relationships and the growth of the sector of the economy providing goods to the military were leading to a dangerous concentration of economic and political power. This could happen even more readily under a monopolistic system.[4]

Many capitalists believe that the competitive pressures of a truly free market will prevent the development of monopolies. They also believe that any monopoly that develops will not last long because of the same pressures. One reason monopolies are expected to collapse is that their dominance of the market will reduce their incentive to innovate or take risks. In these circumstances, people with new ideas and the risk-taking capitalist mentality will bring new goods to the market and undermine the power of the monopoly.

Economic Freedom   Thus even within capitalism the desired extent of economic freedom is the subject of debate. The basic premise is that capitalism allows more freedom for the individual than does any other economic system. Any individual with sufficient interest and funds can buy stock in any number of companies. Stockholders become part owners of a company and can, if time and money permit, participate in some decisions of the company at annual meetings, although this opportunity is limited for the small shareholder.

In addition, there are those like Milton Friedman (b. 1912) who argue that capitalism provides greater political freedom than any other system. "The kind of economic organization that provides economic freedom directly, namely, competitive capitalism, also promotes political freedom because it separates economic power from political power and in this way enables the one to offset the other."[5] This separation can be compared to a checks-and-balances system such as that in the U.S. Constitution. Government power is limited by centers of economic power that also limit one another. These centers of economic power are in turn limited by government, which is also subject to regular elections. If both economic and political power are centralized in government, there is no check on the activities of government except through the vote.

The individual is free to enter the economic system subject to some government regulation and some limitation due to the existence of many large

---

[4] Some critics argue that this happened some time ago. See, for example, Paul A. Baran and Paul M. Sweezy, *Monopoly Capital: An Essay on the American Economic and Social Order* (New York: Monthly Review Press, 1966).

[5] Milton Friedman, *Capitalism and Freedom* (Chicago: University of Chicago Press, 1962), 9.

corporations. The individual succeeds or fails depending on his or her willingness to work hard and the desire of the consumer, manipulated to some extent by advertising, to buy the product. This is economic freedom and shows the relationship of capitalism to equality of opportunity. Every person should be able to become a capitalist and have the potential to get rich.

Equality of Opportunity   To the extent that capitalists support equality, they mean equality of opportunity, and equality of opportunity was one motivation behind the development of a welfare system designed to ensure that everyone can participate in the system. This concern is not based solely on humanitarian ends but also on the recognition that people who cannot provide for themselves can be a burden on society and a waste of potential human resources. In addition, welfare programs have been concerned with the aged, who have contributed to society but who need help to provide for retirement when many costs, such as medical bills, tend to rise while incomes decline.

Criticism of Democratic Capitalism

Critics of capitalism focus on the extremes of wealth and poverty, the power over the political process that such wealth gives its owners, and the extreme inequality between employer and employee that exists under capitalism. Some of these points have also bothered defenders of capitalism. Other criticisms attack the institution of private property, the free market, and the profit motive.

Results   There are two related issues in the criticism of capitalism's results—power and poverty. The power issue can be framed generally by asking how much power one person should have in a democratic society. Great wealth gives potential power in a political system, and critics assert that such wealth makes rule by the people impossible. Defenders of capitalism argue either that this is a nonissue (the rich are a minority, and the majority can always defeat them) or that limited regulation can solve the problem. But the essence of the argument is that the benefits of capitalism outweigh any danger.

Great wealth appears to accompany extreme poverty. Critics of capitalism say that such extremes are inevitable in a capitalist system and are wrong. No one should be condemned to a life of poverty so that a few individuals can be rich. Defenders of capitalism reply either that poverty is the fault of the poor (they have not worked hard enough) or that poverty will be overcome through the economic growth that capitalism makes possible.

Most defenders of capitalism, and in the United States most people, believe the power of an employer over an employee to be simply in the nature of things. But critics of capitalism see this exercise of power as undemocratic and demeaning to the worker. In addition, many people believe that the power relationship between employer and worker fosters undemocratic attitudes, leading to authoritarianism in the employer and servility in the worker. This was clearly the case in Britain in the nineteenth and early twentieth centuries.

Private Property   Critics of capitalism state that the private control of property used to manufacture and distribute goods is wrong because it gives a great deal of power to a few people. Today the power of private property is obvious as many companies relocate their operations for various reasons. Critics contend that such factors as the effect on a community, the well-being of employees, and the economic strength of a country should be taken into account in economic decision making. They usually argue that the creation of the value of property is social, not private—that is, it is created by groups of people working together, including those who invest, those who manage, and those who labor, all working within a structure of legal rules. Therefore social effects should outweigh other factors in decision making. Capitalists respond that if wealth is to be produced, they must consider their competitive situation first in any decision. Giving social factors precedence would make capitalists uncompetitive and ultimately force them out of business to the detriment of all concerned.

The Profit Motive   Capitalists believe that the profit motive drives people to succeed and create wealth; their critics argue that even if that idea is true, it is wrong. They assert that the competition fostered is personally and socially unhealthy. Capitalists reply that competition is natural and healthy, both personally and socially, and that it is the major source of effort and excellence.

The Free Market   Critics of capitalism argue that there is no such thing as a free market and that the whole point of business activity is to control or dominate the market, not compete freely in it. They also say that the free market, to the extent there is one, is inefficient. Capitalists, of course, state that there either is a free market or could be one in most circumstances and that it is the only truly efficient mechanism for producing and distributing goods.

As can be seen, the disagreements are fundamental. They will come up frequently in succeeding pages, particularly because the same issues are often involved in the discussion of socialism.

The Problem of Welfare

In the mid-1990s, politicians in most developed democracies came to the conclusion that the systems designed to provide assistance to the poor had developed fundamental problems and were keeping people out of jobs rather than helping them until they were in a position to enter or reenter the job market. Bolstered by a strong economy and a low unemployment rate, so-called welfare-to-work programs were implemented to force people into the job market by setting dates at which their welfare payments would stop. In the United States the states came up with a wide variety of such programs with different dates for the cutoff, different job training programs, and various incentives to get a job and disincentives to stay on welfare. Initially these programs were huge successes, with large numbers of welfare recipients entering or reentering the workforce and welfare rolls dropping dramatically. Two problems emerged—one expected, the other not planned for. The first is that some people on welfare have serious health problems (both mental and physical) or other issues that make it difficult to get or keep a job. The second problem is that the economy is no longer as strong, and many people recently hired off the welfare rolls are being fired, not through any fault in their job performance but because companies are cutting back.

DEMOCRATIC SOCIALISM

Socialism in all forms is currently under attack, and many democratic socialists are dropping the label because many communists now call themselves democratic socialists. Particularly in Eastern Europe, it is difficult to know what a current political label really means. Democratic socialists are in this position because communism, which they criticized, is a form of socialism and has failed. Thus democratic socialists, while not giving up their beliefs, do not want to be falsely identified with communism and are unsure what to call themselves. *Social democracy* is the most common new label and allows for the incorporation of some elements of the market into democratic socialist theory.

The Principles of Democratic Socialism

Democratic socialism can be characterized as follows:

- Much property held by the public through a democratically elected government, including most major industries, utilities, and the transportation system
- A limit on the accumulation of private property
- Governmental regulation of the economy
- Extensive publicly financed assistance and pension programs
- Social costs and the provision of services added to purely financial considerations as the measure of efficiency

Socialism has a long history, which some advocates like to trace back to biblical sources. It is more accurate to see socialism as originating in response to the excesses of early industrial capitalism; but many socialists, particularly those calling themselves Christian socialists, found their inspiration in the New Testament.

Still, the origins of contemporary democratic socialism are best located in the early to mid-nineteenth century writings of the so-called utopian socialists, Robert Owen (1771–1858), Charles Fourier (1772–1837), Claude-Henri Saint-Simon (1760–1825), and Étienne Cabet (1788–1856). All these writers proposed village communities combining industrial and agricultural production and owned, in varying ways, by the inhabitants themselves. Thus the essence of early socialism was public ownership of the means of production. These theorists all also included varying forms of democratic political decision making, but they all distrusted the ability of people raised under capitalism to understand what was in their own best interest.

Karl Marx, discussed in detail in Chapter 7, rejected these early socialists and developed his own version of socialism, which he called *communism*. There is considerable controversy among scholars regarding Marx's own attitude toward democracy, but two lines of thought developed from Marx: one emphasizing democracy and one, the dominant line, rejecting it. However, other socialists rejected Marx, and later in the century two American writers, Edward Bellamy (1850–98) and Henry George (1839–97), produced versions of public ownership with what they saw as democratic control, although again both placed some limitations on democracy. In his last work, *Equality* (1897), Bellamy dropped most of those limitations.

In Britain a form of socialism developed, called Fabian Socialism (now embodied in the Fabian Society), that emphasizes the democratic elements of democratic socialism: electoral success, the rational presentation of their position (in innumerable publications), careful study of the current social situation, and gradualism.

Since that time many democratic socialist political parties, such as the Labour Party in the United Kingdom and the Social Democratic Party in Sweden, have been elected to office, been defeated and left office, and later returned to office or remained in opposition. In Europe today democratic socialists often call themselves *social democrats*. This label is intended to stress the democratic nature of democratic socialism and to deemphasize links with other forms of socialism, particularly Marxian socialism or communism. The best known adherents of this position have been Willy Brandt (1913–92) of Germany, Olof Palme (1927–86) of Sweden, and Michael Harrington (1928–89) of the United States. Recently, three socialists have been elected to the presidency of countries in South America. Two of them, Luíz Inácio Lula da Silva (b. 1945) of Brazil, who was elected in 2002, and Tabare Vazquez (b. 1940) of Uruguay, who was elected in 2004, are clearly democratic socialists. The third, Hugo Chavez (b. 1954) of Venezuela, elected in 1998, is a controversial figure, and attempts have been made to remove him from office. In all three cases, their campaigns succeeded in part due to the electorates' unhappiness with the extent of poverty in these countries, poverty that was successfully portrayed as the result of the operations of the free market.

If one assumes citizens should control their political lives and contribute to political decision making, it is only a short step to the democratic socialist argument that citizens should have some say in economic decision making. There is no question that economic decisions in connection with, for example, an automobile manufacturing industry have a tremendous impact on an entire country. Therefore, say democratic socialists, there must be some means for the people to oversee such economic decisions through their elected representatives. However, what economic decisions are significant? What are key industries for a national economy? Democratic socialists argue that the elected representatives of the people should answer these questions and that the answers are likely to vary from country to country. In addition, the forms of governmental control and regulation and the extent of public ownership of industry will vary depending on the decisions made by the elected representatives of the people, checked at the polls by the people themselves.

Luíz Inácio Lula da Silva (b. 1945) is the President of the Federative Republic of Brazil. Known in Brazil as Lula (originally a nickname that he added to his legal name), he was a union organizer and strike leader. In 1980 the Partido dos Trabalhadores (PT) or Workers' Party was formed, and in 1986 he was elected to congress. He has run for president in every election since 1989 and was elected in 2002 after campaigning from a somewhat more centrist position than he had previously taken.

Paulo Fridman/Corbis

Another rationale for democratic socialism, perhaps the most appealing one, is what might be called the humanitarian argument. Democratic socialists believe that only when the people control the economic system will solutions to basic social problems, like hunger and disease, be possible. Only under democratic socialism can the people demand solutions; therefore, democratic socialism is essential to overcome the most basic problems of society.

In practice democratic socialist systems vary considerably, particularly in the degree to which industries, utilities, and transportation systems are directly owned by the government. In some countries most of these are governmentally owned, but in most countries the government owns only specific parts of industrial complexes. For example, in Sweden, which most Americans think of as a socialist country, few major industries are governmentally owned.

When we say the public holds much property, this refers to property crucial to the functioning of the economic system. It does not mean there is no private property. Private property is still held by individuals in personal belongings, housing, most small businesses, and, in some cases, large corporations. Some democratic socialists, theorists, and systems do not limit the amount of private property that can be held by an individual, but most do. There is no necessity within democratic socialist theory for such limitations. On the other hand, most approaches suggest some degree of income redistribution and thereby justify limited private property.

Socialism and Democracy

The fundamental assumption underlying democratic socialism is that participation in political decision making should be extended to include economic decision making. Democratic socialists say that because the economy and politics are so closely intertwined, voters should be able to control their economic futures through the government they elect. Such voter control presupposes government's ability to control much of the economy through ownership and/or regulation of its most important parts.

The government of a democratic socialist system regulates the part of the economy it does not own directly. This regulation is designed to ensure that privately owned businesses operate in the best interest of society as a whole rather than simply for private profit. This point illuminates the ethos of democratic socialism. The word *socialism* refers to *social* theories rather than to theories oriented to the individual.

In addition to the democratic proposition proclaimed in the basic assumption outlined earlier, democratic socialism suggests that liberty cannot be maintained without economic security. This argument resembles the democratic capitalist argument for welfare as a means of attaining equality of opportunity, but it is broader in that it demands more than equality of opportunity. The democratic socialist says neither the right to vote nor any other form of liberty is possible unless every person within the society is economically secure. If insecure, citizens will be incapable of exercising personal liberty. Such economic security is possible, it is argued, only with an extensive welfare system.

Welfare The typical democratic socialist welfare system includes an extensive medical care system, which is provided either free or at minimal cost, usually including prenatal care, dental care, and eye examinations, in addition to more typical health services. Access to alternative medical practitioners and procedures like acupuncture or homeopathic treatment was not originally included in most countries but is now being added in some places. An obvious practical rationale for such a system is that a healthy individual can contribute more to society than a sick one. Therefore, it is to the advantage of society to ensure the health of all. This is the fundamental rationale of any welfare system—an individual who is maintained at the minimum level of life can contribute to society. The welfare system also takes care of those who have already contributed to society and cannot now care for themselves. Thus the welfare system provides money for food, housing, and other minimum necessities.

The Problem of Bureaucracy Bureaucracy presents one of the greatest problems for democratic socialism. Whether in business or government, it is difficult for a bureaucracy to be as well informed or as responsive to the needs of the people or industry it serves as would be ideal. Because bureaucracies are not directly responsible to the people, many argue that a large bureaucracy threatens the public control that the democratic socialist is trying to preserve. In democratic capitalism the economy is controlled privately; therefore, powerful people are not directly accountable to the electorate. In democratic socialism bureaucrats who are not directly accountable to the electorate replace these people. In addition, because bureaucrats remain while politicians and governments change, it is not unusual for the bureaucrats to follow their own policies rather than those of the political leaders.

This problem is fundamental to the nature of a bureaucracy. Bureaucracies administer laws (rules) established by the normal processes of legislation. These rules are applied equally (in the same way) to people even though people differ. Attempts to allow flexibility generally produce charges of favoritism, corruption, discrimination, and other forms of illegality. Quite simply, flexibility seems to undermine the equal application of rules even though that equal application may seem unfair. Thus bureaucracy raises a problem: How can rules be applied unequally but fairly? Laws are rules, and rules by their nature are supposed to apply to everyone in the same way. People are different, and they have different needs. How can a bureaucracy do its job in these circumstances?

Therefore, at times democratic socialism faces the same problems for which it criticizes democratic capitalism. Still, the democratic socialist argues that people control the bureaucracy through their elected representatives and that the government can immediately change the operations of the bureaucracy when it becomes cumbersome or ineffective. Democratic capitalists counter that under capitalism people control the economic system through the market.

Many countries, both democratic socialist and democratic capitalist, have instituted an *ombudsman* (the word derives from a Swedish term for deputy or representative) who hears and investigates complaints about a bureaucracy. Sometimes the ombudsman is empowered to make sure the causes of the complaints are corrected. Such a person fills an obvious need because most bureaucracies are unwieldy, operate inefficiently, and find it hard to take individual differences into account. Of course, elected representatives, particularly in the United States, also play this role.

Democratic countries recognize the problem of bureaucracy and have attempted to correct it. At the same time, the relatively independent nature of a bureaucracy may provide some protection for liberty. One agency may force another to respond better than it would on its own. Thus conflicts among parts of the bureaucracy may have a positive result.

Criticism of Democratic Socialism

Critics of democratic socialism have two basic arguments focusing on the destruction of the free market and the centralization of power. Although many socialists now accept "market socialism," critics contend that the free market of competitive capitalism is essential for efficient production and distribution of goods. Socialists have found that a limited market is more efficient and better able to respond to consumer demands than completely centralized regulation and, they argue, fairer than a completely unregulated market.

In related criticism, opponents of socialism say that interference with the free market through government ownership and regulation puts too much power in the hands of government. This, they contend, leads inevitably to even greater centralization of power and the destruction of democracy. A more limited version of the same argument suggests that even if democracy is not destroyed, freedom will necessarily be limited in a democratic socialist regime.

Democratic socialists respond that the electoral process is capable of checking any such tendency if it does occur, but they see no reason that it should occur.

Related to both criticisms is the question, what motivates the socialist bureaucrat? As we saw, the capitalist believes that human beings are motivated by self-interest—the profit motive. Self-interest, capitalists argue, will always make socialism unworkable. The socialist argues that the bureaucrat is motivated by the desire to serve. The capitalist laughs. The socialist responds that while the profit motive—the socialist might call it "greed"—may be necessary under capitalism, socialism makes it possible to be motivated by a desire to serve the public.

There is as much distance between socialism and its critics as between capitalism and its critics. But both socialists and capitalists are making the same claim—each group contends that it is best for democracy.

Market Socialism

Market socialism, a phrase that democratic capitalists see as a contradiction in terms, is the most significant addition to the vocabulary of democratic socialism in many years. Supporters of market socialism accept the democratic capitalist argument that centralized economic power is inefficient, and they agree with democratic capitalists that markets promote greater freedom. But market socialists contend that democratic capitalism places power in the hands of the rich and that large corporations are as inefficient as large government. They contend that such large corporations can function only by controlling the market, and, therefore, that regulated markets protect the weak, prevent monopolies, and produce markets at least as free as those under unregulated democratic capitalism.

In addition, market socialists insist that a functioning welfare system must protect people from the inevitable shifts of a market economy. Thus market socialists have not abandoned the principles of democratic socialism but have moved in the direction of a mixed economy with variously owned enterprises (private, public, worker, and cooperative) competing within a regulated market.[6]

Developmental Socialism

Economic systems have been developed that are neither capitalist nor communist. The most original such creation has been called *African socialism* and *communitarian socialism* but is best known as *developmental socialism*. It was developed by Julius Nyerere (1922–99) of Tanzania, Léopold Sédar Senghor (1906–2001) of Senegal, U Nu (1907–95) of Myanmar (formerly Burma), and India's Vinoba Bhave (1895–1982), and it stresses social solidarity and cooperation as the means of developing the economy. Developmental socialism has also emphasized the

---

[6] The classic studies of market socialism, predating the current interest in it, are Oscar Lange and Fred M. Taylor, *On the Economic Theory of Socialism,* ed. Benjamin E. Lippincott (Minneapolis: University of Minnesota Press, 1938; New York: McGraw-Hill, 1964); and Alec Nove, *Efficiency Criteria for Nationalised Industries* (London: George Allen & Unwin, 1974).

establishment of a network of close social and economic ties to help form national identity. World economic and political realities have brought failure to developmental socialism.

A good illustration of the basic idea of developmental socialism is found in the Swahili word Nyerere uses for socialism, *ujamaa*—familyhood. As he put it, "The foundation, and the objective, of African socialism is the extended family."[7] The extended family—consisting of a wide range of relatives who work cooperatively and share all family resources—is the model for village and tribal socialism. All members of the village are fed, clothed, and housed as well as the group can afford. The aged and the ill are supported. Developmental socialism explicitly rejects the class divisions of communism. All are workers; there is little or no tradition of an indigenous exploiting class.

In Nyerere's socialism all people must recognize that they are part of a single group working together to achieve a common end. This end is designed to achieve economic security and human dignity by changing the distribution system. "There must be something wrong in a society where one man, however hardworking or clever he may be, can acquire as great a 'reward' as a thousand of his fellows can acquire between them."[8] A cardinal principle in Nyerere's socialism reflects the fact that in traditional African society, as in Native American societies, land could not be owned, only used.

These lofty goals remain unmet or only partially met, with a future that looks grim at best. External forces produced conditions that might have made success impossible even if everything had gone perfectly within the countries. Internally, all Third World countries face a multitude of problems. Among the worst problems are rampant corruption, extreme differences of wealth, the threat of military takeover, and tribal and religious conflict. As a result, no Third World country has been in a position to put developmental socialism into practice.

The Third Way

Just as the phrase *Third World* was coined to refer to countries trying to find a position between capitalist and communist countries, *Third Way* refers to the attempt to find a place between capitalism and socialism.[9]

Generally, socialists condemn the Third Way as capitalism and capitalists condemn it as socialism, but what it tries to suggest is that the economy cannot operate effectively under either the free market or state control, however democratically those state controllers have been elected. Thus it has affinities with market socialism, but it is often not socialist enough for supporters of market socialism. It also has affinities with the mixed economy of capitalism, but it is

---

[7] Julius K. Nyerere, *Ujamaa: Essays on Socialism* (Dar Es Salaam, Tanzania: Oxford University Press, 1968), 11.

[8] Nyerere, *Ujamaa*, 3.

[9] The phrase is most associated with Anthony Giddens (b. 1938). See his *The Third Way: The Renewal of Social Democracy* (London: Polity Press, 1998); *The Third Way and Its Critics* (London: Polity Press, 2000); and the collection he edited, *The Progressive Manifesto: New Ideas for the Centre-Left* (Cambridge, England: Polity, 2003).

often not capitalist enough for supporters of the mixed economy. As these comments suggest, the Third Way is rather undefined, and perhaps it is best thought of as taking the position that policy should be based on what works to achieve the desired goal. Political leaders in both Germany and the United Kingdom say that they are basing their policies on the Third Way, and the essence of the Third Way is clearly to be *both* capitalist and socialist, to have both a strong state with a strong public sphere and a strong market economy.

Third Way theorists also take seriously the welfare function of the state. They generally argue that the state should focus on working women, preschool children, and children in single-parent households. They also argue for universal day care and greater work flexibility. All these policies, it is felt, require state implementation.

Economic Democracy

Many people from different ideological perspectives have consistently raised the question of the degree to which democratic approaches can be applied to various aspects of the economy. For example, in many experiments—some successful, some not—companies have been owned and democratically operated by their workers. This means that the workers set policy and hire and fire management. Such businesses are operating successfully in many Western countries, including, most notably, Spain and the United States.

A growing trend is for workers in a company to own a substantial share of the stock, with the company run by a board of directors and managers like any other company. This is not an example of economic democracy unless the workers actively make decisions that give them significant authority.

The argument for economic democracy is the same as that for political democracy outlined in the previous chapter. Robert A. Dahl (b. 1915) has weighed the theoretical arguments for and against economic democracy in *A Preface to Economic Democracy* (1985). He concludes, "A system of self-governing enterprises would be one part of a system of equalities and liberties in which both would, I believe, be stronger, on balance, than they can be in a system of corporate capitalism."[10]

Cooperation

Cooperation, a significant economic movement of long standing that many adherents relate to democratic socialism, is having a recent revival after a temporary decline in interest. Cooperation takes two forms—producer cooperatives and consumer cooperatives (some include both); both are well known and exist throughout the world, although today they are probably most common in the Third World. A third form, the housing cooperative, is currently most visible in the cohousing movement and is discussed in the next section. In all forms of cooperation, decision making within the cooperative is democratic, usually as direct involvement based on majority rule, although some cooperatives use

[10] Robert A. Dahl, *A Preface to Economic Democracy* (Berkeley: University of California Press, 1985).

consensual systems. Larger operations have representative systems, with the representatives checked by regular meetings of the entire membership.

A *consumer cooperative* is a group of people who form a nonprofit organization to purchase goods in large quantities. Thus they can pass on the savings from the bulk purchase, eliminate some levels of distribution, and not add profit to the price. If goods are sold to nonmembers, any profit made by the cooperative is distributed to the members.

A *producer cooperative* is a group of people who form an organization to produce and distribute goods, usually under the management of the workers. Profits are distributed among the workers. Agricultural cooperatives usually involve the processing and distribution of goods together with the joint purchase of expensive equipment but do not normally involve the joint ownership of land. Producer cooperatives frequently establish cooperative financial institutions such as banks, credit unions, and insurance agencies.

Consumer cooperation originated in 1844 with the Rochdale Society of Equitable Pioneers in England. The Rochdale Pioneers, as they are known, established a series of basic principles that cooperatives, with some updating, still follow. These principles include open membership; one member, one vote; limited rate of return on equity capital; surplus returned to the members or reinvested in the business; continuous education; and cooperation among cooperatives.

Communal Living

Communes, now known as *intentional communities,* are generally thought of as a phenomenon of the sixties, but they have experienced a revival. Many communities founded in the sixties are at least forty years old, and others are being founded regularly. Many are religious communities in which people join to practice a particular religious way of life, but in many secular communities the appeal is communal life itself. A subset of these communities that bridges the gap between democratic capitalism and democratic socialism is *cohousing.* The rapidly growing cohousing movement establishes communities in which the dwellings are individually owned but in which there are community-owned land and buildings, where communal interaction is encouraged architecturally and culturally, and where decision making is democratic. Cohousing is both urban and suburban and is a recent development of cooperative housing, which was primarily an urban phenomenon.

CURRENT TRENDS

Most current issues affect both democratic capitalism and democratic socialism.

Corruption

Corruption undermines both capitalism and socialism and is not hard to find in most countries. Capitalists argue that the free market will root out corruption or that limited regulation will uncover it. Socialists argue that regulation and

---

political oversight will root out corruption. Both are right: because corruption is continually being uncovered, there is a good chance that it is more common than we know. Both capitalists and socialists argue that corruption is inevitable in the other system due to the power given to either the wealthy or the bureaucrats. Given the degree of corruption, both may be right, so the question becomes how to ensure that it does not do much damage.

Fordism and Post-Fordism

All economic systems are undergoing a transition from Fordism, named after Henry Ford (1863–1947), which features assembly-line mass production and consumption, to post-Fordism, which relies on flexible production, automation and information technology, niche marketing, just-in-time-delivery, and globalization (discussed in Chapter 2). Some critics of post-Fordism stress the degree to which this approach entails a reorganization of the labor market that requires more part-time work, subcontracting or outsourcing, offshoring, and the need to break labor unions.

Fordist systems still exist throughout the world, but much such production has been shifted from the First to the Third World where labor is cheaper, and such offshoring is an aspect of post-Fordist systems. But post-Fordist production is clearly becoming the norm, and this worries both capitalists and socialists (socialists more than capitalists). Both are concerned that such systems will undermine national economies and produce large-scale unemployment, underemployment (work below the skill level of the worker), and part-time employment, all of which drive down wages so people cannot consume as much. Socialists and some capitalists believe that regulation can solve these problems; but most capitalists argue that the changes are improving the overall productive capacity of the world, raising the standard of living in the Third World, and thus raising the level of consumption in the Third World, which will offset any drop of consumption elsewhere.

Offshoring jobs from one country to another has the potential of developing serious political opposition to the free market in those countries losing jobs. People disagree over whether such job relocation benefits the economy losing jobs. Those in favor point to the lower cost of goods; those against say that the lost wages exceed the savings in consumption costs.

Poverty

According to the International Monetary Find (IMF), the richest 20 percent of the world's population controls over 80 percent of the world's gross domestic product (GDP), and the poorest 20 percent has less than 1.5 percent; the poorest 60 percent of people have only about 7 percent of world GDP. An even more striking statistic is that the richest four people (men) in the world have greater wealth than the poorest seventy-two countries combined. The GDP of those countries is almost 96 billion dollars; the net worth of the four richest men is almost 97 billion dollars.

Poverty is a significant issue throughout the world, and extreme differences between the rich and poor in both income and power can undermine support for any economic system. The poorest of the poor tend to be located in the Third World, and a number of proposals have been made to help these countries. One common suggestion is to forgive the debt of the poorest countries; but although canceling the debt would give the countries a second chance, it would not address the underlying causes, which range from corruption to a poorly educated workforce to a lack of resources. Solving the problem will require active investment in education and infrastructure not simply canceling debt.

Microfinance

A new approach to poverty is *microfinance*—providing credit and savings services to farmers, operators of small enterprises or microenterprises, and, in particular, women who are starting small businesses—at the local level in developing countries. The loans are very small (thus the words *microfinance* and *microenterprise*), but for the people involved they mean the difference between abject poverty and the first step on the very bottom rung of the ladder to independence.[11]

SUGGESTED READING

Democratic Capitalism

Some Classic Works

Friedman, Milton, with the assistance of Rose D. Friedman. *Capitalism and Freedom*. 40th anniversary ed. Chicago: University of Chicago Press, 2002.

Keynes, John Maynard. *The Economic Consequences of the Peace*. New York: Harcourt, Brace & Howe, 1920.

————. *The General Theory of Employment, Interest, and Money*. New York: Harcourt Brace, 1936.

Smith, Adam. *An Inquiry into the Nature and Causes of the Wealth of Nations*. 2 vols. Oxford, England: Clarendon Press, 1976.

Books and Articles

Bhagwati, Jagdish. *Free Trade Today*. Princeton, NJ: Princeton University Press, 2002.

Boswell, Terry, and Christopher Chase-Dunn. *The Spiral of Capitalism and Socialism: Toward Global Democracy*. Boulder, CO: Lynne Rienner, 2000.

Braudel, Fernand. *Civilization and Capitalism, 15th–18th Century*. 3 vols. New York: Harper & Row, 1982–84.

Chapman, John W., and J. Roland Pennock, eds. *Nomos XXXI: Markets and Justice*. New York: New York University Press, 1989.

---

[11] On microfinance, see Sam Daley-Harris, ed. *Pathways Out of Poverty: Innovations in Microfinance for the Poorest Families* (Bloomfield, CT: Kumarian Press, 2002); Malcolm Harper, ed., *Microfinance: Evolution, Achievements and Challenges* (London: ITDG Publishing/New Delhi, India: Samskriti, 2003); Marguerite S. Robinson, *The Microfinance Revolution: Sustainable Finance for the Poor. Lessons from Indonesia. The Emerging Industry* (Washington, DC: The World Bank/New York: Open Society Institute, 2001); and Stuart Rutherford, *The Poor and Their Money* (New Delhi, India: Oxford University Press, 2000).

Chase, Harold W., and Paul Dolan. *The Case for Democratic Capitalism*. New York: Thomas Y. Crowell, 1964.

Dasgupta, Partha, and Ismail Serageldin. *Social Capital: A Multifaceted Perspective*. Washington, DC: World Bank 2000.

Duncan, Graeme, ed. *Democracy and the Capitalist State*. Cambridge: Cambridge University Press, 1989.

Ebenstein, Alan. *Friedrich Hayek: A Biography*. New York: Palgrave, 2001.

Esping-Andersen, Gøsta. *The Three Worlds of Welfare Capitalism*. Princeton, NJ: Princeton University Press, 1990.

Greenfeld, Liah. *The Spirit of Capitalism: Nationalism and Economic Growth*. Cambridge, MA: Harvard University Press, 2001.

Gupta, Suman. *Corporate Capitalism and Political Philosophy*. London: Pluto Press, 2002.

Hayek, Friedrich A. *Economic Freedom and Representative Government*. London: Institute of Economic Affairs, 1973.

Iliffe, John. *The Emergence of African Capitalism*. Minneapolis: University of Minnesota Press, 1983.

Kay, John Anderson. *The Truth about Markets: Their Genius, Their Limits, Their Follies*. London: Allen Lane, 2003.

Kelso, Louis O., and Mortimer J. Adler. *The Capitalist Manifesto*. New York: Random House, 1958.

Kennedy, Paul M. *African Capitalism: The Struggle for Ascendancy*. Cambridge: Cambridge University Press, 1988.

Kirzner, Israel M. *Ludwig von Mises: The Man and His Economics*. Wilmington, DE: ISI Books, 2001.

Kristol, Irving. *Two Cheers for Capitalism*. New York: Basic Books, 1978.

Lane, Robert E. *The Loss of Happiness in Market Democracies*. New Haven, CT: Yale University Press, 2000.

Mueller, John. *Capitalism, Democracy, and Ralph's Pretty Good Grocery*. Princeton, NJ: Princeton University Press, 1999.

Muller, Jerry Z. *The Mind and the Market: Capitalism in Western Thought*. New York: Alfred A. Knopf, 2002. Excellent introductory history of capitalist thought by a sympathetic scholar.

Norberg, Johan. *In Defense of Global Capitalism*. Washington, DC: The Cato Institute, 2003. From a libertarian perspective, capitalism as providing freedom and opportunity to even the poorest peasant.

Novak, Michael. *The American Vision: An Essay on the Future of Democratic Capitalism*. Washington, DC: American Enterprise Institute for Public Policy Research, 1978.

———. *The Spirit of Democratic Capitalism*. New York: American Enterprise Institute for Public Policy Research/ Simon & Schuster, 1982.

Silk, Leonard, and Mark Silk, with Robert Heilbroner, Jonas Pontusson, and Bernard Wasow. *Making Capitalism Work*. New York: New York University Press, 1996.

Stepelevich, Lawrence, ed. *The Capitalist Reader*. New Rochelle, NY: Arlington House, 1977.

Von Mises, Ludwig. *The Anti-Capitalist Mentality*. Princeton, NJ: Van Nostrand, 1956.

———. *Bureaucracy*. New Haven, CT: Yale University Press, 1944; New Rochelle, NY: Arlington House, 1969.

Waligorski, Conrad P. *The Political Theory of Conservative Economists*. Lawrence: University Press of Kansas, 1990.

Wright, David McCord. *Capitalism*. Chicago: Henry Regnery, 1962.

Zmirak, John. *Wilhelm Röpke Swiss Localist, Global Economist*. Wilmington, DE: ISI Books, 2001.

Democratic Socialism

Some Classic Works

Crossman, R. H. S., ed. *New Fabian Essays*. London: Turnstile Press, 1952.

Lange, Oskar, and Fred M. Taylor. *On the Economic Theory of Socialism*. Edited by Benjamin E. Lippincott. Minneapolis:

University of Minnesota Press, 1938;
New York: McGraw-Hill, 1964.

Nove, Alec. *The Economics of Feasible Socialism Revisited.* 2nd ed. London: Harper-
CollinsAcademic, 1991.

———. *Efficiency Criteria for Nationalised
Industries.* London: George Allen &
Unwin, 1973.

Nyerere, Julius K. *Ujamaa: Essays on Socialism.* Dar es Salaam, Tanzania: Oxford
University Press, 1968.

Senghor, Léopold Sédar. *On African Socialism.* Translated by Mercer Cook. New
York: Praeger, 1964.

Shaw, George Bernard, ed. *Fabian Essays
in Socialism.* London: Fabian Society,
1889.

Books and Articles

Albert, Michael. *Parecon: Life after Capitalism.* London: Verso, 2003. Participatory economics.

Archer, Robin. *Economic Democracy: The
Politics of Feasible Socialism.* Oxford,
England: Clarendon Press, 1995.

Bircham, Emma, and John Charlton, eds.
*Anti-Capitalism: A Guide to the Move-
ment.* Rev. ed. London: Bookmarks,
2001.

Bowles, Samuel, and Herbert Gintis.
*Recasting Egalitarianism: New Rules for
Communities, States, and Markets.* Vol. 3
of *The Real Utopias Project.* Edited by
Erik Olin Wright. London: Verso, 1998.

Bronner, Stephen Eric. *Imagining the Possible: Radical Politics for Conservative
Times.* New York: Routledge, 2002.

Busky, Donald F. *Democratic Socialism: A
Global Survey.* Westport, CT: Praeger,
2000.

Callinicos, Alex. *An Anti-Capitalist Manifesto.* Oxford, England: Polity, 2003.

Chua, Amy. *World on Fire: How Exporting
Free Market Democracy Breeds Ethnic
Hatred and Global Instability.* New York:
Doubleday, 2003.

Dahl, Robert A. *A Preface to Economic Democracy.* Berkeley: University of California
Press, 1985.

Giddens, Anthony. *The Third Way and Its
Critics.* London: Polity Press, 2000.

———. *The Third Way: The Renewal of
Social Democracy.* London: Polity Press,
1998.

Gunn, Christopher Eaton. *Workers' Self-
Management in the United States.* Ithaca,
NY: Cornell University Press, 1984.

Harrington, Michael. *Socialism.* New York:
Saturday Review Press, 1972.

Howard, Michael W. *Self-Management and the
Crisis of Socialism: The Rose in the Fist of
the Present.* Lanham, MD: Rowman &
Littlefield, 2000.

Isbister, John. *Capitalism and Justice: Envisioning Social and Economic Fairness.*
Bloomfield, CT: Kumarian Press,
2001.

Jordan, Bill. *The New Politics of Welfare:
Social Justice in a Global Context.* London:
Sage, 1998.

Le Grand, Julian, and Saul Estron, eds.
Market Socialism. Oxford, England:
Clarendon Press, 1989.

Lipset, Seymour Martin, and Gary Marks.
*It Didn't Happen Here: Why Socialism
Failed in the United States.* New York:
Norton, 2000.

Mészáros, István. *Socialism or Barbarism:
From the "American Century" to the
Crossroads.* New York: Monthly Review
Press, 2001.

Nyerere, Julius K. *Freedom and Socialism:
Uhuru na Ujamaa. A Selection from
Writings and Speeches 1965–1967.* Dar
es Salaam, Tanzania: Oxford University Press, 1968.

Ollman, Bertell, ed. *Market Socialism: The
Debate among Socialists.* New York:
Routledge, 1998.

Panitch, Leo. *Renewing Socialism: Democracy,
Strategy, and Imagination.* Boulder, CO:
Westview Press, 2001.

Pencavel, John. *Worker Participation: Lessons
from the Worker Co-ops of the Pacific
Northwest.* New York: Russell Sage
Foundation, 2001.

Pierson, Christopher. *Hard Choices: Social
Democracy in the Twenty-First Century.*
Cambridge, England: Polity, 2001.

———. *Socialism after Communism: The
New Market Socialism.* University Park:
Pennsylvania State University Press,
1995.

Pimlott, Ben, ed. *Fabian Essays in Socialist Thought*. London: Heinemann, 1984.

Roemer, John E. *Equal Shares: Making Market Socialism Work*. Vol. 2 of *The Real Utopias Project,* edited by Erik Olin Wright. London: Verso, 1996.

Russell, Peter H., ed. *The Future of Social Democracy: Views of Leaders from Around the World*. Toronto: University of Toronto Press, 1999.

Tormey, Simon. *Anti-Capitalism. A Beginner's Guide*. Oxford, England: Oneworld Publications, 2004.

Unger, Roberto Mangabeira. *Democracy Realized: The Progressive Alternative*. London: Verso, 1998.

Wood, Ellen Meiksins. *Empire of Capital*. London: Verso, 2003.

———. *The Origin of Capitalism: A Longer View*. London: Verso, 2002.

Websites

Democratic Capitalism

The Capitalism Site: http://www.capitalism.org/

The Center for the Advancement of Capitalism: http://www.moraldefense.com/

Democratic Socialism

California Peace and Freedom Party: http://www.peaceandfreedom.org/mainpage.html

Social_Science/Political_Science/Political_Theory/Marxism/Socialism Yahoo Directory— Political Theory—Socialism http://dir.yahoo.com/

The Socialist Party of Oregon: http://www.thesocialistparty.org/spo/index.html

The Socialism Website: http://home.vicnet.net.au/~dmcm/

5

Conservatism, Liberalism, and Democracy

C onservatism and liberalism within democracy must be treated in three different ways because they are three different things. First, they are general sets of attitudes toward change, human nature, and tradition. Second, they are specific positions taken at different times and places by identifiable groups of people. Third, they have different histories in different countries, although these histories are so complex that the same individuals are sometimes included in the histories of both. Today, we generally trace the histories of Western conservative and liberal traditions back to the seventeenth and eighteenth centuries. For North Americans, the histories are primarily connected with British political thought, with limited French and German influence.

Two related subjects are also discussed here, communitarianism and the extreme right. Libertarianism, which has been both accepted and rejected by American conservatives, is discussed in Chapter 8. While even its most ardent defender, its founder and primary theorist Amitai Etzioni, believes that communitarianism has declined in recent years, it remains as a clear variant of conservatism that has been explicitly rejected by most liberals. Parts of the extreme right are closely related to conservatism and parts are not; the latter are discussed in Chapter 9. What conservatives might want to call the extreme left is discussed in the previous chapter and in Chapter 8.

Some writers choose to treat conservatism and liberalism as separate ideologies rather than as tendencies within democracy, as they are presented here. Neither approach is perfect, but the approach used here captures the complexity of attitudes toward democracy by showing that, in addition to democrats who are capitalist and democrats who are socialist, there are democrats who are liberal and democrats who are conservative. In the United States almost all democrats are capitalists and are either liberal or conservative. In some countries there are liberal and conservative democratic socialists as well as liberal and conservative democratic capitalists.

Conservatism and liberalism also differ from place to place and time to time. For example, a Canadian conservative will emphasize something different than will a Japanese or Swedish conservative. And a conservative in the United States at the beginning of the twenty-first century does not believe the same things as a U.S. conservative in 1890. In fact, the position taken by many conservatives today was called liberalism in the late nineteenth century, and many conservatives believe that they are the true liberals.

Even though conservatives often think of liberals as extremists and vice versa, both liberals and conservatives are found in the middle of the political spectrum; they both want to maintain the basic institutions and processes of the society in which they live. Other terms include *reactionary,* or one who wants to move dramatically in the direction of an idealized past society, and *radical,* or one who wants dramatic change in the direction of a vision of a better society that has not yet existed. Today the term *reactionary* has generally disappeared because both extremes are really radical, desiring a society that has never existed.

CONSERVATISM

Conservatives are interested in conserving something. Conservatism within democracy today has the following characteristics:

1. Resistance to change

2. Reverence for tradition and a distrust of human reason

3. Rejection of the use of government to improve the human condition; ambivalence regarding governmental activity for other purposes

4. Preference for individual freedom but willingness to limit freedom to maintain traditional values

5. Antiegalitarianism—distrust of human nature

These defining principles of conservatism do not change much over time, and later in the chapter we will see how they are applied today in the United States.

Modern Anglo-American conservatism is traceable to Edmund Burke (1729–97), although he had precursors, and a variety of alternative traditions exist in various countries. Burke is most noted for his emphasis on tradition. As he wrote in his most famous book, *Reflections on the Revolution in France* (1790),

> In states there are often more obscure and almost latent causes, things which appear at first view of little moment, on which a very great part of its prosperity or adversity may most essentially depend. The science of

Edmund Burke (1729–97) is best known as the founder of modern conservatism. His most famous work is *Reflections on the French Revolution* (1790), in which he argued that society is a complex web of relationships among the past, present, and future. He contended that social institutions slowly evolve over time to fit needs and conditions and that, therefore, tampering with tradition is likely to bring grief rather than improvement. He was an advocate of slow, gradual change; he did not reject change altogether or argue for the return to some idealized past.

government being therefore so practical in itself, and intended for such practical purposes, a matter which requires experience, and even more experience than any person can gain in his whole life, however sagacious and observing he may be, it is with infinite caution that any man ought to venture upon pulling down an edifice which has answered in any tolerable degree for ages the common purposes of society, or on building it up again, without models and patterns of approved utility before his eyes.[1]

Here we see both Burke's concern with the wisdom of the past and his concern with the complexity of social and political life. This latter concern leads to the conservative rejection of the liberal emphasis on rational planning.[2] Life is too complicated for human beings to comprehend and control, and some factors in society do not lend themselves to rational planning.

Burke also stressed another point that is part of contemporary conservatism—private property. "Nothing is a due and adequate representation of a state that does not represent its ability, as well as its property."[3] And, Burke notes, both ability and property are inherited unequally.

F. A. Hayek (1899–1992), whose *The Road to Serfdom* (1944) provided an ethical defense of free markets, wrote, "Conservatism proper is a legitimate, probably necessary, and certainly widespread attitude of opposition to drastic change."[4] Although his point is correct, it is too specific. Conservatives not only

---

[1] Edmund Burke, *The Works of the Right Honorable Edmund Burke,* rev. ed. (Boston: Little, Brown, 1865), 3:312.

[2] See, for example, Michael Oakeshott, "Rationalism in Politics," in Oakeshott, *Rationalism in Politics and Other Essays* (New York: Basic Books, 1962), 1–36.

[3] Burke, *Works,* 3:297–98.

[4] F. A. Hayek, "Why I Am Not a Conservative," in *The Constitution of Liberty* (London: Routledge & Kegan Paul, 1960), 397.

oppose "drastic change," as he says, but are hesitant about any change. As one writer put it, "the conservative does not oppose change, but he does resist it."[5] Conservatives do not unthinkingly oppose change; they resist and question it because they are wary of social experimentation. They believe that something that has worked, even if not very well, is better than something untried and unknown.

The second characteristic of conservatism, a reverence for tradition, is composed of a number of subsidiary points, including traditional moral standards, religion (with few exceptions), and the assumption that the longer an institution has existed, the more likely it is to be worth preserving. Reverence for tradition springs from the conservative's basic distrust of reason as a means of improving humanity's lot. Conservatives do not reject reason completely, but they would rather trust tradition because they believe that tradition contains the accumulated wisdom of past generations. Note also how closely connected the first and second characteristics are—honoring tradition entails resistance to change.

This point is quite simple and clear-cut. The only really complicating factor is that conservatives (and liberals) change over time regarding the specifics they wish to preserve. The world changes, and conservatives change with it. They do not want to conserve all the past; they want to conserve what they believe is the best of the past.

The third characteristic presents the major dilemma in conservative thought. Overall, conservatives believe governmental power should be reduced and individuals should make their own way in the world. (Note the similarity to traditional capitalism.) But there is ambivalence here. Governmental power to support traditional moral standards and limit an individual's freedom regarding them is perfectly acceptable to many conservatives. Conservatives believe "genuinely ordered freedom is the only sort of liberty worth having: freedom made possible by order within the soul and order within the state."[6]

The case must not be overstated, however. Conservatives reject the use of government to improve the human condition. They do so because (1) they are convinced the use of government does not necessarily improve the human condition, and (2) they believe people left alone can do a better job. The first point is the key. It asserts that the use of government for social betterment will actually produce the opposite. People, according to most conservatives, will come to rely on government and lose the ability to help themselves.

Conservatives have held this position very consistently. Edmund Burke (1729–97), writing in the eighteenth century, held it; Bernard Bosanquet (1848–1923), writing at the beginning of this century, held it; and modern conservatives, such as Russell Kirk (1918–94), continue to hold it. Kirk's *The Conservative Mind* (1953) provided one of the bases for the redevelopment of

---

[5] Jay A. Sigler, introduction to *The Conservative Tradition in American Thought,* ed. Jay A. Sigler (New York: Capricorn Books, 1969), 13.

[6] Russell Kirk, "Prescription, Authority, and Ordered Freedom," in *What Is Conservatism?* ed. Frank S. Meyer (New York: Holt, Rinehart & Winston, 1964), 24.

modern conservatism; and two of the journals he founded, *Modern Age* in 1957 and *University Bookman* in 1960, provided outlets for conservative writers.

Conservatives believe some people are better than other people and, therefore, should be honored more by society. "Aye, men are created different; and a government which ignores this law becomes an unjust government, for it sacrifices nobility to mediocrity; it pulls down the aspiring natures to gratify the inferior natures."[7] This is precisely the reason that conservatives are ambivalent about both government and individual freedom. Governmental help will hurt persons of the better sort; the poorer sort will not be helped.

"The conservative accepts as natural the differences that separate men. Class, intelligence, nationality, and race make men different."[8] This recognition of differences sometimes implies superiority or inferiority, but it does not necessarily do so. The recognition states that inferiority and superiority exist but does not necessarily tie them to race, class, or sex.

LIBERALISM

Some scholars find liberalism in ancient Greece and Rome, but most commonly liberalism is traced to the English revolutions of the seventeenth century. Politically, liberalism originated in the revolution of the 1640s and the Levellers, particularly the Putney debates where Colonel Thomas Rainsborough (1610–48) argued for widening the electoral franchise, saying, "I think that the poorest he that is in England hath a life to live, as the greatest he; and therefore truly, sir, I think it's clear, that every man that is to live under government ought first by his own consent to put himself under that government; and I do think that the poorest man in England is not at all bound in a strict sense to that government that he hath not had a voice to put himself under."[9] Intellectually, liberalism stems from the writings of John Locke (1632–1704), who developed the arguments for consent, majority rule, and rights, particularly property rights.

Today most liberals argue that liberalism is primarily concerned with liberty and trace their roots to John Stuart Mill (1806–73) and his little book *On Liberty* (1859), which stressed freedom of thought and speech. But the liberal emphasis on liberty has taken two differing routes from Mill to the present. One approach is really a continuation of Locke's concern with rights, including property rights. The other approach developed in the late nineteenth and early twentieth centuries in the writings of T. H. Green (1836–82) and others, who argued that some people need help in order to be able to exercise their liberty. This argument was the beginning of what became known as *welfare liberalism*.

---

[7] Kirk, "Prescription," 34.

[8] Sigler, introduction to *Conservative Tradition*, 13.

[9] From A. S. P. Woodhouse, ed., *Puritanism and Liberty: Being the Army Debates (1647–9) from the Clarke Manuscripts with Supplementary Documents*, 2nd ed. (London: Dent, 1974), 59.

Library of Congress

John Stuart Mill (1806–73) was the most influential philosopher in the English-speaking world in the nineteenth century. His major political works were *On Liberty* (1859), *Considerations on Representative Government* (1861), *Utilitarianism* (1861), and *The Subjection of Women* (1869). Mill developed and modified the philosophy of utilitarianism of Jeremy Bentham (1748–1832), but is best known today for his defense of freedom in *On Liberty*. With his wife, Harriet Taylor (1807–58), Mill began to explore the subordinate role of women in contemporary society, and he became an advocate of women's rights.

These varied strands bring us to a liberalism that today can be described as having the following characteristics:

1. A tendency to favor change

2. Faith in human reason

3. Willingness to use government to improve the human condition

4. Preference for individual freedom but ambivalence about economic freedom

5. Greater optimism about human nature than conservatives

These defining principles of liberalism do not change much over time, and later in the chapter we will see how they are applied today in the United States.

Hubert H. Humphrey (1911–78) once wrote, "Liberals fully recognize that change is inevitable in the patterns of society and in the challenges which confront man."[10] A contemporary liberal theorist recently made the same point in even stronger language, saying, "If there is a fundamental liberal principle it is the recognition of change in all things as an inevitable condition of living."[11] Liberals generally believe people should keep trying to improve society. Somewhat less optimistic about progress than they once were, liberals still believe beneficial change is possible. Such change can come about through the conscious action of men and women, as unforeseen side effects of decisions, or

---

[10] Hubert H. Humphrey, introduction to Milton Viorst, *Liberalism: A Guide to Its Past, Present, and Future in American Politics* (New York: Avon Books, 1963), vii.

[11] Marcus G. Raskin, *Liberalism: The Genius of American Ideals* (Lanham, MD: Rowman & Littlefield, 2004), 15.

through the operation of various social forces. But there will be change, and the liberal is convinced it can be directed and controlled for human benefit.

Liberals do not desire radical change that would do away with the basic structure of the current system. On this point, the difference between liberalism and conservatism is a matter of degree rather than kind. Liberals want more change and tend to favor social experimentation, but they want this only within the framework of the current political, legal, and economic system. Liberals are not radicals.

Change is welcomed because liberals trust human reason to devise solutions to human problems. This faith in the potential of reason is the key to the liberal credo—only with such faith can they accept the use of governmental power to improve the human condition. This faith is not a naïve, unquestioning faith, but it assumes that social experimentation is valid and that it is better to use such powers as we have to control change than to allow change to control us.

Liberals contend that some people must be helped to live better lives and fulfill their individual potential, and they believe such assistance can work. Conservatives believe just the opposite—helping people may make it impossible for them to fulfill their potential as individuals. Liberals argue that people, though capable of reason and reasoned action, are often caught in situations where self-help, even if possible, is difficult and that government should help. This assistance, far from injuring people, can (although it may not) give them the impetus to do more for themselves. The liberal assumption is that, although not everyone will respond, it is better to attempt to help than to do nothing. In contemporary society, liberals believe government is in the best position to provide help.

Liberals believe that help through governmental activity will lead to greater individual freedom. They argue that a person, once relieved of some basic problems, can enlarge his or her sphere of activity and improve both life and mind. Still, liberals are somewhat ambivalent about human nature. They contend that most problems derive from impersonal social and economic forces acting on humanity. Human reason can solve the problems, but an unaided human being cannot. This is why liberals are ambivalent about economic freedom; they are afraid that one result of an unregulated economy would be great differences in individual power, which would be used to the detriment of the weaker members of society.

The tradition of liberalism most strongly stresses individual freedom. The term *liberalism* is closely related to liberty, and the emphasis on liberty has been a major thread in all liberal thought. The role of the government is limited—it cannot invade the rights and freedoms of the individual. Human beings will err, but liberals have always thought that error is far better than the suppression of error. This belief follows from the belief in the value and inevitability of change. If change is good and will always occur, today's error may be tomorrow's truth.

As general tendencies, liberalism and conservatism are primarily attitudes toward change within the democratic tradition, resting uneasily between reaction and radicalism. Too often attempts are made to transform them into major ideologies with rigidly defined beliefs. Doing this is an error. Liberalism and conservatism do not have clear-cut belief systems except in response to current problems, but in such responses they can be identified.

John Rawls

The most important contribution to liberalism in the second half of the twenti-eth century was the publication of *A Theory of Justice* (1971) by John Rawls (1921–2002). In this work, Rawls sets out to establish the fundamental princi-ples of social justice. To do this he undertakes a thought experiment in which he imagines people in what he calls "the original position," in which people are assumed not to know what talents and abilities they have or what position they hold in society. They do not know what race they are, whether they are rich or poor, powerful or weak.[12] They are then asked to choose the principles on which to build a society. Rawls argues that the following principles would be chosen in such a situation:

1. Each person is to have an equal right to the most extensive basic liberty compatible with a similar liberty for others.

2. Social and economic inequalities are to be arranged so they are both (a) reasonably expected to be to everyone's advantage and (b) attached to posi-tions that are open to all.[13]

The second principle is intended to ensure equality of opportunity. These principles are meant to be applied in order. Thus equality of rights has a higher priority than equality of opportunity. Rawls argues that justice requires that everyone have a wide range of basic liberties, including the freedoms discussed in Chapter 3 and those rights that are essential to personal integrity, like the right to personal property.

Rawls contends that these are the fundamental principles of liberalism. The publication of *A Theory of Justice* set off a long debate among political theorists over all aspects of the book, but particularly about the thought experiment and the priorities that Rawls had assigned to the values he believed would result from it. In *Political Liberalism* (1993) Rawls made explicit that he sees his argu-ments as contributions to contemporary political debate as well as contributions to a general theory of justice. He states that we must recognize that our soci-eties are composed of people with irreconcilable fundamental beliefs. As he puts it, "the problem of political liberalism is: How is it possible that there may exist over time a stable and just society of free and equal citizens profoundly divided by reasonable though incompatible religious, philosophical, and moral doctrines?"[14] To answer the question, Rawls subtly modifies the two principles just stated, which now read as follows:

1. Each person has an equal claim to a fully adequate scheme of basic rights and liberties, which scheme is compatible with the same scheme for all; and in this scheme the equal political liberties, and only those liberties, are to be guaranteed their fair values.

---

[12] Rawls and other theorists of justice were criticized by Susan Moller Okin for not recognizing the importance of gender in their theories. Rawls, in particular, was criticized for not seeing how important a lack of knowledge of gender would be in the original position. See Okin's *Justice, Gender, and the Family* (New York: Basic Books, 1989).

[13] John Rawls, *A Theory of Justice* (Cambridge, MA: Harvard University Press, 1971), 60.

[14] John Rawls, *Political Liberalism* (New York: Columbia University Press, 1993), xviii.

2. Social and economic inequalities are to satisfy two conditions: first, they are
   to be attached to positions and offices open to all under conditions of fair
   equality of opportunity; and second, they are to be of the greatest benefit
   to the least advantaged members of society.[15]

One critique of Rawlsian liberalism developed into a debate between liberals and what came to be called *communitarians.*

COMMUNITARIANISM

According to the communitarian critique of liberalism, liberalism overempha-
sizes the individual to the detriment of the community. Liberals say that the
communitarian alternative destroys liberty. In this debate, liberals focus on the
desirability of developing autonomous individuals who are protected from government by universally applicable rights. Communitarians focus on the community rather than the individual as the basis for personal and political identity
and moral decision making. Communitarians argue that to some extent all individuals are created by and embedded in specific communities. Our beliefs, moral
systems, and senses of self come from the community or communities of which
we have been and are a part.

The political conclusions drawn by communitarians vary across the political
spectrum from left to right, although the right has been most clearly identified
with communitarianism. Some left-wing communitarians see it as simply an
extension of participatory democracy with a greater concern for the community
in which the participation takes place. Thus communitarianism could be seen
as a development of the emphasis on community that was found in the New
Left,[16] but this is not how most communitarians see it.

Most communitarians are conservatives who believe that the growth of
legally enforceable individual rights has gone too far to the detriment of society
as a whole. They believe that there must be a renewed focus on personal, family,
and community responsibility. Are individuals responsible to and for themselves? Or, as products of the communities of which they are a part, are they
responsible to the community (and the community to them)? Most important
from the liberal point of view: Should we accept the dominance of community
values if those values include the elimination of minority rights? In a sense, this
is asking who constitutes the community. Is it the current majority in some
geographic area? Are they allowed to simply impose their values on everyone
else in that area?[17]

These questions are at the heart of the confused state of liberalism and conservatism in the United States today. People want to live the lives they choose

---

[15] Rawls, *Political Liberalism,* 5–6.

[16] See Lyman Tower Sargent, *New Left Thought: An Introduction* (Homewood, IL: Dorsey
Press, 1972).

[17] See The Communitarian Network at http://www.gwu.edu/~ccps/ and Amitai Etzioni,
ed., *The Essential Communitarian Reader* (Lanham, MD: Rowman & Littlefield, 1998).

without interference, and they worry about interference from both government and their neighbors, whose vision of the good life may be different than theirs and who might want to impose it on them. This concern is not without justification. There are people who want us all to live their way. We usually call them *extremists*.

THE EXTREME RIGHT

There are a number of groups and individuals on the extreme right, and because extremism is often in the eye of the beholder, some commentators lump together people who have relatively little in common. The most visible act on the extreme right was the bombing of the Alfred P. Murrah Federal Office Building in Oklahoma City in 1995 by Timothy McVeigh (1968–2001). Whatever combination of reasons there may have been for the bombing, one motive was to attack a symbol of the federal government. Many on the extreme right contend that the bombing was in fact a government plot with the bomb set off by government agents to incriminate those on the right, which indicates the attitude toward the national government of the extreme right and the depth of its belief in conspiracies.[18] Generally speaking, those in this part of the extreme right hold that the county is the highest legitimate government. This part of the extreme right also tends to take a strongly anti-international position. While communists have not disappeared as the focus of their concern, the fear of communism has been partially superseded by the perception of a communist-dominated United Nations.

Although the extreme right is strongly in favor of property rights, it has no use for large corporations or financial capitalism, symbolized by Wall Street. They believe that there is a conspiracy among wealthy capitalists to control the economy for their own benefit and that the federal government is part of this conspiracy.

A common theme on the extreme right is racism. Anti-Semitism is common, with both Jews and Arabs grouped together; African Americans are defined as America's major problem. The goal is a purely Caucasian country.

One example of a racist and anti-Semitic program can be found in the novel *The Turner Diaries* (2nd ed., 1980), which a number of far-right groups in the United States treat as a blueprint for a future race war and which Timothy McVeigh had with him when captured. Probably the best known of the contemporary U.S. groups is the Aryan Nations, which was led by Richard Girnt Butler (1918–2004) and which operated from an enclosed compound in Hayden Lake, Idaho. All these groups are very small, but most of them are bigger than Hitler's initial political party.[19]

---

[18] See Michael Barkun, "Religion, Militias and Oklahoma City: The Mind of Conspiratorialists," *Terrorism and Political Violence* 8:1 (Spring 1996): 50–64.

[19] For more on these groups, see Lyman Tower Sargent, ed., *Extremism in America: A Reader* (New York: New York University Press, 1995). For a history, see Michael Barkun, *Religion and the Racist Right: The Origins of the Christian Identity Movement* (Chapel Hill: University of North Carolina Press, 1994.)

The extreme racist right is particularly popular with the group of disaffected people generally called "skinheads." There are music festivals that are all white (and overwhelmingly male), featuring bands with names like The Bully Boys; groups like the National Alliance, headed by William Pierce (1933–2002), receive a lot of their funding through record sales.

Far Right Policy

Many issues that bother the far right are the same as those that bother others, like globalism, the difficulty of surviving on small farms and in small businesses, crime, drugs, big government, the power of large corporations, changing patterns of marriage and family life, education, and so forth. The central difference is that they see these problems through different lenses. They see many issues through the lens of race, very broadly defined. Thus globalization, corporate power, big government, and related issues are often viewed through the lens of anti-Semitism as a Jewish conspiracy. Many other problems are blamed on African Americans, Hispanics, and immigrants. Almost always central to their worldview are conspiracies.

As a result, their solutions tend to be fairly simplistic. If all our problems are due to conspiracies, if we get rid of the conspiracy, the problems will go away. But, of course, if the conspiracy is worldwide and centuries old, as they think some are, it is hard to see how to make it go away. Some have taken to violence, but, for all the headlines, that is fairly rare. Most just want to be left alone. Some achieve this by retreating to an isolated part of the country (Idaho and eastern Washington are favorite spots), homeschooling their children, living as much as possible in a cash-only or barter economy to avoid the attention of government, and generally cutting as many ties with the outside world as possible.

But some find staying out of sight inadequate and want to change the world they reject. Many journals, pamphlets, books, videos, and records are published by the extreme right, but today the Internet is a major means of communication.

CURRENT TRENDS

The divisions between conservatism and liberalism are mostly long-standing but, in some cases, are focusing on new issues. One division that is discussed throughout this book is multiculturalism. On the whole conservatives oppose it and liberals support it, but there are liberals who raise doubts about the rights of individual members of groups versus the rights of groups as a whole, fearing that these could conflict with each other.[20]

Another division is over the Internet. Issues range from free speech to the role of the Internet in fostering democracy, with particular concerns over the

---

[20] See Brian Barry, *Culture and Equality: An Egalitarian Critique of Multiculturalism* (Cambridge, MA: Harvard University Press, 2001); and Susan Moller Okin, with respondents, *Is Multiculturalism Bad for Women?* ed. Joshua Cohen, Matthew Howard, and Martha C. Nussbaum (Princeton, NJ: Princeton University Press, 1999).

degree to which the Internet should be regulated.[21] But here there is no clear conservative–liberal split.

At the time of writing, one issue shows a clear conservative–liberal division—how to stimulate the economy. On the whole conservatives want to give money to large corporations and the wealthy on the assumption that that is the most effective way to get the money into the economy productively and create jobs. Liberals, on the other hand, tend to want to give money to the poorest people both to help them directly and because the poor are most likely to spend the money immediately, thus putting it into the economy. Both want the same result but with very different approaches.

CONTEMPORARY CONSERVATISM
IN THE UNITED STATES

Two groups of people share the label *conservative* in the United States today: traditional conservatives and neoconservatives. At times they disagree with each other, but on the whole they are more united than the liberals. They are defined by their positions on specific issues and therefore can usually be clearly identified.

Three sets of issues can be used to define contemporary conservatives (and liberals): social, fiscal, and foreign policy issues. The mixture of positions on each of these and the emphasis placed on them define the differences among the three types of conservatives. Briefly, these positions can be characterized as follows:

- Social—a belief in traditional values centering on the home, family, and religion. At present this includes the belief that the appropriate place for women is in the home; a strong opposition to abortion; support for required prayer in schools; and opposition to the teaching of sex education and evolution, among other subjects.

- Fiscal—a belief in capitalism, opposition to most government regulation of the economy, and support for a balanced budget.

- Foreign policy—a belief in a strong military, an active opposition to communism (obviously now less important), support for our allies whatever their political position, and opposition to giving authority to international organizations like the United Nations.

Traditional Conservatism

What I call *traditional conservatism* is closest to the general characterization of conservatism outlined previously, but has currently rather faded from view under pressure from neoconservatism. This does not mean that such conservatives don't exist; they have always been the mainstream of conservative thought, both in

---

[21] For a discussion, see Cass Sunstein, *Republic.com* (Princeton, NJ: Princeton University Press, 2001).

numbers and influence, and remain so. They are simply not getting the publicity that the other brands of conservatism are getting.

Traditional conservatives are more likely to support some government regulation of the economy than are neoconservatives, but they are still fiscal conservatives. They are much less likely to be social conservatives than are neoconservatives. While they support traditional moral values, they do not generally favor using government power to enforce them. Traditional conservatives are also foreign policy conservatives, but in all three areas they emphasize gradual change and continuity rather than immediate, radical change.

Neoconservatism

The name *neoconservative* actually originated with former liberals who felt that liberalism had lost its way in the 1960s and 1970s, but what is now called neoconservatism developed through a number of stages under different names and through amalgamation with conservatives of somewhat different outlook. One stream of neoconservatism was originally called the *radical right* and developed in the 1950s in opposition to communism. As such, most radical right programs were negative and oppositional. Later it expanded its outlook, became the *New Right,* and was concerned with social issues, such as abortion, busing to integrate schools, pornography (a concern shared with some feminists), prayer in schools, and local control of education, which are all seen as fundamentally moral questions.

This is now the dominant outlook of neoconservatism. It is primarily concerned with issues centering on the family, religion, and education. All these issues are, they argue, basically about morals. They generally believe that the proper place for women is in the home caring for and educating their children. They strongly oppose any position that can be seen as supporting nontraditional sexual relations, such as the movement for gay rights. The role of the schools is to teach parentally approved values and "the basics" (reading, writing, and arithmetic). Schools should have required Christian prayer, and creationism rather than evolution should be taught in biology classes (the New Right does not believe in the separation of church and state).

These positions might pose a dilemma for neoconservatives. They oppose government activity that imposes moral positions with which they disagree, but they are willing to use government to impose their own moral positions. But there is no dilemma because there is a simple division of right and wrong on moral questions, and government has an appropriate role to support the right morality and oppose the wrong morality. To them, tolerance of what they know to be the wrong positions is unacceptable.

Neoconservatives are strongly conservative on foreign policy, with the conservatism formerly driven by anticommunism now driven by support for a strong military. Patriotism seems to be the motivation behind most New Right foreign policy positions. In the contemporary environment of world politics, they see the United States as the rightly dominant power, and they believe humanitarian military intervention can advance U.S. policy.

On fiscal policy, neoconservatives argue for a free market and against government regulation because they see these positions as essential to political freedom. For many neoconservatives, capitalism and the free market are absolutely central, and reducing nonmilitary government expenses and lowering taxes are among their primary goals.

The differences in these forms of conservatism are primarily ones of emphasis. Members of the New Right stress social questions, neoconservatives stress the free market, and traditional conservatives take a moderately conservative position on those plus fiscal policy. All conservatives support free market capitalism, want the United States to have a strong defense and foreign policy, and are concerned with traditional values.

CONTEMPORARY LIBERALISM
IN THE UNITED STATES

Liberalism is somewhat in disarray today, and liberals are less sure about their policies than they used to be. There has been a movement away from government regulation of the economy to acceptance of the position that less regulation (not *no* regulation) might be a good idea. Liberals have also concluded that the welfare system needs to be redesigned but not entirely scrapped. The old liberal faith that the government could help people to help themselves and the belief that recession and depression could be avoided by stimulating the economy have been challenged but not entirely discarded. Liberalism has not yet found a new faith, but it has not lost its old faith either. Liberals still stand for expanded personal freedom and therefore find themselves constantly at odds with the radical right. Liberals still believe that greater human equality is a desirable and achievable goal and thus usually oppose conservatives, who reject the belief in equality as not reflecting the reality of the human race.

Liberals can be characterized on the same three measures as conservatives, but there is much less agreement on the mix of the three than there is among conservatives. On social, fiscal, and foreign policy, liberals can be characterized roughly as follows:

- Social—a belief in freedom of choice. Today this tends to mean support for the pro-choice position on abortion and advocacy of the rights of women and minorities.
- Fiscal—a belief in the use of government intervention in the economy to regulate it. Deficit spending was once a fundamental tenet of liberal belief; some liberals still hold to it as a means of regulating the economy.
- Foreign policy—a belief in the need to work within the international community for the peaceful resolution of conflicts. The stress is on cooperation and aid with a related reduction in emphasis on defense and the military.

Neoliberalism

Neoliberals have identified themselves as fiscal conservatives while remaining social and foreign policy liberals, albeit with a slight shift to the conservative side in both cases. Neoliberals stress that they are concerned with getting the system to work rather than with ideology. They want to change the pattern of government spending because it is, they say, too high and inefficiently handled. They want a strong defense but more government oversight of military spending. They want efficient and effective welfare programs. Generally they want what they consider to be a realistic liberalism that faces rapid social and economic change. Today neoliberals dominate the Democratic Party.

Traditional Liberalism

Traditional liberalism (in this sense a tradition from the 1930s) is now everybody's scapegoat and is usually described as advocating big government, deficit spending, and expensive welfare programs. Traditional liberals see themselves as advocates of working people, the poor, and minorities against big business and as supporters of civil rights for African Americans, women, and ethnic minorities against the repression of government and business. Thus they see themselves as defenders of freedom and equality. They believe that only government is powerful enough to achieve these goals; therefore, they favor strong government. Liberals are unified on goals but divided on means. All liberals believe in an egalitarian society with protection for civil rights; they are divided on how to achieve it. And in recent years liberals have tried to expand civil rights to the disabled, indigenous groups, and gays and lesbians.

SUGGESTED READING

Conservatism

Some Classic Works

Buckley, William F., Jr. *Up from Liberalism.* 25th anniv. ed. New York: Stein & Day, 1984.

Burke, Edmund. *Reflections on the Revolution in France.* 1790.

Hayek, Friedrich A. *The Constitution of Liberty.* London: Routledge & Kegan Paul, 1960.

———. *The Road to Serfdom.* 50th anniversary ed. Chicago: University of Chicago Press, 1994.

Kendall, Willmoore. *The Conservative Affirmation.* Chicago: Henry Regnery, 1954.

Kirk, Russell. *The Conservative Mind, from Burke to Santayana.* Chicago: Henry Regnery, 1953. 7th rev. ed with the subtitle *from Burke to Eliot.* Washington, DC: Regnery Publishing Co., 1995.

———. *A Program for Conservatives.* Rev. ed. Chicago: Henry Regnery, 1962.

Books and Articles

Bloom, Allan. *The Closing of the American Mind: How Higher Education Has Failed Democracy and Impoverished the Souls of Today's Students.* New York: Simon & Schuster, 1987.

Buchanan, Patrick. *Right from the Start.* Boston: Little, Brown, 1988.

Carey, George W., ed. *Freedom and Virtue: The Conservative/Libertarian Debate.* Rev. and updated ed. Wilmington, DE: Intercollegiate Studies Institute, 1998.

Dahl, Göran. *Radical Conservatism and the Future of Politics.* London: Sage, 1999.

Dunn, Charles W., and J. David Woodard. *The Conservative Tradition in America.* Rev. ed. Lanham, MD: Rowman & Littlefield, 2003.

Durham, Martin. *The Christian Right and the Boundaries of American Conservatism.* Manchester, England: Manchester University Press, 2000.

Eccleshall, Robert. "The Doing of Conservatism." *Journal of Political Ideologies* 5, no. 3 (October 2000): 275–87.

Falwell, Jerry. *Listen America!* Garden City, NY: Doubleday, 1980.

Feulner, Edwin J. Jr., ed. *The March of Freedom: Modern Classics in Conservative Thought.* Dallas: Spence, 1998.

Green, E. H. H. *Ideologies of Conservatism: Conservative Political Ideas in the Twentieth Century.* Oxford: Oxford University Press, 2002. History of the ideologies of the Conservative Party in the UK.

Halper, Stefan, and Jonathan Clarke. *America Alone: The Neo-Conservatives and the Global Order.* Cambridge: Cambridge University Press, 2004.

Huntington, Samuel P. "Conservatism as an Ideology." *American Political Science Review* 51:1 (June 1957): 454–73.

Hurst, David. *On Westernism: An Ideology's Bid for World Domination.* Reading, England: G. Hartley & Co., 2003. Strong attack from a conservative viewpoint on a constellation of ideas he calls Westernism, feminism, multiculturalism, liberalism, egalitarianism, socialism. He argues that this is an ideology and is used to suppress conservatives.

Kekes, John. *A Case for Conservatism.* Ithaca, NY: Cornell University Press, 1998.

Kirk, Russell. *The American Cause.* Edited by Gleaves Whitney. Wilmington, DE: ISI Books, 2002. Originally published in 1957.

———. *The Politics of Prudence.* Bryn Mawr, PA: Intercollegiate Studies Institute, 1993.

———. *Redeeming the Time.* Edited by Jeffrey O. Nelson. Wilmington, DE: ISI Books, 1996.

Kristol, Irving. *Reflections of a Neoconservative: Looking Back, Looking Ahead.* New York: Basic Books, 1983.

McDonald, W. Wesley. *Russell Kirk and the Age of Ideology.* Columbia: University of Missouri Press, 2004.

Moen, Matthew C. *The Transformation of the Christian Right.* Tuscaloosa: University of Alabama Press, 1992.

Schneider, Gregory L., ed. *Conservatism in American since 1930.* New York: New York University Press, 2003.

Schoenwald, Jonathan M. *A Time for Choosing: The Rise of Modern American Conservatism.* New York: Oxford University Press, 2001.

Scotchie, Joseph. *Revolt from the Heartland: The Struggle for an Authentic Conservatism.* New Brunswick, NJ: Transaction, 2002.

Scully, Matthew. *Dominion: The Power of Man, the Suffering of Animals, and the Call to Mercy.* New York: St. Martin's Press, 2002. Animal rights from the point of view of the Christian right.

Stone, Brad Lowell. *Robert Nisbet: Communitarian Traditionalist.* Wilmington, DE: ISI Books, 2000.

Liberalism

Some Classic Works

Hartz, Louis. *The Liberal Tradition in America.* New York: Harcourt Brace, 1955.

Pateman, Carole. *The Problem of Political Obligation: A Critical Analysis of Liberal Theory.* New York: Wiley, 1979.

Rawls, John. *Justice as Fairness: A Restatement.* Edited by Erin Kelly. Cambridge, MA: Harvard University Press, Belknap Press, 2001.

———. *Political Liberalism.* New York: Columbia University Press, 1993.

———. *A Theory of Justice.* Cambridge, MA: Harvard University Press, Belknap Press, 1971. Rev. ed.: Oxford: Oxford University Press, 1999.

Books and Articles

Anderson, Charles W. *A Deeper Freedom: Liberal Democracy as an Everyday Morality.* Madison: University of Wisconsin Press, 2002.

Avnon, Dan, and Avner de-Shalit, eds. *Liberalism and Its Practice.* London: Routledge, 1999.

Birt, Robert E., ed. *The Quest for Community and Identity: Critical Essays in Africana*

Social Philosophy. Lanham, MD: Rowman and Littlefield, 2002.

Brands, H. W. *The Strange Death of American Liberalism.* New Haven, CT: Yale University Press, 2001.

Carens, Joseph H. *Culture, Citizenship, and Community: A Contextual Exploration of Justice as Evenhandedness.* Oxford: Oxford University Press, 2000.

Cumming, Robert Denoon. *Human Nature and History: A Study of the Development of Liberal Thought.* 2 vols. Chicago: University of Chicago Press, 1969.

Dawson, Michael C. *Black Visions: The Roots of Contemporary African-American Political Ideologies.* Chicago: University of Chicago Press, 2001.

De Ruggiero, Guido. *The History of European Liberalism.* Translated by R. G. Collingwood. Boston: Beacon Press, 1959.

Farmer, Paul. *Pathologies of Power: Health, Human Rights, and the New War on the Poor.* Berkeley: University of California Press, 2003.

Flathman, Richard E. *Freedom and Its Conditions: Discipline, Autonomy and Resistance.* New York: Routledge, 2003.

————. *Toward a Liberalism. . . .* Ithaca, NY: Cornell University Press, 1989.

Freeman, Samuel, ed. *Cambridge Companion to Rawls.* Cambridge: Cambridge University Press, 2002.

Galston, William A. *Liberal Pluralism: The Implications of Value Pluralism for Political Theory and Practice.* Cambridge: Cambridge University Press, 2002.

Gaus, Gerald F. "Liberalism at the End of the Century." *Journal of Political Ideologies* 5, no. 2 (June 2000): 179–99.

————. *Value and Justification: The Foundations of Liberal Theory.* Cambridge: Cambridge University Press, 1990.

Gill, Emily. *Becoming Free: Autonomy and Diversity in the Liberal Polity.* Lawrence: University of Kansas Press, 2001.

Gray, John. *The Two Faces of Liberalism.* New York: New Press, 2000.

Guinier, Lani, and Gerald Torres. *The Miner's Canary: Enlisting Race, Resisting Power, Transforming Democracy.* Cambridge, MA: Harvard University Press, 2002.

Gunnell, John G. "The Archaeology of American Liberalism." *Journal of Political Ideologies* 6, no. 2 (June 2001): 125–45.

Ivison, Duncan. *Postcolonial Liberalism.* Cambridge: Cambridge University Press, 2002.

Kaufman, Cynthia. *Ideas for Action: Relevant Theory for Radical Change.* Cambridge, MA: South End Press, 2003.

Krause, Sharon R. *Liberalism with Honor.* Cambridge, MA: Harvard University Press, 2002.

Kymlicka, Will. *Multicultural Citizenship: A Liberal Theory of Minority Rights.* Oxford, England: Clarendon Press, 1995.

Kymlicka, Will, and Magda Opalski, eds. *Can Liberal Pluralism Be Exported? Western Political Theory and Ethnic Relations in Eastern Europe.* Oxford: Oxford University Press, 2001.

Levy, Jacob T. *The Multiculturalism of Fear.* Oxford: Oxford University Press, 2000.

Lowi, Theodore J. *The End of Liberalism: The Second Republic of the United States.* 2nd ed. New York: Norton, 1979.

Phillips, Anne. "Defending Equality of Outcome." *The Journal of Political Philosophy* 12:1 (March 2004): 1–19.

Raskin, Marcus G. *Liberalism: The Genius of American Ideals.* Lanham, MD: Rowman & Littlefield, 2004.

Rawls, John. *The Law of Peoples with "The Idea of Public Reason Revisited."* Cambridge, MA: Harvard University Press, 1999.

Rosanvallon, Pierre. *The New Social Question: Rethinking the Welfare State.* Translated by Barbara Harshaw. Princeton, NJ: Princeton University Press, 2000.

Rosenblum, Nancy, ed. *Liberalism and the Moral Life.* Cambridge, MA: Harvard University Press, 1989.

Russell, Conrad. *An Intelligent Person's Guide to Liberalism.* London: Duckworth, 1999.

Schmidtz, David, and Robert E. Goodin. *Social Welfare and Individual Responsibility.* Cambridge: Cambridge University Press, 1998.

Shweder, Richard A., Martha Minow, and Hazel Rose Markus, eds. *Engaging Cultural Differences: The Multicultural*

PART III DEMOCRACY — page 140.

Challenge in Liberal Democracies. New York: Russell Sage Foundation, 2002.

Sowell, Thomas. *Affirmative Action around the World: An Empirical Study*. New Haven, CT: Yale University Press, 2004.

Unger, Roberto Mangabeira, and Cornel West. *The Future of American Progressivism: An Initiative for Political and Economic Reform*. Boston: Beacon Press, 1998.

Communitarianism

Some Classic Works

Bell, Daniel. *Communitarianism and Its Critics*. Oxford, England: Clarendon Press, 1993.

Etzioni, Amitai. *The Spirit of Community: Rights, Responsibilities, and the Communitarian Agenda*. New York: Crown, 1993.

Books

Bauman, Zygmunt. *Community: Seeking Safety in an Insecure World*. Cambridge, England: Polity Press, 2001.

Etzioni, Amitai. *The Common Good*. Cambridge, England: Polity Press, 2004.

———. *The Monochrome Society*. Princeton, NJ: Princeton University Press, 2001.

———. *The New Golden Rule: Community and Morality in a Democratic Society*. New York: Basic Books, 1996.

———, ed. *The Essential Communitarian Reader*. Lanham, MD: Rowman & Littlefield, 1998.

Tam, Henry [Benedict]. *Communitarianism: A New Agenda for Politics and Citizenship*. New York: New York University Press, 1998.

The Extreme Right

Classic Work

Macdonald, Andrew [William Luther Pierce]. *The Turner Diaries*. 2nd ed. Washington, DC: National Alliance, 1980.

Books and Articles

Barkun, Michael. "Religion, Militias, and Oklahoma City: The Mind of Conspiratorialists." *Terrorism and Political Violence* 8, no. 1 (Spring 1996): 50–64.

Blee, Kathleen M. *Inside Organized Racism: Women in the Hate Movement*. Berkeley: University of California Press, 2002.

Kaplan, Jeffrey. "Right Wing Violence in North America." *Terrorism and Political Violence* 7, no. 1 (Spring 1995): 44–95.

———, ed. *Encyclopedia of White Power: A Sourcebook on the Radical Racist Right*. Walnut Creek, CA: AltaMira Press, 2000.

Kaplan, Jeffrey, and Leonard Weinberg. *The Emergence of a Euro-American Radical Right*. New Brunswick, NJ: Rutgers University Press, 1998.

Mariani, Mack. "The Michigan Militia: Political Engagement or Political Alienation?" *Terrorism and Political Violence* 10, no. 4 (Winter 1998): 122–48.

Merkl, Peter H., and Leonard Weinberg, eds. *The Revival of Right-Wing Extremism in the Nineties*. London: Frank Cass, 1997.

Ryan, Nick. *Homeland: Into a World of Hate*. Edinburgh, Scotland: Mainstream Publishing, 2003. Popular on the far right, mostly European.

Sargent, Lyman Tower, ed. *Extremism in America: A Reader*. New York: New York University Press, 1995.

Swyngedouw, Marc, and Gilles Ivaldi. "The Extreme Right Utopia in Belgium and France: The Ideology of the Flemish Vlaams Blok and the French Front National." *West European Politics* 24:3 (July 2001): 1–22.

White, Jonathan R. "Political Eschatology: A Theology of Antigovernment Extremism." *American Behavioral Scientist* 44:6 (February 2001): 937–56.

Whitsel, Brad. "Aryan Visions for the Future in the West Virginia Mountains." *Terrorism and Political Violence* 7, no. 4 (Winter 1995): 117–39.

Websites

Conservatism

The American Enterprise Institute for Public Policy Research: http://www.aei.org/

The Cato Institute: http://www.cato.org/

The Heritage Foundation: http://www.heritage.org/

Liberalism

The Brookings Institution: http://www.brook.edu/

Human Rights Watch: http://www.hrw.org

Communitarianism

The Communitarian Network: http://www.gwu.edu/~ccps/

Institute for Communitarian Policy Studies: http://www.gwu.edu/~icps/about.html

The Responsive Communitarian Platform: http://www2.gwu.edu/~ccps/platformtext
.html

The Extreme Right

National Alliance: http://www.natvan.com/

National Association for the Advancement of White People: http://www.naawp.com

Panzerfaust Records: http://www.panzerfaust.com/

Resistance Records: http://www.resistance.com/

6

☙

Feminism

Today feminism is a well-established ideology with certain core positions and a range of variants that move in somewhat different directions. Feminism is also an international movement that cuts across class, national, and racial barriers even while those same barriers reveal significant differences.

One subject on which feminists agree is the need to replace what they see as the system of male dominance, or *patriarchy,* that affects all social institutions. Clearly, feminism focuses on the position of women in society and the roles they play, but feminists argue that improving the status of women will also benefit men. Not all men agree. An obvious example of the problems women face were the laws the Taliban imposed in Afghanistan that required most women to stay at home, allowing them to leave only if accompanied by a male relative; prohibited their employment and education; and required them to wear the *burqa,* a traditional head-to-toe covering. The Taliban also restricted men's freedom in many ways but much less severely. Such extreme measures are rare, but women face a wide variety of major and minor restrictions, both customary and legal, throughout the world. Although the Taliban were defeated militarily, they are still influential in many rural areas of Afghanistan, and in some of those areas women face the same conditions they did under Taliban rule.

Feminism focuses on the goal of gender equality. Feminism has long realized that women themselves often do not recognize the restrictions within which they live, and the modern women's movement has often focused on *consciousness-raising,* or helping first women and then men to become aware of the limits imposed on women by both law and custom. In the 1960s, which saw the rapid growth of feminism, there were thousands of consciousness-raising groups in North America and Europe.

THE DEVELOPMENT OF FEMINISM

Debates over the social roles of men and women go back to classical and biblical times. Both the Old and New Testaments contain passages that have been used to argue either that women are inferior or that women are equal. Plato's *Republic* has been interpreted as contending both that women should be treated as equals to men and that they are naturally inferior to men.

Such debates are a constant of Western history. For example, in March 1776 Abigail Adams (1744–1818) wrote to her husband John Adams (1735–1826), who was then involved in the movement for American independence and later was second president of the United States, entreating him to "Remember the Ladies" in the laws drawn up for the newly independent country. John Adams responded, "I cannot but laugh," and continued, "We know better than to repeal our Masculine systems."[1]

At about the same time in England, Mary Wollstonecraft (1759–97) was writing the first major work arguing for rights for women. Her *Vindication of the Rights of Woman* (1792) was part of a European and American movement to develop a theory of individual human rights. Thomas Paine's *The Rights of Man* (1791–92) and the French Declaration of Rights of Man and Citizen (1789) are other expressions of the movement. But in most cases, these rights were only for men. Thus Wollstonecraft's book was an early and generally neglected plea that the radical thinkers of the time should argue for human rights rather than man's rights.

Earlier, writers like Mary Astell (1668–1731) in *A Serious Proposal to the Ladies* (1694) and Sarah Scott (1723–95) in *A Description of Millenium Hall* (1762) had so despaired of being treated as autonomous human beings that they argued that women should separate themselves from men. And, as we shall see, many women still believe today that real freedom for women can come only through separation from men.

In the nineteenth century, the women's movement began as a general movement for sexual equality and ended dominated by a single issue—the campaign for the vote. In the United States this pattern was repeated with the attempt to pass the Equal Rights Amendment (ERA), which was temporarily the sole political focus of the women's movement in this country. In both cases the general feminist arguments tended to get lost in the political campaign.

In the first half of the nineteenth century in the United States women like Angelina Grimké (1805–79), Sarah Grimké (1792–1873), Margaret Fuller

---

[1] L. H. Butterfield, ed., *Adams Family Correspondence,* vol. 1 (Cambridge, MA: Harvard University Press, Belknap Press, 1963), 370, 382.

Culver Pictures, Inc.

The campaign to extend the vote to women was one of the longest-running reform movements in Western democracies. In most countries women did not gain the right to vote until well into the twentieth century. The campaign for the vote included activities such as this parade, along with marches, petitions, fasts, violent protests, and demonstrations in which women chained themselves to the doors of public buildings. Their efforts involved virtually all the tactics used in later protest movements. The suffrage movement was a single-issue campaign; as such, many feminists today believe that it detracted from attempts to bring about more radical changes in the condition of women. At the time, many women felt that women with the vote would be able to bring about greater changes. So far this has not been true.

(1810–50), and Frances Wright (1795–1852) became involved in the abolitionist movement and, from there, moved into other areas of reform including the rights of women. As Angelina Grimké put it, "I recognize no rights but human rights—I know nothing of man's rights and women's rights."[2] Later Elizabeth Cady Stanton (1815–1902), Susan B. Anthony (1820–1906), and others argued for a wide-ranging emancipation of women. As Anthony put it in a famous statement to the court on being found guilty of voting, "You have trampled underfoot every vital principle of our government. My natural rights, my civil rights, my political rights, are all alike ignored. Robbed of the fundamental privilege of citizenship, I am degraded from the status of a citizen to that of a subject."[3]

---

[2] Angelina E. Grimké, *Letters to Catherine E. Beecher in Reply to an Essay on Slavery and Abolitionism Addressed to A. E. Grimké, Revised by the Author* (Boston: Printed by Isaac Knapp, 1838; reprint, New York: Arno Press and *New York Times*, 1965), 118.

[3] Elizabeth Cady Stanton, Susan B. Anthony, and Martha Joslyn Gage, eds., *History of Woman Suffrage*, vol. 2 (New York: Fowler & Wells, 1881; reprint, New York: Arno Press & *New York Times*, 1969), 687.

In 1848 a convention in Seneca Falls, New York, was called "to discuss the social, civil, and religious conditions and rights of woman."[4] This convention passed the famous "Declaration of Sentiments" modeled on the U.S. Declaration of Independence. It stated "that it is the duty of the women of this country to secure to themselves their sacred right to the elective franchise."[5] It also stated, much more radically, in words similar to those of Henry David Thoreau's (1817–62) "On the Duty of Civil Disobedience" (1849), that "all laws which prevent women from occupying such a station in society as her conscience shall dictate, or which place her in a position inferior to that of man, are contrary to the great precept of nature, and therefore of no force or authority."[6]

Similar movements existed in most western European countries, and they generally followed the same pattern of radical demands for equality giving way to the sole demand for the vote. In Britain three works in the nineteenth century were particularly important in establishing the early stages of the women's movement. *Appeal of One-Half of the Human Race, Women, Against the Pretensions of Other Half, Men* (1825) by William Thompson (1775–1833) [and Anna Doyle Wheeler (1785-1848), whom he credited with many of the ideas in the book], *The Enfranchisement of Women* (1851) by Harriet Taylor (1808–58), and *The Subjection of Women* (1869) by John Stuart Mill (1806–73) all pointed to the mistreatment of women. Although these works stressed documenting the status of women legally and socially, they also argued for the vote and equality before the law.

Emmeline Pankhurst (1858–1928) was one of the leaders in the movement for the vote. Her group, the Women's Social and Political Union, used civil disobedience in the campaign. As a result, Pankhurst and many of her followers were repeatedly jailed, thus bringing more attention to the movement. Her daughters Christobel (1880–1958) and Sylvia (1882–1960) were also active feminists. Sylvia attacked the institution of marriage and bore a child out of wedlock.

Before World War I the single most important issue for the women's movement besides the vote was birth control. The most prominent figure in the birth control movement was Margaret Sanger (1883–1966), but others like the anarchist Emma Goldman (1869–1940), whose broad radical agenda included many issues of particular interest to women, supported her. Others who were concerned with more than the vote included Charlotte Perkins Gilman (1860–1935), whose journal *The Forerunner* was a forceful advocate for women, and Jane Addams (1860–1935), who exemplified and argued for an active role for women in improving life in the cities, and who was deeply involved in the peace movement at the time of World War I. Gilman's *Women and Economics* (1898) was a widely acclaimed study that argued for the need to restructure social institutions to permit women to work. Her utopian novel *Moving the Mountain* (1911) fictionally shows such a changed society.

---

[4] *History of Woman Suffrage,* vol. 1, 67.

[5] *History of Woman Suffrage,* vol. 1, 72.

[6] *History of Woman Suffrage,* vol. 1, 72.

When the vote was won, there was little noticeable effect on social policy. But during World War II women were encouraged to join the workforce for the war effort and learned to do things they had been taught were impossible for women. After the war these same women were told to go back home and give up the money and independence they had come to expect. The publication in France in 1949 of Simone de Beauvoir's *Le Deuxième Sexe* (published in English in 1952 as *The Second Sex*), a study of the treatment of women by various academic disciplines, helped fan the anger at this loss.

Still, it wasn't until the 1960s and the publication of *The Feminine Mystique* (1963) by Betty Friedan (b. 1921), combined with the rejection of women's issues by the New Left, that a renewed feminist movement began. Although this early movement was predominantly white, a number of African American women were also active in the burgeoning feminist movement. Today the women's movement is acutely aware of the importance of speaking to the needs of minority women and of women in the developing nations. And, of course, these women are finding their voices and speaking for themselves.

THE PERSONAL IS THE POLITICAL

In opposing all forms of discrimination against women (and men), feminists have argued that the term *political* needs to be redefined. If, as some would have it, politics is about power, there is politics between men and women both individually and as groups. There are power relations between friends and lovers and within families. For example, in the family, who makes decisions and how they are made are political questions, as are questions about who spends how much and on what, who allocates tasks around the house, and the division of labor reflected in such allocation.

An interesting case is housework. This is an important issue because it includes the traditional sexual division of labor in which men work outside the home for a wage and, if a man's wage is high enough, the woman does not work. But if the man's income is not high enough to pay for servants, the woman works at home without a wage. And, of course, if a woman works outside the home, in the traditional division of labor, she still does the housework. Housework is the largest sector of unwaged labor in the economy. Anyone attempting to replace that unpaid labor with paid labor finds that certain aspects of it command substantial wages because, although the work is not well paid, long hours are required. Cooking and child care can be very expensive; regular cleaning is not cheap, and high-quality work is hard to find. Housework is also repetitive and not particularly exciting work. Many people—men and women alike—if given a choice, don't do it.

For these reasons, housework illustrates how political work allocation is in a modern household. Generally, although there is much awareness of a change toward men helping more around the house (the word *help* implies assistance freely donated, not required), the traditional pattern remains common, with the added factor that the woman works outside the home for a wage as well as doing the same work in the home as before. In other words, the pattern of sexual division of labor that once applied only to the poor has spread to the middle class. Thus both the economics and the internal dynamics of housework illustrate the maxim that the personal is the political. Similar questions affect all relations between women and men.

Another way of describing the situation in which women find themselves can be seen in an expansion of the notion of the personal as the political. If all human relationships are power relationships, whatever else they may also be, women as individuals and as a group have been and are among the powerless. An example can illustrate the point. When men were telephone operators and secretaries, these positions were adequately paid and had some prestige; when these positions became "women's work," they changed into low-paid positions with little prestige.

The fact that we are aware of power relations where we previously failed to notice them does not mean that such relations are necessarily subject to public policy, but our changed awareness does raise the complicated question of the relationship between the public and the private and what activities should belong to each sphere. Many things we consider private have entered the public arena. For example, until recently spousal and, to a slightly lesser extent, child abuse were not considered appropriate subjects for public action. In most states in the United States, it was, until the last few decades, legally impossible for a man to rape his wife; he literally owned access to her body, and she had no right to deny him that access. Thus a central debate raised by feminism is what, if anything, remains private and not subject to public/political scrutiny. At present, there is no clear answer, but the boundaries set by both public opinion and the law have clearly moved toward including more life experiences within the public realm. At the same time, there remains significant opposition to such changes.[7]

SEXISM

Sexism is the belief that women are inferior to men. *Racism* is the belief that one group of people is inferior or superior based on factors such as skin color. But sexism and racism are just examples of the much broader point that people are oppressed both individually and as groups by socially constructed patterns of beliefs, attitudes, and practices. Like racism, but to an even greater extent, sexism is pervasive in our languages, art, literature, and religions. More obviously, sexism pervades politics and the economy. Sexism is part of what feminists oppose and hope to eliminate. Eliminating sexism will be extremely difficult because it is, feminists contend, part of all Western languages and part of many dearly held beliefs, including religious beliefs.

---

[7] For an analysis of the position, see Jyl Josephson and Cynthia Burack, "The Political Ideology of the Neotraditional Family," *Journal of Political Ideologies* 3:2 (June 1998): 213–31. For advocacy, see Phyllis Schlafly, *Feminist Fantasies* (Dallas, TX: Spence, 2003).

Socialization

Women have been socialized to believe that only certain narrowly defined roles are acceptable for them, and there is considerable debate over how much this has changed. As was seen in the first chapter, *socialization* is the process by which individuals are given the fundamental values of their society. In the case of women, this means that they internalize the sense of inferiority that has been the dominant image of women. Feminists argue that the process of socialization should not eliminate options for women; women should be allowed to see all the possibilities open to them, not just a few. For example, at one time women could not be secretaries or telephone operators; these jobs were reserved for men, both because women were not thought capable of doing them and because women were not expected to have paid employment. But, of course, poor women have always worked in paid employment, and women on farms have always worked along with other family members. And feminist historians have discovered multitudes of women who refused to be limited by stereotypes of acceptable female behavior. This illustrates how the work of recovering the history of women, African Americans, ethnic minorities, and other groups provides psychological support for individuals living today and a basis for political arguments against discrimination.

In addition, feminists contend that men socialize women to accept both physical and mental mistreatment. Rape has been considered the most underreported crime in the United States, but the "discovery" of the extent of incest and child abuse indicates that there are a number of rarely reported crimes, almost all of which are crimes against women and children. Feminists argue that these crimes are underreported for several reasons. First, women who report rape must still generally deal with male police officers; even if—too rarely—they are sensitive to the woman's trauma, they are still men. Second, the legal system has traditionally treated the woman as the responsible party. Third, women have been taught to accept such abuse from men and to consider it almost normal. This socialization process (along with women's common fear of leaving their abusive homes because of the financial consequences) also encourages women to accept abuse from husbands or companions.

Feminists note that in addition to physical abuse, women are subject to pervasive mental abuse. It consists, in large part, of attacks on women's self-esteem and treating women as objects or things rather than as individuals or persons. Clearly rape is the most extreme form of treating a person as an object, but many other ways of abusing women do not involve physical abuse.

Physical and mental abuse are part of the oppression of women, as is the fact that in many jobs women are not paid the same as men for doing the same work and are frequently sexually harassed at work. In addition, although overt political discrimination has been reduced, more subtle forms are still common.

Religion

Orthodox Judaism makes a rigid division between men and women, with women defined as inferior. Liberal Judaism advocates, but does not always practice, equality. Women have been rabbis in reform congregations for some years but have only recently been allowed to become rabbis in conservative ones, and the acceptance of women as rabbis is spreading slowly even where it is the policy to allow them.[8]

Even though in the New Testament Christ is portrayed as treating men and women equally, the same pattern of gender discrimination holds true in Christianity. Almost as soon as the first Christian churches were organized, women were placed in subordinate roles. In fact, some of the earliest heresies centered on the advocacy of equality for women, and such heresies continued to appear from time to time, particularly around the Reformation and again in seventeenth-century England.[9]

Christian churches today are still divided over the role of women. The Episcopalian Church in the United States decided, after a long, intense debate, to admit women to the priesthood, and an African American woman has been consecrated as a bishop in the United States. Some Episcopalian churches and priests left the denomination as a result. In 2004 almost a quarter of the priests in the church were women, but in three of the church's 100 dioceses women are not allowed to serve as priests because the local bishop does not believe in a female priesthood. The Anglican Church has been deeply divided on the same issue. The Roman Catholic Church excludes women from the priesthood. Most Protestant denominations encourage the ordination of women as ministers, but there are still relatively few women ministers in most churches.

These divisions reflect a deep ambivalence about women in Christianity, particularly in the Roman Catholic Church. Two women, Eve the rebel and temptress and Mary the mother of Christ, can symbolize the conflict. Roughly the position has been that to the extent women emulate Mary and remain subordinate to men they are correctly fulfilling their natures; to the extent that they emulate Eve they are dangerous. As a result, many feminists see Eve, the rebel, as a symbol of the real strength of women, but the message that most churches present to women is one of subordination to men.

Language

Feminists have often been both criticized and laughed at for proposing changes in language use to remove the male bias. But taking the argument seriously and looking at the history (some feminists note that the word *history* itself can be read as "his story," and prefer to use "herstory") of language use, we can see the force of their point. For example, a female first-year university student is called a freshman. Why? Not long ago, women could not attend a university, and the term implies that. Of course, language use changes, and most people now use

[8] See *On Being a Jewish Feminist: A Reader,* ed. Susannah Heschel (New York: Schocken Books, 1983).

[9] See Elaine Pagels, *The Gnostic Gospels* (New York: Random House, 1979); Norman Cohn, *The Pursuit of the Millennium: Revolutionary Millenarians and Mystical Anarchists of the Middle Ages* (London: Granada, 1970); and Christopher Hill, *The World Turned Upside Down: Radical Ideas during the English Revolution* (London: Temple Smith, 1972).

freshman to refer to both male and female first-year students; but the word is a relic of past sexual discrimination.[10]

As another example, when Thomas Jefferson drafted the Declaration of Independence and wrote, "All men are created equal," did he mean all human beings or just male human beings? We don't really know what Jefferson meant, but we do know that for many people at the time the words referred only to white, male human beings. And when we read major thinkers of the past, we often don't know what the word *man* means; we can read it to mean all human beings, but we may miss what the author intended us to understand.

A particularly interesting example can be seen in the novel *The Left Hand of Darkness* (1969) by Ursula K. Le Guin (b. 1929). When *The Left Hand of Darkness* was originally published, there was relatively little awareness of the gendered character of language, and Le Guin called her characters, who changed gender at different points in their lives, "he." The twenty-fifth anniversary edition (1994) of *The Left Hand of Darkness* addresses the criticism she received for her lack of awareness by providing sample chapters with four different sets of pronouns: one using invented pronouns and genderless personal nouns and titles, one using feminine pronouns and personal nouns rather than the masculine of the original, one using pronouns that reflect the changes her characters go through—neuter and gendered at different life stages—and one using masculine and feminine pronouns for the same character as that person goes through a transition. One's understanding of the text varies remarkably depending on the set of pronouns and personal nouns used, which makes this exercise by Le Guin a striking contribution to the debate on language.

THE FEMINIST RESPONSES

Feminists agree on some responses to sexism, but they also disagree. Almost all feminists agree that fundamental answers to the problem of women's position in modern society include freedom and equality, but there are disagreements over both the meaning of these terms and how to achieve the desired result. All feminists agree that any changes should not benefit women alone. They oppose racism and homophobia (the belief in the inferiority of homosexuals) as well as sexism, and they argue that discrimination against any human being is an attack on all human beings. And they agree, men will also benefit from a free and egalitarian society.

There are a number of ways to classify the feminist responses; none is entirely satisfactory because all of them tend to group people who have important disagreements and separate people who agree on significant questions. No set of categories is currently acceptable, and many of the suggested categories are nonpolitical. The categories I use are reform or liberal, Marxist, socialist,

---

[10] See Dale Spender, *Man Made Language,* 2nd ed. (London: Routledge & Kegan Paul, 1985).

integrative or transformative, and separatist or radical. Some commentators add a term to describe conservative antifeminists, but because they are antifeminists, I do not include them here.[11] In addition, ecofeminism is discussed in Chapter 12. I have chosen, following Angela Miles (b. 1946),[12] to call the middle group *integrative* or *transformative* feminists because they generally try to recognize and incorporate the concerns of all feminists while taking a strong political stand.

Reform or Liberal Feminism

Reform feminists argue that the basic pattern of society is generally acceptable but that changes are needed so women are not put at a disadvantage by their sex. Reform feminists want an equal opportunity to compete with men. Reform feminists propose that means be found, such as improved and expanded day care facilities and improved parental leave policies, to more readily allow women to combine paid employment and motherhood. Obviously, these proposals also suggest that men must change their attitude toward sharing responsibility for child rearing, housework, and all other aspects of women's traditionally unpaid labor.

Reform feminists in the United States were particularly supportive of the Equal Rights Amendment:

Section 1. Equality of rights under the law shall not be denied by the United States or by any State on account of sex.

Section 2. The Congress shall have the power to enforce, by appropriate legislation, the provisions of this article.

Section 3. This amendment shall take effect two years after the ratification.

Forces that considered the amendment dangerously radical or unnecessary defeated its passage.

Marxist Feminism

In its earliest manifestations, Marxism had a split personality regarding women. Marxists often said that women's issues must wait until after the class revolution. On the other hand, in 1884 Friedrich Engels (1820–95) published *Origins of the Family, Private Property, and the State,* in which he noted the central role of women and the family in the development and maintenance of the social system. Engels thereby put what was called "the woman question" at the forefront of issues Marxists needed to solve, and many women were attracted to Marxism because of this.

In the last quarter of the twentieth century, feminists noted both of these tendencies within Marxism, and, while many believed that Marx's analysis of

---

[11] None of these terms are ideal, and others use different terms to describe the same categories.

[12] See Angela Miles, *Integrative Feminisms: Building Global Visions 1960s–1990s* (New York: Routledge, 1996).

capitalism was correct and pointed in useful directions, most concluded that Marxists in the twentieth century had generally ignored the insights of Engels and others and adopted the "wait until after the revolution" approach. And because the so-called Marxist revolutions in China, Russia, and other countries did not produce the significant changes in women's roles that had been promised, considerable disillusionment resulted. Today many Marxists argue that the insights of feminism need to be added to Marxism.

Socialist Feminism

Contemporary socialist feminists are perhaps best seen as democratic socialists with a focus. They reject the Marxist tendency to put class before gender, race, sexual identification, ethnicity, and the other ways in which human beings identify and classify themselves. And in doing so, they stress democratic decision making and the acceptance of difference within community. In this they are quite close to what Angela Miles has called *integrative feminism*.

Integrative or Transformative Feminism

Integrative feminists have shown how men have created a male-centered way of understanding the world that severely limits our ability to conceptualize human relations that are not hierarchical and patriarchal. These feminists' goal is to break through those mental barriers as well as the political, economic, and cultural barriers that keep all human beings from becoming fully human. For example, Nancy Hartsock (b. 1943) has noted that feminists have begun to reconceptualize the notion of power. Power as dominance will give way to power as "energy and competence."[13] All our ways of thinking need to undergo a similar revolution.

Hence integrative feminists are arguing for a fundamental transformation of not only our political and economic lives but our social, cultural, and personal lives as well. As Angela Miles says, "The alternative value core of integrative feminisms in all their variety is the holistic, egalitarian, life-centered rejection of dominant androcentric, dualistic, hierarchical, profit-centered ideology and social structures."[14] The goal is to achieve equality while recognizing difference or specificity.

Separatist or Radical Feminism

Separatist feminism, with some exceptions, argues for lesbianism and a woman-centered culture. Lesbian communes exist in all Western countries. Shulamith Firestone (b. 1945) argues for the abandonment of the biological family in *The Dialectic of Sex* (1970), and the development of a woman's culture can be seen in the works of Judy Chicago (b. 1939) and others.

---

[13] Nancy C. M. Hartsock, *Money, Sex, and Power: Toward a Feminist Historical Materialism* (New York: Longman, 1983), 224–25.

[14] Miles, *Integrative Feminisms*, xi.

CURRENT TRENDS

Feminism is developing a critical apparatus for analyzing contemporary society that is challenging all contemporary ideologies. Feminist philosophers and political philosophers are proposing new ways of understanding the world. Feminist economists are analyzing the economic roles of women and suggesting a transformation of economic life. Specifically, feminists have discovered the central role that women play in the agricultural economies of Third World countries and are arguing that the bias-rooted failure to recognize this fact has undercut all attempts to improve agricultural production in developing countries. Feminist writers and artists are developing a substantial body of literature and art that speaks to different concerns than had been previously addressed.

Feminists are encouraging all human beings to envision the possibility of a society rid of sexism, racism, homophobia, and all the other ways in which human beings have subjugated other human beings. At present feminists are divided over exactly how to go about this transformation, and reform feminists are not convinced that it is either necessary or desirable, but feminism is potentially the most radical of ideologies and the most likely to change the way most of us live today.

Votes for Women

For much of the twentieth century women were concerned with achieving the right to vote.[15] But the franchise did not translate into many women being elected to office, and while the number slowly rose in most developed countries in the last quarter of the twentieth century, the number of women elected to office has never come close to the percentage of women of voting age in the electorates. While there are many arguments about both the causes and cures for this situation, one cure that is gaining ground is to set aside a certain number of positions to which only women can be elected. There are precedents for this practice in New Zealand, in which seats are set aside for Maori, and India, where seats are reserved for Untouchables.

In France, where the practice is called *parity,* a constitutional amendment has passed that states "the law favors equal access for men and women to electoral mandates and elective offices."[16] This amendment is being implemented by requiring that in certain circumstances political parties must put forward an equal number of men and women as candidates for office. This does not, of course, guarantee election, but it is believed that more women will be elected under this system than have been previously. Anne Phillips has developed proposals for a similar system designed for Britain.[17] Today 25 countries allocate

---

[15] The first country to grant women the vote was New Zealand, which did so in 1893 while still excluding women from running for office; the first country to allow women to run for office was Finland in 1906 with 19 women elected to Parliament in 1907; the United States granted the vote in 1920.

[16] Sylviane Agacinski, *Parity of the Sexes,* trans. Lisa Walsh (New York: Columbia University Press, 2001), viii.

[17] See Anne Phillips, *Engendering Democracy* (University Park: Pennsylvania State University Press, 1991); and Phillips, *The Politics of Presence* (Oxford: Oxford University Press, 1995).

access to political power (either setting aside seats in the legislature or through electoral representation) based on gender, 15 countries do so based on ethnicity, and 9 do so on both gender and ethnicity.

Freedom and Equality

A number of feminist theorists say that feminists need to shift the emphasis from equality to freedom. This argument reflects older wording like that in the U.S Declaration of Independence, where people are said to be equal "in that they are endowed by their Creator with certain inalienable rights." In other words, having the same freedoms generates equality. The contemporary feminist arguments recognize that the relationship between freedom and equality is more complicated than this.

Feminism and Legal Theory

Catherine A. MacKinnon (b. 1946) has developed a legal theory that stresses that male dominance has been accepted in American law.[18] She contends that the male has always been the standard, even if not stated as such, and presents a position generally called *nonsubordination,* which argues for the recognition of the woman's actual lived experience as opposed to the supposed "objective" model, which has turned out to be the male perspective.

MacKinnon's initial work was on sexual harassment, which when she began was considered not sexual discrimination but merely what should be expected between men and women. It is easy to see that looking at sexual harassment from the point of view of the harassed is essential to seeing the entire picture. MacKinnon's analysis provided the basis for changes in case law and legal codes so that today sexual harassment is seen as sexual discrimination.[19]

MacKinnon's work on pornography as discrimination based on sex has been much more controversial. MacKinnon argues that freedom of expression is based on the false assumption of general equality and that the fact of gender inequality invalidates negative liberty, or the right of people to be left alone. Thus pornography is not, for MacKinnon, a question of civil liberties, but an issue "central to the institutionalization of male dominance."[20] Opponents of MacKinnon's position, which on this issue include many feminists, argue that

[18] A parallel movement regarding race, called "critical race theory," has also developed within legal theory. See Richard Delgado and Jean Stefancic, *Critical Race Theory: An Introduction* (New York: New York University Press, 2001); Richard Delgado and Jean Stefancic, eds., *Critical Race Theory: The Cutting Edge* (Philadelphia, PA: Temple University Press, 2000); and Dorothy A. Brown, *Critical Race Theory: Cases, Materials, and Problems* (St. Paul, MN: West, 2003).

[19] See Catherine A. MacKinnon, *The Sexual Harassment of Working Women* (New Haven, CT: Yale University Press, 1979). See also *Directions in Sexual Harassment Law,* ed. Catharine A. MacKinnon and Reva B. Siegal (New Haven, CT: Yale University Press, 2004).

[20] Catherine A. MacKinnon, "Pornography," in MacKinnon, *Feminism Unmodified: Discourses on Life and Law* (Cambridge, MA: Harvard University Press, 1987), 146.

freedom of the press is too important a negative liberty to be compromised to get rid of pornography, however desirable that might be.

Multiculturalism

Given the emphasis on difference by many feminists, multiculturalism would appear to be an obvious position for feminists to take, and many do. But in a recent essay, Susan Moller Okin (1947–2004) asked the question "Is Multiculturalism Bad for Women?" In her essay she suggests that accepting multiculturalism may lead to the acceptance of cultures with gender divisions that disadvantage women.[21] Okin's argument poses a serious question for both feminists and multiculturalists. The assertion of universal human rights has been central to the arguments feminists have made that such rights belong equally to both women and men. On the other hand, the recognition of important differences between and among men and women has become central to the argument that equality of rights can go hand in hand with respect for differences among human beings. The problem is that if difference includes cultural differences, then some of those differences include the rejection of equal rights. The valuing of differences can allow differences to be used to undermine gender equality, through the argument that valued differences require differential treatment. Okin contends that equality of rights must not be sacrificed in the name of multicultural respect.

Clearly, as Okin points out, multiculturalism poses a major issue for feminists, but the issue is important not just for feminists. As is noted throughout this book, in the past all ideologies posited certain universal values; but with the advent of postmodernism, universals of all sorts are now being questioned. The problem, acutely stated by Okin, is how can we keep important universals while respecting differences among human beings.[22]

Women of Color The multicultural argument reflects a central, long-standing problem for feminists, particularly in the United States—the fact that most feminists are white. African American author bell hooks (Gloria Watkins, b. 1952), in her *Ain't I a Woman? Black Women and Feminism* (1981), and the collection of essays *This Bridge Called My Back: Writings by Radical Women of Color* (1983), made early statements that the "universal" claims of white feminists did not necessarily apply to them. The title of the former was taken from the famous speech "Ain't I a Woman" (1851) given by Sojourner Truth (ca. 1797–1883) at a women's rights convention and illustrates that the issue is not a new one.

Third World Feminism The multicultural issue, seen through a different lens, is one that continues to be a problem within feminism—the appropriate

---

[21] For the essay and a number of responses, both pro and con, see Susan Moller Okin, with respondents, *Is Multiculturalism Bad for Women?* ed. Joshua Cohen, Matthew Howard, and Martha C. Nussbaum (Princeton, NJ: Princeton University Press, 1999).

[22] In her *The Futures of Difference: Truth and Method in Feminist Theory* (Cambridge, England: Polity Press, 1999), Susan J. Hekman argues that it is necessary to find a middle ground between the erasure of difference and the emphasis on difference.

approach to take toward Third World women. Many Western feminists such as Okin point to the obvious mistreatment of women in the Third World, the Taliban being only the most glaring case, and argue that the Western model of individual rights is the appropriate solution. On the other hand, both a growing number of Western feminists and many Third World feminists see this as an attempt to impose Western, and particularly American, values where they are not appropriate.[23]

Reproductive Rights

All feminists share a concern with freeing women from unwanted childbearing. This concern has been called *reproductive rights,* the right of a woman to control her own body, or, more recently, *reproductive freedom* in an attempt to separate it from the narrow, legal concept of rights. For most feminists this means that all methods of birth control should be available and either free or inexpensive and, because no system of birth control is 100 percent effective, that safe, affordable abortions should be available to all women. For a few radical feminists this means the end of biological motherhood and the development of artificial means of reproduction, but for most feminists it means the transformation of society to allow full participation by women. They envision a remodeling of all institutions of socialization so that all human beings can participate fully in all life activities as they freely and independently choose.

There is a difference among feminists on this issue. Some feminists assume that men are capable of the changes needed; others argue that a much more radical transformation of social institutions, with a resulting change in men, will be necessary before men can participate fully in raising children. They argue that without this change increased male participation in child rearing will only reduce women's power.

Third Wave Feminism

Feminism in the United States is usually described as having experienced two "waves" and is now in its third "wave." The first wave was the period of the vote in the early part of the twentieth century. The second wave was the rapid growth of and attention to feminism in the 1980s and 1990s. Much literature sees the waves as generational, with a certain amount of tension between mothers and daughters, thought of as both biological and intellectual. The waves can also be seen as responses to the differing issues that woman faced at these times.

Third wave feminism is primarily characterized by much more consciously extending the concerns raised by feminism to gay and lesbian issues

---

[23] For a forceful argument against Western feminist hegemony, see Chilla Bulbeck, *Re-orienting Western Feminisms: Women's Diversity in a Postcolonial World* (Cambridge: Cambridge University Press, 1998). For a broader consideration of these issues that includes both the arguments against Western dominance and for women in the Third World taking control of their own lives, see Marjorie Agosín, ed., *Women, Gender and Human Rights: A Global Perspective* (New Brunswick, NJ: Rutgers University Press, 2001).

("queer theory," the name adopted by the gay and lesbian movement even though it applies to all identities, not just gay and lesbian ones), postcolonial issues (postcolonial theory), and racial issues (critical race theory). The inclusion of postcolonial issues reflects an awareness that globalization is a feminist issue as well as an economic and political issue. Third wave feminists are also likely to say that feminism today is much less of a political movement than was second wave feminism; it is more cultural and local, which may reflect the influence of postmodernism with its emphasis on viewing the world from specific standpoints.

SUGGESTED READING

Some Classic Works

Brownmiller, Susan. *Against Our Will: Men, Women, and Rape*. New York: Simon & Schuster, 1975.

Daly, Mary. *Beyond God the Father: Toward a Philosophy of Women's Liberation*. Boston: Beacon Press, 1973.

Davis, Angela Y. *Women, Race, and Class*. New York: Random House, 1981.

De Beauvoir, Simone. *The Second Sex*. Translated and edited by H. M. Pashley. New York: Knopf, 1952. Originally published as *Le Deuxième Sexe*. Paris: Gallimard, 1949.

Dworkin, Andrea. *Intercourse*. New York: Free Press, 1987.

Firestone, Shulamith. *The Dialectic of Sex: The Case for Feminist Revolution*. New York: Morrow, 1970.

Friedan, Betty. *The Feminine Mystique*. New York: Norton, 1963.

Gilligan, Carol. *In a Different Voice: Psychological Theory and Women's Development*. Cambridge, MA: Harvard University Press, 1982.

Greer, Germaine. *Female Eunuch*. London: MacGibbon & Kee, 1970.

hooks, bell [Gloria Watkins]. *Ain't I a Woman: Black Women and Feminism*. Boston: South End Press, 1981.

Millett, Kate. *Sexual Politics*. Garden City, NY: Doubleday, 1970.

Moraga, Cherríe, and Gloria Anzaldúa, eds. *This Bridge Called My Back: Writings by Radical Women of Color*. Exp. and enl.

3rd ed. Berkeley, CA: Third Woman Press, 2001.

Morgan, Robin, ed. *Sisterhood Is Powerful: An Anthology of Writings from the Women's Liberation Movement*. New York: Random House, 1970.

Pateman, Carole. *The Sexual Contract*. Stanford, CA: Stanford University Press, 1988.

Books and Articles

Ackerly, Brooke A. *Political Theory and Feminist Social Criticism*. Cambridge: Cambridge University Press, 2000.

Afshar, Haleh. *Women and Politics in the Third World*. London: Routledge, 1996.

———, ed. *Women, Work, and Ideology in the Third World*. London: Tavistock, 1985.

Agacinski, Sylviane. *Parity of the Sexes*. Translated by Lisa Walsh. New York: Columbia University Press, 2001.

Agosín, Marjorie, ed. *Women, Gender and Human Rights: A Global Perspective*. New Brunswick, NJ: Rutgers University Press, 2001.

Alaimo, Stacy. *Undomesticated Ground: Recasting Nature as Feminist Space*. Ithaca, NY: Cornell University Press, 2000.

Ali, Suki, Kelly Coate, and Wangui wa Goro, eds. *Global Feminist Politics: Identities in a Changing World*. London: Routledge, 2000.

Andermahr, Sonya, Terry Lovell, and Carol Wolkowitz. *A Concise Glossary of Feminist Theory*. London: Arnold, 1997.

Anzaldúa, Gloria E., and AnaLouise Keating, eds. *This Bridge We Call Home: Radical Visions for Transformation*. New York: Routledge, 2002.

Beasley, Chris. *What Is Feminism? An Introduction to Feminist Theory*. London: Sage, 1999.

Bell, Diane, and Renate Klein, eds. *Radically Speaking: Feminism Reclaimed*. London: Zed Press; Melbourne: Spinifex, 1996.

Blasius, Mark, ed. *Sexual Identities, Queer Politics*. Princeton, NJ: Princeton University Press, 2001.

Brownmiller, Susan. *In Our Time: Memoir of a Revolution*. New York: Dial Press, 1999.

Bryson, Valerie. *Feminist Debates: Issues of Theory and Political Practice*. New York: New York University Press, 1999.

Bulbeck, Chilla. *Re-orienting Western Feminisms: Women's Diversity in a Postcolonial World*. Cambridge: Cambridge University Press, 1998.

Card, Claudia, ed. *On Feminist Ethics and Politics*. Lawrence: University Press of Kansas, 1999.

Charles, Nickie, and Helen Hintjens, eds. *Gender, Ethnicity, and Political Ideologies*. London: Routledge, 1998.

Christ, Carol P. *Rebirth of the Goddess: Finding Meaning in Feminist Spirituality*. Reading, MA: Addison-Wesley, 1997.

———. *She Who Changes: Re-imagining the Divine in the World*. London: Palgrave Macmillan, 2003.

Cobble, Dorothy Sue. *The Other Women's Movement: Workplace Justice and Social Rights in Modern America*. Princeton, NJ: Princeton University Press, 2004.

Code, Lorraine, ed. *Encyclopedia of Feminist Theories*. London: Routledge, 2000.

Cornell, Drucilla. *At the Heart of Freedom: Feminism, Sex, and Equality*. Princeton, NJ: Princeton University Press, 1998.

Crow, Barbara A., ed. *Radical Feminism: A Documentary Reader*. New York: New York University Press, 2000.

Dalla Costa, Mariarosa, and Giovanna F. Dalla Costa, eds. *Women, Development, and Labor of Reproduction: Struggles and Movements*. Trenton, NJ; Asmara, Eritrea: Africa World Press, 1999.

De Oliveira, Rosiska Darcy. *In Praise of Difference: The Emergence of a Global Feminism*. Translated by Peggy Sharpe. New Brunswick, NJ: Rutgers University Press, 1998.

Dicker, Rory, and Alison Piepmeier, eds. *Catching a Wave: Reclaiming Feminism for the 21st Century*. Boston: Northeastern University Press, 2003.

Donaldson, Laura E., and Kwok Pui-lan, eds. *Postcolonialism, Feminism, and Religious Discourse*. New York: Routledge, 2002.

Donovan, Josephine. *Feminist Theory: The Intellectual Traditions*. 3rd ed. New York: Continuum, 2000.

Dworkin, Andrea. *Heartbreak: The Political Memoir of a Feminist Militant*. New York: Basic Books, 2002.

Eagleton, Mary, ed. *A Concise Companion to Feminist Theory*. Malden, MA: Blackwell Publishing, 2003.

Eaton, Heather, and Lois Ann Lorentzen, eds. *Ecofeminism and Globalization: Exploring Culture, Context, and Religion*. Lanham, MD: Rowman & Littlefield, 2003.

El Saadawi, Nawal. *The Hidden Face of Eve: Women in the Arab World*. Translated and edited by Sherif Hetata. London: Zed Books, 1980.

Elshtain, Jean Bethke. *Public Man, Private Woman: Women in Social and Political Thought*. 2nd ed. Princeton, NJ: Princeton University Press, 1993.

———, ed. *The Family in Political Thought*. Amherst: University of Massachusetts Press, 1982.

Evans, Judith. *Feminist Theory Today: An Introduction to Second-Wave Feminism*. London: Sage, 1995.

Fricker, Miranda, and Jennifer Hornsby, eds. *The Cambridge Companion to Feminism in Philosophy*. Cambridge: Cambridge University Press, 2000.

Gal, Susan, and Gail Kligman. *The Politics of Gender after Socialism: A Comparative-Historical Survey.* Princeton, NJ: Princeton University Press, 2000.

Gamble, Sarah, ed. *The Routledge Companion to Feminism and Postfeminism.* London: Routledge, 2001.

García, Brígida, ed. *Women, Poverty, and Demographic Change.* Oxford: Oxford University Press, 2000.

Haraway, Donna. *Simians, Cyborgs, and Women: The Reinvention of Nature.* New York: Routledge; London: Free Association, 1991.

Hartsock, Nancy C. M. *The Feminist Standpoint Revisited and Other Essays.* Boulder, CO: Westview Press, 1998.

———. *Money, Sex, and Power: Toward a Feminist Historical Materialism.* New York: Longman, 1983.

Hawthorne, Susan. *Wild Politics: Feminism Globalisation Bio/Diversity.* North Melbourne, Vic, Australia: Spinifex Press, 2002.

Hekman, Susan J. *The Futures of Differences: Truth and Method in Feminist Theory.* Cambridge, England: Polity Press, 1999.

———, ed. *Feminism, Identity, and Difference.* Special issue of *Critical Review of International Social and Political Philosophy* 2, no. 1 (Spring 1999). London: Frank Cass, 1999.

Henry, Astrid. *Not My Mother's Sister: Generational Conflict and Third-Wave Feminism.* Bloomington: Indiana University Press, 2004.

Hirschmann, Nancy J. *The Subject of Liberty: Toward a Feminist Theory of Freedom.* Princeton, NJ: Princeton University Press, 2002.

hooks, bell [Gloria Watkins]. *Talking Back: Thinking Feminist, Thinking Black.* Boston: South End Press, 1989.

Inglehart, Ronald, and Pippa Norris. *Rising Tide: Gender Equality and Cultural Change around the World.* Cambridge: Cambridge University Press, 2003.

Jackson, Stevi, and Jackie Jones, ed. *Contemporary Feminist Theories.* New York: New York University Press, 1998.

Jaggar, Alison M., and Iris Marion Young, eds. *A Companion to Feminist Philosophy.* Oxford: Blackwell, 1998.

Jayawardena, Kumari. *Feminism and Nationalism in the Third World.* London: Zed Books, 1993.

Kaplan, Caren, Norma Alarcón, and Minoo Moallem, eds. *Between Woman and Nation: Nationalisms, Transnational Feminisms, and the State.* Durham, NC: Duke University Press, 1999.

Kaplan, Temma. *Taking Back the Streets: Women, Youth, and Direct Democracy.* Berkeley: University of California Press, 2004.

King, Ursula, ed. *Feminist Theology from the Third World: A Reader.* Maryknoll, NY: Orbis Books, 1994.

Kristeva, Julia. *Revolt, She Said. An Interview by Philippe.* Edited by Sylvère Lotringer. Translated by Brian O'Keeffe. Los Angeles, CA: Semiotexte 2002.

Labaton, Vivien, and Dawn Lundy Martin, eds. *The Fire This Time: Young Activists and the New Feminism.* New York: Anchor Books, 2004.

Lacey, Nicola. *Unspeakable Subjects: Feminist Essays in Legal and Social Theory.* Oxford, England: Hart, 1998.

MacKinnon, Catharine A. *Only Words.* Cambridge, MA: Harvard University Press, 1993.

———. *Toward a Feminist Theory of the State.* Cambridge, MA: Harvard University Press, 1989.

Mazur, Amy G. *Theorizing Feminist Policy.* Oxford: Oxford University Press, 2002.

Merchant, Carolyn. *The Death of Nature: Women, Ecology, and the Scientific Revolution.* San Francisco: Harper & Row, 1980.

Miles, Angela. *Integrative Feminism: Building Global Visions, 1960s–1990s.* New York: Routledge, 1996.

Minow, Martha. *Making All the Difference: Inclusion, Exclusion, and America Law.* Ithaca, NY: Cornell University Press, 1990.

Moghissi, Haideh. *Feminism and Islamic Fundamentalism: The Limits of Postmodern Analysis.* London: Zed Books, 1999.

Naples, Nancy, and Manisha Desai, eds. *Women's Activism and Globalization: Linking Local Struggles and Transnational Politics*. New York: Routledge, 2002.

Nasta, Susheila, ed. *Motherlands: Black Women's Writings from Africa, the Caribbean, and South Asia*. London: The Women's Press, 1991; New Brunswick, NJ: Rutgers University Press, 1992.

Not a Minute More: Ending Violence against Women. New York: UNIFEM United Nations Development Fund for Women, 2003.

Nussbaum, Martha C. *Sex and Social Justice*. New York: Oxford University Press, 1999.

O'Brien, Mary. *The Politics of Reproduction*. Boston: Routledge & Kegan Paul, 1981.

Okin, Susan Moller, with respondents. *Is Multiculturalism Bad for Women?* Edited by Joshua Cohen, Matthew Howard, and Martha C. Nussbaum. Princeton, NJ: Princeton University Press, 1999.

Parsons, Susan Frank, ed. *The Cambridge Companion to Feminist Theology*. Cambridge: Cambridge University Press, 2002.

Penn, Michael L., and Rahel Nardos, in collaboration with William S. Hatcher and Mary K. Radpour of the Authenticity Project. *Overcoming Violence against Women and Girls: The International Campaign to Eradicate a Worldwide Problem*. Lanham, MD: Rowman & Littlefield, 2003.

Phelan, Shane. *Sexual Strangers: Gays, Lesbians, and Dilemmas of Citizenship*. Philadelphia, PA: Temple University Press, 2001.

Phillips, Anne. *Engendering Democracy*. University Park: Pennsylvania State University Press, 1991.

———. *The Politics of Presence*. Oxford: Oxford University Press, 1995.

Roth, Benita. *Separate Roads to Feminism: Black, Chicana, and White Feminist Movements in America's Second Wave*. Cambridge: Cambridge University Press, 2004.

Scanzoni, Letha Dawson, and Nancy A. Hardesty. *All We're Meant to Be; Biblical Feminism for Today*. 3rd rev. ed. Grand Rapids, MI: William B. Eerdmans, 1992.

Schiebinger, Londa L. *Has Feminism Changed Science?* Cambridge, MA: Harvard University Press, 1999.

Schlafly, Phyllis. *Feminist Fantasies*. Dallas, TX: Spence, 2003. Feminism viewed from the right.

Solanas, Valerie. *SCUM Manifesto*. Edinburgh: AK Press, 1996. Originally published by author, New York, 1967.

Squires, Judith. *Gender in Political Theory*. Cambridge, England: Polity Press, 1999.

Sturgeon, Noël. *Ecofeminist Natures: Race, Gender, Feminist Theory, and Political Action*. New York: Routledge, 1997.

Tong, Rosemarie. *Feminist Thought: A More Comprehensive Introduction*. 2nd ed. Boulder, CO: Westview Press, 1998.

Warren, Karen J. *Ecofeminist Philosophy: A Western Perspective on What It Is and Why It Matters*. Lanham, MD: Rowman & Littlefield, 2000.

Young, Iris Marion. *Intersecting Voices: Dilemmas of Gender, Political Philosophy, and Policy*. Princeton, NJ: Princeton University Press, 1997.

Websites

Convention on the Elimination of All Forms of Discrimination against Women (CEDAW): http://www.unhchr.ch/html/menu3/b/e1cedaw.htm

Directory: http://www.wwwomen.com/category/femini1.html

Equal Rights Amendment: http://www.equalrightsamendment.org/

Feminist majority: http://www.feminist.org

Feminist theory: http://www.cddc.vt.edu/feminism/

General feminism: http://www.feminist.com/

Michigan Womyn's Music Festival: http://www.michfest.com

Society_and_Culture/Cultures_and_Groups/Women/Feminism/ Yahoo Directory—
   Feminism http://dir.yahoo.com/

United Nations Division for the Advancement of Women: http://www.un.org/
   womenwatch/daw/

7

Marxism

K arl Marx (1818–83) and his followers produced one of the dominant ideologies from World War I into the early 1990s—communism—and a number of variants that have been influential in many parts of the world. This chapter considers the roots of communism in the writings of Marx and Friedrich Engels (1820–95)[1] and the theoretical structure based on these writings, which is still widely respected. In addition to communism, a number of other Marxist traditions developed and will be discussed here.

Communism was the result of a line of intellectual and political development from Marx and Engels through V. I. Lenin (original name Vladimir Ilyich Ulyanov, 1870–1924) and others that emphasized the authoritarian and centralist aspects of Marx's thought. An alternative Marxist tradition has always been available that stressed the decentralist and democratic aspects of Marx's thought, but it has always been a minority position. This latter tradition, together with what are widely recognized as Marx's fundamental insights into social relations in general and the effects of capitalism in particular, explains Marx's continuing importance.

---

[1] On the Marx–Engels relationship, see Terrell Carver, "The Engels–Marx Question: Interpretation, Identities, Partnership, Politics," in *Engels after Marx,* ed. Manfred B. Steger and Terrell Carver (University Park: Pennsylvania State University Press, 1999), 17–36. On Engels, see J. D. Huntley, *The Life and Thought of Friedrich Engels* (New Haven, CT: Yale University Press, 1991); and Christopher J. Arthur, ed., *Engels Today: A Centenary Appreciation* (London: Macmillan; New York: St. Martin's Press, 1996).

The partial demise of communism does not mean the end of Marxism. The inability of capitalism to rapidly overcome the failures of communist regimes has caused many people in former communist countries to regret the passing of communism and to vote for the former communists, now under new names. Although no informed person expected capitalism to quickly correct communism's legacy, many people believed it would, and self-serving anticommunists oversold capitalism. The required restructuring of the economies involved means that many people are significantly worse off than they were under communism: jobs have been lost; pensions have been radically reduced by inflation; and social services and health care that people relied on have disappeared. Thus it is no surprise that former communists are being elected to office.

Another reason for the difficulties encountered in the transition from communism is the lack of certain aspects of a civil society in the former communist countries. Such countries have no tradition of meaningful elections, no private banking system, and no nonstate social institutions like the Red Cross/Red Crescent, scouts, the National Organization of Women, and so forth. Thus people in these countries traditionally turn to the state for most of their social activities, and all the needed new practices and organizations take time to grow.

Marxism remains a powerful tool for understanding social relations and change. Many thinkers still find the Marxist critique of capitalism to contain considerable truth. Social classes largely based on economic power remain even though Marxist and other theoreticians have been arguing for some time that this class analysis needs to be complicated by adding such factors as gender and race. In this and other ways, Marxist thinkers still contribute significantly to our understanding of the world around us. In addition, the collapse of communism has not convinced all communists that communism has failed. Thus it is important to understand the various parts of the Marxist tradition.

KARL MARX AND FRIEDRICH ENGELS

To understand the branches of the Marxist tradition, it is essential to look first at the philosophic basis found in the thought of Karl Marx and Friedrich Engels and then to turn to the developments and changes made by others.

Alienation—The Young Marx

In his twenties Marx wrote a number of works that are controversial to this day. Most writers now argue that these early writings are central to any understanding of Marx and that the later writings grow out of and develop the themes of the early writings. Those who stress the early writings argue that authoritarian communism lost sight of the human concerns that motivated Marx and that are central to these early writings.

The central concept in these early writings is alienation, particularly found in the work known as *The Economic and Philosophic Manuscripts of 1844* (first published in full in 1932). *Alienation* refers to a relationship between two or more people or parts of oneself in which one is cut off from, a stranger to, or alien to the others. It has been a major theme in modern literature, in works such as Albert Camus's *The Stranger* (1942; *The Outsider* in the United Kingdom), Jean-Paul Sartre's *Nausea* (1938) and *No Exit* (1945), and Samuel Beckett's *Waiting for Godot* (1952), to name four of the best known depictions of various forms of alienation.

For Marx it meant something more specific. He argued that in capitalism, for reasons that will become apparent later, individuals become cut off from—out of tune with—themselves, their families and friends, and their work. They are not and cannot be whole, fully developed human beings in a capitalist society.[2]

For Marx, private property and alienation are intimately linked because the most basic form of alienation is alienated labor, or labor that is sold like an object. A worker sells her or his strength, effort, skill, and time; so for much of the worker's life someone else has purchased and thus has the use of the worker (and in Marx's time this was usually a minimum of twelve to fourteen hours a day, six or seven days a week). Alienated labor produced an alienation of self; no longer whole human beings, workers could not establish full human relationships with others, who were in the same situation. This is the human meaning of capitalism for Marx: people cut off from self, others, and work. It is this condition that Marx was determined to change; it was the reason for his writings and his revolutionary activity.

Marx's Critique of Capitalism

The Marxian analysis of society and the forces operating in it is a commentary on and condemnation of industrial capitalism. Marx argued both that capitalism was the most progressive economic system developed so far and that capitalism was an essential stage in the development to socialism. Marx also attributed most of the ills of contemporary society to the capitalist system. Many evils were inherent in developing industrialism, and Marx was not the only one to point them out. His comments are interesting, though, because they indicate a great deal about Marx and how he viewed the world; much of the appeal of Marxism is found in these criticisms of the industrial system.

For Marx, economic relationships are the foundation of the entire social system; therefore, his economic criticism must be considered first. For Marx, the most fundamental fact of life is that people must produce goods before they can do anything else. They must also reproduce themselves, but they cannot even do that unless they are capable of feeding themselves. Thus material production or economic relationships are basic to all life.

The primary points in Marxian economics are the *labor theory of value*, the doctrine of *subsistence wages*, and the theory of *surplus value*. Marx used *value* in

---

[2] For extended commentaries, see István Mészáros, *Marx's Theory of Alienation* (London: Merlin Press, 1970); Bertell Ollman, *Alienation*, 2nd ed. (Cambridge: Cambridge University Press, 1976); and Adam Schaff, "Alienation as a Social and Philosophical Problem," *Social Praxis* 3, nos. 1–2 (1975): 7–26.

the sense of real costs in labor. Nothing else was considered. In other words, the value (not the price) of any manufactured object was based on the amount of labor time consumed in producing it.

Marx argued that nothing had value without labor. Neither capital nor land is of any value until labor is added. This is the *labor theory of value*. An individual has to work a certain number of hours or days to produce enough to provide a living. Marx assumed that the capitalist would pay workers only enough to keep them alive, a *subsistence wage*. Marx made this assumption for the following reasons:

1. There was a surplus of laborers, and there was no need to pay more.

2. He could not conceive of the capitalist paying more than absolutely necessary.

3. He assumed that the capitalist would be faced with a series of economic crises that would make it impossible for the capitalist to pay more.

In addition, Marx believed that the profit of the capitalist was taken from the amount produced over and above the wages paid the worker. This is the theory of *surplus value* and can be used to explain more fully the doctrine of subsistence wages. As capitalists replaced workers with machines (sometimes called *dead labor*), they would have to reduce wages to keep up their rate of profit because profit came only from surplus value extracted from labor. They would also be able to reduce wages because replacing workers with machines produces a pool of unemployed workers who must compete for whatever wages the capitalists choose to pay. Of course, the real reason that capitalists are constantly pushing down wages is to maximize profits, and Marx was certainly aware of that fact.

Hence Marx's major economic criticism revolved around the exploitation of the majority, the *proletariat* or workers, by the minority, the *bourgeoisie* or capitalists. His concern was not purely economic but also centered on the extent to which the system kept proletarians from ever fulfilling their potential as individuals. It was impossible for them to improve themselves in any way, and they were denied education and were thereby kept from any real understanding of their deplorable position.

At the same time Marx noted that the growing need for literate workers meant that some workers had to be educated and that education had the potential of teaching some proletarians about their situation, who then might teach others, thus undermining bourgeois dominance. The same thing happened in the Third World when the colonial powers started to educate some of the colonized to fill jobs needing literate workers; these same workers became part of the successful overthrow of colonial regimes.

The state was the tool of the dominant class (the bourgeoisie) and was used to suppress, violently if necessary, any attempt by the proletariat to better themselves. To Marx and most other radical theorists of the day, the *state* referred to all the officials, such as the police, the army, bureaucrats, and so forth, who could be, and were, used to suppress workers. In addition, Marx contended that as long as the bourgeoisie was the dominant class, the government would be its

Karl Marx (1818–83) was the father of modern communism. His work as a philosopher, political thinker, and economist has made him one of the most influential thinkers of all time. Born in Germany, Marx spent much of his life in England studying contemporary society and actively working for revolution. In association with Friedrich Engels (1820–95), he published their famous call for revolution, *Manifesto of the Communist Party,* in 1848. He published the first volume of his study of contemporary economics, *Capital,* in 1867; Engels undertook the publication of the other volumes. Today, every word that Marx wrote is carefully studied by a wide range of scholars and revolutionists for clues to his thought.

tool and could not be made responsive to the needs of other classes. Marx always saw the state or the government as the tool of the dominant class, whatever class that might be, and he believed the state would so remain as long as there was more than one class. For many radicals the state is the epitome of evil, the symbol of all that is bad about society. This is particularly true among the anarchists and will be discussed further in the chapter on anarchism (Chapter 8), but it is also true of Marx and some of Marx's followers, particularly those prior to Lenin. This notion probably developed because the state, through the bureaucracy, the police, and the army, represents and controls the forces regularly used to oppose workers' demands. The history of the labor movement in the United States, for example, reveals the frequent use of the police, the army, and the National Guard to put down strikes and break up demonstrations.[3] Thus Marx's ultimate goal, full communism, has no state. In this he is similar to the anarchists.

The religious system was also in the hands of the dominant class, the bourgeoisie, and Marx said religion was used to convince the proletariat that if they obeyed the state and their bosses they would be rewarded in another life. This is what Marx meant by his famous statement that religion is the opium of the

---

[3] For studies from differing viewpoints, see John R. Commons et al., *History of Labor in the United States,* 4th ed. (New York: Kelly, 1955); and Louis Adamic, *Dynamite: The Story of Class Violence in America,* rev. ed. (New York: Viking Press, 1934).

people. The proletariat is lulled into accepting its way of life by the vision of heaven. This life might well be harsh, but, if the workers stand it for a brief time, they will be rewarded in the next life. Marx believed this kept the workers from actively seeking to change the system. In this way, the religious system was a major focus of Marx's criticism of contemporary society. He saw religion used by the dominant class, the bourgeoisie, to hold the proletariat in its downtrodden position. As a result, Marx made many scathing attacks on religion and argued that the future society in which the proletariat would rule would have no need for religion. At the same time, Marx argued that religion contains the highest expression of the human ethical sense. The fact that the institution of the church and the beliefs of the masses were used to control people did not mean that Marx rejected all aspects of religious belief.

The state and the religious system were both part of what Marx called the *superstructure.* They were not fundamental economic structures of society; they were a reflection of economic relations and would change as these relations changed. Thus, as class antagonism was overcome, both the state and religion would begin to disappear.

The capitalist system degraded workers in all of their relationships. Because they had to fight against others of their own class for bare subsistence, they could never hope to establish any sort of valid relationship with another person. For example, Engels wrote bitterly of the effect capitalism had on marriage and the family. To him, the family system of his day was a repetition of the class struggle. The husband symbolized the bourgeoisie and the wife the proletariat. The contemporary marriage system under capitalism was monogamy supplemented by adultery and prostitution, and it could not change until capitalism ceased to exist. This marriage system had originated as an institution of private property at about the same time private property in land and goods originated. It developed to ensure that a man's property would be handed on to his sons. The only way this could be done was to endow the sons of one woman with a particular legal status. This did not limit the man's relationships with other women; it supposedly limited the wife's relationships with other men. In practice, as shown by the incidence of adultery, this latter proscription did not work. It failed because of "individual sex–love." Sometime after the development of monogamous marriage, there developed the tendency to find one sex–love partner and no other. This could, of course, occur after marriage, and it explained the existence of adultery. But, as will be seen later, it also provided the basis for the true monogamous marriage, which Marx believed would develop after the revolution.[4]

It is easy to see how many of Marx's criticisms of capitalism stemmed from the concerns found in his early writings. He was also impressed by Engels's description of the position of industrial workers in *The Condition of the Working Class in England* (1845), which depicted the extreme poverty in which the workers lived and the dehumanizing lives they led as mere extensions of the

---

[4] Engels discussed the family at length in *The Origin of the Family, Private Property, and the State* (Harmondsworth, England: Penguin, 1985). For a modern Marxist commentary, see Juliet Mitchell, *Women's Estate* (Baltimore: Penguin, 1971).

machines they tended. Thus both Marx and Engels saw capitalism as destroying the humanity of the workers and the bourgeoisie, because wage slavery was degrading to both buyer and seller. Marx and Engels set out to understand capitalism, to destroy it, and to found a new, better world in its place.

Materialism

For Marx, general theoretical positions must always be related to the concrete, material world and vice versa. Questions of theory are never separated from practice; they are always closely related.

The basis of Marx's philosophy is found in the influence of the conditions of life on people. Although Marx did not develop the basis of this notion thoroughly himself, he once spelled out in capsule form the fundamental thesis, saying it "served as the guiding thread in my studies." Although the jargon is a bit difficult to follow, it is best to have this statement in Marx's own words; it summarizes thoroughly his basic ideas. The meaning will become clearer later.

> In the social production of their means of existence men enter into definite, necessary relations which are independent of their will, productive relationships which correspond to a definite state of development of their material productive forces. The aggregate of these productive relationships constitutes the economic structure of society, the real basis on which a juridical and political superstructure arises, and to which definite forms of social consciousness correspond. The mode of production of the material means of existence conditions the whole process of social, political, and intellectual life. It is not the consciousness of men that determines their existence, but, on the contrary, it is their social condition that determines their consciousness. At a certain stage of their development the material productive forces of society come into contradiction with the existing productive relationships within which they had moved before. From forms of development of the productive forces these relationships are transformed into their fetters. Then an epoch of social revolution opens. With the change in the economic foundation the whole vast superstructure is more or less rapidly transformed.[5]

The fundamental point, which is a truism today, is that how people think is greatly affected by how they live. As was noted in Chapter 1, the whole process known as *socialization* is the means by which an individual takes on the values of his or her particular society. The point made there was that an individual, by her or his position in life economically, socially, and so forth, and by family and religious background, educational experiences, and such daily influences as the mass media, is presented with a picture or a group of pictures of the world that helps form his or her basic value system. In other words, the way an individual lives does quite clearly affect how she or he thinks.

---

[5] Karl Marx, "Preface," in *A Contribution to the Critique of Political Economy*, trans. N. T. Stone (Chicago: Charles H. Kerr, 1913), 11–12.

But the point generally accepted today is not quite the same as the point Marx was making. Marx argued that the forms taken by the law, religion, politics, aesthetics, philosophy, and so forth, which he called the *superstructure,* are largely determined by the economic structure and processes of society.

Marx is often, with considerable truth, called an *economic determinist,* and taken at face value, that is the meaning of the phrase "their social condition . . . determines their consciousness." But earlier in the same passage Marx uses the word *conditions* instead of *determines.* In the simplest formulation, Marx can be read as saying there is a cause-and-effect relationship between the economic structure of society and the superstructure. However, Marx thought in terms of interactions, not simple cause-and-effect relationships. In this case there is a continuing interaction between economic structure and superstructure, where changes in one produce changes in the other back and forth constantly. Marx's analysis is of a continuing process of change, with all aspects of both the economic structure and the superstructure constantly interacting. The economic structure is the driving force of social and intellectual change, but it is not a simple cause-and-effect relationship—even though Marx can be, has been, and still is read as a simple economic determinist.

The distinction here is subtle but important. For Marx, economic relationships are the most important factor determining the social forms produced at any time and place; but these economic relationships interact with aspects of the superstructure, opening up possibilities for changes in economic relationships that will then further change the superstructure, and so on. Thus Marx is almost a simple determinist, but not quite. Today, based mostly on the original insights of Marx, we tend to say that economic relationships are among the most important factors influencing the social and intellectual forms produced, but they are not always the most important factors.

In developing his materialistic approach, Marx was attacking a school of German philosophy known as *idealism.* Its major exponent had been Georg Wilhelm Friedrich Hegel (1770–1831), and it was particularly against Hegel that Marx directed his attack. Hegel's ideas and the diverse influence they had on Marx are a complex subject and cannot be explored thoroughly here. But some attempt at explanation must be made because Hegel's influence on Marx, both in what Marx accepted and what he rejected, was so great. Hegel's basic proposition, from Marx's viewpoint, was the existence of an Absolute Spirit—sometimes Hegel called it God—that gradually revealed more and more of itself in the form of higher and higher stages of human freedom. In Hegel's philosophy the ideal and the material, or *concrete* as he called it, were intimately connected, but not as cause and effect. The two were closely bound together, each influencing the other, even though ultimately the ideal was more important than the material.

Marx directed his main attack against Hegel's idealism. As Marx put it, he set Hegel on his feet by emphasizing the material rather than the ideal. Marx, of course, stressed economic relationships in his definition of the material, rather than physical nature or the like. By stressing the material, Marx was able to argue that his position was scientific (Marx's approach is often called *scientific socialism*)[6] because matter, the material, is subject to objective scientific analysis and laws; it behaves in a predictable manner. Marx was one of the first to say that economics could be treated scientifically, that it followed certain laws. He also contended history followed certain patterns and these patterns could be discovered and projected into the future. Marx did not claim he could predict the future with certainty; he simply stated that, if conditions continued as they were at the present, certain things would probably happen in the future. If conditions changed, which they did (Marx had argued that they probably would not), the future would be different. Because they did change even within his lifetime, some of Marx's positions changed. Finally, it must be noted that Marx believed history was moving not only to a different stage but also to a better one.

Dialectical Materialism The pattern Marx found in history, which he thought was a basic tool of analysis, was the dialectic. Hegel, too, had argued that history was moving to different and better stages; he also used the dialectic as his basic tool of analysis.

Marx's position is sometimes referred to as *dialectical materialism*. The *dialectic* seems to have originated in ancient Greece as a means of attaining truth through a process of questions and answers. In answer to an original question, such as the meaning of courage, beauty, justice, or the like, a position is stated. The questioner then criticizes this position through the question–answer process until an opposite or significantly different position is taken. Then, by a continuation of the process, an attempt is made to arrive at the truth contained in both positions. The process is continued until all are satisfied that the correct answer has been reached. The most famous illustrations of this process can be found in the dialogues of Plato (427?–347 B.C.), such as the *Republic*.

Marx took the dialectic from Hegel, who argued that all ideas develop through this dialectical process of thesis (first position), antithesis (second position), and synthesis (truth of the opposites), which becomes a new thesis and thus continues the process. An illustration (see Figure 7.1) shows us something of what both Hegel and Marx are saying. Starting at the bottom with the original thesis (first position), we see its "opposite" antithesis (second position). This opposition is not one of complete difference; it is produced from the thesis in one of two ways, which are spelled out in the first two laws of the dialectic.

1. *The transformation of quantity into quality.* Changes in degree gradually produce a change in quality or kind. The usual example is the change in water from a solid (ice), to a liquid, to a gas. The changes Hegel had in mind were more basic, say H_2O to H_2O_2. In this process the combination of oxygen and hydrogen first produces H_2O, which is totally different from either hydrogen or oxygen. The continued addition of oxygen produces H_2O_2, which is again different.

---

[6] The best statement of his argument is still Friedrich Engels, *Socialism: Utopian and Scientific* (1880). Many editions are available.

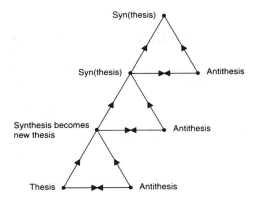

FIGURE 7.1 The Dialectic

2. *Unity or identity of opposites.* Contradictions in the thesis become the antithesis. Thus the opposites are actually similar because they are composed of similar elements. In addition, the thesis and antithesis become unified, differently, in the synthesis. This unification of the thesis and the antithesis is produced through the third law of the dialectic.

3. *Negation of the negation.* Contradictions continue to accumulate until another qualitative change occurs and the synthesis is reached. The synthesis, or the unity of the opposites, is a qualitative change, as was the original step from the thesis to the antithesis. In other words, a new position is reached that is not simply the combination of the thesis and antithesis. In a similar way, chemists sometimes speak of synthesizing a new product from two or more products. Thus water (H_2O) is a synthesis of two parts hydrogen with one part oxygen to produce a product that is significantly different from the original components. The synthesis is then treated as a new product, and the process continues in the same manner.

These three laws are often neglected or slighted by students of Marx; but, as will be seen later, they help provide an understanding of the pattern taken by his analysis of history. Marx did not attempt to apply the dialectic systematically to the material world. Some of his followers, such as Engels and Lenin, tried to view nature as changing dialectically and spoke vaguely of scientific laws operating dialectically, but their attempts were not very successful.[7]

The general form of the dialectic is the interaction and intermingling of ideas, beliefs, and positions, not the specific form used here as an example of the dialectic. The dialectic is a way of understanding the constant interaction that characterizes the world. For a particularly relevant example, none of the ideologies presented here is, by itself, an accurate reflection of the world; but on the other hand, each of them has something valuable to contribute to the

---

[7] For a modern consideration, see Richard Levins and Richard Lewontin, *The Dialectical Biologist* (Cambridge, MA: Harvard University Press, 1985).

Library of Congress

Vladimir Ilyich Lenin (1870–1924, born Vladimir Ilyich Ulyanov) was a follower of Karl Marx. He is remembered primarily as the leader of the successful Bolshevik section of the Communist Party of the Soviet Union and as the first leader of the USSR, which he headed from the time of the Russian revolution in 1917 to his death. He was a major theorist of revolution as well as one of its successful practitioners. His books *What Is to Be Done?* (1902) and *One Step Forward, Two Steps Back* (1904) presented the case for a highly disciplined body of revolutionists as the only approach to a successful revolution. His *Imperialism: The Highest Stage of Capitalism* (1916) and *State and Revolution* (1918) were his major contributions to Marxist theory.

understanding of how people behave. Ideological positions constantly interact in the world and are changed by that interaction. This complex, constant interaction and change are a more accurate description of the dialectic.

Historical Materialism Marx applied the dialectic to his interpretation of history. Because any change in the economic system is reflected in changes in the entire superstructure, Marx argued that it would be possible to interpret all history from this perspective. He also contended it might be possible to make some general statements about the future on the same basis, arguing that history contained patterns that would in all probability continue into the future. Thus an understanding of history should make it possible to argue that if conditions remain the same, certain things are likely to take place in the future.

Although Marx contended economics is an exact science and is basic to an understanding of his scientific socialism, he nowhere clearly and unambiguously defined the most important element in his economics, the *modes of production*. Most of the time they consist of (1) available natural resources and (2) productive techniques. At times Marx includes the organization of production as a third element, but this is more properly part of the superstructure.

Natural resources become available as we learn how to use them. Human knowledge is basic to both of the modes of production; this illustrates the interactive nature of Marx's materialism. Tools and knowledge grow together, each improvement in tools adding to knowledge and each improvement in knowledge making it possible to improve tools. Through this process more natural resources become available for use, and techniques of production change.

As humans learn the uses of natural resources, their modes of production change, and they begin to develop more tools and manufacturing processes. They begin to produce pottery or weave baskets; they learn to form metals into tools and weapons. These changes in turn lead to further changes in both the modes of production and the superstructure.

Changes in productive techniques are brought about because previous changes were made. In other words, each development sets the stage for a further development. Also, major changes in productive techniques, such as the shift from herding to agriculture, produce comprehensive changes in the organization and belief system of society. In the case cited, Marx is right. If we look at any civilization where we know the pattern, we can see that the change from herding to agriculture was accompanied by new political, religious, and social systems, as different activities became important. Although the change from herding to agriculture is an obvious case where major changes in productive techniques do alter the organization of society, and specifically the political system of that society, Marx is probably correct in assuming that any such change significantly modifies society. It is again obviously true that the change from a predominantly agricultural society to a predominantly industrial society has produced many far-reaching changes in contemporary society, and many argue that similar far-reaching changes will occur as production becomes more and more highly automated.

Part of the superstructure is a set of relations of production, or property relations. These constitute the second key to Marx's theory of history. *Property relations* in Marx's terminology refer to the ownership of the means of production: land, factories, and so on. These property relations change more slowly than do the modes of production, and thereby a conflict is formed that can be solved only by a change in the property relations. This point is important for an understanding of Marx's analysis of the changes in history and his criticism of contemporary society. Marx argued that property relations evolve more slowly than modes of production, and property relations will not change to meet changing needs. Because his analysis states that property relations are a product of the modes of production, it is clear that the property relations must change to meet the new modes of production rather than the reverse. But in the meantime, there is tension between the modes of production and the property relations, which cannot be resolved until the more slowly changing property relations have changed.

This tension produces conflict within society and is a primary reason for Marx's prediction of a revolution and his certainty that the proletariat will win the revolution. According to Marx, property owners will not be willing to give up their ownership, even though that is dictated by a change in the modes of production. At the same time, they ultimately must give up such ownership because of the change in the modes of production. Thus one can see in operation the three laws of the dialectic mentioned earlier. There is the transformation of quantity into quality in the changes in the modes of production. There is the unity of opposites in the growing contradiction between the economic foundation and the superstructure. And finally, there is the negation of the negation in arriving at the new synthesis of modes of production and superstructure.

In addition, Marx uses the dialectic in his concept of progress to higher and higher, or better and better, stages of society. This is an aspect of the idea of progress or the notion that the human race and society are inevitably moving to better things. An extremely popular idea in Marx's time, the idea of progress has fallen into disrepute today; but Marx's use of the idea of progress deserves further comment.

The idea of progress was not simply the notion of the world getting better and better every day in every way. Some believers in progress did think the world was constantly getting better, and the human race had nothing to do with it. They argued that the world was moving in a straight line from some primitive state to some ultimate, perfect society in which everything would be good and beautiful; all people had to do was wait and things would get better. But most believers in progress did not accept this simple formulation. They believed that the world, although improving, constantly fell away from the line of progress into some sort of corruption; and then only by great effort, perhaps a revolution, could the world be brought back onto the correct path.

People could affect the path taken by the world in its gradual betterment both for good and evil. Marx seems to have assumed the world would gradually get better in spite of whatever humans did, but he contended that through concerted action people make a tremendous difference in the speed of improvement. Thus humanity's position would improve, but knowledgeable people such as Marx were in a position to recognize the direction that must be taken to achieve this.

The Class Struggle

A central part of Marxism is the class struggle, a hypothesis Marx used to explain change. The *class struggle* is produced by the contradiction between the modes of production and the relations of production. Marx said that in the mid-nineteenth century the means of production were controlled by a class he called the *bourgeoisie.* This class did little if any work but reaped immense profits from its control of the means of production. The actual labor was done by a class Marx called the *proletariat.* The modes of production required the proletariat, but did not, according to Marx, require the bourgeoisie; therefore, a struggle between these two classes resulted. For Marx there was no question concerning the result—the proletariat was necessary, the bourgeoisie was not. Although both he and later Marxists applied the theory of class struggle to all history, Marx argued that the best example of class struggle existed in the mid-nineteenth century, in which society was clearly split into these two classes, the bourgeoisie (capitalists) and the proletariat (workers).

It is important to clearly understand the nature of classes and of these two classes in particular. Classes are economic groups ordered according to their relationship to the nonhuman powers of production and to each other. The proletariat is the class that makes its living from the sale of its labor power. The bourgeoisie owns the productive resources on which the proletariat works. The bourgeoisie makes its living primarily from profit, interest, and rent, although it may earn some of its income from wages paid for managerial work and for coordinating risk-taking ventures.

Many other smaller classes existed, but they were generally irrelevant to the unfolding conflict. In addition, Marx had a few problems with the manner in which he included certain groups within the class system. For example, he was always unclear as to exactly where the peasantry fit within his system. He often included the peasantry in a group loosely known as the *petite bourgeoisie* because they were landowners. At other times he split his definition of the peasantry into a variety of groups ranging from the bourgeoisie to the proletariat, but he was never sure exactly where to place peasants who owned their land and worked it themselves. This problem of classification has plagued Marxist theorists ever since: no one is certain where to place the peasant. In addition to the peasantry, Marx also added at the bottom of his classification scheme another class called the *lumpenproletariat,* which was composed of the dregs of society who made no contribution to production. Marx never clarified whether it would be possible to include this group within the proletariat itself, but one would assume from his writings that he thought that at some point after the revolution it would be possible to incorporate the lumpenproletariat into the proletariat in the same way the bourgeoisie was to be incorporated. For Marx in the nineteenth century, however, the most important classes were the proletariat and the bourgeoisie.

Revolution

The class struggle will, according to Marx, ultimately produce a revolution; and Marx worked for that revolution, arguing that we must move beyond simply understanding society to changing it. Marx was a revolutionary because he believed a revolution was both necessary and inevitable. The revolution would develop as a result of a series of crises capitalism was to experience. These failed to appear as regularly or as seriously as Marx had expected, and thus the revolution did not develop, although some contemporary Marxists prefer to say it has not yet developed as anticipated.

In a small book titled *Imperialism: The Highest Stage of Capitalism* (1916), Lenin attempted to show why these crises failed to occur as predicted. He argued that by colonizing and exploiting underdeveloped countries, the capitalists were temporarily able to stave off the crises. Colonial exploitation made it possible to pay workers slightly better by providing capitalists with (1) cheap raw materials, (2) cheap labor, and (3) markets for manufactured goods and excess capital. Lenin believed imperialism merely postponed the revolution; it did not put it off permanently, but it lulled the proletariat into believing revolution will not be necessary.

This position is particularly relevant today, and some Marxists say that Lenin's analysis was correct, with the results only now developing. Cheap raw materials were provided for Western factories and higher wages were paid in the West by exporting exploitation to the colonies, where very low wages were paid. Today Third World countries are beginning to control their own resources and are insisting on high prices, in part because of past exploitation. Some contemporary Marxists believe capitalism will now experience the crises that Marx predicted and that Lenin argued had been put off temporarily through imperialism. According to this argument, the capitalist system will collapse and the revolution will come. So far this has not happened, and the price of raw materials has fluctuated dramatically. Marxists argue that this is only temporary and caused by the capitalists, who still control the markets for raw materials. And, Marxists argue, capitalists continue to control the labor market, as can be seen by the regular movement of jobs to countries with lower labor costs.

In discussing the Marxian approach to revolution, it is instructive to distinguish between two different types of revolution—political and social. Political revolution takes place when political power is seized by the proletariat. Social revolution takes place later, first through changes made in society's property relations and then as the superstructure adjusts to these changes.

Marx thought the political revolution would be violent, although he allowed for the possibility of peaceful change. The revolution would probably be violent for two reasons. First, Marx argued that achieving synthesis would be sudden; thus the gradualness implicit in peaceful change was ruled out by the dialectic. Second, the bourgeoisie would never agree to its disappearance as a class and would force the proletariat into a violent revolution.

Lenin Marx was a revolutionary. He believed revolution was necessary and good, and throughout his life he was involved in groups that tried to bring about revolutions in various countries. He was expelled from a number of countries for his activities. But it was his followers, particularly Lenin and Mao Zedong, who developed the tactics for and led successful communist revolutions.

Lenin's contribution was the development of the revolutionary party—an organizational weapon in the struggle to overthrow capitalism. Lenin argued that such a party was necessary because the proletariat was incapable of recognizing its role as the revolutionary class, whereas the party provided this necessary consciousness. As one scholar stated, "The party is conceived as the organization, incarnation, or institutionalization of class consciousness."[8] The party would be made up of those who had achieved this consciousness and had also become professional revolutionists. In the popular phrase, the party was to be the "vanguard of the proletariat"; it would point the way and lead the proletariat to its goal. The party would bring together the divided masses of workers and would express what they truly felt but could not express. It would mold them and unify them into a force for change.

Proletarians as individual class members would be unlikely to recognize their historic role. They would be much too busy attempting to stay alive to be concerned with class questions. In addition, few would ever identify themselves as class members. Thus it would be left up to those who became aware, the party members, to prepare for the great role the proletariat would play.

The importance of Lenin's party is found in the idea of the professional revolutionary and in the organizational principle of *democratic centralism*. The party would be composed of a small, conspiratorial group of professional revolutionists. But because no revolution could succeed without the support of, or at least little direct opposition from, the largest part of the population of a country, Lenin believed it should develop contacts throughout the society as a whole. This meant party members would need a variety of organizational skills. They would have to be experts at agitation and propaganda. Because they had to be able to establish

[8] Alfred G. Meyer, *Leninism* (New York: Praeger, 1962), 31–33.

and maintain a vast network of "front" organizations, they would have to be expert administrators. Ideally, before the revolution, the majority of the population should be organized into a variety of these groups that would also provide the basis for organization once the revolution succeeded. In addition, the party members would have to prepare constantly for the revolution, because it would come only when the masses suddenly revolted against their oppressors.

The party might light the spark that set the masses afire, but the spark could come from anywhere at any time, and the party had to be ready to ride the revolution into power. The theory of the spark was important to Lenin. One of his newspapers was called *The Spark* (*Iskra*), and he often referred to the necessity of some incident igniting the masses. Lenin believed it was possible for the party to produce the necessary conditions for a revolution, but he believed it was impossible to be absolutely sure when the revolution would come. So the party always had to be prepared for the revolution to come at an unexpected time, perhaps even at a time that was not favorable to the party.

The principle of organization making all this possible is *democratic centralism,* which combines free discussion with centralized control and responsibility. Before any decision is made by the party, there should be complete freedom to dissent; after the decision is made, it must be accepted unanimously. Lenin believed this principle could work because all party members started from a position of agreement regarding goals. In practice, freedom of discussion was often forgotten. Democratic centralism would also serve as the principle of organization in the period immediately following the revolution, which will be discussed more completely later.

As a technique of revolutionary organization, democratic centralism has important characteristics. In planning a revolution, care must be taken to organize in order to act at a moment's notice. Everyone must also be able to act in a completely concerted manner without disagreements or squabbles over what is to be done now and what is to be done later, or arguments about the correct techniques of taking over the government or who is to do this or that at a particular moment. It is essential there be complete agreement among the revolutionists over the techniques of the revolution and the organization of society immediately after the successful revolution. Democratic centralism provides this by giving the leaders complete control over the actions of the revolutionists and at the same time allowing all members of the party to participate freely and openly in the process of reaching the appropriate decisions. Again, democratic centralism has usually been used in ways that stressed centralism.

Mao Zedong   Other Marxist theorists have also contributed to the tactics of revolution. For example, Mao Zedong's (1893–1976) theory of guerrilla warfare is also an organizational weapon. Mao's theory can be divided into two parts: the strictly military principles and some political principles derived from one of the military principles. Militarily, Mao developed what are now the commonly recognized principles of guerrilla warfare. These stress a hit-and-run approach, fighting only when fairly certain of victory, and keeping constant pressure on the enemy.[9]

---

[9] Mao Zedong, *Selected Works* (Bejing: Foreign Language Press, 1961), 4:161–62.

According to Mao, this style of fighting requires a territorial base where the guerrillas will be virtually free from attack so they will be able to rest, train, and so on. To achieve this, they must have the positive support of the people in that area. This support is gained by (1) establishing a peasant government, (2) allowing the peasants to redistribute the land, and (3) helping the peasants in whatever rebuilding activities they undertake. The territorial base will provide food, people, and, perhaps most important, experience in organization. The network of tunnels used by the Vietcong during the Vietnam War provided a similar resting place. Thus Mao's theory of guerrilla warfare fulfills the same function as Lenin's theory of the revolutionary party. Mao's tactics are designed for the same purposes as Lenin's strategies.

Marx had said that revolution required an *industrial* proletariat. But the revolutions brought about by both Lenin and Mao took place in countries that were primarily agricultural; this was particularly the case in China. Lenin still argued that he was sparking a proletarian revolution and worked to develop a base of industrial workers. Mao, while believing that China needed to industrialize quickly, knew that he had no industrial proletariat and changed his analysis to include the peasantry.

Dictatorship of the Proletariat

Marx envisioned a brief transitional period after the revolution, known as the *dictatorship of the proletariat*. This stage was to be characterized by consolidation of proletarian power through the gradual disappearance of the bourgeoisie and the minor classes, as they became part of the proletariat.

The bourgeoisie and the members of other classes would be given jobs that would, over time, change their outlook and make them good members of the proletariat. During the dictatorship of the proletariat, the superstructure would change to adjust to the socialist mode of production. Loosely, the dictatorship of the proletariat should have the following characteristics:

1. Distribution of income according to labor performed.
2. Gradual disappearance of classes.
3. The state in the hands of the proletariat.
4. Increasing productivity.
5. Increasing socialist consciousness—people work with few incentives.
6. Increasing equality.
7. A command economy.
8. The economy managed by the state.

All of these characteristics were expected to change fairly rapidly, and the dictatorship of the proletariat was to be brief. In practice, no country that has followed Marx's ideas has moved beyond the dictatorship of the proletariat. Contrary to Marx's vision, this "transitional" period does not seem to focus on the economic system; as practiced it is based on the political system, with all else as superstructure.

Marx refused to make specific predictions about the future. He argued that people who had been shaped by new experiences would create the new social forms of the future. Except in the most general sense, those socialized in the old, bad society could have no notion of what the new, better society would look like; therefore, Marx never described the dictatorship of the proletariat in any detail. In addition, the dictatorship of the proletariat was to be a short transition period and would be characterized more by change than by stable institutions. Still, it is possible to say something about the society of the dictatorship of the proletariat because Marx gave enough suggestions to allow some elaboration on the eight points listed previously.

During the dictatorship of the proletariat, the state, as always, will be the tool of the dominant class (in this case the proletariat). The state will be used to achieve a number of related goals. First, the economic system will be reorganized; the means of production must be taken from the capitalists and become the property of the state. The state must also establish a new way of administering the means of production so the economy is kept running and goods are produced, distributed, and consumed. As part of this process, the workers will all become employees of the state (public employees) and will be paid by the state on the basis of the quantity and quality of the work they perform, just as they had been by the previous owners. These previous owners and all other members of the bourgeoisie and the other classes will gradually be absorbed into the proletariat. They will be given jobs, and working for a living will resocialize them into the proletariat's way of thought and belief.

Together these show the operation of a command economy managed by a state in the hands of the proletariat, distribution of income on the basis of work performed, and the gradual disappearance of classes. With the gradual disappearance of classes, there should be greater productivity because there will be more workers available, no unproductive bourgeoisie, and no profit. As a result, equality will increase, and people will become more aware of their roles in society and will require fewer incentives to work.

The dictatorship of the proletariat, it can be seen, represents a unified view of a society in a period of transition. All these factors must be thought of as in a state of change. Some things will change quickly, others more slowly. In practice, of course, a command economy was established that was managed by the state, but in no communist country has the state ever been in the hands of the proletariat, and none of the other changes have occurred. No communist country has even come close to the goals of the dictatorship of the proletariat, let alone the next, final stage—full communism.

Full Communism

The changes in contemporary communism brought about by the fusion of nationalism, the early writings of Marx, and existentialism have given rise to a resurgence of utopian thinking by Marxists. But they have not significantly changed the characteristics of Marx's ideal system, full or pure communism. Full communism has the following characteristics:

1. Distribution of income according to need, no longer according to labor performed.
2. No classes.

3. The state withers away.

4. Very high productivity, so that there is plenty for all.

5. High socialist consciousness—people work without incentives.

6. More equality but not absolute equality.

7. No money.

8. A command economy.

9. The economy managed by a free and equal association of producers.

10. The differences between occupations disappear, so that there is no social distinction between town and country.

11. Each person does about as much physical as intellectual labor.

12. The system, as Stalin was the first to show, is worldwide.[10]

Full communism is the goal of the entire system—the utopia or better society toward which all else is aimed. Its general characteristics are not much different from the utopias created by a variety of other socialists throughout the centuries, but some of these characteristics are worth further mention.

The similarities and differences between full communism and the dictatorship of the proletariat can be seen by comparing this list with the one in the previous section. The command economy still exists, but it is no longer controlled by the state. Marx was primarily concerned with abolishing exploitation, and in full communism there are no exploiters, only workers. With the exploiters gone and the people working without incentives, there should be plenty so that all can be rewarded according to need.

The most direct effect of a change to full communism would be on the social stratification and mobility systems. Because classes would no longer exist and no distinction would be made among types of labor, there would be little social stratification. In the classless or single-class society, there would be no basis for any significant distinctions among people. *Significant* for Marx meant economic; he did not foresee a complete leveling. Individual differences would remain, but they no longer would be detrimental to the individual or the society as they had been under capitalism and all the other socioeconomic systems preceding it. Occupational mobility would be increased greatly because an individual would be able to move freely among positions.

Marx envisioned other significant changes in the social system. There would, of course, be no religion. There would be education for all. All crime would disappear because there would be no reason for it. With the coming of full communism, prostitution and adultery would disappear, and the monogamous family would become a reality. The new family would be based on a love–sex relationship that Marx believed could have only one focus. At the same time, he wanted to free women from housework. A Marxist scholar has suggested that under full communism there will be a change from personal

---

[10] Adapted slightly and reprinted by permission of the author and the publishers from
P. J. D. Wiles, *The Political Economy of Communism* (Cambridge, MA: Harvard University
Press, (c) 1962, by Basic Blackwell & Mott Ltd.), 332–33.

housekeeping functions, such as cooking and cleaning, to public or communal services, thus freeing women to choose among occupations in the same way men can.[11]

With the coming of the classless society, the state would no longer be necessary and would disappear. It would be replaced by "the administration of things," which means the economic system would have to be organized and somebody would have to administer it. It would be administered by "a free and equal association of producers" that would have the authority to direct, according to the needs of the people, what should be produced and in what amounts, and how it should be distributed. This "free and equal association of producers" could conceivably take a wide variety of forms, depending on the size of the territory and the complexity of the industries within the territory. Most such associations would undoubtedly take some pattern like the following. A committee would be selected, probably by election, that would collect data on the productive capacity of the region and the needs of the people. It would establish priorities and goals for the various manufacturing plants, farms, and craft industries. This assumes an economy based on abundance and thus would be more concerned with collecting accurate data on needs than with establishing priorities. The process would be continuous, and certainly the composition of the committee would change periodically. The committee would hold no coercive power, still assuming abundance, and would merely administer the economy.

This is the goal of Marxism. Many communists today believe full communism will never come. Others believe it is still possible. But whichever position one takes, it illustrates some of the appeal communism has had and will continue to have in the future.

ALTERNATIVE MARXIST TRADITIONS

As mentioned earlier, an alternative tradition within Marxism emphasizes decentralist and humanitarian aspects of Marx's thought. These alternative traditions provide the basis for the continuation of Marxism as a creative and useful social theory. The line of authoritarianism that Lenin developed was successful only after an intellectual and political struggle, and even Lenin regularly expressed reservations about the direction he took. But the centralization of authority that took place under Joseph Stalin (original name Iosif Vissarionovich Dzhugashvili, 1879–1953) became the model for all communist countries and could be justified within the writings of Marx and Lenin. Lenin had rejected Stalin as his successor, but Stalin won the struggle for power after Lenin's death.

---

[11] E. G. Balagushkin, "The Building of Communism and the Evolution of Family and Marital Relations," *Soviet Sociology* 1 (Winter 1962–63): 43. Originally published in 1962 in *Voprosy Filosofii*. For some similar early U.S. plans, see Dolores Hayden, *The Grand Domestic Revolution: A History of Feminist Designs for American Homes, Neighborhoods, and Cities* (Cambridge, MA: MIT Press, 1981).

Those who lost the early struggle with Lenin, however, remained influential in Western Europe. The first stage of development of an alternative Marxism can be seen in the debate between Eduard Bernstein (1850–1932) and Rosa Luxemburg (1870–1919).

Eduard Bernstein

Bernstein argued, in a work variously translated as *Evolutionary Socialism* and *The Preconditions of Socialism* (1899), that capitalism was more adaptable than Marx had thought, and, as result, evolution from capitalism to socialism was possible. This position, called *revisionism,* led to the development of democratic socialism (see Chapter 4) and poses one of the central dilemmas for revolutionaries: whether to encourage or discourage reform. If reform is successful, the revolution is delayed; but opposing reform is likely to lose support from those who care more for immediate improvement than for a possible revolution. Bernstein's analysis gave strong support to those advocating reform.

Rosa Luxemburg

Luxemburg was one of Bernstein's strongest opponents. In her *Social Reform and Revolution* (1899) she argued that revolution was essential. She advocated mass strikes as the best route to the revolution, but she explicitly rejected Lenin's notion of a centralized revolutionary party, believing that such a party would undermine the creativity of the mass of the workers.

Other opponents of the emphasis on centralism emerged in various countries. Three of the most important were Antonio Gramsci (1891–1937) of Italy, Georg Lukács (1885–1971) of Hungary, and Anton Pannekoek (1873–1960) of the Netherlands.

Antonio Gramsci

Gramsci advocated democracy within factories. For example, he proposed that each factory be organized into workshops and each workshop into work crews based on similar skills. Each work crew would elect a delegate. These delegates would meet and elect an executive committee; and, in a federal structure above the individual factories, elected representatives from the various factories in the area would meet in a variety of groupings. This system is democratic centralism with the emphasis on democracy, and it has similarities with the idea of workers' control (discussed in the next chapter).

Also, Gramsci rejected what he saw as Marx's overemphasis on materialism, particularly rejecting dialectical materialism. In this he was similar to Georg Lukács. (See also the discussion of Gramsci's concept of *hegemony* in Chapter 1.)

Georg Lukács

In his book *History and Class Consciousness* (1923), which was rejected by orthodox Marxists of the time, Lukács stressed the need to recognize the role of human creativity in bringing about social change. He argued, against what came to be called "vulgar Marxism," that human beings can think and act freely independent of their material and class positions. Lukács is often given credit for the rebirth of Marxist philosophy in the late twentieth century and is seen as a forerunner of post-Marxism.

Anton Pannekoek and Council Communism

Marxists like Gramsci and Pannekoek provided the basis for the continuation of an alternative Marxist tradition among Western European and American Marxist theoreticians. Pannekoek suggested that full communism be taken seriously and that there be no governing authority, arguing that workers would achieve freedom and security only when they controlled the means of production directly rather than through the state. The councils that he proposed would not be able to require obedience from the people. In this Pannekoek was close to the type of federal communist anarchism described by Pyotr Kropotkin and discussed in the next chapter.

The Frankfurt School

The Frankfurt Institute for Social Research was founded in 1923, and, under the leadership of Max Horkheimer (1895–1973) and Theodor Adorno (1903–69), it became the foremost center in the West for Marxist research. The school is most noted for the development of *critical theory,* a general theory that views society from the point of view of the need to change it; it intended to show how modern society functions but also at what cost to human lives. Marx saw himself as always being both a social theorist and a revolutionary, or someone who believed in the need to transform society. In his famous "Eleventh Thesis on Feuerbach," he even emphasized that change was more important than theory: "The philosophers have only *interpreted* the world in various ways; the point is to *change* it."[12] Thus the Frankfurt School followed Marx's example in advocating social change.

Although there was great variety among the members, the Frankfurt School's most influential members have been Herbert Marcuse (1898–1979) and Jürgen Habermas (b. 1929). Marcuse combined the insights of Marx with those of Sigmund Freud to develop a vision of a nonrepressive society in his *Eros and Civilization* (1955) and *One-Dimensional Man* (1964). He greatly influenced the New Left. Habermas has focused on the concept of rationality as the basis of his theory. He has worked to develop a broad concept of rationality as a means of criticizing contemporary culture and as the foundation for positive social change. In doing so he developed a theory of communicative action that he used to critique the concept of modernity while keeping those parts of modernity that he considered most valuable: universal rationality and morality. In his most recent work he explores the tension between law as a means of achieving stability and its normative role in each society. He argues that *discursive*

---

[12] Karl Marx, "Theses on Feuerbach," in Karl Marx and Friedrich Engels, *Collected Works* (New York: International Publishers, 1976), 5:5. Emphasis in the original.

or *deliberative democracy,* in which there is a continuing process of discussion involving substantial parts of the population, will overcome this tension.

Ernst Bloch

Ernst Bloch (1885–1977) was a German Marxist philosopher who emphasized the utopian aspects of Marxism. In his magnum opus, *Das Prinzip Hoffnung* (*The Principle of Hope*) (1959), and other works, Bloch explored the various manifestations of hope in human history. He argued that the desire for betterment must be brought back to the center of Marxist thought as the real engine of social change. With the recent translation of his works into English, Bloch's writings are beginning to influence contemporary Marxist thought. Bloch also influenced the development of Liberation Theology.

CURRENT TRENDS

Communism has disappeared as the official ruling force in Eastern Europe and the former Soviet Union. Although modified, it still exists in China, Cuba, and Vietnam and among numerous parties and groups throughout the world, including dominant parties with new names but the same leaders in parts of Eastern Europe and the former Soviet Union. But in general, communism as we have known it is coming to an end. It seems appropriate to ask what happened.

The central problem is that the supposedly short-lived dictatorship of the proletariat, during which the various capitalist classes were to become one class, became a permanent dictatorship in the name of the proletariat but not actually of the proletariat. As Milovan Djilas (1911–95) pointed out in *The New Class* (1955), communism simply replaced capitalist bosses with bureaucratic bosses who ruled in their own interest rather than in the interest of the proletariat. Some have actually called communism *state capitalism.*

Other problems include the fact that it is almost impossible to manage all the details of an economy from the center. As a result, many inefficiencies were built into the Soviet economy, gradually developing into the total breakdown we now see. On the other hand, central planning and control worked in rebuilding the Soviet Union after World War II and in their space program. We should not forget that the Soviet Union put the first person into space.

The Relevance of Marxism Today

In the past few years a small body of work has developed exploring the current situation of Marxism, particularly as a tool of social analysis. Most commentators see the greatest relevance of contemporary Marxism in the application of Marx's insight into capitalist exploitation to contemporary economic relationships in capitalism. For some, this analysis is particularly relevant to the Third World and neocolonialism. For others, it is most important for understanding developed capitalist societies like the United States, which most people are convinced have demonstrated the success of capitalism and the failure of Marxism. Marxists, to the contrary, argue that capitalism has succeeded only in convincing people of its success, rather than in overcoming exploitation. They point to the problems of contemporary American society, where the distance between the rich and the poor continues to grow and where many people find it necessary to work two jobs to earn enough to maintain the standard of living they believe they need. As a result, many people work as many long hours today as they did in Marx's time. And, although in many marriages both spouses choose to work outside the home, many couples feel that both spouses must work, even though they would prefer that one of them be able to stay at home with the children. In these ways and others, contemporary Marxist theorists contend that Marxism is still a relevant tool of analysis.[13]

There are three schools of thought regarding Marxism today, which are often labeled post-Marxism, analytical Marxism, and ecological Marxism.

Post-Marxism There are two forms of post-Marxism, which are generally called *post*-Marxism and post-*Marxism,* although it is reasonable to see the end results as not that different. *Post*-Marxism simply rejects Marxism as a way of thinking and uses whatever insights Marxists may have had without adopting a "Marxist" way of thinking. Jean-François Lyotard (1924–98) was an early *post*-Marxist who is best known for his exposition of postmodernism.[14]

The major theorists of post-*Marxism* are Ernesto Laclau and Chantal Mouffe, whose book *Hegemony and Socialist Strategy: Towards a Radical Democratic Politics* (1985) was an early challenge to Marxism as usual. Post-*Marxism* grafts developments in poststructuralism, deconstruction, postmodernism, and feminism onto Marxism.

As can be seen, Marxists of various types argue that postmodernism is compatible with Marxism.

Analytical Marxism Analytical Marxism is particularly associated with Jon Elster (b. 1940) and John Roemer. They apply the methodology of analytical philosophy and contemporary economic theory to Marxism. This admixture produces a complex, economically sophisticated form of market socialism.

Ecological Marxism Ecological Marxism tends to focus on a critique of the capitalist mode of production's negative impact on the environment. In this way, it might be considered little different from such critiques advanced from within capitalism by environmentalists. But ecological Marxism, or *ecosocialism* as some prefer to call it, has had a political impact, particularly in Europe, where

---

[13] For discussions of the applicability of Marxism to a wide range of topics, see Andrew Gamble, David Marsh, and Tony Tant, eds., *Marxism and Social Science* (Urbana: University of Illinois Press, 1999).

[14] On Marxism and postmodernism, see Terrell Carver, *The Postmodern Marx* (University Park: Pennsylvania State University Press, 1998).

so-called Red–Green alliances have, in Germany, been able to form a national government.

Marxism and Globalization

In general Marxists take the position that globalization equals the spread of capitalism to the detriment of workers in both developed and developing countries and the environment. They also argue that globalization, rather than showing the strength of capitalism, shows its weakness in an increasingly desperate search for cheaper and cheaper labor made necessary by rising wages in formerly low-wage areas. A case can be made for both sides. Capitalists argue that the increase in wages is the result of the spread of capitalism; Marxists actually agree but say that such a pattern fits Marx's argument that once capitalism is fully developed it must inevitably collapse.

Some Marxists take a different approach to globalization, saying that the development of a worldwide market gives rise to international agreements to protect workers. While such agreements do exist,[15] they are rarely enforced.

SUGGESTED READING

Classic Works

Bernstein, Eduard. *Evolutionary Socialism: A Criticism and Affirmation.* Translated by Edith C. Harvey. New York: Schocken Books, 1961. As *The Preconditions of Socialism.* Edited and translated by Henry Tudor. Cambridge: Cambridge University Press, 1993. Both are translations of *Die Voraussetzungen des Sozialismus und die Aufgaben der Sozialdemokratie.* Stuttgart: J.H.W. Dietz, 1899.

Bloch, Ernst. *The Principle of Hope.* Translated by Neville Plaice, Stephen Plaice, and Paul Knight. 3 vols. Oxford, England: Basil Blackwell, 1986. Originally published as *Das Prinzip Hoffnung.* 3 vols. (Berlin: Aufbau-Verlag, 1955–59).

Debray, Régis. *Revolution in the Revolution? Armed Struggle and Political Struggle in Latin America.* Translated by Bobbye Ortiz. New York: Monthly Review Press, 1967.

Djilas, Milovan. *The New Class: An Analysis of the Communist System.* New York: Harcourt Brace Jovanovich, 1955.

Engels, Friedrich. *The Origin of the Family, Private Property, and the State* (1884).

———. *Socialism: Utopian and Scientific* (1880).

Gramsci, Antonio. *The Modern Prince and Other Writings.* New York: International Publishers, 1957.

Lenin, V. I. *Imperialism: The Highest State of Capitalism* (1916).

———. *State and Revolution* (1918).

———. *What Is to Be Done?* (1902).

Lukács, György. *History and Class Consciousness: Studies in Marxist Dialectics.* Translated by Rodney Livingstone. Cambridge, MA: MIT Press, 1971.

Marx, Karl. *Capital* (1867).

———. *Economic and Philosophic Manuscripts of 1844* (first published in 1932).

Marx, Karl, and Friedrich Engels. *The Communist Manifesto* (1848).

Pannekoek, Anton. *Workers' Councils.* San Francisco: AK Press, 2003. Originally published in Dutch in 1946.

---

[15] For some such agreements, see the sections on freedom of association and employment at http://www.unhchr.ch/html/intlinst.htm.

Books and Articles

Althusser, Louis. "Ideology and Ideological State Apparatuses (Notes towards an Investigation)." In his *Lenin and Philosophy and Other Essays,* 121–73. Translated by Ben Brewster. London: NLB, 1971.

———. "Marxism and Humanism." In Althusser, *For Marx,* translated by Ben Brewster, 219–47. New York: Pantheon, 1969.

Barlow, Tani E., ed. *New Asian Marxisms.* Durham, NC: Duke University Press, 2002.

Berman, Marshall. *Adventures in Marxism.* London: Verso, 1999.

Burkett, Paul. *Marx and Nature: A Red and Green Perspective.* New York: St. Martin's Press, 1999.

Callinicos, Alex. *An Anti-Capitalist Manifesto.* Oxford, England: Polity, 2003.

Carver, Terrell. *The Postmodern Marx.* University Park: Pennsylvania State University Press, 1998.

Carver, Terrell, and Paul Thomas, eds. *Rational Choice Marxism.* University Park: Pennsylvania State University Press, 1995.

Cohen, G. A. *If You're an Egalitarian, How Come You're So Rich?* Cambridge, MA: Harvard University Press, 2000.

Cowling, Mark, ed. *The Communist Manifesto: New Interpretations.* New York: New York University Press, 1998.

Cowling, Mark, and Paul Reynolds, eds. *Marxism, the Millennium and Beyond.* Basingstoke, England: Palgrave, 2000.

Djilas, Milovan. *Fall of the New Class: A History of Communism's Self-Destruction.* Edited by Vasilije Kalezic. New York: Knopf, 1998.

Elster, Jon. *Making Sense of Marx.* Cambridge: Cambridge University Press; Paris: Éditions de la Maison des Sciences de l'Homme, 1985.

Eriksen, Erik Oddvar, and Jarle Weigård. *Understanding Habermas: Communicative Action and Deliberative Democracy.* Translated by Frøydis Wiik, Kristin Killie, Anne Elizabeth Stie, and the authors. London: Continuum, 2003.

Foster, John Bellamy. *Marx's Ecology: Materialism and Nature.* New York: Monthly Review Press, 2000.

Gal, Susan, and Gail Kligman. *The Politics of Gender after Socialism: A Comparative-Historical Survey.* Princeton, NJ: Princeton University Press, 2000.

Gamble, Andrew, David Marsh, and Toby Tant, eds. *Marxism and Social Science.* Urbana: University of Illinois Press, 1999.

Gramsci, Antonio. *Letters from Prison.* Translated and edited by Lynne Lawner. New York: Harper & Row, 1973.

———. *Pre-Prison Writings.* Edited by Richard Bellamy. Cambridge: Cambridge University Press, 1994.

———. *Selections from Political Writings (1910–1920).* Translated by Quinton Hoare and John Mathews. London: Lawrence & Wishart, 1977.

———. *Selections from Political Writings (1921–1926).* Translated and edited by Quinton Hoare. Minneapolis: University of Minnesota Press, 1978.

Habermas, Jürgen. *Communication and the Evolution of Society.* Translated by Thomas McCarthy. Boston: Beacon Press, 1979.

Howorth, David. "Post-Marxism." In *New Political Thought: An Introduction,* edited by Adam Lent, 126–42. London: Lawrence & Wishart, 1998.

Hughes, Jonathan R.T. *Ecology and Historical Materialism.* Cambridge: Cambridge University Press, 2000.

Kagarlitsky, Boris. *New Realism, New Barbarism: Socialist Theory in the Era of Globalization.* Translated by Renfrey Clarke. London: Pluto Press, 1999.

Kolakowski, Leszek. *Main Currents of Marxism.* Translated by P. S. Falla. 3 vols. Oxford, England: Clarendon Press, 1978.

Laclau, Ernesto, and Chantal Mouffe. *Hegemony and Socialist Strategy: Towards a Radical Democratic Politics.* Translated by Winston Moore and Paul Cammack. 2nd ed. London: Verso, 2001.

Levine, Andrew. *A Future for Marxism? Althusser, the Analytical Turn and the Revival of Socialist Theory.* London: Pluto Press, 2003.

Lipset, Seymour Martin, and Gary Marks. *It Didn't Happen Here: Why Socialism*

Failed in the United States. New York: Norton, 2000.

Lukács, György. *A Defence of "History and Class Consciousness": Tailism and the Dialectic*. Translated by Esther Leslie. London: Verso, 2000.

Luxemburg, Rosa. *The Accumulation of Capital*. Translated by Agnes Schwarzschild. New York: Monthly Review Press, 1964.

Lyotard, Jean-François. *Libidinal Economy*. Translated by Iain Hamilton Grant. London: Athlone Press; Bloomington: Indiana University Press, 1993. Originally published as *Economie libidinale*. Paris: Les Éditions de Minuit, 1974.

Marcuse, Herbert. *An Essay on Liberation*. Boston: Beacon Press, 1969.

Megill, Allan. *Karl Marx: The Burden of Reason (Why Marx Rejected Politics and the Market)*. Lanham, MD: Rowman & Littlefield, 2002.

Marx, Karl, and Friedrich Engels. *Collected Works*. 50 vols. New York: International Publishers, 1975–2004.

Munck, Ronaldo. *Marx @ 2000 Late Marxist Perspectives*. London: Macmillan; New York: St. Martin's Press, 2000.

O'Connor, James. "What Is Ecological Socialism?" In O'Connor, *Natural Causes: Essays in Ecological Marxism*, 324–39. New York: Guilford Press, 1998.

Ollman, Bertell. *Dance of the Dialectic: Steps in Marx's Method*. Urbana: University of Illinois Press, 2003.

Rethinking MARXISM 1–current (founded 1988).

Robinson, Cedric J. *Black Marxism: The Making of the Black Radical Tradition*. London: Zed Books, 1983.

Roemer, John. *Analytic Foundations of Marxian Economic Theory*. New York: Cambridge University Press, 1981.

———. *A General Theory of Exploitation and Class*. Cambridge, MA: Harvard University Press, 1982.

Sakwa, Richard. *Postcommunism*. Buckingham, England: Open University Press, 1999.

Service, Robert. *Lenin: A Biography*. Cambridge, MA: Harvard University Press, 2000.

Sim, Stuart. *Post-Marxism: An Intellectual History*. London: Routledge, 2000.

———, ed. *Post-Marxism: A Reader*. Edinburgh: Edinburgh University Press, 1998.

Wilde, Lawrence, ed. *Marxism's Ethical Thinkers*. Basingstoke, England: Palgrave, 2001.

Zyuganov, Gennady. *My Russia: The Political Autobiography of Gennady Zyuganov*. Edited by Vadim Medish. Armonk, NY: M.E. Sharpe, 1997.

Websites

Communist Party of America: http://www.cpusa.org/

Communist Party of Canada (Marxist–Leninist): http://www.communist-party.ca/

The Marxism Mailing List: http://www.marxmail.org/

Marxism with links to texts: http://www.anu.edu.au/polsci/marx/marx.html

Marxist sites on the WWW: http://www.shebeen.com/marx.htm

Marxist Writers: http://www.marxists.org/archive/

8

Anarchism and Libertarianism

Although its roots reach back to classical Greece, anarchism emerged as a major modern ideology at about the same time as Marxism. The word *anarchy* means without a chief or ruler, or rule by no one; but today it suggests disorder or chaos, and people connect it to violent protests. As a result, the words *anarchy* and *anarchist* are used indiscriminately to condemn protesters, whether or not any among the protesters are anarchists. This dual perception of anarchism originated in the nineteenth century along with the first statements by anarchist theorists.

Today forms of anarchism exist on the far left and far right of the political spectrum. Although anarchism is traditionally identified with the left, a variant that is rooted in mid-nineteenth-century America, *anarcho-capitalism,* is generally identified with the right. And an offshoot of anarchism that developed mostly in the second half of the twentieth century, *libertarianism* or *minimalism,* is also generally identified with the right, although left-libertarians have recently attacked the social agenda of the right in the United States.

This chapter examines the principles of both anarchism and libertarianism and shows how anarchism, in particular, has changed recently. Libertarianism, because its followers have been willing to be involved in the political process, rests on the border between anarchism and some form of democracy; but its roots, particularly in the United States, are clearly in the anarchist tradition, and therefore it is discussed here rather than as another subtype of democracy.

PRINCIPLES OF ANARCHISM

The ideology we call *anarchism* has a variety of forms and includes a number of different ideas. Most studies of anarchism have focused on a select group of men: Prince Pyotr Kropotkin (1842–1921), Pierre-Joseph Proudhon (1809–65), Mikhail Bakunin (1814–76), Count Leo Tolstoi (1828–1910), Max Stirner (1806–56), William Godwin (1756–1836), and William Morris (1834–96), who rejected the label—with sometimes a bow in the direction of a few lesser-known figures such as Errico Malatesta (1850–1932), Élisée Réclus (1830–1905), Benjamin Tucker (1854–1939), and Josiah Warren (1798?–1874). Today anarchists and scholars of anarchism recognize the significant contribution made to the anarchist movement and anarchist theory by women. Emma Goldman (1869–1940) is generally recognized as the most important, but women have always been involved in all aspects of anarchism.

This approach, focusing on individual anarchists, may produce a valid presentation and analysis of the clusters of ideas that make up anarchism, but it is just as likely to result in a misunderstanding of the important similarities and the equally important differences among anarchists. The best approach, therefore, seems to be to select those parts of the anarchist tradition that are most important today while striving to maintain a balanced presentation.

Kropotkin once defined *anarchism* as

> the name given to a principle or theory of life and conduct under which society is conceived without government—harmony in such a society being obtained, not by submission to law or by obedience to any authority, but by free agreements concluded between the various groups, territorial and professional, freely constituted for the sake of production and consumption, as also for the satisfaction of the infinite variety of needs and aspirations of a civilized being.[1]

Anarchism is, then, a political philosophy that says no group in society should be able to coerce anyone, and society should contain a wide variety of groups arranged to coordinate social functions. Anarchists differ somewhat on the relationships among these groups and on the importance of particular groups in the social system, but most would agree with this definition. As another anarchist, Alexander Berkman (1870–1936), stated, "Anarchism teaches that we can live in a society where there is no compulsion of any kind. A life without compulsion naturally means liberty; it means freedom from being forced or coerced, a chance to lead the life that suits you best."[2] Anarchists envision a peaceful, free life without rules and regulations. But many believe anarchism would result in chaos rather than the peaceful, noncoercive society of the vision.

The basic assumption of anarchism is that power exercised by one person or group over another causes most contemporary problems. As one anarchist says,

---

[1] Peter Kropotkin, "Anarchism," *Encyclopaedia Britannica*, 11th ed. (New York: Encyclopaedia Britannica Co., 1910), 1: 914.

[2] Alexander Berkman, *ABC of Anarchism,* 3rd ed. (London: Freedom Press, 1964), 10.

Pyotr (Peter) Kropotkin (1842–1921) was born into the Russian aristocracy but became the most important anarchist thinker of all time. Kropotkin's ideas originated during a long trip in Siberia as a geographer and naturalist. Intending to demonstrate that there was a "struggle for survival" and "survival of the fittest," he found instead cooperation and what he came to call "mutual aid." He published his findings in a series of essays between 1890 and 1896 and then collected them as *Mutual Aid* (1902). His argument that cooperation rather than competition is the basis of evolution became the foundation of all his thought. From this position he contended that anarchism, not Marxism, was scientific. After escaping from a Russian prison, he spent most of his life in western Europe, primarily in England where he published his most famous books, *The Conquest of Bread* (1892), *Memoirs of a Revolutionist* (1898–99), and *Fields, Factories and Workshops* (1899). He returned to Russia after the revolution in 1917 but quickly came into conflict with Lenin, whom he criticized for centralizing power.

"Many people say that government is necessary because some men cannot be trusted to look after themselves, but anarchists say that government is harmful because no man can be trusted to look after anyone else."[3] All anarchists would agree with this statement. They all focus on the corrupting nature of power, and they believe that human beings are capable of organizing their affairs without anyone exercising authority over others. This does not mean there will be no order in society, except temporarily; it means people can cooperatively produce a better system than can be produced by any authority. "Given a common need, a collection of people will, by trial and error, by improvisation and experiment, evolve order out of chaos—this order being more durable than any kind of externally imposed order."[4] This order—this organization—will be better designed for human needs than any imposed system could be because it will be "(1) voluntary, (2) functional, (3) temporary, and (4) small."[5]

Each of these last points is important for an understanding of anarchism. First, basic to all anarchism is the voluntary nature of any association. Second, an association will develop only to fill a fairly specific need and thus will be designed to fill that need alone. Therefore (third) it will disappear after the need

---

[3] Nicolas Walter, *About Anarchism* (London: Freedom Press, 1969), 6. Originally published as *Anarchy* 100, vol. 9 (June 1969).

[4] Colin Ward, "Anarchism as a Theory of Organization," *Anarchy* 62, vol. 6 (April 1966): 103.

[5] Ward, "Anarchism," 101. See also Terry Phillips, "Organization—The Way Forward," *Freedom* 31 (August 22, 1970): 3.

is met. Finally, it must be small enough so people can control it rather than be controlled by it. Many examples of such organizations function within contemporary society, such as the cooperatives discussed in Chapter 4.

The belief that it is possible to replace a coercive society with voluntary cooperation is about the only thing anarchists agree on. But "the essence of anarchism, the one thing without which it is not anarchism, is the negation of authority over anyone by anyone."[6] Or as another theorist put it, "Nobody is fit to rule anybody else. It is not alleged that people are perfect, or that merely through his/her natural goodness (or lack of same) he/she should (or should not) be permitted to rule. Rule as such causes abuse."[7]

Beyond this, anarchism divides loosely into two categories: (1) collectivist, with emphasis on the individual within a voluntary association of individuals; and (2) individualist, with emphasis on the individual separate from any association. The former is sometimes divided into communist anarchism and anarcho-syndicalism; the latter is usually divided into individualist anarchism and anarcho-capitalism. In each case, though, the similarities are more important than the differences.

Collectivist Anarchism

Communist anarchism, traditionally associated with Kropotkin, is the most developed and comprehensive anarchist theory. It starts, as does all anarchism, with the assumption that coercion in any form is bad. As the solution to the problem of order in a society without a government, it suggests establishing a series of small, voluntary communes or collectives. These communes would join together into a federation to deal with any common problems. As George Woodcock (1912–95) wrote, "The village would appoint delegates to the regional federations, which in their turn would appoint delegates to the national federations. No delegate would have the power to speak for anything but the decisions of the workers who elected him and would be subject to recall at any time."[8] He goes on to say that the delegates would be elected for a short period, and although expenses might be paid, the delegate would receive exactly the same salary as if still working at his or her regular job. In this way, the anarchist delegate is a very restricted representative.

Anarcho-syndicalists take essentially the same approach, except that they refer specifically to the work situation, particularly industrial work. Here are the basic principles:

1. Each industry is organized into a federation of independent syndicates.

2. The workers in each industry control that industry.

3. Policy questions and questions of relations among syndicates are handled by a coordinating council.

---

[6] Walter, *About Anarchism*, 8.

[7] Albert Meltzer, *Anarchism, Arguments For and Against* (Edinburgh: AK Press, 1996), 19.

[8] George Woodcock, *New Life to the Land* (London: Freedom Press, 1942), 26.

Rudolf Rocker (1873–1958), one of the theorists of anarcho-syndicalism, described the system as follows:

> The workers in each locality join the unions of their respective trades, and these are subject to the veto of no Central but enjoy the entire right of self-determination. The trade unions of a city or a rural district combine in a so-called labour cartel. The labour cartels are grouped according to districts and regions to form the National Federation of Labour Cartels, which maintain the permanent connection between the local bodies, arranges for free adjustment of the productive labour of the members of the different organizations on co-operative lines, provide for the necessary co-ordination in the work of education, in which the stronger cartels will need to come to the aid of the weaker ones, and in general support the local groups with counsel and guidance.[9]

Although the idea of syndicalism originated as part of the trade union movement in France, anarcho-syndicalism has moved away from the union movement. Some anarcho-syndicalists argue that the basis for the new society is found in the organization of the present trade unions, but most anarcho-syndicalists view trade unions as conservative. Modern anarcho-syndicalists oppose the existing union movement and contend that it fails to support workers against management and government.

The key to understanding anarcho-syndicalism is its industrial base. The central element of anarcho-syndicalism is workers' control,[10] in which workers organize society based on control of each industry. *Industry* here includes such activities as the building industry, which would be controlled by all the different workers who participate in building any structure. These individuals meet to resolve the particular problems of that industry; then representatives of each industry assemble to administer the economic life of the entire country. The key word here is *administer.*

This is the same as Friedrich Engels's statement that in the final stage of communism, the government of people will become the administration of things, and it is the position held by all collectivist anarchists. People will no longer be governed. They will be free from government, but they will participate in administering the economic life of the country. The contention is that there need be no such thing as a political decision. The administration of things should be a fairly simple and mechanical operation not giving rise to many conflicts.

In anarcho-syndicalism, when conflicts do arise because of, for example, problems in allocating scarce goods, the workers will be in the best position to know what is most important, what can be produced least expensively, and how to improve production. Therefore, workers rather than managers who are not in contact with the actual work should be making such decisions. Anarcho-syndicalists argue that putting workers in control will enable them to produce

---

[9] Rudolf Rocker, *Anarcho-Syndicalism* (1938; London: Pluto Press, 1989), 93.

[10] There is a vast literature on workers' control. For a sampling, see Ken Coates and Tony Topham, ed., *Workers' Control* (London: Panther Books, 1970), and *Anarchy* 2, vol. 1 (April 1961).

more, thus lessening the problem of the allocation of scarce goods. In addition, anarcho-syndicalists contend that workers' control acts as a work incentive. In communist anarchism, when social decisions must be made, they will be made consensually by the community.

The differences between communist anarchism and anarcho-syndicalism are not great. Anarcho-syndicalism is more directly concerned with the organization of industry than is communist anarchism, but both arrive at fundamentally the same conclusions. Both accept the notion that the people in a given area should administer that area for the benefit of society as a whole. It is assumed in both cases that the entire population will be workers in that everyone will participate to some degree in the economic life of the society. Both believe that if coercion is removed, a viable society can develop. The primary difference is found in the emphasis in anarcho-syndicalism on the operation of the industrial system.

Anarcho-syndicalism and communist anarchism developed a secondary level of organization that is important for understanding the course of anarchist thought. Both stress the need for some way of developing cooperation among communes or industries as well as within the commune or industry. Although the focus of most studies of anarchist thought has been on individual freedom, anarchists have always argued that it is not possible to stop there. The primary focus of collectivist anarchism is not the isolated individual, but an individual within a noncoercive society. Anarchists recognize that the small commune or industry is not sufficient for individuals in contemporary society, and that cooperation among communes and industries is necessary to produce enough goods in sufficient diversity.

In anarcho-syndicalism, to give each individual the goods necessary for life, there must be a high degree of cooperation among industries to provide an efficient distribution system for the goods produced by individual industries. The only way to handle this is through cooperation by the workers within the various industries. To some extent, this is simply a form of enlightened self-interest because each worker in a particular industry needs the products of a wide variety of industries. Therefore, all workers will cooperate because they all need the products of each and every industry. Anarcho-syndicalists believe this cooperation can develop readily once coercion disappears. To achieve this, government and, for the collective anarchist, capitalism must go.

The abolition of capitalism is a central concern for most anarchists because they believe workers are exploited by the capitalist in about the same ways Marx believed. Collectivist anarchists argue for common ownership of the means of production and distribution of goods according to need. Getting rid of government and capitalism raises the question of means, and this raises the question of violence. Anarchists believe no established authority will simply give up without a fight; therefore, revolution is likely to be the means of change.[11] But some anarchists are deeply bothered by the connection with violence, and there is a strong current of pacifist anarchism associated with thinkers like Leo Tolstoi (1828–1910) and, for some, Mohandas K. Gandhi (1869–1948). Other anarchists

---

[11] For a discussion, see Vernon Richards, ed., *Violence & Anarchism: A Polemic* (London: Freedom Press, 1993).

accept the connection with violence, believing that only through a violent rev-olution will significant change be possible.

Anarcho-capitalists, discussed shortly, believe that this system would exploit the best workers. Collectivist anarchists respond that capitalism exploits all workers. It may be that this disagreement cannot be solved, but to put it in per-spective, let us look at the individualist position.

Individualist Anarchism

> The individualist anarchist recognizes nothing above his ego and rebels against all discipline and all authority, divine or human. He accepts no morality and when he gives himself to the feelings of love, friendship, or sociability, he does so because it is a personal need, an egoistic satisfaction—because it pleases him to do it.[12]

Individualist anarchism is traditionally associated with Max Stirner. Essen-tially the position is as just stated: individuals determine for themselves, out of their own needs and desires, what is right for them. Stirner even applies this to murder.[13]

Individualist anarchists do not completely reject cooperation. They argue that cooperation is essential for the fulfillment of some needs. But they contend that only the individualist of their own definition is capable of genuinely form-ing a voluntary association with others. In addition, they never see this associa-tion as an end in itself but merely as useful for a temporary purpose. It must serve the members, not dominate them.

Individualist anarchists argue against collective ownership of goods, but not all are convinced the capitalist system is any better. Here one finds a major split in the ranks of individualist anarchists. Some reject both capitalism and social-ism and are not convinced that either system is valid. On the other hand, there are anarcho-capitalists.

Anarcho-Capitalism

Anarcho-capitalists contend that the only form of economic life compatible with individualism is capitalism. Usually their approach is connected with a view of life similar to that of the social Darwinist. They see life as a struggle for survival and hold that a socialist economic system supports those who do not deserve to survive. Anarcho-capitalists take the position that all essential social services can be better operated privately for profit than by any government or commune; this includes the police, education, the military, and so forth.

Anarcho-capitalists trace their origins to Max Stirner and the individualist anarchist tradition; in the United States one of the earliest anarcho-capitalists was Lysander Spooner (1808–87), who argued for the abolition of slavery on

---

[12] Enzo Martucci, "Individualist Amoralism," *Minus One,* no. 16 (November–December 1966): 5, trans. J.-P.S. from *L'Unique,* no. 37.

[13] See Max Stirner [Johann Kasper Schmidt], *The Ego and His Own,* ed. David Leopold, trans. Steven T. Byington, 167–68 (Cambridge: Cambridge University Press, 1995).

anarchist grounds and, after the Civil War, wrote tracts opposing all government. In the twentieth century, much U.S. anarcho-capitalism and libertarianism stems from Ayn Rand (1905–82), whose novels *Anthem* (1938), *Atlas Shrugged* (1957), and *Fountainhead* (1943) and many essays became the most popular expressions of these positions.[14] Less well known, but generally considered the ablest advocate of anarcho-capitalism, was Murray Rothbard (1926–95), whose *For a New Liberty* (1973, republished in 1985 with the subtitle *The Libertarian Manifesto*), *Ethics of Liberty* (1982), and numerous other books were uncompromising defenses of the inviolability of private property; they constitute a consistent moral defense of anarcho-capitalism.

LIBERTARIANISM

Closely related to anarcho-capitalism is libertarianism, sometimes called *minimalism* because some theorists include a role for government. Probably the best-known libertarian/minimalist text is *Anarchy, State, and Utopia* (1974)[15] by Robert Nozick (1938–2002). Nozick argues for a minimal government, saying, "Our main conclusions about the state are that a minimal state, limited to the narrow functions of protection against force, theft, fraud, enforcement of contracts, and so on is justified; that any more extensive state will violate persons' rights not to be forced to do certain things, and is unjustified; and the minimal state is inspiring as well as right."[16] His ideal system consists of a number of small communities where the members have agreed on a particular way of life; many different communities would allow a wide variety of ways of living. But in 1989 Nozick at least partially backed away from his libertarian position, saying, "The libertarian position I once propounded now seems to me seriously inadequate, in part because it did not fully knit the humane considerations and joint cooperative activities it left room for more closely into its fabric."[17] As a result, its author has undermined the most sophisticated and well worked out defense of libertarianism.

In the United States, one form taken by libertarianism is the Libertarian Party, a political party supporting candidates for office who pledge to severely reduce government. The "Preamble" to the Libertarian Party platform for the 2004 election says, "As Libertarians, we seek a world of liberty; a world in which all individuals are sovereign over their own lives, and no one is forced to

[14] On Rand's popularity, see Jerome Tuccille, *It Usually Begins with Ayn Rand* (New York: Stein and Day, 1971).

[15] For discussions of this book, see Jeffrey Paul, ed., *Reading Nozick: Essays on Anarchy, State, and Utopia* (Totowa, NJ: Rowman & Littlefield, 1981); and J. Angelo Corlett, ed., *Equality and Liberty: Analyzing Rawls and Nozick: Property, Justice, and the Minimal State* (Stanford, CA: Stanford University Press, 1991).

[16] Robert Nozick, *Anarchy, State, and Utopia* (New York: Basic Books, 1974), ix.

[17] Robert Nozick, "The Zigzag of Politics," in Nozick, *The Examined Life: Philosophical Meditations* (New York: Simon & Schuster, 1989), 186–87.

sacrifice his or her values for the benefit of others."[18] In language repeated from previous platforms, the 2004 platform says,

> We, the members of the Libertarian Party, challenge the cult of the omnipotent state and defend the rights of the individual. We hold that all individuals have the right to exercise sole dominion over their own lives, and have the right to live in whatever manner they choose, so long as they do not forcibly interfere with the equal right of others to live in whatever manner they choose.[19]

And the platform stresses that to achieve these goals, government power must be strictly limited:

> [W]here governments exist, they must not violate the rights of any individual: namely, (1) the right to life—accordingly we support the prohibition of physical force against others; (2) the right to liberty of speech and action—accordingly we oppose all attempts by government to abridge the freedom of speech and press, as well as government censorship in any form; and (3) the right to property—accordingly we oppose all government interference with private property, such as confiscation, nationalization, and eminent domain, and support the prohibition of robbery, trespass, fraud, and misrepresentation.[20]

The platform specifies many areas in which government should not be involved, such as the use of drugs, alcohol, consensual sexual relations (both heterosexual and homosexual), pornography, and gambling, all of which are called "victimless crimes"; but much of the platform is concerned with property. Regarding property, in language again repeated from earlier platforms, the 2004 platform says, "There is no conflict between property rights and human rights. Indeed, property rights are the rights of humans with respect to property and, as such, are entitled to the same respect and protection as all other human rights."[21] All human rights are property rights based on self-ownership. "Our bodies are our property every bit as much as is justly acquired land or material objects. The owners of property have the full rights to control, use, dispose of—or in any manner enjoy—their property without interference, until and unless the exercise of their control infringes the valid rights of others."[22]

While the Libertarian Party platform stresses economic issues and property rights, it applies the principles that underlie these concerns to many other issues. Because the most basic principle might be stated as "no governmental interference," it is not surprising that the Libertarian Party opposes U.S. involvement in any international organization and says no taxes should go to

---

[18] 2004 Libertarian Party Platform: http://www.lp.org/issues/platform/ Preamble.

[19] Ibid.

[20] Ibid.

[21] 2004 Libertarian Party Platform, Section I.12 Property Rights.

[22] Ibid.

foreign aid, which should be funded entirely privately. They extend this principle to rejecting U.S. intervention economically or militarily in the affairs of other countries.

The only role for government should be to physically protect U.S. citizens, particularly at home, and to ensure that the free market is actually free. In both cases, government activity should be the least possible to achieve the desired result: thus the use of the word *minimalism* to describe this position.

ANARCHIST SOCIAL THOUGHT

Anarchism and libertarianism are concerned with individual freedom. Anarchism rejects control by any group, but particularly by the organized group we call the state or government. Anarchists argue that people are capable of both freedom and cooperation. They believe human beings are willing and able to help each other. They believe human beings' best instincts are destroyed by the present organization of society. They believe, as did Marx, that true love between individuals is impossible, or virtually impossible, under contemporary conditions. They believe a morality system that rejects physical relationships without the sanction of church and state destroys the possibility of developing what Marx called the love–sex relationship. The anarchist does not insist on or reject the simple monogamous marriage relationship. Individuals, they contend, must decide what kind of relationship they want. They must be free to live their lives as they choose.

The anarchist also contends that parents have a real responsibility to ensure freedom for their children. Anarchists believe the contemporary educational system destroys freedom, creativity, and learning; they want an educational system directed to the individual child, whatever her or his needs. Education directed to the individual child cannot be found, they contend, in the highly organized, overly complex system we have today. It can be found in the small group concerned with educating for freedom. Anarchists believe a child, given the freedom to choose and the encouragement to follow his or her own bent, will gradually find distinct interests and, getting interested, will apply to those interests the tremendous energies children can develop. Children will learn more this way than by traditional methods.

Much of what we are taught in our schools, the anarchist believes, is irrelevant to our lives; we waste many years in attempting to learn things that will never interest us or be of any use to us. A child should be encouraged to look at the world and interpret it on her or his own rather than being given answers. This approach to education puts a tremendous burden on parents and teachers. Teachers must develop a close relationship with each child to be able to understand the child's changing interests and to suggest ways in which the child might best fulfill them. This must be done without too much direction. Parents must be capable of giving their children freedom and must not control them too much. Anarchist theories of child rearing and education have been some of the most innovative, instructive, and successful of any of the anarchist approaches to

Library of Congress

Emma Goldman (1869–1940), also known as "Red Emma," was a leading anarchist, lecturer, popularizer of the arts, and agitator for birth control, women's rights, and free speech. Born in Russia, she emigrated to the United States in 1885. In 1889 she moved from Rochester, New York, to New York City, where she met Johann Most (1846–1906) and Alexander Berkman (1870–1936) and became active with them in anarchist circles. In 1892 she and Berkman attempted to assassinate the industrial leader Henry Clay Frick. She edited the journal *Mother Earth* (1906–17) and wrote a number of books, including *Anarchism and Other Essays* (1911), *The Social Significance of Modern Drama* (1914), and *Living My Life* (1931). She was involved in most radical activities in the United States until she was deported as an undesirable alien in 1919. After she was deported she traveled in the Soviet Union and wrote *My Disillusionment with Russia* (1923) and *My Further Disillusionment with Russia* (1924), both of which discussed the authoritarian nature of the Soviet government. After leaving Russia she continued her career as a radical agitator through involvement in the Spanish civil war.

contemporary life.[23] Related to these theories is the *homeschooling* movement, in which parents educate their children at home rather than expose them to public education. For some parents the motivation is religious; for some it is concern over the quality of education; and for others it centers on educating their children for freedom.[24] Thus homeschooling has produced some odd partnerships among people with very different motivations defending the right to remove their children from public schools to educate them at home (not in a private school).

There is no anarchist proscription of or support of religion. Within anarchist circles, considerable debate takes place over the question of religious affiliation. Many say that such affiliation is incompatible with anarchism, while others argue that it depends on the type of organization or church. Still others, including Catholic anarchists such as Dorothy Day (1897–1980) and Ammon Hennacy (1893–1970) (who left the church shortly before he died), have argued that faith in the doctrines of the church did not affect them as anarchists. They held that the church speaks only on matters of faith and morals. Outside these areas, Catholic anarchists consider themselves free of

---

[23] See, for example, Herbert Read, *The Education of Free Men* (London: Freedom Press, 1944); A. S. Neill, *Summerhill: A Radical Approach to Child Rearing* (New York: Hart Publication, 1960); Neill, *A Dominie's Log* (1915; London: Hogarth Press, 1986); Ivan D. Illich, *Deschooling Society* (London: Calder; New York: Harper & Row, 1971); and Peter Buckman, ed., *Education without Schools* (London: Souvenir Press, 1973).

[24] See the list of homeschooling websites at the end of this chapter.

the church. The Catholic anarchist is merely a special case of contemporary anarchism. Individuals such as Day and Hennacy, who accepted an authoritarian religion and at the same time considered themselves anarchists, were merely accepting the dictates of the church in one part of their lives—that part dealing with questions of religious faith. As long as this acceptance is restricted to religious and, perhaps, moral questions, it does not necessarily affect the social and political positions of the anarchist. Today Dorothy Day's Catholic Worker Movement continues in cities and country communities devoted to assisting those at the very bottom of the social ladder. Recently church authorities, who opposed Day during her lifetime, have suggested that she be considered for sainthood.

Anarchist theory has developed mostly as a series of commentaries on specific areas of life that are believed to be coercive and that could be improved by providing a free atmosphere. The ultimate goal is a truly free life in a commune that weaves together the various ways of being free.

Anarchism will probably always remain a minor ideology. Although unlikely to ever succeed in this world, anarchism is the ideology that has the most faith in people. It believes, more than any other ideology does, that people are capable of freedom and cooperation. As Colin Ward wrote, "Anarchism in all its guises is an assertion of human dignity and responsibility."[25]

CURRENT TRENDS

In the last quarter of the twentieth century a number of creative anarchist thinkers have published innovative applications of anarchist theory to current issues of public policy. The most important of these writers is Colin Ward (b. 1924), a freelance writer who has been particularly concerned with transportation policy, housing and town planning, and environmental policy. Ward's most recent work has focused on architecture. Alex Comfort (1920–2000) is best known for his writings advocating a freed sexuality, which he believed was essential to the ability of people to act freely. Later he contributed substantially to anarchist theory in the area of aging.

Recently Murray Bookchin (b. 1921), in *Social Anarchism or Lifestyle Anarchism* (1995), argued that anarchism is in serious danger of losing its value because many anarchists are what he calls "lifestyle anarchists" rather than being seriously involved in trying to change social policy. "Lifestyle anarchists" are, according to Bookchin, committed to individual autonomy rather than to a collective vision of social freedom for all. The issue Bookchin raises is important; many people who believe in anarchism do not think that a fully anarchist society is possible. As a result, they try to live their own lives as freely as possible, but with little or no concern for others. But unless anarchism remains a major critic of contemporary social and political policy, it will lose all claim to be taken seriously as a living ideology.

---

[25] Colin Ward, *Anarchism in Action*, 2nd ed. (London: Freedom Press, 1982), 143.

Bookchin, who will also be discussed in Chapter 12, is a critic of contemporary technology and an advocate of what he calls *social ecology*. Bookchin writes that "social ecology 'radicalizes' nature, or more precisely, our understanding of natural phenomena, by questioning the prevailing marketplace image of nature from an ecological standpoint: nature as a constellation of communities that are . . . freed of all anthropocentric moral trappings, a *participatory* realm of interactive life-forms whose most outstanding attributes are fecundity, creativity, and directiveness, marked by complementarity that renders the natural world the *grounding* for an ethics of freedom rather than domination."[26]

Anarchism and Globalism

Anarchism has been making headlines in the past few years. Those producing the violence at the WTO (World Trade Organization) meeting in Seattle, the G-8 (Group of 8) meeting in Genoa, Italy, and at other economic and political meetings designed to foster globalism have identified themselves as anarchists and, in a few cases, have worn black clothes and carried the black flag symbolic of anarchism. Most protesters tried to distance themselves from these anarchists, but officials, particularly in Genoa, used the anarchists as an excuse for a violent attack on all the protesters.

Anarchists have long had an ambivalent attitude toward the use of violence. Many anarchists have argued that violence is most often ineffective and commonly counterproductive. It may give the violent demonstrators the feeling that they are personally doing something about the evil they oppose, and it certainly gets the attention of the media (these days this is the main reason for its use); but it rarely changes policy and frequently produces a backlash against the position being advocated.

The supporters of violence as a tool contend that it is the only way to get the attention of the media, who without it would ignore the opposition at such meetings. Indeed, violence staged for the cameras, sometimes with the collusion of the media, is a regular feature of demonstrations. Violence is also used by the ignored powerless simply as an expression of frustration. Those whose beliefs fall outside the dominant ideologies and paradigms of the countries in which they live rarely have ways to be heard. They may come to believe that the only way to get attention is to throw a stone through the window of a shop, attack the police, or trash a city center.

There is some merit to the argument. When a protester in Genoa was killed by a police officer, the G-8 leaders all said that they were responsive to the concerns expressed by the protesters, that they were actually trying to solve the problems the protesters raised. The protesters' response was that they wanted action, not talk, and that the leaders would not even have said they were aware of the issues without the protests. Therefore, both peaceful and violent protesters will be at future meetings.

[26] Murray Bookchin, *The Modern Crisis,* 2nd rev. ed. (Montreal: Black Rose Books, 1987), 55.

TAZ, or Temporary Autonomous Zones

One interesting development within anarchism is what Hakim Bey (Peter Lamborn Wilson) calls *TAZ, or temporary autonomous zones,* and George McKay (b. 1950) called *DiY (do-it-yourself) culture.* Both labels suggest a free space in which people can temporarily create the life they want—where one can, briefly, be free.

The collection *DiY Culture* (1998) uses, among other examples, the long-term protests against military bases and construction projects in the United Kingdom as instances in which free communities were established. Other examples include New Age Travelers and the Rainbow Gatherings.[27] A much more temporary version are the "raves," or music and dance festivals, that occur apparently spontaneously (actually mostly by word of mouth) in urban and rural settings and usually last for one night. In Britain there has been a collective creating them; in the United States they are often quasi-commercial enterprises.

TAZ opens up a space in which it is possible for believers to live their beliefs for a while. Julia "Butterfly" Hill lived in a tree for two years to prevent its being cut down; a few of the women protesting the placement of nuclear missiles at Greenham Common Air Base stayed for years, but most were there for short periods. Woodstock and other music festivals are short-lived but still provide a different space for that length of time. There is a lesbian music camp and some lesbian communes that are re-created each summer (other lesbian communes are permanent) in which the women say that they are able to truly be themselves, as they cannot be the rest of the year.

For some, the temporary can become permanent. New Age Travelers are noticed only when they gather in groups for one of their periodic festivals. While for some the Rainbow Gatherings are a once-a-year festival, others travel from gathering to gathering, which now occur in Europe as well as in North America.

These are people who used to be called "dropouts," although most of them prefer to say that they "dropped in" to a better life. But the most common way anarchism is practiced is through individual life choices—for example, to teach in a school in which pupils are given freedom as opposed to teaching in a traditional, hierarchical public or private school.[28]

LETS, or Local Exchange and Trading Systems

An example of TAZ is *LETS, or local exchange and trading systems,* in which "a number of people get together to form an association. They create a unit of exchange, choose a name for it, and offer each other goods and services priced in these units. These offers and wants are listed in a directory, which is circulated

---

[27] Richard Lowe and William Shaw, *Travellers: Voices of the New Age Nomads* (London: Fourth Estate, 1993); Michael I. Niman, *People of the Rainbow: A Nomadic Utopia* (Knoxville: University of Tennessee Press, 1997).

[28] Colin Ward describes DiY culture (although he does not call it that) at work in a community in "Anarchy in Milton Keynes," *The Raven,* no. 18 (5:2) (April–June 1992): 116–31.

periodically to members. Members decide who to trade with and how much trading they want to do."[29] There are many LETS groups, ranging from child care groups in which parents in a neighborhood exchange taking care of children so that they can sometimes have a night out, to Womanshare in New York City, which has created a "Skill Bank" in which each woman gains credit for the work she contributes,[30] to local currency schemes like Ithaca HOURS, BloomingHours, the Maine Time Dollar Network, and Bread Hours in the San Francisco Bay area.[31] Hundreds of such groups exist today.

SUGGESTED READING

Some Classic Works

Bakunin, Mikhail. *God and the State.* New York: Mother Earth Press, 1916.

Berkman, Alexander. *ABC of Anarchism.* 3rd ed. London: Freedom Press, 1964.

Bookchin, Murray. *Post-Scarcity Anarchism.* 2nd ed. Montreal: Black Rose Books, 1986.

Freire, Paulo. *Pedagogy of the Oppressed.* Translated by Myra Bergman Ramos. 30th anniversary ed. New York: Continuum, 2000.

Godwin, William. *Enquiry Concerning Political Justice and Its Influence on Morals and Happiness.* Edited by R. E. L. Priestley. 3 vols. Toronto: University of Toronto Press, 1946. Originally published 2 vols., London: Printed for G. G. J. and J. Robinson, 1793.

Goldman, Emma. *Anarchism and Other Essays.* New York: Mother Earth Press, 1910.

———. *Living My Life.* 2 vols. New York: Dover, 1970.

Kropotkin, Peter. *The Conquest of Bread.* New York: Putnam's, 1907.

———. *Fields, Factories, and Workshops.* New York: Benjamin Blom, 1968.

———. *Fields, Factories, and Workshops Tomorrow.* Edited by Colin Ward. London: George Allen & Unwin, 1974.

———. *Kropotkin's Revolutionary Pamphlets.* Edited by Roger N. Baldwin. New York: Dover, 1970.

———. *Memoirs of a Revolutionist.* Edited by James Allen Rogers. Garden City, NY: Doubleday, 1962.

———. *Mutual Aid: A Factor of Evolution.* Boston: Extending Horizons Books, 1955.

Malatesta, Errico. *Anarchy.* 8th ed. London: Freedom Press, 1949.

Neill, A. S. *Summerhill: A Radical Approach to Child Rearing.* New York: Hart Publications, 1960.

Nozick, Robert. *Anarchy, State, and Utopia.* New York: Basic Books, 1974.

Proudhon, Pierre-Joseph. *What Is Property? An Inquiry into the Principle of Right and of Government.* Edited and translated by Donald R. Kelley and Bonnie G. Smith. 1840. Cambridge: Cambridge University Press, 1994.

Stirner, Max [Johann Kasper Schmidt]. *The Ego and His Own.* Edited by David Leopold. Translated by Steven T. Byington. Cambridge: Cambridge University Press, 1995.

Tolstoy, Leo. *The Law of Love and the Law of Violence.* Translated by Mary Koutouzow Tolstoy. London: Anthony Blond, 1970.

---

[29] Harold Sculthorpe, "LETS: Local Exchange and Trading Schemes," *The Raven,* no. 31 (8:3) (Autumn 1995): 237.

[30] http://www.angelfire.com/ar2/womanshare/.

[31] See the list of LETs websites at the end of this chapter.

Tucker, Benjamin R. *Individual Liberty: Selections from the Writings of Benjamin R. Tucker.* Edited by C. L. S. New York: Vanguard Press, 1926.

Ward, Colin. *Anarchy in Action.* 2nd ed. London: Freedom Press, 1982.

Books and Articles

Aldridge, Theresa, Jane Tooks, Roger Lee, Andrew Leyshon, Nigel Thrift, and Colin Williams. "Recasting Work: The Example of Local Exchange Trading Schemes." *Work, Employment & Society* 15:4 (2001): 565–79.

Avrich, Paul. *Anarchist Portraits.* Princeton, NJ: Princeton University Press, 1988.

———. *Bakunin & Nechaev.* London: Freedom Press, 1974.

———. *The Modern School Movement: Anarchism and Education in the United States.* Princeton, NJ: Princeton University Press, 1980.

Berneri, Camillo. *Peter Kropotkin: His Federalist Ideas.* London: Freedom Press, 1942.

Bey, Hakim [Peter Lamborn Wilson]. *Immediatism.* Edinburgh: AK Press, 1994. Originally published as *Radio Sermonettes.* New York: Libertarian Book Club, 1992.

———. *Millennium.* Brooklyn, NY: Autonomedia; Dublin: Garden of Delight, 1996.

———. *T. A. Z. The Temporary Autonomous Zone, Ontological Anarchy, Poetic Terrorism.* Brooklyn, NY: Autonomedia, 1991.

Boaz, David. *Libertarianism: A Primer.* New York: Free Press, 1997.

Bookchin, Murray. *Anarchism, Marxism, and the Future of the Left: Interviews and Essays, 1993–1998.* San Francisco: A.K. Press, 1999.

———. [as by Lewis Herber]. *Crisis in Our Cities.* Englewood Cliffs, NJ: Prentice-Hall, 1965.

———. *The Modern Crisis.* 2nd rev. ed. Montreal: Black Rose Books, 1987.

———. *Social Anarchism or Lifestyle Anarchism: An Unbridgeable Chasm.* San Francisco: AK Press, 1994.

Brooks, Frank H., ed. *The Individualist Anarchists: An Anthology of "Liberty" (1881–1908).* New Brunswick, NJ: Transaction, 1994.

Carter, April. *The Political Theory of Anarchism.* London: Routledge & Kegan Paul, 1971.

Christie, Stuart, and Albert Meltzer. *The Floodgates of Anarchy.* Rev. ed. London: Kahn & Averill, 1979.

Debord, Guy. *The Society of the Spectacle.* Translated by Donald Nicholson-Smith. New York: Zone Books, 1994.

De Cleyre, Voltairine. *Selected Works of Voltairine de Cleyre.* Edited by Alexander Berkman. New York: Mother Earth Press, 1914.

DeLeon, David. *The American as Anarchist: Reflections on Indigenous Radicalism.* Baltimore: Johns Hopkins University Press, 1978.

DuBrul, Sascha Altman. *Carnival of Chaos: On the Road with the Nomadic Festival.* Philadelphia: Bloodlink Press, 1997.

Freire, Paulo. *Pedagogy of the City.* Translated by Donaldo Macedo. New York: Continuum, 1993. Interviews that Freire gave while head of the school system in São Paulo, Brazil.

———. *Pedagogy of Freedom: Ethics, Democracy, and Civic Courage.* Translated by Patrick Clarke. Lanham, MD: Rowman & Littlefield, 1998.

———. *Pedagogy of Hope: Reliving Pedagogy of the Oppressed. With Notes by Ana Maria Araújo Freire.* Translated by Robert R. Barr. New York: Continuum, 1999.

Gladstein, Mimi Reisel. *The Ayn Rand Companion.* Westport, CT: Greenwood Press, 1984. Rev. and exp. as *The New Ayn Rand Companion.* Westport, CT: Greenwood Press, 1999.

Graeber, David. *Fragments of an Anarchist Anthropology.* Chicago: Prickly Paradigm Press, 2004.

Guérin, Daniel. *Anarchism from Theory to Practice.* Translated by Mary Klopper. New York: Monthly Review Press, 1970.

————, ed. *No Gods No Masters*. Translated by Paul Sharkey. 2 vols. Edinburgh: AK Press, 1998.

Hennacy, Ammon. *The Book of Ammon*. Author: 1965.

————. *The One-Man Revolution in America*. Salt Lake City: Ammon Hennacy Publications, 1965.

Holterman, Thom, and Henc van Maarseveen, eds. *Law in Anarchism*. Rotterdam: Erasmus University, 1980.

Hospers, John. *Libertarianism: A Political Philosophy for Tomorrow*. Santa Barbara, CA: Reason Press, 1971.

Illich, Ivan. *Celebration of Awareness: A Call for Institutional Revolution*. Garden City, NY: Anchor Books, 1971.

————. *Deschooling Society*. New York: Harper & Row, 1971.

————. *The Right to Useful Unemployment and Its Professional Enemies*. London: Marion Boyars, 1978.

————. *Tools for Conviviality*. London: Calder & Boyars, 1973.

Illich, Ivan, Irving Kenneth Zola, John McKnight, Jonathan Caplan, and Harley Shaiken. *Disabling Professions*. London: Marion Boyars, 1977.

Jackson, Corrine. *The Black Flag of Anarchy: Antistatism in the United States*. New York: Scribner, 1968.

Kornbluth, Joyce L. *Rebel Voices: An I.W.W. Anthology*. Ann Arbor: University of Michigan Press, 1968.

Lacey, A.R. *Robert Nozick*. Princeton, NJ: Princeton University Press, 2001.

Marshall, Peter H. *Demanding the Impossible: A History of Anarchism*. London: HarperCollins, 1992.

Martin, James J. *Men against the State: The Expositors of Individualist Anarchism in America, 1827–1908*. Colorado Springs, CO: Ralph Myles, 1970.

Mbah, Sam, and I. E. Igariwey. *African Anarchism: The History of a Movement*. Tucson, AZ: See Sharp Press, 1997.

McKay, George. *Senseless Acts of Beauty: Cultures of Resistance since the Sixties*. London: Verso, 1996.

————, ed. *DiY Culture: Party & Protest in Nineties Britain*. London: Verso, 1998.

Meltzer, Albert. *Anarchism Arguments, For and Against*. 7th ed. rev. Edinburgh: AK Press, 2000.

Morland, David. *Demanding the Impossible? Human Nature and Politics in Nineteenth-Century Social Anarchism*. London: Cassell, 1997.

O'Hara, Craig. *The Philosophy of Punk: More Than Noise*. 2nd ed. Edinburgh, Scot.: AK Press, 1999.

Narveson, Jan. *The Libertarian Idea*. Philadelphia: Temple University Press, 1988.

Piehl, Mel. *Breaking Bread: The Catholic Worker and the Origin of Catholic Radicalism in America*. Philadelphia: Temple University Press, 1982.

Purchase, Graham. *Anarchism and Environmental Survival*. Tucson, AZ: See Sharp Press, 1994.

Purkis, Jon, and James Bowen, eds. *Twenty-first Century Anarchism: Unorthodox Ideas for a New Millennium*. London: Cassell, 1997.

Raimondo, Justin. *An Enemy of the State: The Life of Murray Rothbard*. Amherst, NY: Prometheus Books, 2000.

Rand, Ayn. *Anthem*. Exp. 50th anniv. ed. New York: Dutton, 1995.

————. *Atlas Shrugged*. New York: Random House, 1957.

————. *Capitalism, the Unknown Ideal*. With additional articles by Nathaniel Branden, Alan Greenspan, and Robert Hessen. New York: New American Library, 1966.

————. *For the New Intellectual: The Philosophy of Ayn Rand*. New York: Random House, 1961.

————. *The Fountainhead*. Indianapolis: Bobbs-Merrill, 1943.

————. *The Virtue of Selfishness: A New Concept of Egoism*. With additional articles by Nathaniel Branden. New York: New American Library, 1964.

————. *We the Living*. 60th anniversary ed. New York: Signet, 1996.

Read, Herbert. *Anarchy and Order: Essays in Politics*. London: Faber & Faber, 1954.

————. *The Philosophy of Anarchism*. London: Freedom Press, 1940.

————. *Poetry and Anarchism*. 2nd ed. London: Freedom Press, 1947.

Reichert, William O. *Partisans of Freedom: A Study in American Anarchism*. Bowling Green, OH: Bowling Green State University Popular Press, 1976.

Richards, Vernon, ed. *Violence & Anarchism*. London: Freedom Press, 1993.

Roberts, Nancy L. *Dorothy Day and the "Catholic Worker."* Albany: State University of New York Press, 1984.

Rocker, Rudolf. *Anarcho-Syndicalism*. 1938. London: Pluto Press, 1989.

————. *Nationalism and Culture*. Translated by Ray E. Chase. Los Angeles: Rocker Publications Foundation, 1937.

Rothbard, Murray. *The Ethics of Liberty*. Atlantic Highlands, NJ: Humanities Press, 1982.

————. *For a New Liberty: The Libertarian Manifesto*. Rev. ed. New York: Vollier Books, 1978.

Roussopoulos, Dimitrios I., ed. *The Anarchist Papers*. 3 vols. Montreal: Black Rose Books, 1986–90.

Schmidtz, David, ed. *Robert Nozick*. Cambridge: Cambridge University Press, 2002.

Schuster, Eunice Minette. *Native American Anarchism: A Study of Left-Wing American Individuals*. 1932. New York: AMS Press, 1970.

Sheehan, Seán M. *Anarchism*. London: Reaktion Books, 2003. L

Stevens, Mitchell L. *Kingdom of Children: Culture and Controversy in the Homeschooling Movement*. Princeton, NJ: Princeton University Press, 2001.

Taylor, Michael. *Anarchy and Cooperation*. New York: Wiley, 1976. Rev. ed. as

The Possibility of Cooperation. Cambridge: Cambridge University Press, 1987.

————. *Community, Anarchy, and Liberty*. Cambridge: Cambridge University Press, 1982.

Tuccille, Jerome. *It Usually Begins with Ayn Rand*. New York: Stein and Day, 1971.

Tullock, Gordon, ed. *Explorations in the Theory of Anarchy*. Blacksburg, VA: Center for the Study of Public Choice, Virginia Polytechnic Institute and State University, 1972.

————, ed. *Further Explorations in the Theory of Anarchy*. Blacksburg, VA: University Publications, 1974.

Vallentyne, Peter, and Hillel Steiner, eds. *Left Libertarianism and Its Critics: The Contemporary Debate*. London: Palgrave, 2000.

————. *The Origins of Left Libertarianism: An Anthology of Historical Writings*. London: Palgrave, 2000.

Ward, Colin. *Cotters and Squatters: Housings Hidden History*. Nottingham, England: Five Leaves Publications, 2002.

————. *Housing: An Anarchist Approach*. London: Freedom Press, 1982.

————. *Reflected in the Water: A Crisis in Social Responsibility*. London: Cassell, 1997.

————. *Social Policy: An Anarchist Response*. Rev. ed. London: Freedom Press, 2000.

Weishaar, Wayne, and Wayne W. Parrish. *Men without Money: The Challenge of Barter and Scrip*. New York: G.P. Putnam's Sons, 1933.

Wolff, Robert Paul. *In Defense of Anarchism*. New York: Harper & Row, 1970.

Worpole, Ken, ed. *Richer Futures: Fashioning a New Politics*. London: Earthscan, 1999.

Websites

A-Infos: http://www.ainfos.org/

Anarchist Action Network: www.zpub.com/notes/aadl.html

Anarchist Communitarian Network: http://www.anarchistcommunitarian.net/

Anarchist Yellow Pages: www.flag.blackened.net/agony/ayp.htm

Catholic Worker Movement: http://www.catholicworker.org/

Critiques of libertarianism: http://world.std.com/~mhuben/libindex.html

Freedom Portal: http://www.buildfreedom.com/portal/category.php/52

Green Anarchist (UK): http://website.lineone.net/~grandlaf/Sotiga.htm

Institute for Anarchist Studies: www.flag.blackened.net/ias

Institute for Humane Studies: http://www.libertarian.org/

Institute for Social Ecology: http://www.social-ecology.org/

Libertarian information: http://www.libertarianism.com/

Libertarian Party: http://www.lp.org/

Libertarian Party of Canada/Parti Libertarien du Canada: http://www.libertarian.ca/

Ludwig von Mises Institute: http://www.mises.org/

The Sacco-Vanzetti Project: http://www.saccovanzettiproject.org/

South African Anarchism: http://www.zabalaza.net/

LETS

breadhours.org—What you need, when you need it: http://www.breadhours.org

E.F. Schumacher Society, Local Currency Groups: http://www.schumachersociety.org/cur_grps.html

International Journal of Community Currency Research vols. 1–8 (1997–2004): http://www.le.ac.uk/ulmc/ijccr/

Ithaca Hours Local Currency: http://www.ithacahours.org/

LETS Linkup, International LETS Groups Directory: http://www.lets-linkup.com

LETSLINK UK LETS and Complementary Currencies Development Agency: http://letslinkuk.org/

LETSystems The Home Page: http://www.gmlets.u-net.com/

Project LETS list, a database of community currencies: http://lentils.imagineis.com/letslist/index.html

Transaction Net: LETS—Local Exchange Trading Systems: http://www.transaction.net/money/lets

Vancouver—LETS development: http://www.alternatives.com/lets/

Womanshare: http://www.angelfire.com/ar2/womanshare/

Youth Information: Employment, training and volunteering—Types of work: http://www.youthinformation.com/infopage.asp?snID=371

Homeschooling

A to Z Home's Cool Homeschooling Website: http://homeschooling.gomilpitas.com/

About Homeschooling: Homeschooling Information and Homeschool Resources: http://homeschooling.about.com/

Classical Christian Homeschooling—Classical Education at Home: http://www.classicalhomeschooling.org/

Classical Homeschooling Magazine: http://www.classicalhomeschooling.com/

Eclectic Homeschool Online—A Creative Homeschool Community: http://www.eho.org/

Family Education—Homeschooling: http://familyeducation.com/channel/0,2916,58,00.html

Home Education Magazine: http://www.home-ed-magazine.com/wlcm_HEM.html

Home School Legal Defense Association: http://www.hslda.org/Default.asp?bhcp=1

Homefires, The Journal of Homeschooling Online: http://www.homefires.com/

Homeschool World: http://www.home-school.com

Homeschooling Today: http://www.homeschooltoday.com/

Homeschooling Zone Main Page: http://www.homeschoolzone.com/main.htm

Montessori Homeschooling: http://www.montessori.edu/homeschooling.html

National Home Education Research Institute: http://www.nheri.org/

Pagan Homeschooling—Watching Our Children Grow: http://www.goddessmoon.org/
education/pagan.html

The Teaching Home, a Christian Magazine for Home Education, Written for Homeschooling Families:
http://www.teachinghome.com/

9

⚜

Fascism and National Socialism

Fascism and national socialism are similar enough to be called one ideology, with national socialism best seen as one of a number of varieties of fascism rather than different in kind. Fascism developed early in the twentieth century in France and Italy, and the first successful fascist movement was in Italy in the 1920s. The movements in Germany and Italy before World War II provided the ideological basis for later movements.

For the generation that lived through World War II, the words *fascism, national socialism,* and *Nazism* raise indescribably horrible pictures of brutality and inhumanity. Today the words *fascist* and *Nazi* are used loosely to refer to various authoritarian countries and individuals, but such loose usage obscures both the history and the fact that fascism and national socialism exist today in movements in many countries, including the United States.

THE THEORETICAL BASE

Any discussion of fascism and national socialism must stress the seven ideas listed here. Although the emphasis can vary, these ideas are found in almost all fascist and national socialist writing:

1. Irrationalism
2. Social Darwinism
3. Nationalism

4. Glorification of the state

5. The leadership principle

6. Racism

7. Anticommunism

The first two are basic themes that are rarely explicitly stated. All seven concepts are interrelated but can be separated for analysis.

Irrationalism

Irrationalism permeates the approach of fascism and national socialism but by its nature is difficult to analyze. In the nineteenth and early twentieth centuries, reason and science were the central tenets of liberal and Marxist approaches to social change, and irrationalism specifically rejects those approaches and replaces them with myth, emotion, and hate. National socialism in particular had an affinity for astrology, the occult, and various pseudosciences, and that affinity continues into contemporary neo-Nazi movements.[1]

The basic assumption is that humans are not rational beings, who need not be reasoned with; they can only be led and manipulated. Other ideologies take note of the irrational aspects of human psychology and behavior, but only fascism and national socialism emphasize the irrational and treat it as a central part of the ideology.

The emphasis in national socialism is on myths of blood (racism) and soil (nationalism) and on violence as a constant, normal part of political life. Those who did not fit Hitler's image of racial purity were executed; Jews, homosexuals, and the physically and mentally disabled were specifically targeted.

Paradoxically, racial hatred and intense nationalism are part of the appeal of fascism and national socialism. If you are insecure—financially, socially, or emotionally—an appeal based on racial hatred and intense nationalism, one that promotes a feeling of worth in you as a member of a superior race or nation and that identifies other people as inferior, can be very effective. Fascism and national socialism give a sense of belonging, superiority, and security to those who feel cut off, inferior, or insecure.

Social Darwinism

Social Darwinism is the name generally given to social theories viewing life as a "struggle for survival" within each species as well as between species, with the key to success being the "survival of the fittest"—a phrase first used by Herbert Spencer (1820–1903). In *On the Origin of Species by Means of Natural Selection* (1859), Charles Darwin (1809–82) stated that life evolved through a struggle for survival between species. The social Darwinists took this idea and applied it to

---

[1] See Nicholas Goodrick-Clarke, *The Occult Roots of Nazism: Secret Aryan Cults and Their Influence on Nazi Ideology. The Ariosophists of Austria and Germany, 1890–1935* (New York: New York University Press, 1992); Goodrick-Clarke, *Hitler's Priestess: Savitra Devi, the Hindu–Aryan Myth, and Neo-Nazism* (New York: Oxford University Press, 2000); and Goodrick-Clarke, *Black Sun: Aryan Cults, Esoteric Nazism, and the Politics of Identity* (New York: New York University Press, 2001).

each species. In other words, rather than seeing a struggle for survival *between* species, they saw a struggle for survival *within* each species. Fascists and national socialists applied social Darwinism to their theories of nationalism and racism.[2] Arguing against the social Darwinists, Pyotr Kropotkin (1842–1921), who was discussed in the previous chapter, argued in his book *Mutual Aid* (1902) that there is considerable evidence for cooperation within species.

Nationalism

The most important basic characteristic of fascism and national socialism is nationalism, which was discussed in Chapter 2. The nation is the key unit to which fascists relate, whereas for the national socialist race is the key factor, with the nation second. For the fascist, individuals are primarily members of the nation to which they give all of their loyalty, dedication, and love. The fascist ideal is for the individual to not exist apart from his or her existence in the nation; there is almost no such thing as an individual within fascist ideology. An individual is one small part of the nation, and the individual and the nation are inseparable. Individuals should not be able to conceive of themselves as distinct entities, separate from existence in the nation. People should be completely wrapped up in the nation. Of course, not all fascists felt this strongly, but this was the ideal.

For the national socialist, nationalism and racism were so closely connected that they formed one concept rather than two. For example, among the basic principles on which the national socialists intended to reform the legal system, race is considered the most important:

> The legal protection of the race, which has created a new concept of nationality [*Volkszugehörigkeit*], is consciously put in first place, for the most significant historical principle which has been established by the victory of National Socialism is that of the necessity for keeping race and blood pure. All human mistakes and errors can be corrected except one: "the error regarding the importance of maintaining the basic values of a nation."
>
> The purpose of this legal protection of the basic value of *race* must be the prevention for all time of a further mixture of German Blood with foreign blood, as well as the prevention of continued procreation of racially unworthy and undesirable members of the people.[3]

Many fascists distanced themselves from national socialism on the issue of race. But contemporary fascism tends to have a strong concern with characteristics like ethnicity that sometimes appear to be very similar to race.

---

[2] For further analysis of the role of social Darwinism in national socialism, see Hajo Holborn, "Origins and Political Character of Nazi Ideology," *Political Science Quarterly* 74 (December 1964): 542–54.

[3] Otto Gauweiler, *Rechtseinrichtungen and Rechtsaufgaben der Bewegung* (Munich: Zentralverlag der NSDAP, Franz Eher, Nachfolger, 1939); trans. in *National Socialism: Basic Principles. Their Application by the Nazi Party's Foreign Organization, and the Use of Germans Abroad for Nazi Aims,* prepared in the Special Unit of the Division of European Affairs by Raymond E. Murphy, Francis B. Stevens, Howard Trivers, and Joseph M. Roland (Washington, DC: GPO, 1943), 208–9.

Nonracist fascism holds a strongly nationalist position, usually in connection with the concept of the state. The following statement by Benito Mussolini (1883–1945) is a good example: "The keystone of the Fascist doctrine is the conception of the State, of its essence, of its functions, its aims. For Fascism the State is absolute, individuals and groups relative."[4] Mussolini continued in the same vein, contending that the state is the carrier of the culture and spirit of the people or nation; that it is the past, present, and future; that it represents the "immanent conscience of the nation"; and that it educates the citizens in all the virtues.[5] The nation is embodied in the state; the state brings together the ideas and ideals that form the basis of nationalism.

Glorification of the State

Nationalism and the state cannot be easily separated for the fascist. The state, as Mussolini said, is the carrier of the culture and spirit of the people, the driving force that welds the people together. The state is capable of focusing the spirit of the people and the nationalism of the country. The state, therefore, must be strong; it must have the power necessary to achieve these goals. The state is the vehicle through which the attributes of the nation, the nationality, or the race are expressed. In other words, the people or the nation is the locus of emotion, and the state is the structure through which that emotion is expressed. The theory of the state as presented by fascists and national socialists combines these two notions into the idea of an organic or corporate state. The state, at least as seen by Hitler, is a "rigid formal organization," and the people or the nation is a "living organism."[6]

This conception of the state stresses the continuity of the entire society over generations. In this context, the word *organic* means "social groups as fractions of the species receive thereby a life and scope which transcends the scope and life of the individuals identifying themselves with the history and finalities of the uninterrupted series of generations."[7] Put somewhat differently, this means society, represented by the state, is a separate entity having a life or existence at once different from, and greater than, the life of any individual within that society. This also means (this is the important point) that the life of the individual is less important than the life of the society.

This point is best illustrated by the idea of the folkish state expressed by Hitler in *Mein Kampf:* "Thus, the highest purpose of a *folkish* state is concern for the preservation of those original racial elements which bestow culture and create the beauty and dignity of a higher humanity."[8] The folkish state is a racial

---

[4] Benito Mussolini, "The Doctrine of Fascism," in Mussolini, *Fascism: Doctrine and Institutions* (New York: Howard Fertig, 1968), 27.

[5] Mussolini, "Doctrine of Fascism," 27–28.

[6] Adolf Hitler, *The Speeches of Adolf Hitler, April 1922–August 1939,* ed. Norman H. Baynes (London: Oxford University Press, 1942), 1:178, speech of September 1930.

[7] Alfredo Rocco, "The Political Doctrine of Fascism," trans. D. Bigongiari, *International Conciliation,* no. 223 (October 1926): 402. Some fascists reject the idea that they are presenting the "organic theory of the state."

[8] Adolf Hitler, *Mein Kampf,* trans. Ralph Manheim (Boston: Houghton Mifflin, 1943), 394. Emphasis in the original.

state; only the members of the true Aryan race may participate, but they participate only in the sense of giving of themselves to the state. They do not govern.
The folkish state, then, is a state based on racial purity and on ideas of soil—
myths of racial content connected with the particular history of the German
nation. Here race and nationalism, blood and soil, combine in the folkish state.
An understanding of national socialism as it developed in Germany cannot be
separated from an understanding of race and nationalism and the combination
of the two in a folkish state.

Mussolini said the state is the source of the life of the people of all generations that compose it.[9] The state is owed supreme loyalty by the individuals
who live in it, but the state is also something more than what these somewhat
mechanical notions imply. It is also a "spiritual" unit, but this "spiritual" side is
closely related to the authority controlling the state. The state "enforces discipline and uses authority, entering into the soul and ruling with undisputed
sway."[10] It does this through the leadership principle.

The Leadership Principle

The state is the mechanism for enforcing fascist beliefs, and the state is run on
the *leadership* or *Führer principle,* under which each subordinate owes absolute
obedience to his or her immediate superior, with everyone ultimately subordinate to the absolute leader, the *Führer,* which was Hitler's title. Mussolini's title
was *Il Duce,* which also means "the leader." This hierarchy of leaders with a
single, absolute leader at the top is an important characteristic of fascism and
national socialism. The only limit on the leader's power is that the leader must
reflect the collective will of the people. In practice, this does not limit power
because the leader's will is, by definition, the same as the collective will. "His
will is not the subjective individual will of a single man, but the collective
national will."[11] The leader's authority is absolute. Hitler and Mussolini were
both charismatic leaders able to attract people by sheer force of personality (the
word charismatic comes from *kharisma,* meaning favor or divine gift). Few fascist movements have survived the death of the leader.

The *Führer* principle on which Hitler based his power and organization
seems, on the surface, to be complicated. But it is similar to the notion of a
representative as embodying the will of the constituency, which was discussed
in Chapter 3. Hitler, as leader, was the representative of the German nation and
the Aryan race in that he embodied within himself all the aspirations of the
people. This does not mean that Hitler followed the will of the people, but that
he, by embodying their will, was capable of *rightly* interpreting it. This is the
key to the whole *Führer* principle—the *Führer* is the only one capable of rightly
interpreting the will of the people. When the *Führer* speaks, he represents what

---

[9] Mussolini, "Doctrine of Fascism," 11–12.

[10] Mussolini, "Doctrine of Fascism," 14.

[11] Ernst Rudolf Huber, *Verfassungsrecht des grossdeutschen Reiches* (Hamburg, 1939), 195;
trans. and quoted in *Readings on Fascism and National Socialism* (Denver, CO: Alan Swallow,
1952), 75.

Culver Pictures, Inc.

Adolf Hitler (1889–1945) was founder and leader of the National Socialist German Workers' Party, chancellor (1933–45), and head of state (1934–45) of Germany. He was the leading figure of the Nazi movement and is still venerated as such by Nazis everywhere. He was violently nationalist and anti-Semitic. He was the author of one of the classic texts of national socialism, *Mein Kampf* (1925–27). The swastika on his uniform is the symbol of national socialism. Standing next to him is Benito Mussolini (1883–1945). In this picture he is giving the Nazi salute. Mussolini, known as *Il Duce* (the Leader), ruled Italy from 1922 until shortly before his death.

the people truly want. In this sense he is virtually infallible, and this is clearly how Hitler viewed himself. Hitler as *Führer* could do no wrong.

But no one person, even a *Führer,* can rule an entire country; even an absolute ruler needs some apparatus to enforce rules. This apparatus is the party. Party members in national socialism are separate from and above the rest of the population. Some clearly recognizable sign, such as a uniform, usually identifies them. Finally, there is a corps within this elite to check on the rest of the party. The two groups that served this function within the National Socialist German Workers' Party (the official name of Hitler's party) were the SA (*Sturmabteilung*) and the SS (*Schutzstaffel*). Hitler defined the task of the SA as follows: "The SA on behalf of our German people must educate the young German in mind and body so that he becomes a man hard as steel and ready to fight. Out of hundreds of thousands of individuals it must forge one united, disciplined, mighty organization."[12] The party was the effective ruling mechanism. But as Hitler said, "Every member of the Party has to do what the leader orders."[13]

The word *totalitarian* emerged in the 1920s and 1930s as a way of characterizing governments in Italy under fascism and then Germany under national socialism. It was later extended to the Soviet Union under communism, particularly the regime of Joseph Stalin. It refers to a government that controls or attempts to control the totality of human life and completely subordinates the individual to the state.[14]

---

[12] Adolf Hitler, "Introduction to the Service-Order of the SA," quoted in Hitler, *Speeches,* 1:169.

[13] Hitler, *Speeches,* 1:459, speech of May 21, 1930.

[14] For different perspectives on the concept of totalitarianism, see Carl J. Friedrich, Michael Curtis, and Benjamin R. Barber, *Totalitarianism in Perspective: Three Views* (New York: Praeger, 1969).

In fascism and national socialism the party plays a role similar to that of the Communist Party in Lenin's thought, as discussed in Chapter 7. The party is the vanguard of the nation or the race rather than of the proletariat, but the general notion is the same. The party is the forerunner of the new order to come. The national socialist believes the new order is based on race.

Racism

Probably the single best-known part of national socialism is its racism. The words *racism* and *racist* were first used in the 1930s to refer to the beliefs of the national socialists, and they reflect the belief that the human species can be sub-divided into *races,* or subgroups with similar cultural and/or physical character-istics, and that one of these races is superior to the others. Modern science does not provide support for these beliefs.[15]

For national socialism, racism represents the underlying current of social Darwinism and is a mechanism of social control: negatively by destroying the Jews and others identified by the regime—primarily Gypsies and homosexuals—and thus instilling fear in the Germans, and positively by instilling pride in the Germans in their so-called racial heritage. Nazi policy stressed what was known as both negative and positive eugenics. Negative eugenics was aimed at keeping those perceived to be unfit from having children. Positive eugenics was aimed at encouraging the fit to have children.

Hitler based racism originally on the right of the stronger, and he believed that from the very beginning the Aryan, or Nordic, or white, or sometimes German, race was the strongest. He contended this domination was good for all because it was natural and founded on reason, and ultimately the dominated races would accept it; but the social Darwinian struggle for survival as inter-preted by the national socialists does not include the survival of the dominated races. The national socialist position is that the inferior races will be eliminated, not merely dominated.

The racial policies of Hitler were not limited to extermination and breed-ing. They included the belief that all that is good in culture stems from the Aryan race and that, therefore, the Germans as the representative of the Aryans had the best cultural heritage of the Western world and would have an even better culture in the future. One of Hitler's great loves was the operas of Richard Wagner because Wagner's operas could be seen as operas of the folkish state representing the myths of blood and soil that were so important to Hitler. In particular, they represented what he saw as a high point in German culture—an illustration that the Germans had a great culture and particularly that Wagner, as a representative of German culture, seemed to agree with some of the ideas

---

[15] For the history of the concept and current understandings of race, see Bernard Boxill, ed., *Race and Racism* (Oxford: Oxford University Press, 2001); George M. Fredrickson, *Racism: A Short History* (Princeton, NJ: Princeton University Press, 2002); Joseph L. Graves, Jr., *The Emperor's New Clothes: Biological Theories of Race at the Millennium* (New Brunswick, NJ: Rutgers University Press, 2001); and Paul C. Taylor, *Race: A Philosophical Introduction* (Cambridge, England: Polity, 2004).

put forth by Hitler. Therefore, Hitler was able to present national socialism as a logical outgrowth of German culture and the German nation.

The relationship of the state to racism is seen in *Mein Kampf,* where Hitler wrote, "The state is a means to an end. Its end lies in the preservation and advancement of a community of physically and psychically homogeneous creatures."[16] The effect of racism on other aspects of the society is obvious. For example, social stratification would be based on racial purity and party membership. Also taken into account would be positive support for the regime and contributions to the country. In addition, the racist ideology would control marriage, and the desire to control the minds of children would dictate control of the family system. Along these lines, German women were encouraged to have many children—that is, if they were of the correct racial type. As Goebbels put it, "The mission of woman is to be beautiful and to bring children into the world."[17] German women were also supposed to be athletic and to refrain from wearing makeup or from such things as smoking in public. But, above all, they were to have children. The educational system, the family, and religion were all used to develop the correct values in children. Parents were to teach their children the true national socialist ideas from birth. National socialism also contended God supported it; thus religion was used for the same purpose.[18]

Anticommunism

One aspect of fascism and national socialism that made them acceptable to many was their anticommunism. As one scholar of fascism put it, "Before all else, it was anticommunist. It lived and throve on anticommunism."[19] This was an aspect of fascism's antirationalist approach and its general rejection of the modern world, but it became a significant element in the appeal of fascism.[20]

Fascism and national socialism were not only anticommunist, but also antiintellectual, antirational, and antimodern because they glorified the past with myths of blood and soil. Fascism and national socialism developed first as practice and were never tightly tied together by theory, but their lack of rational coherence is an integral part of the ideologies and part of their rejection of what was seen as the overly intellectual, overly rational approach of communism.

---

[16] Hitler, *Mein Kampf,* 393.

[17] Joseph Goebbels, quoted in Mosse, *Nazi Culture: Intellectual, Cultural, and Social Life in the Third Reich* (New York: Grosset & Dunlap, 1966), 41. A good introduction to the socialization process is Fritz Brennecke, *The Nazi Primer: Official Handbook for Schooling the Hitler Youth,* trans. Harwood L. Childs (New York: Harper & Brothers, 1938; New York: AMS Press, 1972).

[18] A recent book on religion under national socialism is Richard Steigmann-Gall, *The Holy Reich: Nazi Conceptions of Christianity, 1919–1945* (Cambridge: Cambridge University Press, 2003).

[19] H. R. Trevor-Roper, "The Phenomenon of Fascism," in S. J. Woolf, ed., *European Fascism* (New York: Vintage Books, 1969), 24.

[20] See, for example, Alastair Hamilton, *The Appeal of Fascism: A Study of Intellectuals and Fascism 1919–1945* (New York: Macmillan, 1971).

THE ECONOMIC SYSTEM

The economic theory of fascism and national socialism was never developed systematically, and there were marked differences in the countries involved. Even though socialism is part of the name *national socialism* and Mussolini was originally a socialist, neither fascism nor national socialism was actually socialist. National socialism began from that position, but it quickly changed as it gained the support of capitalists.[21] Probably the best statement of the general economic theory of national socialism is this: "All property is common property. The owner is bound by the people and the Reich [government] to the responsible management of his goods. His legal position is only justified when he satisfies this responsibility to the community."[22] Thus property was held privately, but it had to be used as the government dictated or it would be confiscated. The economic system of national socialism clearly states that even though an individual may have temporary control of some economic good (land, capital, or whatever), this control must serve the interests of the collectivity as interpreted by the *Führer,* or the control must be terminated. Here again is the idea of the people as a whole acting for the best interests of the state.

A major concern in the economic theory is to establish economic self-sufficiency. For fascism and national socialism to achieve their goals, the countries involved must be self-sufficient; they must not depend on other countries for supplies.[23] All the stress on the nation, the state, the race, and the people would lose considerable force if these entities were dependent on other nations, states, races, and peoples.

The economic system of fascism includes the idea of state-controlled *syndicates.* The state creates all economic organizations, as the Labour Charter of April 21, 1927, says: "Work in all its forms—intellectual, technical and manual—both organizing or executive, is a social duty. On this score and only on this score, it is protected by the State. From the national standpoint the mass of production represents a single unit; it has a single object, namely, the well-being of individuals and the development of national power."[24] All economic organization under fascism is ultimately controlled by the state and is designed to include both workers and employers in the same organization; this is called *corporatism* or the *corporate economy.* In this way, the state is made superior to every part of the economy. The syndicates are designed to ensure that production continues as long as the state requires it. The right to strike is taken away from the workers, but at the same time the syndicate, operating as an arm of the state, has the power to set wages; thus the syndicate acts as a policymaking arm of the state in economic affairs. As in Germany, the Fascist Party in Italy with Mussolini at the head had ultimate power. In many

---

[21] On this point, see Martin Broszat, *German National Socialism 1919–1945,* trans. Kurt Rosenbaum and Inge Pauli Boehm (Santa Barbara, CA: CLIO Press, 1966), 22–24.

[22] Huber, *Verfassungsrecht,* 372–73, quoted in *Readings on Fascism,* 91.

[23] See the discussion in Paul M. Hayes, *Fascism* (London: George Allen & Unwin, 1973), 89–105.

[24] "The Labour Charter," in Benito Mussolini, *Four Speeches on the Corporate State* (Rome: "Laboremus," 1935), 53.

ways, the syndicates were merely administrative arms of the Fascist Party and of Mussolini rather than having any real power to make decisions. The leadership principle was not abrogated in Italy. It was maintained, and the syndicates acted as lower-level leaders following the dictates of the leader.

CURRENT TRENDS

Neofascism

In the past few years fascism and national socialism have revived in a number of countries, including Germany, Italy, the United Kingdom, Russia, a number of the countries of the former Soviet Union, China, and the United States.[25] In Italy parties associated with fascism have made substantial electoral gains. In Germany direct reference to national socialism is rare, but opposition to immigration has produced groups that are quite similar to early national socialism. This is particularly true in the former East Germany, where the unification of Germany has produced substantial unemployment and poverty in contrast to the obvious wealth of the former West Germany. In the United States a number of groups, most fairly small, either identify with national socialism through the use of its traditional symbols (mostly the swastika) or support social and political traditions closely associated with national socialism.

Although these small groups clearly exist, most of the extreme right political movements are not necessarily fascist, and were discussed under the heading "The Extreme Right" in Chapter 5. If we take the seven points with which the chapter began, most of the movements are anticommunist, racist, and nationalist, but they generally do not stress the other four points. Because anticommunism, racism, and nationalism are the most important of the seven, there is certainly a close affinity between the contemporary extremist groups and fascism, and perhaps that is enough for us to use the word *neofascism* to describe them. Such groups are particularly strong in France, where the National Front led by Jean-Marie Le Pen (b. 1928) has gained considerable electoral success, and in the United States, where various groups on the extreme right continue to flourish.

Some groups in the United States are clearly fascist, and others explicitly align themselves with national socialism. For example, the Creativity Movement, formerly the World Church of the Creator, currently led by Matt Hale (b. 1971), preaches what it calls RAHOWA or RAcial HOly WAr, uses the Nazi salute, and is virulently anti-Semitic.[26] One of its members, Benjamin Nathaniel Smith, killed two people, wounded seven, and shot at many more in Illinois and Indiana on July 4, 1999, before committing suicide. All of his targets and victims were black, Jewish, or ethnic minorities. He was lauded by

---

[25] A. James Gregor, *Phoenix: Fascism in Our Time* (New Brunswick, NJ: Transaction, 1999). See also Peter Davies and Derek Lynch, eds., *The Routledge Companion to Fascism and the Far Right* (London: Routledge, 2002).

[26] On April 6, 2005, Hale was found guilty of soliciting the murder of a Federal judge and sentenced to forty years in prison.

Matt Hale as a "martyr for free speech."[27] The former leader of the National Alliance, William L. Pierce (1933–2002), was once an associate of George Lincoln Rockwell (1918–67), the longtime leader of the American Nazi Party, which still exists, together with other U.S. groups that explicitly align themselves with national socialism. The National Alliance, although experiencing conflicts after Pierce's death, controls a number of white racist music companies and supports various white racist music festivals. It is also closely connected to "skinhead" groups.

Fascism is emerging in Russia, the states of the former Soviet Union, and China. In Austria, Jörg Haider (b. 1950), chairman of the Freedom Party (FPÖ), was briefly a member of a coalition government in 2000 but resigned in part as a result of controversy that arose from his oft-stated sympathies with national socialism. As head of the Freedom Party in that province, he was elected prime minister of Carinthia. In April 2005, Haider resigned his membership in the Freedom Party and founded a new party, the Alliance for the Future of Austria. He intends to remain prime minister of Carinthia, and Freedom Party members serving in the provincial government also resigned from the party and joined the new party. He says that the new party will be less ideological and more pragmatic.

In Europe the issue that seems to most attract people to the neofascist ranks is immigration. The focus of the neofascist right in the United States was, until recently, race followed by internationalism, the power of the Federal Reserve and the Internal Revenue Service, and the perceived desire of the central government to restrict the freedoms of dissenters on the right. But in the past couple of years there has been a growing concern with immigration, with a particular focus on Muslims.

Another issue of interest to neo-Nazi groups around the world is a revival in the Nazi interest in eugenics, brought about in part by the possibility of genetic engineering and cloning. They see the possibility of these new or potential technologies being used for racist purposes.

SUGGESTED READING

Some Classic Works

Hitler, Adolf. *Mein Kampf.* Translated by Ralph Manheim. Boston: Houghton Mifflin, 1943.

Mussolini, Benito. *Four Speeches on the Corporate State.* Rome: "Laboremus," 1935.

——. *My Autobiography.* New York: Scribner, 1928.

Books and Articles

Barkun, Michael. *Religion and the Racist Right: The Origins of the Christian Identity Movement.* Rev. ed. Chapel Hill: University of North Carolina Press, 1997.

Bosworth, R[ichard] J. B. *Mussolini.* London: Arnold, 2002.

Boxill, Bernard, ed. *Race and Racism.* Oxford: Oxford University Press, 2001.

Brennecke, Fritz. *The Nazi Primer: Official Handbook for Schooling the Hitler Youth.* Translated by Harwood L. Childs. New York: Harper & Brothers, 1938; New York: AMS Press, 1972.

---

[27] Duncan Campbell, "Hate Spawned on the Fourth of July," *Guardian* (London), 6 July 1999: 3.

Campbell, Duncan. "Hate Spawned on the Fourth of July." *Guardian* (London), 6 July 1999: 3.

Davies, Peter, and Derek Lynch, eds. *The Routledge Companion to Fascism and the Far Right*. London: Routledge, 2002.

De Grand, Alexander. *Italian Fascism: Its Origin & Development*. 3rd ed. Lincoln: University of Nebraska Press, 2000.

Durham, Martin. *Women and Fascism*. London: Routledge, 1998.

Eatwell, Roger. *Fascism: A History*. London: Chatto & Windus, 1995.

Fraser, Nicholas. *The Voice of Modern Hatred: Tracing the Rise of Neo-Fascism in Europe*. Woodstock, NY: Overlook Press, 2000.

Furet, François, and Ernst Nolte. *Fascism and Communism*. Translated by Katherine Golsan. Lincoln: University of Nebraska Press, 2001.

Gentile, Giovanni. *Origins and Doctrine of Fascism with Selections from Other Works*. Translated and edited by A. James Gregor. New Brunswick, NJ: Transaction Publishers, 2002.

Golsan, Richard J. *Fascism's Return: Scandal, Revision, and Ideology since 1980*. Lincoln: University of Nebraska Press, 1998.

Gonen, Jay Y. *The Roots of Nazi Psychology: Hitler's Utopian Barbarism*. Lexington: University Press of Kentucky, 2000.

Goodrick-Clarke, Nicholas. *Black Sun: Aryan Cults, Esoteric Nazism, and the Politics of Identity*. New York: New York University Press, 2002.

——. *Hitler's Priestess: Savitra Devi, the Hindu–Aryan Myth, and Neo-Nazism*. New York: New York University Press, 1998.

——. *The Occult Roots of Nazism: Secret Aryan Cults and Their Influence on Nazi Ideology. The Ariosophists of Austria and Germany, 1890–1935*. New York: New York University Press, 1992.

Gregor, A. James. *Giovanni Gentile: Philosopher of Fascism*. New Brunswick, NJ: Transaction, 2001.

——. *Interpretations of Fascism*. New Brunswick, NJ: Transaction, 1997.

——. *Phoenix: Fascism in Our Time*. New Brunswick, NJ: Transaction, 1999.

Griffin, Roger. *The Nature of Fascism*. New York: St. Martin's Press, 1991.

——, ed. *Fascism*. Oxford: Oxford University Press, 1995.

——, ed. *International Fascism: Theories, Causes, and the New Consensus*. London: Arnold, 1998.

Guernsey, Lisa. "Mainstream Sites Serve as Portals to Hate." *New York Times*, 30 November 2000: D1, D12.

Hamm, Mark S. *Apocalypse in Oklahoma: Waco and Ruby Ridge Revenged*. Boston: Northeastern University Press, 1997.

Hilliard, Robert L., and Michael C. Keith. *Waves of Rancor: Tuning in the Radical Right*. Armonk, NY: M. E. Sharpe, 1999.

Hitler, Adolf. *The Speeches of Adolf Hitler, April 1922–August 1939*. Edited by Norman H. Baynes. 2 vols. London: Oxford University Press, 1942.

Kallis, Aristotle A.. *Fascist Ideology: Territory and Expansionism in Italy and Germany, 1922–1945*. London: Routledge, 2000.

——, ed. *The Fascism Reader*. London: Routledge, 2003.

Kaplan, Jeffrey, ed. *Encyclopedia of White Power: A Sourcebook on the Radical Racist Right*. Walnut Creek, CA: AltaMira Press, 2000.

Kershaw, Ian. *Hitler*. 2 vols. New York: Norton, 1999–2000.

Kettle, Martin. "Church of Hates Hand Seen in Killing of Gays." *Guardian* (London), 12 July 1999: 13.

Kühl, Stefan. *The Nazi Connection: Eugenics, American Racism, and German National Socialism*. New York: Oxford University Press, 1994.

Lee, Martin. *The Beast Reawakens: Fascism's Resurgence from Hitler's Spymasters to Today's Neo-Nazi Groups and Right-Wing Extremists*. Boston: Little, Brown, 1997.

Mann, Michael. *Fascists*. Cambridge: Cambridge University Press, 2004.

Mariani, Mack. "The Michigan Militia: Political Engagement or Political Alienation?" *Terrorism and Political Violence* 10, no. 4 (Winter 1998): 122–48.

Mosse, George L. *The Crisis of German Ideology: Intellectual Origins of the Third*

Reich. New York: Grosset & Dunlap, 1964.

————. *The Fascist Revolution: Toward a General Theory of Fascism.* New York: Howard Fertig, 1999.

Mussolini, Benito. *Fascism: Doctrine and Institutions.* New York: Howard Fertig, 1968.

————. *My Rise and Fall.* New York: Da Capo Press, 1998.

Nolte, Ernst. *Three Faces of Fascism: Action Française, Italian Fascism, National Socialism.* Translated by Leila Vennewitz. New York: Holt, Rinehart & Winston, 1965.

Paxton, Robert O. *The Anatomy of Fascism.* New York: Alfred A. Knopf, 2004.

Perlmutter, Philip. *Legacy of Hate: A Short History of Ethnic, Religious, and Racial Prejudice in America.* Armonk, NY: M.E. Sharpe, 1999. Rev. ed. of *Divided We Fall: A History of Ethnic, Religious, and Racial Prejudice in America.* Ames: Iowa State University Press, 1992.

Renton, Dave. *Fascism: Theory and Practice.* London: Pluto Press, 1999.

Rocco, Alfredo. "The Political Doctrine of Fascism." Translated by D. Bigongiari. *International Conciliation,* no. 223 (October 1926): 393–415.

Sargent, Lyman Tower, ed. *Extremism: A Reader.* New York: New York University Press, 1995.

Schnapp, Jeffrey T., ed. *A Primer of Italian Fascism.* Translated by Jeffrey T. Schnapp, Olivia E. Sears, and Maria G. Stampino. Lincoln: University of Nebraska Press, 2000.

Shenfield, Stephen D. *Russian Fascism: Traditions, Tendencies, Movements.* Armonk, NY: M.E. Sharpe, 2001.

Simonelli, Frederick J. *American Fuehrer: George Lincoln Rockwell and the American Nazi Party.* Urbana: University of Illinois Press, 1999.

Steigmann-Gall, Richard. *The Holy Reich: Nazi Conceptions of Christianity, 1919–1945.* Cambridge: Cambridge University Press, 2003.

Steinweis, Alan E., and Daniel E. Rogers, eds. *The Impact of Nazism: New Perspectives on the Third Reich.* Lincoln: University of Nebraska Press, 2003.

Viereck, Peter. *Metapolitics: The Roots of the Nazi Mind.* Rev. and enl. ed. New York: Capricorn Books, 1965.

Wolin, Richard. *The Seduction of Unreason: The Intellectual Romance with Fascism from Nietzsche to Postmodernism.* Princeton, NJ: Princeton University Press, 2004.

Websites

American Nazi Party: http://www.americannaziparty.com/

Libertarian National Socialist Green Party: http://www.nazi.org/

National Alliance: http://www.natvan.com/

National Association for the Advancement of White People: http://www.naawp.com/

National Socialist Movement: http://www.nsm88.com/

Panzerfaust Records: http://www.panzerfaust.com/

10

Political Islam

I slam is a religion that has become a major political force in the contemporary world.[1] *Islam* is an Arabic word meaning submission, specifically submission to the will of God or *Allah* (the Arabic word meaning God); *Muslim* means one who submits. Islam is the second largest world religion, after Christianity, with about a billion adherents. They live mostly in a wide belt from Senegal on the west coast of Africa, east to Indonesia on the western edge of the Pacific Ocean, and reaching south into sub-Saharan Africa and north into the southern

---

[1] Islamic political thought has not yet been studied much in the West. The following sources in English include works both for the beginner and for someone wanting some depth. Good places for the neophyte to start are Aziz Al-Azmeh, "Islamic Political Thought," in *Blackwell Encyclopedia of Political Thought,* ed. David Miller (Oxford, England: Blackwell Reference, 1987), 249–53; and Phil Marfleet, "Islamist Political Thought," in *New Political Thought: An Introduction,* ed. Adam Lent (London: Lawrence & Wishart, 1998), 89–111. The best and most recent systematic study is Antony Black, *The History of Islamic Political Thought: From the Prophet to the Present* (New York: Routledge, 2001). Other works to consult include Hamid Enayat, *Modern Islamic Political Thought: The Response of the Shi'i and Sunni Muslims to the Twentieth Century* (London: Macmillan, 1982); Abdulrahman Abdulkadir Kurdi, *The Islamic State: A Study Based on the Islamic Holy Constitution* (London: Mansell, 1984); Bernard Lewis, *The Political Language of Islam* (Chicago: University of Chicago Press, 1988); E. I. J. Rosenthal, *Political Thought in Medieval Islam: An Introductory Outline* (Cambridge: Cambridge University Press, 1962); and W. Montgomery Watt, *Islamic Political Thought: The Basic Concepts* (Edinburgh: Edinburgh University Press, 1968). Some texts can be found in "Political Philosophy in Islam," ed. Muhsin Mahdi, in *Medieval Political Philosophy: A Sourcebook,* ed. Ralph Lerner and Muhsin Mahdi (New York: Free Press, 1963), 22–186; and Kemal H. Karpat, ed., *Political and Social Thought in the Contemporary Middle East,* rev. and enl. ed. (New York: Praeger, 1982).

part of the former Soviet Union. Although many equate Islam with the Arab Middle East, only about 18 percent of Muslims are Arabs, and most Muslims do not speak or read Arabic. About fifty countries are predominantly Islamic, with Indonesia the largest. In addition, Muslim communities are growing throughout the rest of the world, including the United States and Europe.

Similarities of belief among Muslims allow us to identify a community of believers, just as there are similarities of belief among the widely divergent sects of Christianity. But just like Christianity, Islam is not a single, unified religion. There is one major division between two sects, the Sunni with about 85 percent of all Muslims and the Shiite with the other 15 percent, which will be discussed in this chapter; and there are a number of smaller sects. Equally important, there are significant differences in Islamic practice from country to country as well as from individual to individual.

For most of the twentieth century Islam was not a significant political force in world affairs. Most Islamic countries were attempting to modernize and join the developed world. Four things changed this:

1. The establishment of the state of Israel in 1948 on land then occupied by Palestinians united Islamic countries that had been previously divided.

2. The rapid rise in the price of oil made some poor countries suddenly rich.

3. The Iranian revolution, combined with Iranian attempts to foment revolution in other Islamic countries, led to a much greater focus on Islamic thought both in the Middle East and elsewhere.

4. The process of decolonization and the connected revitalization of national cultures revived divisions in Islam that had lain dormant during the colonial period.

Many Muslims reject modernization and Westernization, seeing it as corrupting basic Islamic values. This rejection is most frequently labeled *Islamic fundamentalism*. Although *Islamic revivalism* or *re-Islamization* are better labels because they avoid the too easy identification with Christian fundamentalism, these terms are currently used interchangeably with *Islamic fundamentalism*.[2]

BELIEFS

It is neither possible nor relevant to discuss Islamic theology here, but a few points of religious belief are necessary as background to help understand Islam. Islam is unified by its faith in Allah, the holy book the Qur'an (Koran), and the teachings of its prophet, Muhammad. Islam sprang from the same roots

---

[2] There are fundamentalist currents in Christianity, Hinduism, and Judaism as well as Islam, but the word was first used in 1920 to describe debates within Protestantism in the United States. See Gabriel Almond, R. Scott Appleby, and Emmanuel Sivan, *Strong Religion: The Rise of Fundamentalisms around the World* (Chicago: University of Chicago Press, 2003), 14–17, for a discussion of the word. See also Malise Ruthven, *Fundamentalism: The Search for Meaning* (Oxford: Oxford University Press, 2004).

and the same geographic area as Christianity and Judaism, and Islam accepts the Jewish prophets and Jesus as great religious teachers who were forerunners to Muhammad. Islam, like both Judaism and Christianity, is monotheistic. Christians, Jews, and Muslims are all thought of as "People of the Book."

Every pious Muslim must perform five "pillars" of Islam:

1. In a lifetime the believer must at least once say, "There is no god but God and Muhammad is the messenger of God," in full understanding and acceptance.

2. The believer must pray five times a day (at dawn, noon, midafternoon, dusk, and after dark).

3. The believer must give alms generously.

4. The believer must keep the fast of Ramadan (the ninth month of the Muslim year).

5. The believer must once make the pilgrimage (*hajj*) to Mecca (officially Makkah-tul-Mukarramah, usually shortened to Makkah, but *Mecca* is still used outside Islam).

A sixth pillar is sometimes included, the *jihad,* usually thought of in the West as denoting "holy war" but actually meaning "to struggle" and signifying that believers must struggle with themselves and their communities to be good Muslims and to proselytize to enlarge the Muslim community.[3] Today *jihad* is being used by radical Islamic sects to describe a holy war against the West.

Beyond these basic beliefs and duties, the believer refers for guidance to the *Shari'a* (path or way), the religious law.[4] Islamic law gives both legal and moral guidance and has provided an additional point of reference for the widely divergent cultures represented by the many Islamic countries. For radical Muslims, one central goal is the adoption of the *Shari'a* as the law of the land. Of course, any law requires interpreters, and who is to interpret the law is the basis for certain disagreements within Islam.

Islamic law is derived from the Qur'an, the *Sunna* of the Prophet (the life of Muhammad), legal reasoning, and the consensus of the community.[5] It is more like a set of moral and ethical principles than what Westerners today think of as law; it was, and in many Muslim countries is, interpreted and applied by a variety of courts and officials. In addition, in most countries the *Shari'a* was gradually supplemented and, in the eyes of some, supplanted by laws designed to address changing economic and political conditions.

Islamic countries have traditionally been theocratic (*theo* = God, *kratos* = rule) societies where there is no separation of church and state and politics is subordinate to religion. Part of Islamic liberalism is the result of the political leaders in some countries changing or trying to change that relationship.

---

[3] John L. Esposito, *Islam: The Straight Path,* exp. ed. (New York: Oxford University Press, 1991), 93.

[4] Esposito, *Islam: The Straight Path,* 75–76.

[5] Esposito, *Islam: The Straight Path,* 79–85.

HISTORY

It is impossible to understand contemporary Islam without a little history. Muhammad lived from about A.D. 570 to 632, and the major division in Islam relates to his succession. Most Islamic groups accept that the first four *caliphs* (successors) were correctly chosen. The dispute involves the line of succession after the fourth caliph. The main Shiite sect, the Twelvers (believers in the Twelfth Imam), believe that the correct succession was through the fourth caliph's descendants by his wife Fatima, Muhammad's daughter, through a line of infallible imams—beginning with Ali ben Abi Talib, the fourth caliph, and his two sons to the Twelfth Imam, who disappeared while still a boy. The Twelvers believe that the Twelfth Imam is waiting for the right time to return, when he will bring justice to the earth and overthrow oppression. The Sunni, on the other hand, believe that the caliphs that followed Ali were correctly chosen. They also accept a different basis for the choice—consensus—whereas the Shiites believe in divine appointment.

Although the division between the Sunni and the Shiite is the most important division within Islam, there are many other subgroups. For example, Saudi Arabia is ruled by followers of Wahabism, which was named after Muhammad bin Abd al-Wahab (1703–91), an eighteenth-century clan leader. His descendants unified the country in 1932 and still rule; they consider Wahabism a purified form of Islam. Another important group within Islam is the Sufi, a mystical sect that exists throughout Islam, and there are numerous other distinct sects within Islam.

The Great Mosque, or *Haran,* at Mecca, Saudi Arabia, is the spiritual center of Islam. At the center of the mosque is the Kaaba or Caaba, the most sacred sanctuary in Islam. Mecca and the mosque are the destination of the *hajj,* or the pilgrimage that every Muslim is required to make in his or her lifetime. The towers are minarets, and from them a *muezzin* calls the faithful to prayer five times a day.

It should be clear from this that Islam has gone through a variety of periods of reformation. The Shiites in particular have splintered; the Sunni have followed one of two paths—literalists and those trying to break away from the texts. Literalism is based on the belief that the *Qu'ran* is the unaltered word of God, and the success of the literalists has narrowed the Sunni canon. Sufism has remained, and some of the other schools of thought remain influential.

The great division within Islam that is relevant to the contemporary political situation was brought about by the impact of the West. As with most other colonized areas, Islamic countries went through a process of combined acceptance and rejection of Western values and practices. While it was clear that Western technology, which allowed colonization to take place, was useful, perhaps even necessary, there was a deep division over the acceptance of Western values, particularly those related to individual freedom and equality.

Islamic thought has no concept of individual freedom or rights.[6] The emphasis is on the community of believers rather than the individual. An Islamic government is expected to provide the internal and external security that will allow the believer to worship and earn a living. But these are not rights that an individual can claim against a government. The process of government is dependent on the *Shari'a,* which means that religious teachers and interpreters are very powerful, as was the Imam Khomeini (1900–1989) in Iran during his lifetime.

The ideas of freedom, rights, and equality proved appealing to some believers, however, and groups of Westernizers, Islamic liberals, Islamic socialists, and advocates of women's rights began to appear in the nineteenth and early twentieth centuries. Thus, in practice the ideals of Islam have been challenged and compromised, particularly through contact with the West and its emphasis on individual liberty, the rights of the individual against the state, and the equality of women and men.

ISLAM TODAY

Politically, Islam is deeply divided between those who accept modernization and those who reject it. In the West today we mostly hear about the latter. The primary issue is not technology but the attitudes and beliefs of the West, and the modernizers are under great pressure to reject Western beliefs and attitudes even while encouraging the use of modern technologies.

Islamic Liberalism or Modernism

In the nineteenth and early twentieth centuries Islam went through a lengthy transformation similar to the changes Christianity experienced in the seventeenth through nineteenth centuries. Specifically, Islamic liberal thinkers accepted the

---

[6] Watt, *Islamic Political Thought,* 96. The Arab version of the "Universal Declaration of Human Rights" differs from the English version and has more exceptions; see Ann Elizabeth Mayer, *Islam and Human Rights: Tradition and Politics,* 2nd ed. (Boulder, CO: Westview Press/ London: Pinter Publishers, 1995).

notion of historical change and, in particular, the idea that Islamic texts could be reinterpreted to meet changing conditions. The key texts of Islam have undergone critical analysis by scholars throughout the history of Islam, but today that sort of analysis tends to remain with academics and not penetrate the mosques. There are no seminaries of the "higher criticism."

These thinkers also argued for the reconciliation of reason and faith, religious freedom within Islam, recognition that religious practices need to change to meet changed conditions, the need for educational reform to take advantage of Western science and technology, democracy, and the desirability of greater equality for women.[7] For quite some time and in many countries, Islamic liberalism was dominant. But in the second quarter of the twentieth century a shift began to take place, based on the experience of colonialism, that rejected Islamic liberalism as too Western. The identification of Islamic liberalism with the West and colonialism provided the ideological basis for the emergence of Islamic revivalism.

Islamic liberalism or modernism survives as a strong intellectual force throughout Islam and in movements that stem from the earlier liberal period, but it has made compromises with Islamic revivalism.[8] Today Islamic liberalism or modernism is an active force throughout Islam but is particularly strong in the West.

In Egypt the movement started by Gamal Abdel Nasser (1918–70) still exists but is much less important than it once was, even though the current leaders of Egypt see themselves as the heirs of Nasser. Nasserism was essentially secular but used Islamic symbols. In Libya, Colonel Mu'ammar Gadafi (al-Qaddafi) (b. 1942) established a highly idiosyncratic version of Islam that hides a dictatorship behind most of the policies of Islamic liberalism. In Syria the Baath Party, which was founded in 1940 by Michel Aflaq (1910–89), a Christian, and Salah al-Din Baytar (1911–80), a Muslim, is essentially secular while using Islamic symbols. It rejects both capitalism and communism because both are based on materialism; economically the Baath Party is socialist. Its greatest emphasis, though, is on Arab nationalism and the desirability of a single Arab nation; the party finds Islamic origins for this position.

Intellectually, Islamic liberalism or modernism centers on democratization and what Western intellectuals and a growing number of Islamic scholars see as related issues, freedom and equality, the latter particularly as it relates to the status of women. Although they approach the question from a number of different angles, many Islamic scholars argue that democracy, with its attendant elections and the loss and gain of power, is completely acceptable within Islam as a way of fulfilling the traditional obligation that rulers have to consult widely.[9]

---

[7] See Nader Saiedi, "What Is Islamic Fundamentalism?" in *Prophetic Religions and Politics: Religion and the Political Order,* ed. Anson Shupe and Jeffrey K. Hadden (New York: Paragon House, 1986), 179–82.

[8] See, for example, Charles Kurzman, ed., *Liberal Islam: A Sourcebook* (New York: Oxford University Press, 1998).

[9] See, for example, Azzam Tamimi, ed., *Power-Sharing Islam?* (London: Liberty for Muslim World Publications, 1993), particularly the essays by Rachid Ghannouchi, Muhammad Salim Al-Awa, and Hassan Al-Alkim.

One commentator notes that the Qur'an does not specify a form of government but requires "pursuing justice through cooperation and mutual assistance (49:13, 11:119); establishing a nonautocratic, consultative method of governance; and institutionalizing mercy and compassion in social interactions (6:12, 6:54, 21:107, 27:77, 29:51, 45:20)."[10]

Islamic Revivalism or Fundamentalism

In the West revivalism is usually associated with the Shiites, but revivalism is also strong among the Sunni. Although there are significant differences between Sunni and Shiite revivalists, there are also major agreements. In particular, all revivalists want to reestablish the *Shari'a*, which they believe will result in an Islamic theocracy and full realization of the ideal Islamic community.

The intellectual grounding of Islamic revivalism is usually traced to Ayatollah Ruhollah Khomeini (1900–1989), Abu al-A'la al-Mawdudi (1903–79), and Sayyid Qutb (1906–66). Qutb is best known for the concept of *jahiliyya,* which originally referred to the period of "ignorance" or "barbarism" that existed before Muhammad preached in Arabia. Qutb used *jahiliyya* to refer to the present day, explicitly to the influence of the West. Although these revivalists had serious differences, they all wanted to create theocracies in which Allah delegated political power to the current rulers. In other words, all temporal power was to be held in the name of Allah, and the leader was to be responsible to Allah for his use of that power (none of them could conceive of a woman as a ruler).

The Muslim Brotherhood   The fact that revivalism can combine modernization with rejection of Westernization is demonstrated best by the Muslim Brotherhood (al-Ikhwan al-Muslimun), the first major revivalist movement, founded in 1928 in Egypt by Hasan al-Banna (1906–49). The Muslim Brotherhood, which became one of the most powerful movements ever within Islam and still exists today, emphasizes both a return to Islamic traditions and scientific and technical education. The Muslim Brotherhood also argues for major social and economic reforms within the framework of Islam. In addition, the Brotherhood seeks the unification of all Muslims.

Politics   For Muslims, Allah is the only legislator; any earthly ruler is only to ensure that God's laws are practiced. Therefore, any such ruler is an administrator, not a lawgiver. Sunni and Shiite revivalists disagree on who should rule. The most extreme Sunni believe that a caliph (successor) should administer the Divine Law. Shiite Islam requires the presence of the Mahdi, or Twelfth or Hidden Imam, for the correct government to be established. In his absence a monarch or sultan who rules with the consent of the *ulama*—religious teachers or those who are learned in the divine law—is the best possible solution.

As was seen in Iran under Ayatollah Khomeini, a legislature composed of the *ulama* operating with the advice of an imam (leader) can replace the

[10] Khaled Abou El Fadl, *Islam and the Challenge of Democracy. A Boston Review Book,* ed. Joshua Cohen and Deboarah Chasman (Princeton, NJ: Princeton University Press, 2004), 5.

monarch or sultan, but that legislature is still subordinate to the *Shari'a*. Khomeini believed that the clergy were the appropriate rulers. He also argued that the most preeminent among the clergy—that is, the most learned, just, and pious—should hold the highest office, that of deputy to the Hidden or Twelfth Imam. Khomeini saw himself in that role and was accepted as such.

Social Organization   The traditional, patriarchal family with the man as its head is at the center of the Islamic community. A Muslim man may have up to four wives as long as he can support them. Under the law the testimony of two women is equal to that of one man. However, the Qur'an gives women specific rights. Most important, women can hold and inherit property, although these rights have been frequently violated and some revivalists would like them limited. But women are to function only in the private sphere; only men are to act publicly.

In traditional Islam, which the revivalists want to see reestablished, equality between women and men is impossible—the concept is meaningless. According to one scholar's interpretation, the functions of men and women could be divided into privileges and duties. Men have the privileges of social authority and mobility and the duty of economic responsibility.[11] Women have three privileges:

1. "A woman in traditional Islamic society does not have to worry about earning a living."

2. "A woman does not have to find a husband for herself."

3. A woman "is spared direct military and political responsibility." Her primary duty "is to provide a home for her family and to bring up her children properly."[12]

The Taliban   In September 2001 Americans suddenly became aware of the Taliban (spelled Taleban in the U.K.), an obscure sect of Islam then ruling most of Afghanistan.[13] The word *taliban* means "student," and the movement is sometimes called the "Religious Students' Movement." The goal of the Taliban was to create a pure Islamic state in Afghanistan under its founder and leader Mullah Mohammad Omar Akhund (b. 1959/61).

Although mostly representing one of the many ethnic groups in the country (the Pashtuns, the largest ethnic group in Afghanistan), the Taliban was initially

---

[11] Seyyad Hossein Nasr, *Ideals and Realities of Islam,* 2nd ed. (London: George Allen & Unwin, 1975), 112.

[12] Nasr, *Ideals and Realities of Islam,* 112–13.

[13] On the Taliban, see M. J. Gohari, *The Taliban: Ascent to Power* (Karachi, Pakistan: Oxford University Press, 2000); Peter Marsden, *The Taliban: War, Religion, and the New Order in Afghanistan* (Karachi, Pakistan: Oxford University Press; London: Zed Books, 1998); Kamal Matinuddin, *The Taliban Phenomenon: Afghanistan 1994–1997* (Karachi, Pakistan: Oxford University Press, 1999); Ahmed Rashid, *Taliban: Militant Islam, Oil, and Fundamentalism in Central Asia* (New Haven, CT: Yale University Press, 2000); and *The Taliban's War on Women: A Health and Human Rights Crisis in Afghanistan. A Report by Physicians for Human Rights* (Boston: Physicians for Human Rights, 1998).

very popular because it brought relative peace to a country that had been at war with its neighbors and within itself since 1978. The Soviet Union invaded Afghanistan in 1979 and was finally forced to withdraw in 1988, at which time a struggle for power among various factions within Afghanistan began. The Taliban captured the capital, Kabul, in 1996 and began to enforce its very narrow interpretation of the Islamic rule of law—one in which women must wear the *burqa,* a dress that covers them completely from head to toe, and men must grow beards. Women, in particular, were severely restricted in that few were allowed to work or be educated, and, with almost no women doctors, their access to health care was almost nonexistent.[14] The ultimate goal appears to be to abolish all contemporary political boundaries and reestablish the rule of the caliphs.

After the 2001 U.S. invasion of Afghanistan, the Taliban leaders escaped and remain in hiding either in Afghanistan or in a remote part of neighboring Pakistan. Some areas of Afghanistan are only nominally under the rule of the central government in Kabul, and the Taliban has reestablished its authority in some areas.

ISLAM IN THE UNITED STATES

Islam has deep roots in the United States and is growing rapidly, with about five million adherents (about the same as Lutherans and Mormons); they came mostly from south Asia rather than the Middle East. In fact, 90 percent of Arab Americans are Christian.

Muslims were among the earliest explorers and settlers in North America, but significant numbers began to arrive in the late 1800s, with later waves of immigrants in the periods 1947 to 1960 and 1967 to the present. As a result, there are Islamic communities in the United States that are 100 years old. In addition, many African Americans converted to Islam. This movement began early in the twentieth century, but its greatest growth was in the 1950s and 1960s with the development of the Nation of Islam under the leadership of Elijah Muhammad (1897–1975) and Malcolm X (1925–65). It continues today in a variety of groups that emerged from the Nation of Islam. About 30 percent of the Muslims in America today are African American.

Immigrant Islam

Islam is among the fastest-growing religions in both Europe and the United States. Although estimates of the number of Muslims in the United States vary widely and are considered unreliable, there are more Muslims in the United States than in a number of Islamic countries in the Middle East. In the United States Islam tends to center on local mosques, which generally operate quite independently, although there are the beginnings of a number of regional and countrywide federations of mosques, mostly based on the country of origin of

---

[14] For some of the actual rules, see "A Sample of Taliban Decrees Relating to Women and Other Cultural Issues, after the Capture of Kabul, 1996," in Rashid, *Taliban,* 217–19.

the immigrant community attending the mosques.[15] At present there are about 1,200 mosques in the United States.

Because many Islamic students come to the United States to attend university, there are also a number of Muslim student groups, the Muslim Student Association being the largest. There are also a number of immigrant Islamic sectarian communities.[16] The largest and best established of these is the Sufi.

American Muslims have the full range of immigrant responses that have been experienced by immigrants of other faiths. Some return to the home country (sometimes with the idea of building an Islamic state); others work to establish Islamic communities in the United States so that it will be possible to live an Islamic life within the United States; and yet others assimilate. As with other immigrants, the second and third generations tend toward the third option, but often, again as with other immigrants, with the desire to reconnect with their national and religious roots.[17] An indication of the adjustment to U.S. conditions is that women now head the boards running two mosques in the United States. It is, of course, entirely possible that the attacks on Muslims in the United States since September 11, 2001, will produce future terrorists of people who were good, loyal American citizens until they and their fellow Muslims were targeted by U.S. ethnic nationalists.

African American Islam

African Americans have been affiliated with Islam from at least 1913, when the Moorish American Science Temple was founded in Newark, New Jersey. But African American Islam is most commonly identified with the Nation of Islam (better known as the Black Muslims), which was a direct response to the conditions of African Americans in the twentieth century in the United States. As taught by Elijah Muhammad, the Nation of Islam combined traditional Islamic teachings with an interpretation of the African American experience in the United States that saw whites as the devil.

---

[15] On Islam in America, see Yvonne Yazbeck Haddad and Jane Idleman Smith, *Mission to America* (Gainesville: University Press of Florida, 1993), which discusses Islamic groups in America outside the mainstream; Haddad and Smith, eds., *Muslim Communities in North America* (Albany: State University of New York Press, 1994), a collection of essays on many specific Muslim communities in the United States and Canada; Haddad, ed., *The Muslims of America* (New York: Oxford University Press, 1991); Gilles Kepel, *Allah in the West: Islamic Movements in America and Europe*, trans. Susan Milner (Stanford, CA: Stanford University Press, 1997); Michael A. Koszegi and J. Gordon Melton, eds., *Islam in North America: A Sourcebook* (New York: Garland, 1992); Jane I. Smith, *Islam in America* (New York: Columbia University Press, 1999); and Earle H. Waugh, Sharon McIrvin Abu-Laban, and Regula Burckhardt Qureshi, eds., *Muslim Families in North America* (Calgary: University of Alberta Press, 1991).

[16] For a list of Islamic organizations in North America, see the Suggested Reading and "A Directory of Islamic Organizations and Centers in North America," in Koszegi and Melton, *Islam in North America*, 291–395. For a list of Internet sources (though be aware that many of these will have changed), see Smith, *Islam in America*, 225–26.

[17] On the immigrant experience, see Yvonne Yazbeck Haddad and Adair T. Lummis, *Islamic Values in the United States: A Comparative Study* (New York: Oxford University Press, 1987); Haddad and John L. Esposito, eds., *Muslims: The New Generation* (New York: Continuum, 2000).

After the death of Elijah Muhammad and the assassination of Malcolm X, who, after a pilgrimage to Mecca, rejected the racial message of the Nation of Islam, the Nation of Islam fragmented. One of Elijah Muhammad's sons, Warith Deen Mohammad (b. 1933), rejected the racial message of his father, decentralized the organization, changed its name to the American Muslim Mission, and encouraged African American Muslims to join mainstream Islam. The best-known contemporary descendent of the Nation, Louis Farrakhan (b. 1933), kept both the name and centralized structure of the Nation of Islam and, although not consistently, has kept at least some of its racial message.[18]

CURRENT TRENDS

Looked at internationally, Islam today is remarkably diverse, with advocates of capitalism and socialism, authoritarianism and democracy, feminism and antifeminism all within its boundaries. But the issue that has the greatest potential for bringing about change in Islam is the movement to develop an Islam appropriate for Muslims living in the West. The primary theorist of this position, Tariq Ramadan (b. 1962), who had been hired to teach at Notre Dame, had his visa revoked just days before he and his family were to move to the United States from Switzerland. Ramadan argues for a Western Islam tied to the classic roots of Islam; he also argues that Western Islam is beginning to influence Muslims throughout the entire Islamic world.

Ramadan says that the social message of Islam includes the following:

1. The right to life and the minimum necessary to sustain it
2. The right to family
3. The right to housing
4. The right to education
5. The right to work
6. The right to justice
7. The right to solidarity or the right to participate in social life[19]

The arguments of Ramadan and a growing group of Islamic theorists and theologians for an Islam that fits the West illustrates the revival of Islamic modernism in a form that aims at remaining true to Islam while adjusting to the West.

Other issues include the status of women. In the West, probably the best-known aspect of traditional Islam is the veiling of women. Veiling—which can

[18] On the Nation of Islam, see Essien Udosen Essien-Udom, *Black Nationalism: A Search for Identity in America* (Chicago: University of Chicago Press, 1962); Mattias Gardell, *In the Name of Elijah Muhammad: Louis Farrakhan and the Nation of Islam* (Durham, NC: Duke University Press, 1996); C. Eric Lincoln, *The Black Muslims in America* (Boston: Beacon Press, 1973); and Vibert L. White, Jr., *Inside the Nation of Islam: A Historical and Personal Account by a Black Muslim* (Gainesville: University Press of Florida, 2001).

[19] Tariq Ramadan, *Western Muslims and the Future of Islam* (Oxford: Oxford University Press, 2004), 149–52. (In italics in original.)

range from a scarf covering the hair to the *burqa* required by the Taliban—is not found in the Qur'an but developed differently within the different Islamic countries. In fact, most of the rules that keep women in an inferior position in some Islamic countries are not found in either the Qur'an or the *Shari'a*. As a result, Islamic feminists argue that there are strong grounds for an Islamic version of female–male equality. It must be recognized, though, that many modern Islamic women accept the veil or scarf covering the head as a way of respecting their religion; for many it is definitely not a symbol of inferiority.[20]

It is difficult to generalize about Islam. For example, in March 2001 I flew from New Zealand to Europe and back on Air Malaysia, and I spent a few hours in each direction waiting in the airport in Kuala Lumpur. Malaysia is an Islamic country, and one of the most striking things in the airport was that women, both those working in the airport and those traveling, wore clothes that ranged from blue jeans and short skirts to complete coverings, including face masks or the *burqa*.

Today the issue in France and Turkey is not the *burqa* but the scarf. Both countries are legally secular countries, and France has banned the use of any obvious religious symbols in schools. While the rule includes such Christian symbols as large crosses, it is clearly aimed at the scarves worn by some Islamic girls. Turkey, which illustrates that a country can be both Islamic and secular, has banned the wearing of such scarves in its legislative assembly and removed a duly elected woman member because she wore one. In both cases, protests and negotiations continue.

An issue that reemerges regularly is the extent to which Islamic law or the *Shari'a* should replace the legal codes currently in place. Most of these codes are based on Western models, either left over from colonial times or put into place by the first postindependence governments; putting the *Shari'a* in place would serve the dual purpose of rejecting the West and enhancing the Islamic identity of the country. But non-Muslims are afraid that they will lose the rights they had under the previous codes and become an oppressed minority. In Nigeria and a growing number of other countries, this dispute has led to sporadic violence.

Another issue is the dominance of the Middle East in training Islamic religious leaders. The typical pattern in founding a mosque in the West is that a small group gets together (often including both men and women) and rotates leading the prayers or chooses a member who is thought to be wise; the group buys a house or some other building and continues the community-based services. Then the group decides it wants a "proper" mosque with an imam. Mosques tend to be funded by Saudi Arabia or other Gulf states, and the imams are mostly trained in the Gulf and brought from there to mosques around the world. Even if the mosque is funded locally, the imam usually comes from the Arab world because Saudi Arabia and other Gulf states are willing to both pay to build a mosque almost anywhere in the world and pay the imam. Having trained in the conservative Islam of that region, the imam changes the entire pattern of

---

[20] On veiling specifically, see Fadwa El Guindi, *Veil: Modesty, Privacy, and Resistance* (Oxford, England: Berg, 1999); and Nancy J. Hirschmann, "Eastern Veiling, Western Freedom?" *Review of Politics* 59, no. 3 (summer 1997): 461–88.

behavior in the mosque. Islam is multicultural and multilinguistic, but given the Middle Eastern funding, much of the preaching is in Arabic and not understood by the average members. I have been told of a mosque where the imam speaks in Arabic, which is translated into the local language (English in this case) by someone who regularly skips those parts of the imam's talk thought to be too radical for the members.

Some Western Muslims believe that change can come from two sources. The first is a growing feminist movement within Islam, which insists that Islam must not reflect the ancient practices of particular ethnic groups but become a religion of all its believers. The second is Sufism, which although rejected by the many extremists, is generally respected by Muslims of all persuasions. Thus it is felt that Sufis may be able to help reconcile believers and reject the extremes. At present, there is no evidence of this actually happening, and mystics are rarely political leaders.

For most people in the West, Islam is still identified with the radical fringe of the religion and with terrorism. In a real sense, this is simply wrong. Islam is a rich and varied religion, and we should not identify one small part of it as the whole. At the same time, it is hard for most people in the West, who know little or nothing about Islam, to get beyond the daily news and understand that such events represent groups that are rejected by the majority of believers.

SUGGESTED READING

Some Classic Works

Ahmad, Jalal Al-E. *Gharbzadegi (Weststruckness)*. Translated by John Green and Ahmad Alizadeh. Lexington, KY: Mazdâ Publishers, 1982. Rpt. with the title *Occidentosis: A Plague from the West*. Berkeley, CA: Mizan Press, 1984.

Banisadr, Asbolhassan. *The Fundamental Principles and Precepts of Islamic Government*. Translated by Mohammad R. Ghanoonparvar. Lexington, KY: Mazdâ Publishers, 1981.

El Saadawi, Nawal. *The Hidden Face of Eve: Women in the Arab World*. Translated and edited by Sherif Hetata. London: Zed Books, 1980.

Hourani, Albert. *Arabic Thought in the Liberal Age 1798–1939*. London: Oxford University Press. Issued under the auspices of the Royal Institute of International Affairs, 1967.

Khomeini, Ayatollah Sayyed Ruhollah Mousavi. *Islam and Revolution*. Translated by Hamid Algar. Berkeley, CA: Mizan Press, 1981.

————. *Islamic Government*. Translated by Joint Publications Research Service. New York: Manor Books, 1979.

The Koran. With Parallel Arabic Text. Translated by N. J. Dawood. London: Penguin Books, 1990.

Books and Articles

Abdo, Geneive. *No God but God: Egypt and the Triumph of Islam*. Oxford: Oxford University Press, 2000.

Abou El Fadl, Khaled. *Islam and the Challenge of Democracy. A Boston Review Book*. Edited by Joshua Cohen and Deborah Chasman. Princeton, NJ: Princeton University Press, 2004. Statement of the democratic aspects of Islam and comments.

Abrahamian, Ervand. *Khomeinism: Essays on the Islamic Republic*. Berkeley: University of California Press, 1993.

Abu-Hamdiyyah, Mohammad. *The Qur'an—An Introduction*. London: Routledge, 2000.

Abu-Rabi', Ibrahim M. *Intellectual Origins of Islamic Resurgence in the Modern Arab World.* Albany: State University of New York Press, 1996.

Abu Zaid, Nasr, with Esther R. Nelson. *Voice of an Exile: Reflections on Islam.* Westport, CT: Praeger. 2004.

Afshar, Haleh. *Islam and Feminisms: An Iranian Case Study.* London: Macmillan; New York: St. Martin's Press, 1998.

———, ed. *Women and Politics in the Third World.* London: Routledge, 1996.

Ahmad, Khurshid. *Islam: Its Meaning and Message.* 2nd ed. Leicester, England: The Islamic Foundation, 1976. Conservative; includes articles by some of the founders of fundamentalism like Qutb and Mawdudi.

Ahmed, Akbar S. *Islam Today: A Short Introduction to the Muslim World.* London: I. B. Tauris, 1999.

AlSayyad, Nezar, and Manuel Castells, eds. *Muslim Europe or Euro-Islam: Politics, Culture, and Citizenship in the Age of Globalization.* Lanham, MD: Lexington Books, 2002.

Baker, Raymond William. *Islam without Fear: Egypt and the New Islamists.* Cambridge, MA: Harvard University Press, 2003. Liberal Islam.

Barlas, Asma. *"Believing Women" in Islam: Unreading Patriarchal Interpretations of the Qur'an.* Austin: University of Texas Press, 2002. Argues that the Qur'an is radically egalitarian and antipatriarchal.

Black, Antony. *The History of Islamic Political Thought: From the Prophet to the Present.* New York: Routledge, 2001.

Blank, Jonah. *Mullahs on the Mainframe: Islam and Modernity among the Daudi Bohras.* Chicago: University of Chicago Press, 2001. A community of Sh'ite Muslims in south Asia but with members throughout the world balance traditional Islam and the modern world.

Brown, Daniel. *A New Introduction to Islam.* Malden, MA: Blackwell, 2004.

Brown, L. Carl. *Religion and State: The Muslim Approach to Politics.* New York: Columbia University Press, 2000.

Brumberg, Daniel. *Reinventing Khomeini: The Struggle for Reform in Iran.* Chicago: University of Chicago Press, 2001. Argues that Khomeini was sufficiently vague that all the current factions can legitimately draw from him.

Butterworth, Charles E., and I. William Zartman, eds. *Between the State and Islam.* Washington, DC: Woodrow Wilson Center Press; Cambridge: Cambridge University Press, 2001.

Choueiri, Youssef. *Arab Nationalism: A History. Nation and State in the Arab World.* Oxford, England: Blackwell, 2000.

Cook, Michael. *Forbidding Wrong in Islam.* Cambridge: Cambridge University Press, 2001. This is a summary for the general reader of Cook, *Commanding Right and Forbidding Wrong in Islamic Thought.* Cambridge: Cambridge University Press, 2000.

———. *The Koran: A Very Short Introduction.* Oxford: Oxford University Press, 2000.

Davidson, Lawrence. *Islamic Fundamentalism.* Rev. and updated ed. Westport, CT: Greenwood Press, 2003.

DeLong-Bas, Natana J. *Wahhabi Islam: From Revival and Reform to Global Jihad.* New York: Oxford University Press, 2004.

Diamond, Larry; Marc F. Plattner; and Daniel Brumberg, eds. *Islam and Democracy in the Middle East.* Baltimore, MD: Johns Hopkins University Press, 2003.

El Guindi, Fadwa. *Veil: Modesty, Privacy, and Resistance.* Oxford, England: Berg, 1999.

Ernst, Carl W. *Following Muhammad: Rethinking Islam in the Contemporary World.* Chapel Hill: University of North Carolina Press, 2003. Islam as a religion.

Esposito, John L. *The Islamic Threat: Myth or Reality.* 3rd ed. New York: Oxford University Press, 1999.

———. *The Oxford Encyclopedia of the Modern Islamic World.* 4 vols. New York: Oxford University Press, 1995.

———. *What Everyone Needs to Know about Islam.* Oxford: Oxford University Press, 2003. Questions and short answers.

————, ed. *The Oxford History of Islam.* New York: Oxford University Press, 1999.

Esposito, John L., and John O. Voll. *Makers of Contemporary Islam.* Oxford: Oxford University Press, 2001.

Essien-Udom, Essien Udosen. *Black Nationalism: A Search for Identity.* Chicago: University of Chicago Press, 1962.

Euben, Roxanne L. *Enemy in the Mirror: Islamic Fundamentalism and the Limits of Modern Rationalism. A Work of Comparative Political Theory.* Princeton, NJ: Princeton University Press, 1999.

Fluehr-Lobban, Carolyn, ed. *Against Islamic Extremism: The Writings of Muhammad Sa'id al-'Ashmawy.* Gainesville: University Press of Florida, 1998. Secularist (former chief justice of the High Court of Cairo); opposes politicizing Islam and violence as a political tool. Al-'Ashmawy calls himself a humanist.

Foltz, Richard C., Frederick M. Denny, and Azizan Baharuddin, eds. *Islam and Ecology: A Bestowed Trust.* Cambridge, MA: Harvard University Press for the Center for the Study of World Religions, Harvard Divinity School, 2003. Collection of essays arguing that Islam is ecologically sensitive. The argument is that the Prophet prohibited wastefulness, which led to many rulings on water management that could be extended to other resources. Others argue that sustainability is a basic tenet. The Prophet encouraged planting trees, even on doomsday.

Fuller, Graham E. *The Future of Political Islam.* New York: PalgraveMacmillan, 2003.

Gardell, Mattias. *In the Name of Elijah Muhammad: Louis Farrakhan and the Nation of Islam.* Durham, NC: Duke University Press, 1996.

Gerges, Fawaz A. *America and Political Islam: Clash of Cultures or Clash of Interests?* Cambridge: Cambridge University Press, 1999.

Gohari, M. J. *The Taliban: Ascent to Power.* Karachi, Pakistan: Oxford University Press, 2000.

Goodson, Larry P. *Afghanistan's Endless War: State Failure, Regional Politics, and the Rise of the Taliban.* Seattle: University of Washington Press, 2001.

Goody, Jack. *Islam in Europe.* Cambridge, England: Polity, 2004.

Haddad, Yvonne Yazbeck. *Muslims in the West.* Oxford: Oxford University Press, 2002.

————, ed. *The Muslims of America.* New York: Oxford University Press, 1991.

Haddad, Yvonne Yazbeck, and John L. Esposito, eds. *Islam, Gender, and Social Change.* New York: Oxford University Press, 1998.

————, eds. *Muslims on the Americanization Path?* Atlanta: Scholars Press, 1998.

Haddad, Yvonne Yazbeck, and John L. Esposito, with Elizabeth Hiel and Hibba Abugideiri. *The Islamic Revival since 1988: A Critical Survey and Bibliography.* Westport, CT: Greenwood Press, 1997.

Haddad, Yvonne Yazbeck, and Adair T. Lummis. *Islamic Values in the United States: A Comparative Study.* New York: Oxford University Press, 1987.

Haddad, Yvonne Yazbeck, and Jane Idleman Smith. *Mission to America: Five Islamic Sectarian Communities in North America.* Gainesville: University Press of Florida, 1993.

————, eds. *Muslim Communities in North America.* Albany: State University of New York Press, 1994.

————, eds. *Muslim Minorities in the West: Visible and Invisible.* Walnut Creek, CA: Alta Mira, 2002.

Halliday, Fred. *Nation and Religion in the Middle East.* Boulder, Colo.: Lynne Rienner, 2000.

Hasan, Asma Gull. *American Muslims: The New Generation.* 2nd ed. with study guide. New York: Continuum, 2002.

Hassan, Riaz. *Faithlines: Muslim Conceptions of Islam and Society.* Oxford: Oxford University Press, 2002.

Hekmat, Anwar. *Women and the Koran: The Status of Women in Islam.* Amherst, NY: Prometheus Books, 1997.

Kepel, Gilles. *Allah in the West: Islamic Movements in America and Europe.* Translated by Susan Milner. Stanford, CA: Stanford University Press, 1997. Originally published as *A l'Ouest d'Allah* (Paris: Éditions du Seuil, 1994).

————. *Jihad: The Trail of Political Islam.* Translated by Anthony F. Roberts. Cambridge, MA: Belknap Press of Harvard University Press, 2002.

Khadduri, Majid. *The Islamic Conception of Justice.* Baltimore: Johns Hopkins University Press, 1984.

Khuri, Richard K. *Freedom, Modernity, and Islam: Toward a Creative Synthesis.* Syracuse, NY: Syracuse University Press, 1998.

Koszegi, Michael A., and J. Gordon Melton, eds. *Islam in North America: A Sourcebook.* New York: Garland, 1992.

Kurzman, Charles, ed. *Liberal Islam: A Sourcebook.* New York: Oxford University Press, 1998.

Lapidus, Ira M. *A History of Islamic Societies.* 2nd ed. Cambridge: Cambridge University Press, 2002.

Lawrence, Bruce B. *Shattering the Myth: Islam beyond Violence.* Princeton, NJ: Princeton University Press, 1998.

Lee, Martha F. *The Nation of Islam: An American Millenarian Movement.* Lewiston, NY: Edward Mellen Press, 1988. Reprint, Syracuse, NY: Syracuse University Press, 1996.

Leonard, Karen Isaksen. *Muslims in the United States: The State of Research.* New York: Russell Sage Foundation, 2003.

Lincoln, C. Eric. *The Black Muslims of America.* 3rd ed. Grand Rapids, MI: W.B. Eerdmans; Trenton, NJ: Africa World Press, 1994.

Malcolm X. *The Autobiography of Malcolm X.* New York: Grove Press, 1965.

Mamdani, Mahmood. *Good Muslim, Bad Muslim: America, the Cold War, and the Roots of Terror.* New York: Pantheon Books, 2004.

Marfleet, Phil. "Islamist Political Thought." In *New Political Thought: An Introduction,* edited by Adam Lent, 89–111. London: Lawrence & Wishart, 1998.

Martin, Vanessa. *Creating an Islamic State: Khomeini and the Making of a New Iran.* New ed. London: I.B. Tauris, 2003. On Khomeini's political theory.

Strong, centralized government capable of ensuring an Islamic state (theocracy).

Mayer, Ann Elizabeth. *Islam and Human Rights: Tradition and Politics.* 3rd ed. Boulder, CO: Westview Press, 1999.

Mernissi, Fatima. *Beyond the Veil: Male–Female Dynamics in Modern Muslim Society.* Rev. ed. Bloomington: Indiana University Press, 1987.

Messaoudi, Khalida. *Unbowed: An Algerian Woman Confronts Islamic Fundamentalism.* Interviews with Elisabeth Schemla. Translated by Anne C. Vila. Philadelphia: University of Pennsylvania Press, 1998. Originally published as *Une Algérienne Debout* (Paris: Flammarion, 1995).

Moaddel, Mansoor, and Kamran Talattof, eds. *Contemporary Debates in Islam: An Anthology of Modernist and Fundamentalist Thought.* New York: St. Martin's Press, 2000.

Moghissi, Haideh. *Feminism and Islamic Fundamentalism: The Limits of Postmodern Analysis.* London: Zed Books, 1999.

Moin, Baqer. *Khomeini: Life of the Ayatollah.* New York: Thomas Dunne Books, 1999.

Moses, Wilson Jeremiah, ed. *Classical Black Nationalism: From the American Revolution to Marcus Garvey.* New York: New York University Press, 1996.

Moussalli, Ahmad S. *Moderate and Radical Islamic Fundamentalism: The Quest for Modernity, Legitimacy, and the Islamic State.* Gainesville: University Press of Florida, 1999.

Norton, Augustus Richard, ed. *Civil Society in the Middle East.* 2 vols. Leiden, The Netherlands: E. J. Brill, 1995–96.

Physicians for Human Rights. *The Taliban's War on Women: A Health and Human Rights Crisis in Afghanistan. A Report by Physicians for Human Rights.* Boston: Author, 1998.

Pipes, Daniel. *Miniatures: Views of Islamic and Middle Eastern Politics.* New Brunswick, NJ: Transaction, 2004.

Qureshi, Emran, and Michael A. Sells, ed. *The New Crusades: Constructing the Muslim Enemy.* New York: Columbia University Press, 2003.

Rahnema, Ali. *An Islamic Utopian: A Political Biography of Ali Shari'ati.* London: I.B. Tauris, 1998.

———, ed. *Pioneers of Islamic Revival.* London: Zed Books, 1994.

Ramadan, Tariq. *Western Muslims and the Future of Islam.* Oxford: Oxford University Press, 2004.

Rashid, Ahmed. *Taliban: Militant Islam, Oil, and Fundamentalism in Central Asia.* New Haven, CT: Yale University Press, 2000.

Roberson, B.A., ed. *Shaping the Current Islamic Reformation.* London: Frank Cass, 2003.

Robinson, Dean E. *Black Nationalism in American Politics and Thought.* Cambridge: Cambridge University Press, 2001.

Rouse, Carolyn Moxley. *Engaged Surrender: African American Women and Islam.* Berkeley: University of California Press, 2004.

Ruthven, Malise. *Islam: A Very Short Introduction.* Oxford: Oxford University Press, 1997.

Sadri, Mahmoud, and Ahmad Sadri, eds. and trans. *Reason, Freedom, and Democracy in Islam: Essential Writings of 'Abdolkarim Soroush.* Oxford: Oxford University Press, 2000. Tries to combine reason and faith, spiritual authority and political liberty.

Safi, Omid, ed. *Progressive Muslims on Gender, Justice, and Pluralism.* Oxford, England: Oneworld, 2003.

Saliba, Therese, Carolyn Allen, and Judith A. Howard, eds. *Gender, Politics, and Islam.* Chicago: University of Chicago Press, 2002.

Sciolino, Elaine. *Persian Mirrors: The Elusive Face of Islam.* New York: Free Press, 2000.

Shadid, Anthony. *Legacy of the Prophet: Despots, Democrats, and the New Politics of Islam.* Boulder, CO: Westview, 2001.

Shay, Shaul. *The Shahids: Islam and Suicide Attacks.* Translated by Rachel Lieberman. New Brunswick, NJ: Transaction, 2004.

Shehadeh, Lamia Rustum. *The Idea of Women in Fundamentalist Islam.* Gainesville: University Press of Florida, 2003.

Sidahmed, Abdel Salam, and Anoushiravan Ehteshami, eds. *Islamic Fundamentalism.* Boulder, CO: Westview, 1996.

Smith, Jane I. *Islam in America.* New York: Columbia University Press, 1999.

Suleiman, Yasir. *A War of Words: Language and Conflict in the Middle East.* Cambridge: Cambridge University Press, 2004.

Tamimi, Azzam, ed. *Power-Sharing Islam?* London: Liberty for Muslim World Publications, 1993.

Tamimi, Azzam, and John L. Esposito, eds. *Islam and Secularism in the Middle East.* New York: New York University Press, 2000.

Tibi, Bassam. *The Challenge of Fundamentalism: Political Islam and the New World Disorder.* Updated ed. Berkeley: University of California Press, 2002. Strongly antifundamentalist from an Islamic perspective.

Turner, Richard Brent. *Islam in the African American Experience.* 2nd ed. Bloomington: Indiana University Press, 2003.

Van Deburg, William L., ed. *Modern Black Nationalism: From Marcus Garvey to Louis Farrakhan.* New York: New York University Press, 1997.

Wadud-Muhsin, Amina. *Qur'an and Woman.* 2nd ed. New York: Oxford University Press, 2001.

Waines, David. *An Introduction to Islam.* 2nd ed. Cambridge: Cambridge University Press, 2003.

Waugh, Earle H., Baha Abu-Laban, and Regula B[urckhardt] Qureshi, eds. *The Muslim Community in North America.* Calgary: University of Alberta Press, 1983.

Waugh, Earle H., Sharon McIrvin Abu-Laban, and Regula Burckhardt Qureshi, eds. *Muslim Families in North America.* Calgary: University of Alberta Press, 1991.

Waugh, Earle H., and Frederick M. Denny, eds. *The Shaping of an American Islamic Discourse: A Memorial to Fazlur Rahman.* Atlanta: Scholars Press, 1998.

Webb, Gisela. "Expressions of Islam in America." In *America's Alternative Religions,* edited by Timothy Miller, 233–42. Albany: State University of New York Press, 1995.

————. "Sufism in America." In *America's Alternative Religions,* edited by Timothy Miller, 249–58. Albany: State University of New York Press, 1995.

White, Vibert L. Jr. *Inside the Nation of Islam: A Historical and Personal Account by a Black Muslim.* Gainesville: University Press of Florida, 2001.

Websites

Dar al Islam: http://www.daralislam.org/

Islam in America: http://global.globale.net/~mag/

Islamcity news, shopping, and contact site for African American Muslims: http://www.islamiccity.com

Liberal Islam: http://www.unc.edu/~kurzman/LiberalIslamLinks.htm

Osama bin Laden, World Islamic Front Statement: http://www.fas.org/irp/world/para/docs/980223-fatwa.htm

Muslim Organizations in the United States

Ahmadiyyas: Ahmadiyya Muslim Community: http://www.alislam.org/

American Muslim Alliance (AMA): http://www.amaweb.org/

American Muslim Council (AMC): See the American Muslim Council, Chicago Chapter: http://www.amcchicago.org/index.asp

Council on American-Islamic Relations (CAIR): http://www.cair-net.org/default.asp

Federation of Islamic Associations (FIA: has been disassociated from the Department of Public Information at the UN because it "no longer meets the criteria for associations"): http://www.islamerica.com/

International Sufi Movement, America: http://www.universalsufism.com/

Islamic Assembly of North America: http://www.iananet.org/

Islamic Center of North America: http://www.icofa.com/

Islamic Circle of North America (ICNA): http://www.icna.org/

Islamic Foundation of North America: http://www.islamicedfoundation.com/

Islamic Society of North America (ISNA): http://www.isna.net/

Moorish Science Temple: No website, but they have their interpretation of the Koran online: http://www.hermetic.com/bey/7koran.html.

Muslim Public Affairs Council (MPAC): http://www.mpac.org/

Muslim Students' Association (MSA)/MSA of the United States and Canada: http://www.msa-natl.org/

Nation of Islam: http://www.noi.org/

11

⚜

Liberation Theology

L iberation Theology began as a movement within the Roman Catholic Church in Latin America and is now a worldwide movement found within most Christian denominations. As a movement it struggled to define itself against the opposition of most of the church hierarchy in Latin America and against the opposition of the papacy, particularly that of Pope John Paul II (1920–2005; elevated to the papacy in 1978). From these roots Liberation Theology spread to Protestantism and to Africa, Asia, Ireland, and the United States. Because of the continuing opposition of the Roman Catholic Church, today Liberation Theology may be most dynamic in Protestantism, particularly in Black Theology in the United States; but it remains of great significance, although quietly, within Roman Catholicism, particularly in Latin America. In addition, Christian women throughout the world have been inspired by Liberation Theology while also finding it lacking sensitivity to women's issues. These women have spoken of the need to "engender" Liberation Theology and have, largely, succeeded in doing so. Coordination among liberation theologies is provided by the Ecumenical Association of Third World Theologians (EATWOT).

Liberation Theology has a conflicted relationship with European theology, which clearly provided some of its ideas and early thinkers. Particularly outside Latin America, the European, or in the United States the white, nature of theology is seen as a problem to be overcome. This is so because European/white theology ignored or, to some degree, opposed the concerns of the poor, minorities, colonized peoples, and women. As one Asian theologian put it, "we find that many elements in the Christian teachings are not relevant to us."[1]

Liberation Theology is based on the message that Jesus was and is a liberator. It brings "the good news of liberation" from unjust social structures, the power of fate, and personal sin and guilt through divine mercy and the action of people to transform their own lives. It brings hope to and requires commitment from its adherents—hope that the Kingdom of God can be created on earth and commitment to the effort to prepare the way.

Liberation Theology developed as a response to the poverty found in Latin America. The phrase "the preferential option for the poor," which means that all actions should be judged on whether or not they help the poor, is one of the identifying marks of Liberation Theology and has had a major impact on Christian thinking throughout the world. As one writer recently said, "The preferential option for the poor has been one of the most significant developments in theology and the church in the twentieth century, signaling a broad shift in theological sensitivities."[2]

The Roman Catholic Church, the dominant church in Latin America, was identified with the rich and powerful. The Church was having difficulty providing priests for rural areas where most of the poor lived. As a result, those who were concerned with these problems began, first in Brazil as early as the late 1950s, to encourage community-based organizations (later to be called base communities, base Christian communities, or base ecclesial communities) to provide for their own religious needs. In the absence of priests, this involved the laity taking responsibility for their own religious activity, which led to these same groups identifying social, economic, and political needs and organizing themselves to meet those needs.

As the movement developed, intellectuals began to look for theological and theoretical justification. They found the French worker–priest movement,[3] and they found Western Marxism with its concern for the poor. The worker–priest movement helped them encourage priests to work in communities as equals with laypeople. Marxism, but particularly the so-called Marxist–Christian dialogue of the late 1960s, provided a theory that could be integrated with the theological movements that had produced the Ecumenical Council of 1962–65, better known as Vatican II, with its emphasis on modernizing the Church and making it more responsive to laypeople. Vatican II also stressed collective

---

[1] Tissa Balasuriya, "Toward the Liberation Theology of Asia," in *Asia's Struggle for Full Humanity: Toward a Relevant Theology. Papers from the Asian Theological Conference, January 7–20, 1979, Wennappuwa, Sri Lanka,* ed. Virginia Fabella (Maryknoll, NY: Orbis Books, 1980), 19.

[2] Joerg Rieger, "Introduction: Opting for the Margins in a Postmodern World," in *Opting for the Margins: Postmodernity and Liberation in Christian Theology,* ed. Joerg Rieger (New York: Oxford University Press, 2003), 3.

[3] The worker–priest movement was a movement in French Catholicism in which priests took factory jobs so they would experience the lives of the people more completely.

responsibility in the Church, which fit nicely with the community organizations that Liberation Theology was developing.

THE MARXIST–CHRISTIAN DIALOGUE

Much of the Marxism found in Liberation Theology came through Ernst Bloch (1885–1977), who was discussed in Chapter 7. Bloch, a Marxist who spent much of his life in what was then East Germany, argued that Christianity had a tremendous radical potential, and theologians within Liberation Theology found that Marx's emphasis on the poor resonated with their concerns and the needs of their people. Thus Christian theologians and Marxist theorists found common ground.[4]

In 1965 the French Roman Catholic Marxist Roger Garaudy (b. 1913) published a book titled *From Anathema to Dialogue: The Challenge of Marxist–Christian Cooperation.*[5] The publication of this book began a long-lasting debate on the degree to which Marxists and Christians could learn from each other or even actively cooperate. The basis of the developing dialogue was the writings of the young Marx (discussed in Chapter 7), which focused on human alienation and the dehumanizing effects of capitalist society. These writings attracted theologians with similar concerns, and some Marxists found in Christianity both a deep concern with the oppressed and a message of hope for the future in this life. As a result, both Marxists and Christians began to consider what they could say to each other without losing the essential characteristics of their beliefs.

For Liberation Theology the key is found in accepting that Marx made major contributions to our understanding of capitalism and helped illuminate the position of the poor in modern society, but also in recognizing that he was limited by his rejection of God. Thus "Marx (like any other Marxist) can be a companion on the way . . . but he can never be the guide, because 'You have only one teacher, the Christ' (Matt. 23:10)."[6] In addition to Marx, one of the most important nontheological sources of Liberation Theology is the work of the Brazilian Paulo Freire (1921–97), particularly his *Pedagogy of the Oppressed* (1970). Freire advocated what he called *conscientization,* or consciousness-raising (also discussed in Chapter 6), a process in which the oppressed become aware of their oppression through participation in group discussion with others in similar circumstances. Anarchists also claim Freire as an important theorist, and he is best known as an educational theorist who successfully headed the school system in São Paulo, Brazil.

---

[4] For a recent statement on the relations between Christian thinkers and Marxists, see Andrew Collier, *Christianity and Marxism: A Philosophical Contribution to Their Reconciliation* (London: Routledge, 2001).

[5] Garaudy converted to Islam in 1982 and is now known both for his books extolling Muslim culture and his 1995 book denying the Holocaust, for which he was tried and fined.

[6] Leonardo Boff and Clodovis Boff, *Introducing Liberation Theology*, trans. Paul Burns (Maryknoll, NY: Orbis Books, 1987), 28.

Most conservatives within the Roman Catholic Church reject Liberation Theology. Although at one point Pope John Paul II condemned Liberation Theology, he later accepted some of its positions.

THE PRINCIPLES OF LATIN AMERICAN LIBERATION THEOLOGY

Liberation Theology arose out of the dialogue just described. It has also been said that "Liberation theology was born when faith confronted the injustice done to the poor."[7] In broad outline, the position of Liberation Theology is as follows:

1. The church should be concerned with poverty.
2. The church should be concerned with political repression.
3. The church should be concerned with economic repression.
4. Priests should become actively involved in trying to solve these problems.
5. Priests should move beyond general activity to
   a. Direct political action, and, possibly,
   b. Direct involvement in attempts to change political and economic systems, even by actual participation in revolutionary activity.
6. *Base communities*, or communities that include both religious (priests and nuns) and laypeople, should be established. These communities should be designed to overcome the division between religious and laypeople.

The Roman Catholic Church specifically rejects item five and is not sure about item three. Pope John Paul II once rejected item six but later accepted it in some circumstances. Camilo Torres (1929–66) was one of the priests who took the political messages to heart and became an active revolutionary.[8]

One of the earliest theorists of Liberation Theology was Gustavo Gutiérrez (b. 1928) of Chile. His *Theology of Liberation* (1971, English trans. 1973) was the first work to bring together the elements of Liberation Theology. Gutiérrez argued, based on Freire and Bloch, that the Church must recognize the positive function of the idea of utopia. Utopia includes condemnation of the evils of the present and affirmation of the possibilities of the future. As Gutiérrez put it,

> The theology of liberation attempts to reflect on the experience and meaning of the faith based on the commitment to abolish injustice and to build a new society; this theology must be verified by the practice of that commitment, by active, effective participation in the struggle which the exploited social classes have undertaken against their oppressors. Liberation from

---

[7] Boff and Boff, *Introducing Liberation Theology*, 3.

[8] For his writings, see *Revolutionary Priest: The Complete Writings and Messages of Camilo Torres*, ed. John Gerassi (New York: Random House, 1971).

every form of exploitation, the possibility of a more human and more dignified life, the creation of a new man—all pass through this struggle.[9]

Another well-known Liberation Theology theologian, Leonardo Boff (b. 1938), argued that Liberation Theology developed as and where it did because Latin Americans are both poor and Christian. As Boff and his brother Clodovis Boff (b. 1944) wrote, "we can be followers of Jesus and true Christians only by making common cause with the poor and working out the gospel of liberation."[10] The poor are, for the Boffs, "the Disfigured Son of God,"[11] and they argue that the idea of the poor must be expanded to include all the oppressed.

Liberation Theology, like other radical movements in the 1960s and 1970s, stressed consciousness-raising, the direct participation of the people, and socialism, but Liberation Theology differs from other radical movements in that it is, of course, religious. Liberation Theology is first and foremost a theology and bases its political and economic message on an understanding of the Bible and, particularly, the mission of Christ.

Like many radical theologians and spiritual leaders of the past, the leading thinkers of Liberation Theology see the Christian message as directed particularly to the poor and oppressed. One earlier spiritual leader to whom the Liberation Theologians look is St. Francis of Assisi (1182–1226), who, it should be remembered, insisted on the absolute poverty of his followers.[12] St. Francis was too radical for the church of his day, and many consider Liberation Theology to be too radical today.

Liberation Theology holds out hope for the transformation of the world in which we live today. "The holy city, the new Jerusalem that comes down from heaven (Rev. 21:2), can be established on earth only when men and women filled with faith and passion for the gospel, united with each other, and hungry and thirsty for justice, create the human dispositions and material conditions for it."[13] This desired transformation will be a gift from God, but people can prepare the way for it.

Base Communities

In a phrase reminiscent of Karl Marx's statement, "The philosophers have only *interpreted* the world in various ways; the point is to *change* it,"[14] Boff says, "More important than to see and to judge is to act."[15] A key to action in Latin American

---

[9] Gustavo Gutiérrez, *A Theology of Liberation: History, Politics, and Salvation*, 15th anniv. ed., trans. and ed. Sister Caridad Inda and John Eagleson (Maryknoll, NY: Orbis Books, 1988), 174.

[10] Boff and Boff, *Introducing Liberation Theology*, 7.

[11] Boff and Boff, *Introducing Liberation Theology*, 31.

[12] Leonardo Boff, *Saint Francis: A Model for Human Liberation*, trans. John W. Diercksmeier (New York: Crossroad Press, 1982).

[13] Boff and Boff, *Introducing Liberation Theology*, 95.

[14] See Chapter 7.

[15] Boff, *Saint Francis*, 87.

Antonio Scorza/AFP/Getty Images

Leonardo Boff (b. 1938) is Emeritus Professor of Ethics, Philosophy of
Religion, and Ecology at the State University of Rio de Janeiro. For
twenty years he was Professor of Systematic Theology at the Institute for Philosophy and Theology in Petrópolis, Brazil. He is one of
the best-known theologians of Liberation Theology. He was a member
of the Franciscan order who left the order after twice being "silenced"
(meaning he could not publish) by the Vatican for his writings on
Liberation Theology.

Liberation Theology has been the establishment of base communities or base
ecclesial communities. These communities both aid consciousness-raising and
provide a setting in which people learn to take control of their own lives.
"These base communities have an immediate and direct religious value, but
they also achieve social importance because they are places for the formation of
social conscience, responsibility, and the desire for change."[16] In 1979 Latin
American bishops meeting at Puebla, Mexico, recognized the base communities as an important new form of both evangelizing and liberating the poor and
oppressed.[17] They have also become central to the development of Liberation
Theology in the Philippines, where Liberation Theology is known as the Theology of Struggle.[18]

Since Vatican II (1962–65) there has been a movement within the Roman
Catholic Church to involve the laity more fully in the Church, although the

---

[16] Boff, *Saint Francis*, 87.

[17] *Puebla and Beyond: Documentation and Commentary*, ed. John Eagleson and Philip Scharper
(Maryknoll, NY: Orbis Books, 1979), 211.

[18] See Kathleen M. Nadeau, *Liberation Theology in the Philippines: Faith in a Revolution*
(Westport, CT: Praeger, 2002).

hierarchy of the church has not always supported this movement.[19] The development of base communities is one response to this movement. Boff describes a typical community as follows:

> The base ecclesial community is generally made up of fifteen to twenty families. They get together once or twice a week to hear the Word of God, to share their problems in common, and to solve those problems through the inspiration of the Gospel. They share their comments on the biblical passages, create their own prayers, and decide as a group what their tasks should be. After centuries of silence, the People of God are beginning to speak. They are no longer just parishioners in their parish; they have their own ecclesiological value; they are recreating the Church of God.[20]

This sense of participation is a radical departure for the Roman Catholic Church, which has traditionally been hierarchical and authoritarian. Many in the Church have difficulty accepting the empowerment of the laity and the degree of control over the forms of worship that are being demanded.

LIBERATION THEOLOGY IN IRELAND

Eire (Ireland) was the first British colony, gaining its independence only in 1922. The existence of Northern Ireland as a part of the United Kingdom of Great Britain and Northern Ireland constantly reminds the Irish of this colonial past and, as many see it, the continuing colonial status of this part of their country. Until quite recently, Ireland was one of the poorest countries in Europe, and therefore both the sense of still being a colony and the stress on poverty in Liberation Theology appealed to some Irish theologians. At the same time, Ireland, like Latin America, had a church hierarchy opposed to Liberation Theology, and the closeness of Rome and the Papacy appears to have led to an almost complete suppression of Liberation Theology in Ireland in the recent past.[21]

---

[19] In the United States, the most recent manifestation of this movement has been in response to the crisis caused by the widespread scandal of sexual abuse. The involvement of laypeople has been officially sanctioned at the national level, but actions by laypeople at the local level have met both support and opposition. Similar scandals have emerged in Australia, Canada, and Ireland.

[20] Leonardo Boff, *Church: Charism and Power—Liberation Theology and the Institutional Church,* trans. John W. Diercksmeier (New York: Crossroad Press, 1985), 125–26. From *Church: Charism and Power—Liberation Theology and the Institutional Church* by Leonardo Boff, trans. John W. Diercksmeier. English translation © 1985 by T. C. P. C. Reprinted by permission of The Crossroad Publishing Company.

[21] On Irish Liberation Theology, see, for example, Dermot Lane, ed., *Liberation Theology: An Irish Dialogue* (Dublin: Gill and Macmillan, 1977), reprinted as *Ireland, Liberation, and Theology* (Maryknoll, NY: Orbis Books, 1978); and Joe McVeigh, *Renewing the Irish Church: Toward an Irish Liberation Theology* (Dublin: Mercier Press, 1993). An interesting sidelight on Irish Liberation Theology is found in the recognition by a Protestant minister from Northern Ireland that Liberation Theology may also speak to their concerns. See Sidney John Garland, "Liberation Theology: An Irish Perspective" (master's thesis, Westminster Theological Seminary, Philadelphia, 1984).

PROTESTANT LIBERATION THEOLOGY

Although Liberation Theology originated within the Roman Catholic Church, it moved to Protestantism and may now be most dynamic within Protestant denominations in the United States and the Third World.

Black Liberation Theology in the United States

From the perspective of the United States, the most interesting development is the spread of Liberation Theology within African American Protestantism. James H. Cone (b. 1938), certainly one of the most important theologians of the twentieth century, was the first exponent of Black Theology, a distinct movement not initially connected to Liberation Theology, and is still its best-known advocate. For a time, Cone kept his distance from Latin American Liberation Theology because it was rooted in Roman Catholicism and because he saw its proponents as white. But Cone quickly recognized the commonalities between his position and theirs, and he also helped introduce Asian Liberation Theology to U.S. theologians and Black Theology to both Latin American and Asian theologians. Cone has been a key figure internationally in bringing together the various strands of Liberation Theology. He has recognized and corrected weaknesses in his own initial analysis, particularly regarding women and class.

Cone stresses that Black Theology derives from the lived experiences of African Americans in racist America and their experiences in the black church. He calls white theology *ideology* and means it negatively, saying, "Christ *really* enters into our world where the poor, the despised, and the black are, disclosing that he is with them, enduring their humiliation and pain and transforming oppressed slaves into liberated servants. Indeed, if Christ is not *truly* black, then the historical Jesus lied."[22] This strong language emphasizes Black Theology's alienation from the dominant theological culture in Europe and North America, in which Christ is always depicted as white. It also stresses that for African Americans, Christ as liberator reflects their community.

Currently the best-known exponent of Black Liberation theology is Dwight N. Hopkins, Professor of Theology at the University of Chicago Divinity School. Hopkins, drawing explicitly on Gutiérrez, argues, "Indeed, we need the preferential option for the poor more than ever these days because postmodernity includes an intensification of worker exploitation, racial oppression, discrimination against women, and sexual-identity exclusion."[23] He writes, "Black theology is the interplay between the pain of oppression and the promise of liberation found in the Bible, on the one hand, and a similar existence experienced by African Americans and poor people today."[24]

---

[22] James H. Cone, *God of the Oppressed* (New York: Seabury Press, 1975), 136. Emphasis in the original.

[23] Dwight N. Hopkins, "More Than Ever: The Preferential Option for the Poor," in *Opting for the Margins: Postmodernity and Liberation in Christian Theology,* ed. Joerg Rieger (New York: Oxford University Press, 2003), 138.

[24] Dwight N. Hopkins, *Heart and Head: Black Theology—Past, Present, and Future* (New York: Palgrave, 2002), 7.

James H. Cone (b. 1938) is the Charles A. Briggs Distinguished Professor of Systematic Theology at Union Theological Seminary. His book *A Black Theology of Liberation* (1970) founded the school of thought now known as Black Theology. Over the years, he has enriched his thought by incorporating work by theologians from North America, Africa, Asia, and Latin America, including black women theologians, and later editions of *A Black Theology of Liberation* (1986 and 1990) illustrate the evolution of his thought. His books *Black Power and Black Theology* (1969, new ed. 1989), *The Spirituals and the Blues* (1972), *God of the Oppressed* (1975, rev. ed. 1997), *For My People: Black Theology and the Black Church* (1984), *Speaking the Truth: Ecumenism, Liberation, and Black Theology* (1986), *My Soul Looks Back* (1986), and *Martin and Malcolm and America: A Dream or a Nightmare?* (1991) reflect his growing stature as both a theologian and a cultural critic.

He bases the "Liberation of the Least" on Matthew 25:31–46, in which Christ says, "Come, O blessed of my Father, inherit the kingdom prepared for you from the foundation of the world; for I was hungry and you gave me food, I was thirsty and you gave me drink, I was a stranger and you welcomed me, I was naked and you clothed me, I was sick and you visited me, I was in prison and you came to me" (RSV 34–39); and continues, "Truly, I say to you, as you did it to one of the least of these my brethren, you did it to me" (RSV 40).

Womanist Theology As just indicated, Cone was criticized for ignoring gender issues, and although he responded positively to the criticisms, African American women have developed a variant of Black Liberation Theology known as Womanist Theology. *Womanist* comes from Alice Walker's (b. 1944) *In Search of Our Mothers' Gardens* (1983).[25] Womanist theologians argue, as did Cone, that "Christ is Black. That is to say, Christ has Black skin and features and is committed to the Black community's struggle for life and wholeness."[26] Womanist theologians are explicit that African American women must free themselves from their own acceptance "of sexist oppression, the black man's acceptance of patriarchal privilege, and the white woman's acceptance of white racist privilege."[27]

[25] Alice Walker, "Womanist," in *In Search of Our Mothers' Gardens: Womanist Prose* (San Diego: Harcourt Brace Jovanovich, 1983).

[26] Kelly Brown Douglas, *The Black Christ* (Maryknoll, NY: Orbis Books, 1994), 106–7.

[27] Marcia Y. Riggs, *Awake, Arise, and Act: A Womanist Call for Black Liberation* (Cleveland: Pilgrim Press, 1994), 2.

Womanist theologians also argue, as do most feminists, that liberation must be for all peoples regardless of race, gender, and ethnicity.[28]

Minjung Theology

Minjung theology is a Korean Liberation Theology that emerged initially within the Korean Methodist Church in the 1970s in response to oppression by the Korean government. The central theologian of Minjung theology is Ahn Byung-mu (1922–96). Minjung is Korean, derived from Chinese *min* = "people" and *jung* = "mass," but the word cannot be translated into English.[29] Minjung theology is millenarian, believing that the Kingdom of God will be established on earth in the near future.

Minjung refers to the common people oppressed by an elite. "Minjung are the people of God, and their experience of suffering owing to the injustice of the ruling group has to be eliminated from this world. Therefore, the act of liberation becomes the central focus of Minjung theology. Moreover, the realization of the fruits of liberation produces the establishment of the Messianic Kingdom or the Reign of God on earth."[30] The key concepts are *Han* and *Dan*. "*Han* is the feeling of resentment, depression, repressed anger, helplessness, just indignation, and so forth, which is combined with a desire for a better future."[31] *Dan* is a more complex and more clearly political concept that refers to the ability to overcome *Han* with the help of God by breaking through the repression that creates *Han*. Thus, using different concepts, Minjung theology is quite similar to Latin American Liberation Theology. It focuses on the poor and repressed and fashions a theology that energizes people to help themselves overcome their situation. It is different from Latin American Liberation Theology in being millenarian and in relying on local congregations rather than base ecclesial communities. A women's movement has developed within Minjung to address the specific oppression of Korean women.

LIBERATION THEOLOGY IN AFRICA

Contemporary Christian theology in Africa can be divided into liberation, most obviously in South Africa, and inculturation, found throughout the rest of Christian Africa. *Inculturation* means that indigenous African religious practices have been

---

[28] A Roman Catholic variant of womanist theology is *mujerista theology,* which has developed to appeal specifically to Latina women in the United States. See Ada María Isasi-Díaz, *En la Lucha/In the Struggle: Elaborating a Mujerista Theology,* 10th anniv. ed. (Minneapolis, MN: Fortress Press, 2004).

[29] David Suh Kwang-sun, "A Biographical Sketch of an Asian Theological Consultation," in *Minjung Theology: People as the Subjects of History,* ed. Commission on Theological Concerns of the Christian Conference of Asia (CTC-CCA), rev. ed. (Maryknoll, NY: Orbis Books; London: Zed Books, 1983), 16.

[30] Jung Young Lee, "Minyung Theology: A Critical Introduction," in *An Emerging Theology in World Perspective: Commentary on Korean Minjung Theology,* ed. Jung Young Lee (Mystic, CT: Twenty-Third Publications, 1988), 11.

[31] Michael Amaladoss, S. J., *Life in Freedom: Liberation Theologies from Asia* (Maryknoll, NY: Orbis Books, 1997), 4.

grafted onto Christian theology. This has generally been easier within Protestantism, but is also found in Roman Catholicism. Liberation Theology took hold in South Africa because it provided a response to the oppression of the black majority by the white majority.[32] The best known of the South African Liberation Theologians is Allan Boesak (b. 1946), who in *Farewell to Innocence* (1976, English trans. 1977) argued that African theology, Latin American Liberation Theology, Black Theology in the United States, and Black Theology in South Africa are all expressions of the same fundamental theology of liberation.

Liberation Theology in Africa is similar to and different from Latin American Liberation Theology in much the same ways as Minjung theology, with the added ingredient of race. The oppressed group was oppressed because it was black, which resonates with the development of Black Liberation Theology in the United States.

CURRENT TRENDS

The Ecumenical Association of Third World Theologians (EATWOT) provides a recurring venue for dialogue among theologians from Africa, Asia, the Caribbean, Latin America, the Pacific Islands, and North America. They are trying to address how Protestants and Roman Catholics, men and women, and peoples of all colors, ethnicities, and nationalities can forge a common understanding within Christianity of a common theology of liberation. Liberation Theology is as active today as at any time in the past.

Liberation Theology is now a worldwide movement, and for all their differences, these theologians agree on the central role of the poor and the oppressed and the need for committed action to achieve their liberation. Thus Liberation Theology is explicitly and consciously a political movement that challenges economic and political oppression as well as the acceptance of such oppression by religious hierarchies.

The Catholic Worker Movement

In the United States, the Catholic Worker Movement (discussed in Chapter 8) now identifies itself with Liberation Theology. Given the movement's tradition of working with the poorest of the poor, specifically alcoholics and drug addicts, the affinity with Liberation Theology is obvious. But the movement also appears to be reemphasizing its connection to the Roman Catholic Church, although some members of the hierarchy still oppose it, while continuing its social and political activity. Because Catholic Worker centers exist throughout the United States, this could signal a strengthened Roman Catholic Liberation Theology within the United States to parallel the still strong Black Liberation Theology.

---

[32] For a discussion of both trends, see Emmanuel Martey, *African Theology: Inculturation and Liberation* (Maryknoll, NY: Orbis Books, 1993).

Ecology and Globalization

Recently a few theologians have begun to integrate ecology into Liberation Theology, again appealing to the image of St. Francis of Assisi, who is often depicted preaching to the birds. Other theologians have added a specific critique of globalization to the mix, arguing that although the rhetoric of globalization suggests inclusion, its practice excludes the poor and minorities and destroys the environment.[33]

SUGGESTED READING

Some Classic Works

Boff, Leonardo. *Jesus Christ Liberator: A Critical Christology for Our Times.* Translated by Patrick Hughes. Maryknoll, NY: Orbis Books, 1981.

————. *Saint Francis: A Model for Human Liberation.* Translated by John W. Diercksmeier. Maryknoll, NY: Orbis Books, 1982.

Cone, James H. *A Black Theology of Liberation.* 20th anniv. ed. Maryknoll, NY: Orbis Books, 1990.

Dussel, Enrique. *History and Theology of Liberation: A Latin American Perspective.* Translated by John Drury. Maryknoll, NY: Orbis Books, 1975.

Gutiérrez, Gustavo. *The Power of the Poor in History.* Translated by Robert R. Barr. Maryknoll, NY: Orbis Books, 1983.

————. *A Theology of Liberation: History, Politics, and Salvation.* 15th anniv. ed. Maryknoll, NY: Orbis Books, 1988.

————. *We Drink from Our Own Wells: The Spiritual Journey of a People.* Translated by Matthew J. O'Connell. 20th anniversary ed. Maryknoll, NY: Orbis Books, 2003.

Isasi-Díaz, Ada María. *En la Lucha/In the Struggle: Elaborating a Mujerista Theology.* 10th anniv. ed. Minneapolis, MN: Fortress Press, 2004.

Míguez Bonino, José. *Doing Theology in a Revolutionary Situation.* Philadelphia: Fortress Press, 1975. Published in the United Kingdom as *Revolutionary Theology Comes of Age.* London: SPCK, 1975.

Segundo, Juan Luis. *Liberation Theology.* Translated by John Drury. Maryknoll, NY: Orbis Books, 1976.

Williams, Delores S. *Sisters in the Wilderness: The Challenges of Womanist God-Talk.* Maryknoll, NY: Orbis Books, 1993.

Books and Articles

Althaus-Reid, Marcella. *Indecent Theology: Theological Perversions in Sex, Gender and Politics.* London: Routledge, 2000.

Amaladoss, Michael S. J. *Life in Freedom: Liberation Theologies from Asia.* Maryknoll, NY: Orbis Books, 1997.

Aquino, María Pilar. *Our Cry for Life: Feminist Theology from Latin America.* Translated by Dinah Livingstone. Maryknoll, NY: Orbis Books, 1993.

Balasuriya, Tissa. "Toward the Liberation Theology of Asia." In *Asia's Struggle for Full Humanity: Toward a Relevant Theology. Papers from the Asian Theological Conference, January 7–20, 1979, Wennappuwa, Sri Lanka,* edited by Virginia Fabella, 16–27. Maryknoll, NY: Orbis Books, 1980.

Boesak, Allan [Aubrey], and Charles Villa-Vicencio. *A Call for an End to Unjust Rule.* Edinburgh: Saint Andrew Press, 1986.

---

[33] Among Leonardo Boff's most recent books are *Ecology and Liberation: A New Paradigm,* trans. John Cumming (Maryknoll, NY: Orbis Books, 1995); and *Cry of the Earth, Cry of the Poor,* trans. Philip Berryman (Maryknoll, NY: Orbis Books, 1997).

————. *Farewell to Innocence: A Socio-Ethical Study on Black Theology and Black Power.* Maryknoll, NY: Orbis Books, 1977.

Boff, Leonardo. *Church, Charism, and Power: Liberation Theology and the Institutional Church.* Translated by John W. Diercksmeier. New York: Crossroad Press, 1985.

————. *Cry of the Earth, Cry of the Poor.* Translated by Philip Berryman. Maryknoll, NY: Orbis Books, 1997.

————. *Ecclesiogenesis: The Base Communities Reinvent the Church.* Translated by Robert R. Barr. Maryknoll, NY: Orbis Books, 1986.

————. *Ecology and Liberation: A New Paradigm.* Translated from the Italian by John Cumming. Maryknoll, NY: Orbis Books, 1995. Originally published in Portuguese.

————. *Liberating Grace.* Translated by John Drury. Maryknoll, NY: Orbis Books, 1979.

————. *The Lord's Prayer: The Prayer of Integral Liberation.* Translated by Theodore Morrow. Maryknoll, NY: Orbis Books, 1983.

————. *Trinity and Society.* Translated by Paul Burns. Maryknoll, NY: Orbis Books, 1988.

————. *Way of the Cross—Way of Justice.* Translated by John Drury. Maryknoll, NY: Orbis Books, 1980.

Boff, Leonardo, and Clodovis Boff. *Introducing Liberation Theology.* Translated by Paul Burns. Maryknoll, NY: Orbis Books, 1987.

————. *Salvation and Liberation: In Search of a Balance between Faith and Politics.* Translated by Robert R. Barr. Maryknoll, NY: Orbis Books; Melbourne, Australia: Dove Communications, 1984.

Boff, Leonardo, and Virgil Elizondo, eds. *Convergences and Differences* [Cover title: *Theologies of the Third World*]. Edinburgh: T. & T. Clark, 1988.

————, eds. *Ecology and Poverty: Cry of the Earth, Cry of the Poor.* London: SCM Press/Maryknoll, NY Orbis Books, 1997.

————, eds. *The People of God amidst the Poor.* Edinburgh: T. & T. Clark, 1986.

Commission on Theological Concerns of the Christian Conference of Asia (CTC-CCA), ed. *Minjung Theology: People as the Subjects of History.* Rev. ed. Maryknoll, NY: Orbis Books; London: Zed Books; Singapore: Christian Conference of Asia, 1983.

Cone, James H. *Black Theology and Black Power.* Maryknoll, NY: Orbis Books, 1997.

————. *God of the Oppressed.* Rev. ed. Maryknoll, NY: Orbis Books, 1997.

————. *Martin and Malcolm and America: A Dream or a Nightmare?* Maryknoll, NY: Orbis Books, 1991.

————. *Risks of Faith: The Emergence of a Black Theology of Liberation, 1968–1998.* Boston: Beacon Press, 1999.

————. *The Spirituals and the Blues: An Interpretation.* New York: Seabury Press, 1972.

Cone, James H., and Gayraud S. Wilmore, eds. *Black Theology: A Documentary History, 1966–1979.* 2nd rev. ed. Maryknoll, NY: Orbis Books, 1993.

————, eds. *Black Theology: A Documentary History, 1980–1992.* Maryknoll, NY: Orbis Books, 1993.

Dawson, Michael C. *Black Visions: The Roots of Contemporary African-American Political Ideologies.* Chicago: University of Chicago Press, 2001.

Douglas, Kelly Brown. *The Black Christ.* Maryknoll, NY: Orbis Books, 1994.

Dussel, Enrique. *Philosophy of Liberation.* Translated by Aquilina Martinez and Christine Morkowsky. Maryknoll, NY: Orbis Books, 1985.

Elwood, Douglas J., ed. *Asian Christian Theology: Emerging Themes.* Rev. ed. of *What Asian Christians Are Thinking.* Philadelphia: Westminster Press, 1980.

Fabella, Virginia, ed. *Asia's Struggle for Full Humanity: Toward a Relevant Theology. Papers from the Asian Theological Conference, January 7–20, 1979, Wennappuwa, Sri Lanka.* Maryknoll, NY: Orbis Books, 1980.

Fabella, Virginia, and R. S. Sugirtharajah, eds. *Dictionary of Third World Theologies.* Maryknoll, NY: Orbis Books, 2000.

Fabella, Virginia, and Sergio Torres, eds. *Irruption of the Third World: Challenge to Theology. Papers from the Fifth International Conference of the Ecumenical Association of Third World Theologians, August 17–29, 1981, New Delhi, India.* Maryknoll, NY: Orbis Books, 1983.

Fagan, Seán, S. M. "Liberation Theology in Ireland." *Doctrine and Life* (Dublin), 27, no. 2 (May 1977): 22–28.

Garland, Sidney John. "Liberation Theology: An Irish Perspective." Master of Theology thesis, Westminster Theological Seminary, Philadelphia, 1984.

Gerassi, John, ed. *Revolutionary Priest: The Complete Writings and Messages of Camilo Torres.* New York: Random House, 1971.

Gilkes, Cheryl Townsend. *"If It Wasn't for the Women . . .": Black Women's Experience and Womanist Culture in Church and Community.* Maryknoll, NY: Orbis Books, 2001.

Gutiérrez, Gustavo. *The Density of the Present: Selected Writings.* Maryknoll, NY: Orbis Books, 1999. Essays have different translators.

Hayes, Diana L. *And Still We Rise: An Introduction to Black Liberation Theology.* New York: Paulist Press, 1996.

Hebblethwaite, Margaret. *Base Communities: An Introduction.* London: Geoffrey Chapman, 1993.

Hopkins, Dwight N. *Down, Up, and Over: Slave Religion and Black Theology.* Minneapolis: Fortress Press, 2000.

———. *Heart and Head: Black Theology— Past, Present, and Future.* New York: Palgrave, 2002.

———. *Introducing Black Theology of Liberation.* Maryknoll, NY: Orbis Books, 1999.

Isasi-Díaz, Ada María. *Mujerista Theology: A Theology for the Twenty-First Century.* Maryknoll, NY: Orbis Books, 1996.

King, Ursula, ed. *Feminist Theology from the Third World: A Reader.* Maryknoll, NY: Orbis Books, 1994.

Kwok, Pui-lan. *Discovering the Bible in the Non-Biblical World.* Maryknoll, NY: Orbis Books, 1995.

———. *Introducing Asian Feminist Theology.* Cleveland, OH: Pilgrim Press, 2000.

Kyung, Chung Hyun. *Struggle to Be in the Sun Again: Introducing Asian Women's Theology.* Maryknoll, NY: Orbis Books, 1990.

Lane, Dermot, ed. *Liberation Theology: An Irish Dialogue.* Dublin: Gill & Macmillan, 1977. Reprinted as *Ireland, Liberation, and Theology* (Maryknoll, NY: Orbis Books, 1978).

Lee, Jung Young, ed. *An Emerging Theology in World Perspective: Commentary on Korean Minjung Theology.* Mystic, CT: Twenty-Third Publications, 1988.

Martey, Emmanuel. *African Theology: Inculturation and Liberation.* Maryknoll, NY: Orbis Books, 1993.

McVeigh, Joe. *Renewing the Irish Church: Toward an Irish Liberation Theology.* Dublin: Mercier Press, 1993.

Nadeau, Kathleen M. *Liberation Theology in the Philippines: Faith in a Revolution.* Westport, CT: Praeger, 2002.

O'Sullivan, Michael S. J., ed. *The Liberation of Theology.* Dublin: Irish Student Christian Movement, 1977.

Park, Jong Chun. *Crawl with God, Dance in the Spirit: A Creative Formulation of Korean Theology of the Spirit.* Nashville, TN: Abingdon Press, 1998.

Rieger, Joerg. *Opting for the Margins: Postmodernity and Liberation in Christian Theology.* New York: Oxford University Press, 2003.

———. *Remember the Poor: The Challenge to Theology in the Twenty-First Century.* Harrisburg, PA: Trinity Press International, 1998.

Riggs, Marcia Y. *Awake, Arise, and Act: A Womanist Call for Black Liberation.* Cleveland: Pilgrim Press, 1994.

Rowland, Christopher, ed. *The Cambridge Companion to Liberation Theology.* Cambridge: Cambridge University Press, 1999.

Setiloane, Gabriel M. *African Theology: An Introduction.* Johannesburg, South Africa: Skotaville Publishers, 1986.

Townes, Emilie M., ed. *Embracing the Spirit: Womanist Perspectives on Hope, Salvation, and Transformation.* Maryknoll, NY: Orbis, Books, 1997.

————, ed. *A Troubling in My Soul: Womanist Perspectives on Evil and Suffering.* Maryknoll, NY: Orbis Books, 1999.

Wilmore, Gayraud S. *Black Religion and Black Radicalism: An Interpretation of the Religious History of African Americans.* 3rd ed., rev. and enl. Maryknoll, NY: Orbis Books, 1998.

Websites

Centre for Liberation Theologies, Faculty of Theology, Katholieke Universiteit Leuven (Belgium): http://www.theo.kuleuven.ac.be/clt/

Ecumenical Association of Third World Theologians (EATWOT): http://www.eatwot.org

Liberation Theology at Believe Religious Information Source Website: http://mb-soft.com/believe/txn/liberati.htm

Mujerista Theology: http://www.users.drew.edu/aisasidi/Definition1.htmSabeel Ecumenical Liberation Theology Center for Palestinian Christians http://www.sabeel.org/

Vatican Statement on Liberation Theology: http://www.osjspm.org/cst/libtheo2.htm

12

Environmentalism

This chapter briefly examines the origins and development of what is variously called *ecologism, environmentalism, Green politics,* or *Green political thought.* Here it is simply called environmentalism because that is what it is most often called in the United States. In Europe the word *environmentalism* reflects a fairly conservative approach, rather like the word *conservationism* does in the United States. Thus European thinkers tend to use words like *ecologism,* which have not caught on in the United States. One aspect of the Green Movement, animal rights, has become important recently both philosophically and politically. In 2004 environmentalism was recognized with the award of the Nobel Peace Prize to the Kenyan environmental activist Wangari Maathai [(b. 1940)] for her "fight to promote ecologically viable social, economic, and cultural development in Kenya and Africa" in a "holistic approach to sustainable development that embraces democracy, human rights and women's rights in particular."[1]

For most people the impact of environmentalism is not found in a radical rethinking of the place of human beings in the biosphere but in smaller things like recycling, buying canned tuna certified as having been caught using methods that do not harm dolphins, eating more organic foods, and greater awareness of the importance of clean air and water. Others focus more on specific issues such as the treatment of animals, genetically modified foods, or the protection of whales, and the environmental movement has certainly changed their lives significantly, as it

---

[1] http://.nobelpeaceprize.org/eng_lau_announce2004.html

has the lives of activists who devote their entire lives to some aspect of the movement. At the same time, radical environmentalism represents the beginning of an entirely new way of conceptualizing the world, one that moves human beings off center stage and puts the biosphere, of which humanity is only a small part, at the center.

In Europe many countries have Green political parties that have elected members to various local and regional legislative bodies, national legislative bodies, and the European Parliament of the European Union. Green political parties are uncommon in North America. Ralph Nader (b. 1934) ran for president in 2000 as the candidate of the Green Party, but he received only 2.7 percent of the votes cast and was blamed or credited for Al Gore (b. 1948) losing the presidency while winning the popular vote. The Green Party did not renominate Nader.

The Green Movement is primarily in the developed North (including Australia and New Zealand in the South but generally excluding Japan) but is beginning to be felt in the rest of the world. Many, but not all, thinkers in the Third World argue that although they would like to encourage environmentally sound policies, they can't afford to; they see the Green Movement as a luxury that only the developed world can afford. However, the Green Movement is beginning to convince some of them that environmentalism is good economic policy.

ORIGINS

In North America two major sources have coalesced in the development of environmentalism. One source is the conservationism that developed in the United States as a result of such works as *Silent Spring* (1962) by Rachel Carson (1907–1964) and out of concern about the effects of overpopulation stemming from works like *The Population Bomb* (1968) by Paul Ehrlich (b. 1932). The other main source is the environmental theorists and activists who give the movement its belief system. It is possible to follow the careers and writings of major figures of this second source back to the ferment of the 1960s.

In North America, protests against the Vietnam War, nuclear weapons, and nuclear power broadened awareness of how these issues interact with political power and social conflict. There was a strong concern with self-sufficiency and a "back-to-the-land" component to some of the movements of the 1960s and 1970s. In the United States, the immensely successful series *The Whole Earth Catalog* (1968–1981) and the related *CoEvolution Quarterly* (1974–84) were evidence of this. A new edition of *The Whole Earth Catalog* was published in 1994, and the *CoEvolution Quarterly* continued as the *Whole Earth Review* until 1996, when it became *Whole Earth,* which was published through 2003. Related materials exist in Europe, Canada, Australia, and New Zealand based on similar earlier activities, and one can easily find publications aimed at similar questions.

In Europe the development of the movement was similar, but the failed revolutions of 1968 in Czechoslovakia and France were of central importance, followed by the campaign against nuclear weapons, a growing recognition of the

cross-national effects of pollution, and an early awareness that political and economic systems were centrally involved in the existing environmental problems
as well as in any possible solutions. The key difference is that in Europe political
parties were formed as well as interest or pressure groups as in North America.

A slightly different path involving the same issues can be traced in the writings of major theorists of environmentalism such as André Gorz (b. 1924), Ivan
Illich (1926–2002), and Murray Bookchin (b. 1921). These theorists usually
started from a position of general radicalism and then focused more and more
on ecological issues.

Environmentalism also has more remote origins that are difficult to define
precisely. In North America these origins can be found in the writings of early
environmentalists like John Muir (1838–1914), who campaigned for forest
reserves and is now a "patron saint" of radical environmentalists, and Henry
David Thoreau (1817–62), a writer whose *A Week on the Concord and Merrimack
Rivers* (1849) and, especially, *Walden, or Life in the Woods* (1854) are imbued
with a sensuous love of nature and a political rebelliousness that are echoed in
many contemporary works.

Ecotopia

In 1975 Ernest Callenbach (b. 1929) self-published a novel that was to become
the classic ecological utopia, particularly after it was republished in 1977 in a
mass-market edition.[2] *Ecotopia* also produced a small body of related literature.[3]

Ecotopia is a fictitious country formed out of the Northwest of the United
States (Washington, Oregon, and Northern California). The story of the revolution that led to this successful secession is told in Callenbach's *Ecotopia Emerging* (1981) and need not detain us here. In 1999, when *Ecotopia* is set, a reporter
is visiting Ecotopia for the first time since the 1980 secession, and his description of a train trip in *Ecotopia* is a good example of what environmentalists hope
to achieve:

> Their sentimentality about nature has even led the Ecotopians to bring
> greenery into their trains, which are full of hanging ferns and small plants I
> could not identify. (My companions however reeled off their botanical
> names with assurance.) At the end of the car stood containers rather like
> trash bins, each with a large letter—M, G, and P. These, I was told, were
> "recycle bins." It may seem unlikely to Americans, but I observed that
> during our trip my fellow travelers did without exception dispose of all
> metal, glass, or paper and plastic refuse in the appropriate bin. That they
> did so without the embarrassment Americans would experience was my

---

[2] Ernest Callenbach, *Ecotopia: The Notebooks and Reports of William Weston* (Berkeley, CA:
Banyan Tree Books, 1975; New York: Bantam Books, 1977).

[3] See Ernest Callenbach, *Ecotopia Emerging* (Berkeley, CA: Banyan Tree Books, 1981); and
Callenbach, *The Ecotopian Encyclopedia for the 80s: A Survival Guide for the Age of Inflation*
(Berkeley, CA: And/Or, 1980). See also Judith Clancy, *The Ecotopian Sketchbook: A Book
for Drawing, Writing, Collaging, Designing, Thinking About, and Creating a New World, Based
on the Novel* Ecotopia *by Ernest Callenbach* (Berkeley, CA: Banyan Tree Books, 1981).

Photographs of Earth taken from outer space make the point that all human beings inhabit a single place. Such photographs have struck a chord in many people and encouraged them to become aware of themselves as part of an international community. In addition, seen from outer space Earth has a fragile beauty that has helped fuel the recognition that ecological and environmental concerns cross all national borders.

NASA

first introduction to the rigid practices of recycling and re-use upon which Ecotopians are said to pride themselves so fiercely.[4]

The principles behind Callenbach's description and the rest of the utopia he presents in *Ecotopia* include closeness to nature, illustrated by the plants inside the train; knowledge of the natural world, as shown by the passengers' ability to name the plants; and recycling. Substantial recycling now exists in the United States; it didn't in 1975, but if the St. Louis area is any indicator, while the programs exists, only a small part of the population participates. A number of cities are trying various means to encourage greater recycling.

THE PRINCIPLES OF ENVIRONMENTALISM

Other writers have explicitly spelled out what they see as the fundamental principles of environmentalism. Lester W. Milbrath (b. 1925) has argued that there is a "new environmental paradigm" that includes a "high valuation on nature"; compassion toward other peoples, generations, and species; planning to avoid technology that is not environmentally sensitive; limiting growth; and, most important for the development of a new ideology, a new social paradigm and a new politics. The latter will require, among other things, greater participation, simpler living, cooperation, public versus private solutions to many issues, and a greater emphasis on worker satisfaction.[5] These principles make a good starting point; most other theorists would generally differ only in degree.

---

[4] Callenbach, *Ecotopia*, 9–10. Reprinted by permission of the author.

[5] Lester W. Milbrath, "Environmental Beliefs and Values," in *Political Psychology* (San Francisco: Jossey-Bass, 1986), 100.

Elsewhere Milbrath has expanded on these characteristics with proposals that are more radical while rejecting any sort of right/left political dichotomy. In later work he insists on the necessity of eliminating the whole concept of dominance over nature; but much more important is his argument that we must both reduce the population in the world and lower the standard of living in the West.[6] Although many agree with this position, it is not frequently stated because of fear that it will frighten people away from the movement.

Another author who has outlined the basic principles is Robert C. Paehlke (b. 1941). His "central value assertions of environmentalism" include recognition of human beings as part of a global ecosystem, political decentralization and participation, concern with the future, simplicity, nonmaterial values, and less concern with technical solutions.[7]

Although there are basic similarities, positions differ within the Green Movement. Here we will look briefly at three of these different positions—ecosocialism, ecofeminism, and Deep Ecology.

ECOSOCIALISM

André Gorz

André Gorz (b. 1924) argues that *"the ecological movement is not an end in itself but a stage in the larger struggle."*[8] That larger struggle is the one against capitalism. Gorz is a Marxist who rejects the centralism of the dominant Marxist tradition and uses Marx's philosophy to argue for a way of life that is no longer dominated by work. He wants a simpler lifestyle for all based on production limited to socially necessary goods. Everyone would work, but people would work less and at more satisfying jobs. To the extent possible, necessary but repetitive work would be replaced by automated machinery, a position that many environmentalists reject.

Gorz also contends that ecology cannot produce an ethic, another argument that is widely rejected by environmentalists. With the existence of journals like *Environmental Ethics* (founded 1979), it would seem that Gorz has lost that part of the argument. Gorz contends that ecology should be seen as a "purely scientific discipline" that "does not necessarily imply the rejection of authoritarian technological solutions."[9]

Most environmentalists argue that ecology does produce an ethic, one that requires the rejection of "authoritarian technological solutions." But Gorz's argument is based on the fact that many environmentalists accept the possibility of using highly technological means to solve some of the world's pollution problems.

---

[6] See Milbrath's argument in *Envisioning a Sustainable Society: Learning Our Way Out* (Albany: State University of New York Press, 1989).

[7] Robert C. Paehlke, *Environmentalism and the Future of Progressive Politics* (New Haven, CT: Yale University Press, 1989), 144–45.

[8] André Gorz, *Ecology as Politics*, trans. Patsy Vigderman and Jonathan Cloud (Boston: South End Press, 1980), 3. Emphasis in the original.

[9] Gorz, *Ecology as Politics*, 17.

Thus, while the left wing of the Green Movement rejects his position and argues for an ethic that is antitechnological, those to Gorz's right generally accept his conclusion and support the use of technology to solve problems brought about by technology.

Murray Bookchin

Murray Bookchin (b. 1921) is best described as an anarchist, but he also fits under the label of ecosocialism. Bookchin described what he calls "an ecological society" in the following terms: "An ecological society would fully recognize that the human animal is biologically structured to live with its kind, and to care for and love its own kind within a broadly and freely defined social group."[10] In the last part of his *Ecology of Freedom* (1982) and in his *Toward an Ecological Society* (1980), Bookchin describes a society that seems to be based on many of the principles outlined by Milbrath, Paehlke, and others. It is radically decentralized, participatory, and has overcome hierarchy, replacing it with a society that respects each individual and the planet on which we live.

ECOFEMINISM

The set of ideas called *ecofeminism* is a combination of feminism, the peace movement, and environmentalism.[11] It springs mostly from the part of feminism that views women as more in tune with nature than men, but it begins with the assertion that our ecological problems stem from the male notion of dominance as applied to nature and other human beings. Thus it explicitly rejects the sort of technological solution accepted by Gorz. An interesting example of this sensibility can be found in Ursula K. Le Guin's short story "She Unnames Them" (1985), in which Eve is depicted as freeing the animals from Adam's domination by unnaming them—that is, giving them back their own identity rather than the identity imposed on them through Adam's names.

Ecofeminism tends to accept what is called the *Gaia hypothesis,* which sees the earth as a living being that must be nourished and protected rather than exploited. Many ecofeminists see this as part of a revived belief in what they call the Goddess, a revived religion that in some ways is close to nature worship.[12] It should be noted that not all self-described ecofeminists are women

---

[10] Murray Bookchin, *The Ecology of Freedom: The Emergence and Dissolution of Hierarchy* (Palo Alto, CA: Cheshire Books, 1982), 318.

[11] See Irene Diamond and Gloria Feman Orenstein, eds., *Reweaving the World: The Emergence of Ecofeminism* (San Francisco: Sierra Club Books, 1990); and Heather Eaton and Lois Ann Lorentzen, eds., *Ecofeminism and Globalization: Exploring Culture, Context, and Religion* (Lanham, MD: Rowman & Littlefield, 2003).

[12] See, for example, Carol P. Christ, *Rebirth of the Goddess: Finding Meaning in Feminist Spirituality* (New York: Routledge, 1999); and Christ, *She Who Changes: Re-imagining the Divine in the World* (London: Palgrave Macmillan, 2003).

and that parts of their beliefs, like the Gaia hypothesis, are widely accepted by other environmentalists.

Ecofeminists are thus using age-old traditions, combined with new understandings contributed by feminism and environmentalism, to give birth to a different way of viewing the relationship between the human race and the rest of the natural world. They argue that technological solutions to environmental problems are male solutions that simply cause different problems in the future without correcting the current ones. Ecofeminists are close to the most controversial movement found in the Green Movement, Deep Ecology, but they contend that Deep Ecology has missed the point that our problems stem from the masculine worldview of domination rather than from the more general human-centeredness that Deep Ecology identifies as the source of our environmental problems.[13]

DEEP ECOLOGY

The single most controversial movement found within environmentalism today is Deep Ecology (a term coined in 1972 by Arne Naess [b. 1912]), sometimes called *biocentrism*. It is controversial because it places the rest of nature above humans. In other words, it is acceptable to damage human interests and even human beings in order to protect nature. One of its popularizers, Dave Foreman (b. 1946), the founder of Earth First!, puts it as follows: "This philosophy states simply and essentially that all living creatures and communities possess intrinsic value, inherent worth. Natural things live for their own sake, which is another way of saying they have value. Other beings (both animal and plant) and even so-called 'inanimate' objects such as rivers and mountains are not placed here for the convenience of human beings."[14]

The "deepness" of Deep Ecology lies in its rejection of the emphasis on human beings found in most of the Green Movement. There are "deeper" values that emphasize the entire biosphere, as opposed to just human beings. For Deep Ecology, nature is not for human use; it has value in and of itself. Nature has rights that need to be protected against human beings. Nature is the standard, and human beings are the problem.

Clearly such a position is not acceptable to many environmentalists. Murray Bookchin, for example, attacked Deep Ecology in his *Remaking Society* (1989). Bookchin argues that the whole approach of biocentrism is wrongheaded. He contends that it simply reverses the domination of nature by humanity to the domination of humanity by nature. He says that the goal should be balance, not domination.

---

[13] See Rik Scarce, *Eco-Warriors: Understanding the Radical Environmental Movement* (Chicago: Noble Press, 1990), 39.

[14] Dave Foreman, *Confessions of an Eco-Warrior* (New York: Harmony Books, 1991), 26–27.

In 1984 Naess and George Sessions (b. 1938) spelled out eight principles to form a platform of Deep Ecology:

1. The flourishing of human and nonhuman life on Earth has intrinsic value. The value of nonhuman life forms is independent of the usefulness these may have for narrow human purposes.
2. Richness and diversity of life forms are values in themselves and contribute to the flourishing of human and nonhuman life on Earth.
3. Humans have no right to reduce this richness and diversity except to satisfy vital needs.
4. Present human interference with the nonhuman world is excessive, and the situation is rapidly worsening.
5. The flourishing of human life and cultures is compatible with a substantial decrease of the human population. The flourishing of nonhuman life requires such a decrease.
6. Significant change of life conditions for the better requires change in policies. These affect basic economic, technological, and ideological structures.
7. The ideological change is mainly that of appreciating *life quality* (dwelling in situations of intrinsic value) rather than adhering to a high standard of living. There will be a profound awareness of the differences between big and great.
8. Those who subscribe to the foregoing points have an obligation directly or indirectly to participate in the attempt to implement the necessary changes.[15]

The proponents of Deep Ecology see it as reflecting a total worldview that requires a commitment to social change. Deep Ecology activists have often been among the most radical of environmentalists.

NEO-LUDDITES AND THE UNABOMBER

In April 1996 Theodore J. Kaczynski (b. 1942) was arrested and identified as the so-called Unabomber who had assembled a number of bombs that killed or injured leading figures in industry and technology. During the bombing campaign, the Unabomber published a manifesto justifying his actions and calling for a return to a more natural, less technological way of life.[16] He and others like him have sometimes been called *neo-Luddites* after Ned Lud (or Ludd), a workman who broke stocking frames in 1779 because he was convinced that the newly introduced machines were taking away jobs. In the early nineteenth

---

[15] See Arne Naess, *Ecology, Community, and Lifestyle: Outline of an Ecosophy,* trans. and ed. David Rothenberg (Cambridge: Cambridge University Press, 1989), 29. Reprinted by permission. Emphasis in the original.

[16] For the Unabomber Manifesto, see http://www.soci.niu.edu/~critcrim/uni/uni.txt

century a group of workmen calling themselves Luddites broke up textile machinery for the same reason, and contemporary neo-Luddites like the Unabomber are also taking direct action against the forces that they see destroying the environment.

"MONKEYWRENCHING"

In the Green Movement in the United States, civil disobedience or direct action is frequently called *monkeywrenching* after Edward Abbey's (1927–90) novels *The Monkey Wrench Gang* (1975+) and *Hayduke Lives!* (1990), which describe a group of environmental activists who destroy things that they believe are damaging the environment. The Deep Ecology group Earth First! follows the precepts of Abbey's novels, as do those who free animals from experiments or from battery farms (farms where animals are kept closely penned for life).

The people who are now being called *ecowarriors* contend that they are trying to break down the wall between the human and the nonhuman. It is their aim to protect biodiversity through direct action, particularly direct action that will play well to the media. There is no central organization in the groups that practice monkeywrenching; monkeywrenchers act either individually or in small groups. A number of ecowarriors practice what they preach by living in voluntary poverty.[17] Many in the Green Movement respect the ecowarriors and monkeywrenching while not believing monkeywrenching to be a good tactic politically.

A particularly famous case is that of Butterfly (Julia Hill, b. 1974), who lived in a tree she called Luna for 738 days (over two years) to protest logging. This act of monkeywrenching was at least partially successful in that she saved Luna and some other old-growth forest.[18]

BIOREGIONALISM AND BIODIVERSITY

Another significant issue is what is called *bioregionalism,* which refers to the recognition that no single policy is appropriate to any political area. Each ecological region has its own unique relationship among land, flora, fauna, and the human inhabitants, and this unique relationship needs to be respected.

In addition, each bioregion is biologically diverse, and environmentalists say that such diversity must be maintained and fostered. The particular target of this concern is monoculture agriculture—the tendency to replace diversity with one cash crop like wheat or corn. The classic depiction of a bioregion is Aldo

---

[17] See Scarce, *Eco-Warriors,* 5–6.

[18] See Julia Butterfly Hill, *The Legacy of Luna: The Story of a Tree, a Woman, and the Struggle to Save the Redwoods* (New York: HarperCollins, 2000).

Leopold's (1886–1948) *A Sand County Almanac* (1949). A more recent look at bioregionalism is William Least Heat-Moon's (b. 1939) *PrairyErth* (1991), which examines the history and ecology of Chase County, Kansas (an area of 744 square miles), in great depth.[19]

GENETICALLY MODIFIED FOODS

One of the most controversial issues today is genetically modified foods. Advocates say that such food is identical to natural foods, that horticulturalists and farmers have used genetic modification through selective breeding for centuries, and that genetic modification can radically increase food production and solve the problem of world hunger. Opponents argue that scientific evidence is not yet established for any of these claims and that until it is, genetically modified crops should be grown only in very carefully controlled experiments or not at all. Particularly in the United Kingdom, groups have been destroying such crops when they can be identified. Proponents argue that Americans have been eating genetically modified foods for over ten years (few Americans know this) with no known side effects. For the last few years, most large European supermarket chains have required their suppliers to certify that no product contains any GM product; large signs in their stores say that everything is, to the extent possible, GM free. Such actions are much less common in the United States. The same approach is growing in restaurants, some of which put notices on their menus that to the extent possible the food served is GM free.

ANIMAL RIGHTS

Closely related to Deep Ecology is an issue that has interested both philosophers and activists: the question of the rights of animals. Do animals have rights? If so, what are they?

On the whole, environmentalists accept the notion that animals have rights at roughly the same level as human beings—that is, at a minimum they have the right to be treated in the way that humans call *humane*. Others argue that animals have more rights, including the right not to be exploited by human beings. This position translates into vegetarianism and the rejection of the use of animals in scientific experimentation. Animal rights are controversial for some environmentalists because they think the issue detracts from what they consider more important questions, such as reducing the actual degradation of the environment. But groups like the Animal Liberation Front (most active in the United Kingdom) and People for the Ethical Treatment of Animals (PETA) believe that animals have rights in exactly the same way as human beings and are willing to use violence against humans to further their position. These

---

[19] William Least Heat-Moon [William Trogdon], *PrairyErth: (A Deep Map)* (Boston: Houghton Mifflin, 1991).

Najah Feanny/Corbis

Peter Singer (b. 1946) is the Ira W. DeCamp Professor of Bioethics at the University Center for Human Values, Princeton University. He is author of *Animal Liberation: A New Ethics for Our Treatment of Animals* (1975); he is credited with beginning the modern animal rights movement. He was the first director of the Center for Human Bioethics at Monash University (Australia). He is the author or coauthor of *Democracy and Disobedience* (1973, 1994), *Practical Ethics* (1979), *The Reproduction Revolution, Should the Baby Live?, Rethinking Life and Death* (1995), *One World: The Ethics of Globalization* (2002), and *The President of Good & Evil: The Ethics of George W. Bush* (2004).

groups act on their beliefs. For example, in the United Kingdom in 2004, under threat from animal rights activists Cambridge University decided not to build an animal research laboratory. Oxford University has continued to build one, but a fake letter purporting to be from the chairman was sent to shareholders of the main construction company suggesting that shareholders sell their shares to avoid being targeted by the activists. Shares dropped 19 percent, and the company later withdrew from the project. In addition, a company that supplied concrete for the project had its depots around the country vandalized with extensive damage to equipment. An indication of the strength of feeling on the part of some animal rights activists is the death of Barry Horne (1952–2001) while on a hunger strike in prison. Horne is consider a martyr to the animal rights cause.

The phrase *animal liberation* was first used April 5, 1973, as a headline for an article by Peter Singer (b. 1946) in *The New York Review of Books*. Today Singer, now a professor of philosophy at Princeton University, says that despite differences, "we share with them [animals] a capacity to suffer, and this means that they, like us, have interests."[20] Singer, probably the best-known advocate of animal rights, argues against speciesism or "the idea that it is justifiable to give preference to beings simply on the grounds that they are members of the species *Homo sapiens*,"[21] saying that arguments in favor of the species are similar to those favoring one race over another, and we now reject those arguments.[22]

---

[20] Peter Singer, "Animal Liberation at 30," *New York Review of Books* (May 15, 2003): 23.

[21] Singer, "Animal Liberation at 30," 23.

[22] Singer, "Animal Liberation at 30," 23–24.

Most environmentalists take a middle ground where animals are concerned, wanting to protect species deemed endangered (a rapidly growing list worldwide), encouraging the reintroduction of species to traditional habitats where they no longer exist, and recognizing that humans regularly upset any balance among animal species so that some species multiply rapidly to the detriment of other species. Many environmentalists believe that this last problem requires human intervention to reestablish balance, while Deep Ecologists point out that it simply demonstrates that humans are the problem and cannot therefore be the solution. Law in the United States has generally followed the more conservative approach.[23]

The concern for animals has influenced behavior and public policy. About half as many animals are used in research today as were used in 1970, and it is easy to buy products, like cosmetics, that used to be tested on animals but are now labeled as not having been tested in this way. And in the European Union, new rules are being put in place on how animals destined to be food are treated; for example, more space for them to live in is one of the new rules.

On the other hand, the World Trade Organization (WTO) does not allow countries to ban importation of products produced by cruel means, even if those means are illegal in the country. For example, the United States was prohibited from barring the importation of tuna from Mexico that were caught using drift nets, which kill dolphins.

CURRENT TRENDS

The most striking development within environmentalism is how it has been picked up by theorists of other ideologies such as political Islam, Liberation Theology, and Marxism where it previously played little or no role.[24] Within environmentalism, most issues are relatively unchanging.

The Eco-Village Movement

A worldwide movement has recently developed to establish small settlements that integrate human life into the natural environment. Such villages already exist throughout the world. The movement stresses learning from how peoples throughout the world have successfully adapted to their environments.

---

[23] Specific laws of importance where animals are concerned include the National Environmental Policy Act of 1969 (83 Stat. 852), the Marine Mammal Protection Act of 1972 (86 Stat. 1027), and the Endangered Species Act of 1973 (87 Stat. 884). For the main laws, see http://www.epa.gov/epahome/laws.htm

[24] See Richard C. Foltz, Frederick M. Denny, and Azizan Baharuddin, eds., *Islam and Ecology: A Bestowed Trust* (Cambridge, MA: Harvard University Press for the Center for the Study of World Religions, Harvard Divinity School, 2003); Leonardo Boff, *Ecology and Liberation: A New Paradigm*, trans. John Cumming (Maryknoll, NY: Orbis Books, 1995); and James O'Connor, *Natural Causes: Essays in Ecological Marxism* (New York: Guilford Press, 1998).

"An eco-village is a human scale, full-featured settlement which integrates human activities harmlessly into the natural environment, supports healthy human development, and can be continued into the indefinite future."[25] Eco-villages can be urban or rural, although so far most are rural. Urban eco-villages tend to be neighborhoods that have either collectively decided to transform themselves into a sustainable community or were purposely built as such. Most rural eco-villages have resulted from changes made to existing villages, but a few have been built from scratch.

Green Political Parties

Germany has the most successful Green Party (Die Grünen). It is part of the ruling coalition government with the Social Democratic Party and holds a number of cabinet posts, but its representatives have found it almost as difficult to effectively advocate for the environment with political power as without it. This comes partially from being the minor party in the coalition and partially from the standard political problem of how to balance competing interests.

The U.S. Green Party states these "Ten Key Values of the Green Party":

1. Grassroots democracy
2. Social justice and equal opportunity
3. Ecological wisdom
4. Nonviolence
5. Decentralization
6. Community-based economics and economic justice
7. Feminism and gender equity
8. Respect for diversity
9. Personal and global responsibility
10. Future focus and sustainability[26]

Although some of these key values are designed to appeal to hoped-for supporters, they are much the same as the statements by Milbrath and Paehlke cited earlier.

Sustainability

A theme that appears throughout the Green Party platform is the central issue for most North American environmentalists: sustainability. Sustainability goes to the heart of the ecological approach in that it sees all aspects of the environment,

---

[25] http://www.gaia.org/

[26] http://gp.org/tenkey.html

including human beings, as capable of being balanced so that the environment can be "sustained" or kept from being significantly damaged or depleted.

One focus of sustainability is energy policy. The Green Party advocates the elimination of nuclear power and the development of renewable energy sources like solar and wind power. Renewable energy sources are symbolic of the sustainability ethic because their use does not damage or deplete any aspect of the environment.

Global Warming

Internationally, one issue currently a focus of attention is global warming. The concern here is that human activity appears to be producing a gradual increase in average temperatures around the globe. Major global temperature fluctuations have occurred in the past, so there is some dispute over the degree to which the observable changes are part of a "normal" cycle or the direct result of human activity; but most scientists agree that warming is occurring and that is potentially disastrous.

The concerns range from significant changes in weather patterns that affect agricultural production to the melting of the polar icecaps (clearly happening) and the flooding of coastal cities that are already below sea level, like New Orleans in the United States and Amsterdam in The Netherlands, as well as cities like New York and London that have not previously been thought vulnerable. Other possible effects include much more severe weather in areas not prepared for such storms, and altered ocean currents that could completely change the climate of countries bordering the currents.

What to do about this phenomenon is in dispute. Some scientists believe that it is already too late or nearly so, but most think that agreements to limit damage to the environment can still work. The United Nations Framework Convention on Climate Change, known as the Kyoto Protocol, agreed to the following objective regarding global warming:

> The ultimate objective of this Convention and any related legal instruments that the Conference of the Parties may adopt is to achieve, in accordance with the relevant provisions of the Convention, stabilization of greenhouse gas concentrations in the atmosphere at a level that would prevent dangerous anthropogenic interference with the climate system. Such a level should be achieved within a time-frame sufficient to allow ecosystems to adapt naturally to climate change, to ensure that food production is not threatened and to enable economic development to proceed in a sustainable manner.[27]

Although the United States withdrew from the agreement and convinced some other countries to do so, the protocol has been signed by enough countries for it to go into effect; it became legally binding on February 16, 2005.

---

[27] http://unfccc.int/resource/convkp.html Article 2.

SUGGESTED READING

Environmentalism

Some Classic Works

Abbey, Edward. *The Monkey Wrench Gang.* Philadelphia: J.B. Lippincott, 1975.

Bookchin, Murray. *Toward an Ecological Society.* Montreal: Black Rose Books, 1980.

Callenbach, Ernest. *Ecotopia: The Notebooks and Reports of William Weston.* Berkeley, CA: Banyan Tree Books, 1975.

Carson, Rachel. *Silent Spring.* 40th anniversary ed. Boston: Houghton Mifflin, 2002.

Club of Rome. *The Limits to Growth.* 2nd ed. New York: Universe Books, 1974.

Ehrlich, Paul. *The Population Bomb.* Rev. and exp. ed. New York: Ballantine, 1989.

Foreman, Dave. *Confessions of an EcoWarrior.* New York: Harmony Books, 1991.

Gorz, André. *Ecology as Politics.* Translated by Patsy Vigderman and Jonathan Cloud. Boston: South End Press, 1980.

Illich, Ivan. *Energy and Equity.* London: Calder & Boyars, 1974.

Leopold, Aldo. *A Sand County Almanac, and Sketches Here and There.* New York: Oxford University Press, 1949.

Muir, John. *The Velvet Monkey Wrench.* Santa Fe, NM: John Muir Publications, 1975.

Naess, Arne. *Ecology, Community, and Lifestyle: Outline of an Ecosophy.* Translated and edited by David Rothenberg. Cambridge: Cambridge University Press, 1989.

Schumacher E[rnst] F[riedrich]. *Small Is Beautiful: A Study of Economics as If People Mattered.* London: Blond and Briggs, 1973.

Books and Articles

Abbey, Edward. *Hayduke Lives!* Boston: Little, Brown, 1990.

Attfield, Robin. *Environmental Ethics: An Overview for the Twenty-First Century.* Cambridge, England: Polity, 2003.

Alaimo, Stacy. *Undomesticated Ground: Recasting Nature as Feminist Space.* Ithaca, NY: Cornell University Press, 2000.

Barry, John. *Rethinking Green Politics: Nature, Virtue, and Progress.* London: Sage, 1999.

Barry, John, and Marcel Wissenburg, eds. *Sustaining Liberal Democracy: Ecological Challenges and Opportunities.* Basingstoke, England: Palgrave, 2001.

Baxter, Brian. *Ecologism: An Introduction.* Washington, D.C.: Georgetown University Press, 1999.

Brown, Lester. *Eco-Economy: Building an Economy for the Earth.* New York: W.W. Norton, 2001.

Bryner, Gary C. *Gaia's Wager: Environmental Movements and the Challenge of Sustainability.* Lanham, MD: Rowman & Littlefield, 2001.

Callenbach, Ernest. *Ecotopia Emerging.* Berkeley, CA: Banyan Tree Books, 1981.

Dasgupta, Partha. *Human Well-Being and the Natural Environment.* Oxford: Oxford University Press, 2001.

Davis, John, ed. *The Earth First! Reader: Ten Years of Environmental Radicalism.* Salt Lake City: Gibbs Smith, 1991.

Deep Ecology and Anarchism: A Polemic, with Contributions by Murray Bookchin, Brian Morris, Rodney Aitchtey, Graham Purchase, Robert Hart, Chris Wilbert. London: Freedom Press, 1993.

Defending the Earth: A Dialogue between Murray Bookchin and Dave Foreman. Montreal: Black Rose Books, 1991.

de-Shalit, Avner. *The Environment between Theory and Practice.* Oxford: Oxford University Press, 2000.

Devall, Bill, and George Sessions. *Deep Ecology.* Salt Lake City: Peregrine Books, 1985.

Diamond, Irene, and Gloria Feman Orenstein, eds. *Reweaving the World: The Emergence of Ecofeminism.* San Francisco: Sierra Club Books, 1990.

Dobson, Andrew. *Citizenship and the Environment.* Oxford: Oxford University Press, 2003.

———. *Green Political Thought.* 3rd ed. London: Routledge, 2000.

———. *Justice and the Environment: Conceptions of Environmental Sustainability and Theories of Distributive Justice.* Oxford: Oxford University Press, 1998.

———, ed. *Fairness and Futurity: Essays on Environmental Sustainability and Social Justice.* Oxford: Oxford University Press, 1999.

Doherty, Brian, and Marius de Geus, eds. *Democracy and Green Political Thought: Sustainability, Rights, and Citizenship.* London: Routledge, 1996.

Dryzek, John, David Downes, Christian Hunold, and David Schlosberg with Hans-Kristian Hernes. *Green States and Social Movements: Environmentalism in the United States, United Kingdom, Germany, and Norway.* Oxford: Oxford University Press, 2003.

Eaton, Heather, and Lois Ann Lorentzen, eds. *Ecofeminism and Globalization: Exploring Culture, Context, and Religion.* Lanham, MD: Rowman & Littlefield, 2003.

Eckersley, Robyn. *Environmentalism and Political Theory: Toward an Ecocentric Approach.* Albany: State University of New York Press, 1992.

———. *The Green State: Rethinking Democracy and Sovereignty.* Cambridge, MA: MIT Press, 2004.

Environmental Ethics 1, no. 1–present (founded 1979).

Foltz, Richard C., Frederick M. Denny, and Azizan Baharuddin, eds. *Islam and Ecology: A Bestowed Trust.* Cambridge, MA: Harvard University Press for the Center for the Study of World Religions, Harvard Divinity School, 2003.

Gillroy, John Martin, and Joe Bowersox, eds. *The Moral Austerity of Environmental Decision Making: Sustainability, Democracy, and Normative Argument in Policy and Law.* Durham, NC: Duke University Press, 2002.

Gottlieb, Roger S., ed. *This Sacred Earth: Religion, Nature and Environment.* 2nd ed. New York: Routledge, 2004.

Grim, John A., ed. *Indigenous Traditions and Ecology: The Interbreeding of Cosmology and Community.* Cambridge, MA: Harvard University Press for the Center for the Study of World Religions, Harvard Divinity School, 2001.

Hawthorne, Susan. *Wild Politics: Feminism Globalisation Bio/Diversity.* North Melbourne, Vic, Australia: Spinifex Press, 2002.

Heinberg, Richard. *The Party's Power: Oil, War, and the Fate of Industrial Societies.* Gabriola Island, BC, Canada: New Society Publishers, 2004. Discussion of the effects of the decline in cheap oil.

Hill, Julia Butterfly. *The Legacy of Luna: The Story of a Tree, a Woman, and the Struggle to Save the Redwoods.* New York: HarperCollins, 2000.

Holden, Barry. *Democracy and Global Warming.* London: Continuum, 2002.

Holland, Stephen. *Bioethics: A Philosophical Introduction.* Cambridge, England: Polity, 2003.

Jamison, Andrew. *The Making of Green Knowledge: Environmental Politics and Cultural Transformation.* Cambridge: Cambridge University Press, 2001.

Kassiola, Joel Jay, ed. *Explorations in Environmental Political Theory: Thinking about What We Value.* Armonk, NY: M.E. Sharpe, 2003.

Katz, Eric, Andrew Light, and David Rosenberg, eds. *Beneath the Surface: Critical Essays of Deep Ecology.* Cambridge, MA: MIT Press, 2000.

Latour, Bruno. *Politics of Nature: How to Bring the Sciences into Democracy.* Translated by Catherine Porter. Cambridge, MA: Harvard University Press, 2004.

Lee, Martha F. "Environmental Apocalypse: The Millennial Ideology of Earth First!" In *Millennialism, Messiahs, and Mayhem,* edited by Tom Robbins and Susan J[ean] Palmer, 119–37. New York: Routledge, 1997.

McNeill, J[ohn] R. *Something New under the Sun: An Environmental History of the Twentieth-Century World.* New York: W.W. Norton & Co., 2000.

Meyer, John M. *Political Nature: Environmentalism and the Interpretation of Western Thought.* Cambridge, MA: MIT Press, 2001.

Milbrath, Lester W. *Envisioning a Sustainable Society: Learning Our Way Out.* Albany: State University of New York Press, 1989.

Minteer, Ben A., and Bob Pepperman Taylor, eds. *Democracy and the Claims of Nature: Critical Perspectives for a New Century.* Lanham, MD: Rowman & Littlefield, 2002.

O'Connor, James R. *Natural Causes: Essays in Ecological Marxism.* New York: Guilford Press, 1998.

Paehlke, Robert C. *Democracy's Dilemma: Environment, Social Equity, and the Global Economy.* Cambridge, MA: MIT Press, 2003.

————. *Environmentalism and the Future of Progressive Politics.* New Haven, CT: Yale University Press, 1991.

Prugh, Thomas, Robert Costanza, and Herman Daly. *The Local Politics of Global Sustainability.* Washington, DC: Island Press, 2000.

Purdue, Derrick A. *Anti-GenetiX: The Emergence of the Anti-GM Movement.* Aldershot, England: Ashgate, 2000.

Radcliffe, James. *Green Politics: Dictatorship or Democracy.* Basingstoke, England: Palgrave, 2000.

Schlosberg, David. *Environmental Justice and the New Pluralism: The Challenge of Difference for Environmentalism.* Oxford: Oxford University Press, 1999.

Shutkin, William A. *The Land That Could Be: Environmentalism and Democracy in the Twenty-First Century.* Cambridge, MA: MIT Press, 2001.

Smith, Mark J. *Ecologism: Toward Ecological Citizenship.* Minneapolis: University of Minnesota Press, 1998.

Stein, Rachel, ed. *New Perspectives on Environmental Justice: Gender, Sexuality, and Activism.* New Brunswick, NJ: Rutgers University Press, 2004.

Sturgeon, Noël. *Ecofeminist Natures: Race, Gender, Feminist Theory, and Political Action.* New York: Routledge, 1997.

Taylor, Bron. "Religion, Violence, and Radical Environmentalism: From Earth First! to the Unabomber to the Earth Liberation Front." *Terrorism and Political Violence* 10, no. 4 (Winter 1998): 1–42.

Torgerson, Douglas. *The Promise of Green Politics: Environmentalism and the Public Space.* Durham, NC: Duke University Press, 1999.

Warren, Karen J. *Ecofeminist Philosophy: A Western Perspective on What It Is and Why It Matters.* Lanham, MD: Rowman & Littlefield, 2000.

Wenz, Peter S. *Environmental Ethics Today.* New York: Oxford University Press, 2001.

Whiteside, Kerry H. *Divided Natures: French Contributions to Political Ecology.* Cambridge, MA: MIT Press, 2002.

Woodin, Michael, and Caroline Lucas. *Green Alternatives to Globalisation: A Manifesto.* London: Pluto Press, 2004.

Animal Rights

Some Classic Works

Singer, Peter. *Animal Liberation.* 2nd ed. New York: New York Review of Books, 1990.

————, ed. *In Defense of Animals.* Oxford: Basil Blackwell, 1985.

Books and Articles

Cavalieri, Paola. *The Animal Question: Why Nonhuman Animals Deserve Human Rights.* Translated by Catherine Woollard; revised by the author. Oxford, England: Oxford University Press, 2001.

Cavalieri, Paola, and Peter Singer, eds. *The Great Ape Project: Equality beyond Humanity.* New York: St. Martin's Press, 1994.

Francione, Gary L. *Introduction to Animal Rights: Your Child or Your Dog?* Philadelphia: Temple University Press, 2000.

————. *Rain without Thunder: The Ideology of the Animal Rights Movement.* Philadelphia: Temple University Press, 1996.

Guither, Harold D. *Animal Rights: History and Scope of a Radical Social Movement.* Carbondale: Southern Illinois University Press, 1998.

Nibert, David. *Animal Rights, Human Rights: Entanglements of Oppression and Liberation.* Lanham, MD: Rowman and Littlefield, 2002.

Scully, Matthew. *Dominion: The Power of Man, the Suffering of Animals, and the Call to Mercy*. New York: St. Martin's Press, 2002.

Singer, Peter. "Animal Liberation at 30." *New York Review of Books* (May 15, 2003): 23–26.

———. *The Animal Liberation Movement: Its Philosophy, Its Achievements, and Its Future*. Nottingham, England: Old Hammond, 2000.

———. *Ethics into Action: Henry Spira and the Animal Rights Movement*. Lanham, MD: Rowman & Littlefield, 1998.

Sunstein, Cass R., and Martha C. Nussbaum, eds. *Animal Rights: Current Debates and New Directions*. New York: Oxford University Press, 2004.

Varner, Gary E. *In Nature's Interests? Interests, Animal Rights, and Environmental Ethics*. New York: Oxford University Press, 1998.

Websites

Environmentalism

"Selected Web Sites for Environmental Issues." In Gary C. Bryner, *Gaia's Wager: Environmental Movements and the Challenge of Sustainability*, 237–39. Lanham, MD: Rowman & Littlefield, 2001.

Circle of Life: http://www.circleoflife.org/about/mission.htm

Earth Island Institute: http://www.earthisland.org/

Earth Liberation Front: http://www.earthliberationfront.com/

The Earth Times: http://www.earthtimes.org/

Earthvision: http://www.earthvision.net/

Ecology and Environment Links: http://www.ecotopia.org/about/ecolinks.html

EcoTopia: http://www.ecotopia.org/index.html

Futures 500: http://www.globalfutures.org/

Global Ecovillage Network: http://www.gaia.org/

Green Alliance: http://www.greenalliance.org.uk

Green Party: http://www.gp.org/

Green Party platform: http://www.gp.org/platform/2004/2004platform.pdf

Institute for Social Ecology: http://www.social-ecology.org/

Kyoto Protocol: http://unfccc.int/resource/convkp.html

National Council for Science and the Environment: http://www.cnie.org/

Sierra Club: http://www.sierraclub.org

Unabomber Manifesto: http://www.soci.niu.edu/~critcrim/uni/uni.txt

Animal Rights

Animal Concerns Community: http://www.animalconcerns.org/

Animal Liberation Front: http://www.animalliberationfront.com/

Animal Rights Canada: http://www.animalrightscanada.com/

Animal Rights FAQ (includes lists of organizations): http://www.animal-rights.com/

Feminists for Animal Rights: http://www.farinc.org/

International Society for Animal Rights: http://www.isaronline.org/

Opposition to the animal rights movement: http://www.animalrights.net/

People for the Ethical Treatment of Animals: http://www.peta.org/

13

Conclusion

A number of sets of ideologies have been discussed in this book, and major disagreements and differences of opinion have been described in connection with all of them. In conclusion, it will be instructive to compare these ideologies with regard to questions of political philosophy (see the questions in Chapter 1 on pages 14–15) and with the various parts of the social system. Any comparison has to be general, while attempting to avoid being too broad and therefore meaningless. A number of points will be relevant only to certain ideologies.

HUMAN NATURE

The first question concerns human nature; thus we ask, (a) What are the basic characteristics of human beings as human beings? and (b) What effect does human nature have on the political system? The first question is answered in surprisingly similar ways by all the ideologies except fascism and national socialism. In Marxism, democracy, anarchism, and feminism we find the position that human beings are capable of a high degree of community spirit and good feeling toward other humans. Hate and fear are stressed in fascism and national socialism. Also underlying much of Marxism, democracy, and anarchism is a belief that humans are fundamentally rational. This is not found in nationalism, fascism, and national socialism; instead our irrational side is stressed. Feminism attempts to recognize both sides. Liberation Theology is also balanced because it recognizes the Christian assumption of original sin but stresses the liberating nature of Christ's message. Both Islam and environmentalism have a mixed view of human nature; people are capable of both great good and great evil.

The question about the effect of human nature on the political system is not answered directly or conclusively by most of the ideologies. In Marxism, fascism, national socialism, anarchism, feminism, Liberation Theology, and political Islam, the concern is with the effect on people of changes in the political system. This is most obvious in anarchism: the development of a noncoercive society will allow the growth of a better, more sociable human being. Democracy has perhaps the most sophisticated approach. The whole complex of ideas focusing on freedom with limits, representation with regular checks by voters, and general equality is based on the position that each individual is capable of both high-minded self-sacrifice and corruption—that the human being is an extremely complex creature who cannot be encompassed by a unidimensional system.

ORIGINS

The second set of questions—(the origin of society and government or the state) is, on the whole, ignored. I have indicated that both traditional Marxism and certain arguments for democracy discuss these origins, but contemporary political ideologies are not often concerned with such questions for the simple reason that most people view them as irrelevant. People everywhere find themselves in society and ruled by government; therefore, the question of how this happened does not seem important.

Anarchist thinkers, because they reject the notion of government and the state, do consider their origins. Generally, the conclusion is that humans at some time or other formed a society for protection. Some anarchists argue that government was also formed out of society for protection or security. Others argue that government came about simply by usurpation on the part of some group within society. Each argument accepts society as a necessary form of cooperation, whereas government is rejected. It can and should be done away with because it stifles our ability to cooperate.

OBLIGATION

Questions in the third set, centering on political obligation, are answered by all the ideologies except feminism, Liberation Theology, and environmentalism. But in some ideologies, such as democracy, the answers are so diverse and varied that it is difficult even to summarize them. Why do or should people obey the government? Or, in order to include anarchism, should they at all? Anarchism gives the simplest answer: there is no reason why anyone should obey government.

For fascists and national socialists, government must be obeyed because it is the government—because the system of leadership demands obedience. People must obey because it is their role to obey. Marxists argue that the dictatorship of the proletariat should be obeyed because it provides security and economic benefits in the period of transition from bourgeois society to a full communist society. At the same time, Marxists contend that the individual living under capitalism has no specific obligation to obey; on the contrary, the proletariat has an obligation to attempt to overthrow capitalism.

Democracy demands a more complicated discussion because of the variety of reasons given for justifying obedience, some of which are similar to the reasons given in other ideologies. These reasons may be summarized as follows: (1) security, (2) other benefits, (3) requirement by the community justifying obedience, and (4) the ability of citizens to change the entire system while still obeying. Democracy raises other problems with regard to revolution and the possibility of disobedience. Some contemporary democratic theory accepts the idea of disobedience without revolution. Most democratic ideology rejects revolution within a democracy for the fourth reason just listed. Political Islam is a theocracy with God's will interpreted by the ruler; therefore, the citizen clearly must obey.

LAW

The fourth set of questions concerns law. All the ideologies, with the exception of anarchism, consider law to be a major means of instituting and maintaining the social norms they support. And even some anarchists see a role for policies and procedures that have been agreed by the members of the community. The sources of law differ greatly among the ideologies. In fascism and national socialism, it is the will of the leader. In Marxism, during the dictatorship of the proletariat, law should reflect the needs of the proletariat as the dominant class. In all forms of democracy, it should come from the people, either directly or through representatives. An area of difference that affects democracy as well as most of the other ideologies is how hard law should be to make and change. For some, law should be easy to make or change to reflect the changing needs of the leadership or the people. For many, there should be fundamental sets of laws or constitutions that should be hard to change so as to maintain the social norms established by the ideology or, in many forms of democracy, to protect the liberties of citizens.

LIBERTY

The fifth set of questions concerns liberty. Marxists argue that under full communism the individual is given complete liberty. Under the dictatorship of the proletariat, the individual must have sharply curtailed liberty in order to achieve the transition from capitalism and then to full communism. Fascists and national socialists consider the question of liberty irrelevant. The individual's freedom, such as it is, is found entirely in giving himself or herself up to the state. Anarchism, because it has no government, offers a system of complete liberty except as people choose to limit themselves as part of a cooperative endeavor. Liberation Theology stresses the need to develop liberty as a means of helping the oppressed.

Democracy again is the most complicated of the ideologies because it provides limited liberty within the system. The problem for democracy is how to maintain a system in which the people are willing and able to limit themselves, both individually and through the legal system, so the liberty of one individual does not infringe on the liberty of another.

Almost equally complex is feminism. Reform feminists argue that freedom is all that is really needed, but most feminists are ambivalent. Shouldn't pornography be eliminated? Is advertising that exploits women acceptable? Hence most feminists, while arguing for the basic freedoms, feel that some limitations may be necessary, particularly to overcome the mental abuse that women suffer. There is no concept of freedom in political Islam.

EQUALITY

The sixth set of questions concerns equality. Clearly fascists and national socialists reject any form of equality. In anarchism all individuals should be equal, but there is considerable debate among anarchists whether economic equality is a worthwhile goal. Marxists stress social equality and include political equality in the ideal of full communism. In the period of the dictatorship of the proletariat, social equality would exist, but political equality would not because of the need for strong power at the top. Limited economic equality is a goal of Marxism in that Marxists argue for overcoming the extremes of economic inequality. In democracy political and legal equality and equality of opportunity are emphasized. Feminists generally favor all forms of equality. Reform feminists would exclude economic equality but stress equality of opportunity. Liberation Theology stresses the need to overcome inequality. Political Islam assumes a hierarchical society; people are equal in the eyes of God but not in society.

COMMUNITY

The seventh set of questions concerns community, which is reemerging as a central concern of some ideologies. In nationalism, developmental socialism, and Islam, community is and always has been a major component of the belief systems. In fascism and national socialism, the idea of the nation has elements of community, as does the vision of community-based authority in full communism. Many of the other ideologies tend to downplay community and stress individual fulfillment.

POWER

The eighth set of questions relates to power. Power for the Marxist varies depending on whether one is concerned with the dictatorship of the proletariat or full communism. In full communism, power would be spread among all individuals. In the dictatorship of the proletariat, power rests in the hands of a few at the very top of the Communist party. Some thinkers contend power resides in the party as such, but it is more accurate to see it in the hands of a few. Fascists and national socialists also invest power in the hands of very few people or one individual at the top. Supporters of democracy argue that power is held collectively by all citizens, but it is more accurate to see power in the hands of those actively concerned with the governmental process and working within it. There is no focus on power in anarchism; power is found in each individual. Many feminists argue for the empowerment of women as a means of balancing male power, but others argue for a transformation of our whole notion of power to one based on competence and cooperation rather than dominance. Liberation Theologians argue for empowerment of the poor and oppressed. They want power in the sense of domination replaced with a concept of social or communal power. In political Islam there is no single attitude about power. Islamic liberals and revivalists differ, as do Sunnis and Shiites.

JUSTICE

The next two sets of questions, justice and the end of society or government, may be conveniently collapsed together because in each ideology justice will be found by achieving the end of the ideology or the ends of the society or government. In Marxism, justice is found in the proletariat owning the means of production and distribution. For the democrat, justice is found in the individual citizen controlling his or her own destiny through the political system. For the fascist and national socialist, justice is found in the individual giving up himself or herself willingly and thoroughly to the state. For the anarchist, justice is found in the end of government and the achievement of a society based on the individual, usually within a community. For the feminist and Liberation Theologian, justice is found in a truly free and equal society. In political Islam most believers find justice in the application of the *Shari'a* or Islamic law.

STRUCTURE

The final set of questions concerns the structural characteristics of government. Clearly this is almost irrelevant in nationalism, anarchism, full communism, feminism, and environmentalism. The other ideologies include answers to the questions but not in any way that makes valid generalization possible.

   In the answers to these questions, we are able to see the variety of positions taken on fundamental political questions. The answers vary considerably from ideology to ideology, but the answers are also sometimes quite divergent even within a given ideology. This overview gives us some basis for comparing the political aspects of the ideologies. In order to understand more fully the value system in each ideology, we must look at certain other social institutions. Therefore, a second stage of comparing the ideologies must look at these other subsystems of the social system.

SOCIAL STRATIFICATION AND MOBILITY

The first is the social stratification and mobility system. Marxists argue that there will be no social stratification and hence no social mobility system within full communism. Under the dictatorship of the proletariat, the only stratification system would be that between the proletariat and the remnants of the bourgeoisie and the peasantry. The only form of mobility would be for the bourgeoisie and the peasantry to move into the proletariat. (In practice, however, the dictatorship of the proletariat has produced a new social stratification system that establishes a class of technocrats who operate the government, the Communist party, and the various important institutions of the country.) The democratic social stratification and mobility system is based primarily on money and education. The primary means of mobility in the democratic system is education. In fascism and national socialism, stratification is based on race, indications of loyalty to the nation, and service in the party and to the state. Mobility is based on the same standards. In anarchism, there should be no social stratification and hence no mobility system. Feminists are mostly concerned with removing sexual, racial, and sexual orientation barriers from the operation of the social mobility system. Liberation Theology is directed at removing barriers to social advancement. Political Islam has a highly structured social stratification system based on birth, wealth, and learning. Liberal Muslims are questioning some of the ways Islamic societies are stratified.

SOCIALIZATION

The socialization system is made up of various institutions in society that help to give an individual the values of that society. The primary institutions of socialization are the family, the education system, the religious system, and in modern societies, the mass media. Children gain ideas about life before they are capable of articulating those ideas themselves. They hear their parents give positive or negative connotations to certain words and phrases the children can identify but for which they have no meaning. For example, a child in the United States might acquire a positive connotation with the word *democratic* and a negative connotation with the word *republican* from parents who were strongly in favor of the Democratic Party and vice versa. Throughout life we hear words given particular connotations. Again, using the United States as an example, the child might hear the word *communism* as denoting something bad. Therefore, before the individual is capable of understanding what communism is about, she or he is convinced that it is bad, and this conviction will be difficult to change. Institutions of socialization are thus extremely important.

It is noteworthy, first, that Marxists, fascists, and national socialists, almost without exception, hold that the mass media must be carefully controlled so they will present a positive picture of the system. Anarchists tend to argue for completely unlimited mass media. Democracy comes close to this, limiting the media only in cases of libel and then only in relatively rare cases. Democracies have found a greater problem, though, in connection with the unwillingness of government officials to give the mass media complete information, thus attempting to control them.

Marxism, fascism, and national socialism also include control of the other institutions of socialization. Marxists argue for control of religion because it is seen as a direct threat to the ideology. Fascists and national socialists tend, on the other hand, to view religion as positive support for the nationalism that is so important to the ideology; in many cases the religious system supported fascism and national socialism or did not actually oppose them. In anarchism and democracy, there is little concern with controlling religion, although in anarchism one often finds an antipathy toward religion. Many anarchists believe religion consistently supports the state and thus is opposed to the anarchist philosophy. Most, but not all, democratic ideologies and democratic systems separate the religious system and the political system. At the same time, in democracy religion is often a support for the political system.

In every ideology the educational system is used to directly support the ideology. For all the ideologies, education is the most potent force of socialization; therefore, the educational system must be used to support the values of the society or the ideology. On the other hand, only feminism and, to a lesser extent, anarchism say much about changing the family system. It is probably better policy to attempt to imbue parents with the values one wishes to have passed on to the children; if the parents accept the values, they will be automatically passed on to the children. Therefore, it is not really necessary to tamper with the family system. Clearly the greatest concern of Liberation Theology is changing the church as a means of socialization. It also wants to change other mechanisms of socialization, but the church is its primary target.

Most feminists feel a need for a completely transformed socialization system. Education, the family, religion, and the mass media must not merely be open to women, but must be changed so that no one will be socialized into submission. In this sense feminism is potentially the most radical of contemporary ideologies.

In Islam religion, the family, and the mosque are the centers of society; socialization takes place there first. Education plays a central role. Socialization is designed to give the person the values of the religion.

THE ECONOMIC SYSTEM

In each of the ideologies we have discussed, a considerable amount of time has been spent analyzing the economic system. It is not necessary here to repeat those arguments, but only to say that each ideology differs regarding the economic system. Marxism combines a state socialist economic system with an authoritarian political system. Democracy combines either a capitalist or a socialist economic system with its political system, although there are variations within each. Fascism and national socialism have authoritarian political systems combined with modified capitalist systems. Developmental socialism is connected to a wide variety of political systems. Anarchists are unclear concerning the appropriate system. Feminists are deeply divided on economic questions. Liberation Theology is primarily concerned with the results of the economic system, not the means, but it is accurate to say that it leans heavily toward socialism. Political Islam encourages private property with a religious duty of charity.

THE POLITICAL SYSTEM

The political system is the mechanism that makes binding decisions on society, and even an anarchist society would have to make some such decisions. Today almost all ideologies play at least lip service to democracy. The only exceptions are fascism and national socialism and some positions within political Islam. The arguments are mostly around the degree of democracy, which relates back to the question of power and to what extent it should be representative or participatory.

It is noteworthy that environmentalism has few positions that fit the categories used here. This fact suggests that environmentalism is still developing the attributes of an ideology.

These comments have been very general, but they provide some basis for comparing the ideologies. It is important for a student of contemporary political ideologies to understand both the similarities and the differences among these ideologies. We do not know what the future holds for any of them, but it is important for us to understand what each of these ideologies accepts so we will be able to evaluate them objectively.

In conclusion, I hope the reader will reflect carefully on the challenges that the variety of belief systems poses for his or her own beliefs. What can be expected of humanity in the future? Are we rational, capable of determining a desirable future and working for it? Or are we irrational, incapable of so choosing or unwilling to work for our goals? Must humans be coerced or can we cooperate without coercion? Can humanity achieve a meaningful equality or is equality of any sort an impossible dream? Can humans be free or is freedom a dangerous fantasy? All these questions and many others are continually being answered. We must reflect on the society in which we want to live. We must ask ourselves, In what ways are we affected by ideologies? Do we have an ideology? What are its elements? How does it affect us? How do the ideologies held by others affect us? The answers to all these questions will affect how we spend our lives.

Glossary

This glossary provides a short definition of certain terms used in the text to help the reader better understand the discussion. Many terms are discussed at some length in the text; the reader is referred to the index to locate that discussion. An asterisk identifies these terms. Because some words have different meanings in different ideologies, it is important, in using the index, to follow the word throughout the text.

Alienation   Estrangement or being cut off.

Al Qaeda   Islamic guerrilla group in Afghanistan that is enforcing a very strict interpretation of the *Shari'a* in the areas it controls.

*Anarchism   A system of social order achieved without government.

Aristocracy   Originally meaning rule by the few best, it now means rule by the few, usually with the implication of a hereditary few.

Authority   Legitimate power (*see* Power).

Ayatollah   A Shiite title meaning "sign of God."

Biocentrism   A theory that argues that the biosphere should be the focus of value as opposed to human beings being the focus (called *anthropocentrism*).

Bourgeoisie   In Marxism, refers to the owners of the means of production as contrasted to the proletariat (*see* Proletariat), who have only their labor power to sell. More generally used to refer to the property-owning middle class.

Bureaucracy   The set of nonelected public officials or administrators in any political system.

Burqa   Clothing, required for women by the Taliban in Afghanistan and in some ethnic groups, that covers the body from the top of the head to the ground with only a mesh opening over the eyes.

Caliph   Successor (Sunni).

*Capitalism   Private ownership of the means of production and the organization of production for profit.

Caste   An exclusive, hereditary class. Most often refers to the system found in Hinduism in which people who are members of specific occupations are separated from other occupations through rigid social divisions that prohibit any kind of contact.

Charismatic leader   A person who is able to gain followers through the force of her or his personality.

Charter schools   Schools established to operate outside the regulation of state and local government to provide an education that fits the needs of specific groups of students.

Civil disobedience   The belief that disobedience to the law (*see* Law) is an appropriate means of forcing a political system to change the law.

Civil society   The set of largely voluntary associations and interactions found in the family, clubs, neighborhood associations, and so forth that operate outside the formal political system.

Class   A way of ranking or ordering society. In Marxism the ranking is based on the relationship to the means of production. Other ideologies rank on the basis of wealth, education, racial purity, service to the state, or some other criterion.

*Class struggle   In Marxism, used to describe the fundamental relationship between or among classes and the driving force of social change.

Cohousing   A modern version of cooperative housing in which a group of people owns individual houses or apartments and collectively owns the land and common buildings.

Colonialism   A system in which one state (*see* State) controls another state for the benefit of the former (*see also* Neocolonialism).

Communal living   A group of people living together in an intentional community. Such communities have a wide range of forms from charismatic or authoritarian leadership to consensual democracy and from complete income sharing to complete private ownership.

*Communism   A social and economic system characterized by an authoritarian political system and a state socialist economic system. Originally meant community of goods or goods publicly held (*see also* Full communism).

Communitarianism   Focus on the community rather than on the individual.

*Community   A sense of common interest.

Consciousness raising   A new type of activism in the feminist and other movements. Rather than implementing formal organizations with elected officers, people meet in small groups to explore their own experiences.

*Conservatism   The belief that social change should take place slowly with due account taken of tradition.

Consociational democracy   A system of power sharing in which each significant group in a country is guaranteed a place in the governing bodies and has a veto on some issues.

Cooperation   An economic theory in which people join together to form an economic unit from which they will all benefit.

*Corporatism   Sometimes called *neocorporatism*. The arrangement of political and economic relationships so that power groups in society are actively involved with government in making public policy.

Cosmopolitanism   *See* Internationalism.

Critical theory   A general theory that views society from the point of view of the need to change it.

Decentralization   A system in which power is moved from a central organization to regional centers or from a large group to small groups composing it.

Deep Ecology   A movement that stresses the importance of the entire biosphere as opposed to human beings.

*Democracy   A political system characterized by direct or indirect rule by the people (*see also* Participatory democracy, Representation, *and* Consociational democracy).

Democratic centralism   A system developed by Vladimir Ilyich Lenin in which discussion within an organization is completely free until a decision is made, at which time all must support the decision.

Democratization The process of developing democratic institutions in societies in which they did not previously exist.

Developmental socialism A theory that proposes to use socialist economic policies to assist the economic development of a country.

Diaspora From a Greek word meaning dispersion, diaspora originally was used to refer to Jews living outside the Holy Land but is now used to refer to any group with large numbers living outside their traditional homeland.

*Dictatorship of the proletariat In Marxism, the transitional stage after a successful revolution in which society is gradually transformed.

Direct democracy Democracy by citizens rather than by representatives.

Ecofeminism A movement that argues that women are closer to nature than men and that the Green Movement fails to recognize the male bias of environmentalism.

Ecosocialism A movement that combines environmentalism and socialism.

Elitism The belief that society is and/or should be ruled by a small group of powerful people.

*Equality Sameness in some defined way.

*Equality of opportunity The situation that exists when an individual can succeed or fail on the basis of his or her own ability and effort with no artificial barriers to that success or failure.

Essentially contested concepts Concepts over which there are fundamental, irreconcilable differences.

Ethnic group A group of people united by race or national origin.

Eugenics The selection or prevention of births.

Extremism The far right and the far left.

False consciousness A phrase within Marxism referring to the results of the class-based socialization process in which an individual gains an incorrect view of the world. Similar to the concept of ideology (*see* Ideology).

*Fascism Originally referred to the principles of the 1922 Italian anticommunist revolution. Now a general term referring to authoritarian political systems characterized by extreme nationalism (*see also* National socialism).

Federalism The division of political power between a central government and governments representing defined territories within the country. These latter units, called *states* in the United States, may be further divided into smaller units, but these smaller units do not have the same standing as the other two levels of government.

*Feminism An ideology centered on eliminating oppression of all human beings while stressing the importance of women.

Fourth World There are two very different meanings in use today. In this book the phrase refers to indigenous peoples; it is also sometimes used to refer to the poorest of the developing countries.

Frankfurt School The school of Marxist thought that developed critical theory (*see* Critical theory).

*Freedom The ability to act without constraint (*see also* Liberty *and* Rights).

Führer German word for leader. Used in national socialism.

*Full communism The final stage of the Marxist theory of history.

Gaia hypothesis Proposes that our planet functions as a single organism that maintains conditions necessary for its survival.

General strike A strike in which all workers engage at the same time. Generally believed to be a major tactic in a revolution or to put pressure on a government.

*Globalization The process by which the world economy is becoming fully integrated. Seen by its opponents as the spread of U.S. power.

Government *See* Political system.

Hajj The pilgrimage to Mecca required at least once of every Muslim.

Han A Chinese word adopted by Koreans to describe a perceived aspect of and split in their character. It refers, on the one side, to accumulated grievances, resentments, frustrations, and the like that build into a deep-seated sense of being wounded. On the other side, it refers to a self-mockery of these very feelings.

Hegemony A word used by Antonio Gramsci and others to refer to the intellectual and cultural dominance of a class.

*Human nature   The essential characteristics of all human beings.

Idea of progress   The belief that the world is getting continually better. May or may not include a role for human action.

Ideologue   A true believer or one who has an extremely limited view of the world based on an ideology; an unusually strong believer in an ideology.

*Ideology   A value system or belief system accepted as fact or truth by some group. It is composed of sets of attitudes toward the various institutions and processes of society.

Imam   Leader (Shiite).

*Immigration   Moving to a new country with the intent of establishing permanent residence.

Impeachment   A method of removing a public official from office that involves a hearing of charges before a body of public officials, most often a legislature.

Initiative   A method of bringing a proposed piece of legislation to a vote of the citizenry through a petition signed by citizens.

Internationalism   A belief in the need to unify the entire world in some way; a love of the world.

Jahiliyya   In Islam the period of "ignorance" or "barbarism" before Muhammad preached in Arabia. Used by Sayyid Qutb to refer to the present day.

Jihad   The struggle to follow Islam. Holy war.

Jingoism   Extreme nationalism.

*Justice   Fairness.

*Law   A rule established through an accepted procedure within a community that permits or prohibits certain actions. The system of rules so established.

Levellers   A seventeenth-century British movement favoring political equality.

*Liberalism   A general tendency to accept the ability of human beings to use their reason to reform the social system; a general tendency accepting change as inevitable but controllable; the advocacy of liberty.

*Liberation Theology   The combination of Marxism and theology in opposition to the oppression of the poor.

*Libertarianism   An ideology related to anarchism (*see* Anarchism) that advocates a radically reduced role for government. Also known as *minimalism*.

*Liberty   Freedom (*see* Freedom). Generally used to refer to legally established freedoms (such as civil liberty) (*see also* Rights).

Luddites   Men who broke up textile machinery in the early nineteenth century because they believed the machines were taking away jobs. *See also* Neo-Luddites.

Lumpenproletariat   The lowest class in the Marxist class analysis.

Majority rule   An electoral system in which 50 percent plus 1 or more of those voting win.

Maori   The minority population of New Zealand. The Maori settled New Zealand, probably from Polynesia, about a thousand years ago.

Market socialism   Socialism that accepts some aspects of the free market.

*Materialism   The belief that matter or the material (as opposed to spirit, the spiritual, or the ideal) is the determining factor in human life.

Minimalism   *See* Libertarianism.

Monetarism   The belief that control of the money supply is the most important tool for manipulating a national economy and avoiding inflation.

Monkeywrenching   Direct action or civil disobedience to protect the biosphere.

Monopoly   An organization that controls trade in some commodity or a sector of the economy of a country.

Mosque   A building for Islamic worship.

Muslim   An adherent of Islam.

Nation   A people or race with common descent, language, history, and/or political institutions.

Nationalism   An ideology based on love for the nation (*see* Nation) or patriotism (*see* Patriotism) together with demands for action.

Nationalization of industries   Taking industries into public ownership.

*National Socialism   An ideology developed in Germany under the leadership of Adolf Hitler emphasizing an authoritarian political system, extreme nationalism, and racism (*see also* Fascism).

Naturalization   A process by which a citizen of one country becomes a citizen of another country.

Negative liberty   Liberty achieved by limitations on government activity.

*Neocolonialism   A system of economic dominance over a former colony by an industrialized nation (*see also* Colonialism).

*Neoconservatism   The position held by former liberals in the United States who have become fiscal and foreign policy conservatives.

Neocorporatism   *See* Corporatism.

Neofascism   Contemporary versions of fascism found throughout the world but particularly common in France, Germany, and the United States.

*Neoliberalism   The position taken by liberals in the United States who have tried to modify the welfare-state image of liberalism.

Neo-Luddites   Contemporary opponents of technology. *See also* Luddites.

Neutralism   *See* Nonalignment.

New Left   The phenomenon of the so-called Sixties (1965–75) that tried to revitalize the old left while not making the same mistakes it had.

*New Right   The most conservative wing in U.S. politics.

Nonalignment   A stance taken in the Third World in which such nations refuse to identify themselves with either of the major power blocs—hence the name Third World.

Ombudsman   A Swedish word that has been adopted into English to refer to a public official whose duties are to protect the rights (*see* Rights) of citizens against government, particularly bureaucracies.

Participation   In democracy, to be actively involved in the political system.

*Participatory democracy   A form of democracy in which individuals who are to be affected by a decision make the decision collectively.

Patriarchy   The system of male dominance that affects all social institutions.

*Patriotism   Love of country (*see also* Nationalism).

Petite bourgeoisie   In Marxist class analysis, the class of small shopkeepers, artisans, and the like who are being pushed down into the proletariat (*see* Proletariat).

Pluralism   In the United States, the political system seen as composed of competing groups.

*Political obligation   The duty to obey the dictates of the political system (*see* Political system).

*Political system   Those parts of the social system that have the ability to make authoritative or binding decisions for a territory.

Popular sovereignty   The belief, central to democracy, that ultimate political authority rests with the people.

Positive liberty   Liberty achieved through government support.

Postcolonialism   A contested concept concerned with the social, economic, political, cultural, and psychological conditions created by colonialism and the resistance to it.

*Postmodernism   A contested concept that rejects universals and emphasizes the multiplicity of viewpoints through which people view the world.

*Power   The ability to compel others to act in the way one wishes (*see also* Authority).

PR   *See* Proportional representation.

Privatization   The movement of activities from public control to private control.

*Proletariat   That class in Marxism that has only its labor power to sell (*see also* Bourgeoisie).

Property   Something owned or possessed. Private property: something owned by an individual. Public property: something owned collectively.

Proportional representation   A system of election in which individuals are elected on the basis of the proportion of the votes received rather than the majority as under majority rule (*see* Majority rule).

Queer theory   A set of ideas based on the idea that identities are not fixed.

Qur'an   The holy book for Muslims.

Ramadan   The ninth month of the Muslim year. A month of fasting.

Reapportionment   The process of realigning the boundaries of electoral districts to bring them more in balance in population.

Recall   A mechanism by which an elected official may be removed from office during his or her term through a vote of the electors in the area he or she represents.

Referendum   A process of deciding political questions by the direct vote of the electorate.

Regionalism   The tendency that exists in a number of parts of the world to form economic and sometimes political agreements among states (*see* State) to form larger and more powerful units.

*Representation   A system in which voters choose other individuals to act in their place in making political decisions.

Republic   A state (*see* State) in which political decisions are made by elected representatives.

*Revolution   The process of bringing about radical political and social change, usually violently.

*Rights   Legally defined and enforceable freedoms (*see* Freedom). More generally, something to which a person is entitled. Traditionally divided into natural rights, or rights that are due a person just because of his or her existence as a human being, and civil rights, or rights that are guaranteed by government (*see also* Liberty).

Rochdale Society of Equitable Pioneers or Rochdale Pioneers   The midnineteenth-century founders of the cooperative movement.

Self-governing socialism   *See* Self-management.

*Self-management   A type of socialism (*see* Socialism), sometimes known as self-governing socialism, in which workers' control (*see* Workers' control) operates in industry and decentralized democracy works in government.

Shari'a   Islamic law.

Sikh   An adherent of a monotheistic religion founded in India around 1500.

Skinheads   A subculture group known for their shaved heads and distinctive style of dress (generally jeans, polos, military flight jackets, and boots). They are most often identified with the far right, but there are antiracist skinheads and apolitical skinheads.

Social construction of reality   A phrase used in Marxism to refer to the socialization process. It means that an individual gains a view of the world based on her or his place in society.

Social Darwinism   The belief that relations among human beings are characterized by a struggle for survival.

*Socialism   Public ownership of the means of production and distribution. May be highly centralized as in communism (*see* Communism) or very decentralized as in self-management (*see* Self-management).

*Socialization   The process by which a society transmits its values from generation to generation.

*Social mobility   The process by which individuals move up or down in a society's social stratification system (*see* Social stratification).

Social stratification   The system by which a society ranks the people within it (*see also* Caste, Class, Equality of opportunity, *and* Social mobility).

*State   An organized community (*see* Community) with its own political system (*see* Political system) and law (*see* Law).

Sufi   A believer in Sufism, an ascetic and mystical movement within Islam.

Sunna   Exemplary behavior of Muhammad.

*Superstructure   In Marxism, all those parts of life that are produced by the basic economic relations of society.

*Surplus value   In Marxism, the value of goods produced above and beyond that needed to support labor.

Syndicalism   A system in which the means of production and distribution are under the control of a federation of trade unions.

Taliban   The former rulers of Afghanistan who were a small, extremely conservative sect within Islam. Spelled *Taleban* in the United Kingdom.

Terrorism   A form of killing for political purposes. It differs from assassination in that it is frequently directed at nonpolitical targets and groups of people rather than individuals. Its purpose, as implied by the word, is to terrorize the people in a country.

Theocracy   Literally, rule by God. Usually refers to a government in which religious leaders rule directly or indirectly based on their claim of divine authority.

Toleration   The recognition and acceptance of differing belief systems, particularly the acceptance of beliefs believed to be wrong.

Totalitarianism An authoritarian government that involves itself in all aspects of society, including the private lives of citizens. The word initially developed to refer to Germany under Hitler and the Soviet Union under Stalin.

Ulama Muslim religious scholar.

Utopia Literally means "no place." Term invented by Thomas More (1478–1535) that now refers to all representations of much better societies.

Utopian socialism Refers to the ideas of a number of nineteenth-century thinkers who proposed ways of changing the world. The phrase was first used by Friedrich Engels (1820–95) and was meant as criticism.

Welfare The system of contributory and noncontributory pension, health, unemployment, and other benefits and social services funded and regulated by government.

Workers' control Power (*see* Power) in the workplace in the hands of workers rather than management; the industrial system produced by such an arrangement.

Workplace democracy Democracy within the working environment.

Biographical Notes

Mahmoud Abbas (b. 1935), commonly known as Abu Mazen, was chosen as chair of the Palestinian Liberation Organization (PLO) on the death of Yasir Arafat. He won election as president of the Palestinian Authority in January 2005.

Edward Abbey (1927–90) is revered by radical environmentalists for his fictional portrayals of environmental direct action.

Abigail Adams (1744–1818) was an early advocate of women's rights in the United States and wife of John Adams, the second president.

John Adams (1735–1826) was the second president of the United States.

Jane Addams (1860–1935) was a social settlement worker and peace advocate. She ran Hull House in Chicago from 1889 to 1935. She was awarded the Nobel Peace Prize in 1931.

Theodor Adorno (1903–69) was one of the founders of the Frankfurt School.

Michel Aflaq (1910–89) was a founder of the Baath Party.

Ahn Byung-mu (1922–96) was the leading theologian of Minjung Theology.

Mullah Mohammad Omar Akhund (b. 1959/61) is the founder and head of the Taliban movement in Afghanistan.

Louis Althusser (1918–1990) was a French Marxist philosopher best known as a theorist of ideology who also contributed more widely to late twentieth-century Marxist thought.

Benedict Anderson (b. 1936) is the Aaron L. Binenkorb Professor of International Relations and Director of the Modern Indonesia Program at Cornell University.

Susan B. Anthony (1820–1906) was one of the leaders of the women's suffrage movement.

Yasir Arafat (1929–2004) was the leader of the PLO (Palestinian Liberation Organization).

John Ashcroft (b. 1942) was the attorney general of the United States from 2000 to 2004. He was Governor of Missouri from 1985 to 1993. He was elected to the U.S. Senate from Missouri in 1994 and served until he lost the 2000 election.

Mary Astell (1668–1731) was an English author who proposed a separate community of women in her *A Serious Proposal to the Ladies* (1694).

Daw Aung San Suu Kyi (b. 1945) won the Nobel Peace Prize in 1991 for her efforts to reestablish democracy in Myanmar (formerly Burma), where she was under house arrest off and on since 1989.

Mikhail Bakunin (1814–76) was a leading Russian anarchist theorist who spent most of his life in western Europe.

Hasan al–Banna (1906–49) was the founder of the Muslim Brotherhood.

Salah al–Din Baytar (1911–80) was a founder of the Baath Party.

Simone de Beauvoir (1908–86) was a French author best known for her reflections on the status of women, *Le Deuxième Sexe* (1949, in English as *The Second Sex* in 1952).

Samuel Beckett (1906–1989) was an Irish playwright who moved to Paris in the 1930s. He is famous for his depictions of alienation, particularly in *Waiting for Godot*. He won the Nobel Prize in Literature in 1969.

Edward Bellamy (1850–98), a U.S. author, is remembered for his best-selling utopian novel *Looking Backward 2000–1887* (1888). A movement for social change was founded to promote Bellamy's ideas and was influential both in the United States and abroad.

Alexander Berkman (1870–1936) was a friend of Emma Goldman and an activist in the American anarchist movement who spent many years in prison in the United States.

Isaiah Berlin (1909–97) was a British historian of ideas and social theorist.

Eduard Bernstein (1850–1932) was a follower of Marx who rejected revolutionary socialism. He was a major Marxist revisionist, arguing for evolutionary socialism and political activity.

Hakim Bey is a pseudonym of Peter Lamborn Wilson, who is coeditor of *Autonomedia* and *Semiotext(e)* and has written extensively on Sufism, Persian poetry, and Irish literature. As Bey he is known as one of the foremost theorists of contemporary anarchism.

Homi K. Bhabha (b. 1949) is an Indian-born professor at Harvard University and a major theorist of postcolonialism.

Vinoba Bhave (1895–1982) was an Indian spiritual leader.

Osama bin Laden (b. 1957) is the leader of a worldwide terrorist network called Al Qaeda.

Ernst Bloch (1885–1977) was a German Marxist philosopher best known for his book *Das Prinzip Hoffnung (The Principle of Hope)* (1959).

Allan Aubrey Boesak (b. 1946) is a South African minister, theologian, and activist. He was found guilty of fraud in his use of funds intended for the victims of apartheid and served a year in prison before being released on parole. He is currently Visiting Professor of Theology, Church, and Society at American Baptist Seminary of the West.

Clodovis Boff (b. 1944) is a Servite priest and a professor of theology at the Catholic University of São Paulo. He is the brother of Leonardo Boff.

Leonardo Boff (b. 1938) is Emeritus Professor of Ethics, Philosophy of Religion, and Ecology at the State University of Rio de Janeiro. For twenty years he was Professor of Systematic Theology at the Institute for Philosophy and Theology in Petrópolis, Brazil. He is one of the best-known theologians of Liberation Theology. He was a member of the Franciscan order who left the order after twice being "silenced" (meaning he could not publish) by the Vatican for his writings on Liberation Theology.

Murray Bookchin (b. 1921) is a major anarchist theorist who has recently been a major contributor to environmentalism in the United States.

Bernard Bosanquet (1848–1923) was an English conservative philosopher.

Willy Brandt (1913–92) was active in German politics throughout the postwar period. He was best known for his period as governing mayor of Berlin (1957–66) and as chancellor of the Federal Republic of Germany.

John J. Breuilly (b. 1946) holds the Chair in Nationalism in the Department of Government at the London School of Economics and Political Science.

Edmund Burke (1729–97) is best known as the founder of conservatism.

George W. Bush (b. 1946) is the forty-third president of the United States and was elected to a second term in 2004.

Richard Girnt Butler (1918–2004) was the neo-Nazi founder of Aryan Nations.

Étienne Cabet (1788–1856) was a French utopian socialist and founder of the Icarian movement that established a number of communities in the United States.

Ernest Callenbach (b. 1929) is the author of a series of books describing a fictional society emphasizing ecology.

Albert Camus (1913–60) was an Algerian-born French novelist and exponent of existentialism who won the Nobel Prize in literature in 1957. He was part of the French Resistance movement during World War II.

Rachel Carson (1907–64) was an early writer on environmental issues.

Hugo Chavez (b. 1954) is the controversial president of Venezuela elected in 1998.

Judy Chicago (b. 1939) is a feminist artist.

Robert Coles (b. 1929) is James Agee Professor of Social Ethics at Harvard and a research psychiatrist for Harvard University Health Services, was awarded the Medal of Freedom by President Clinton in 1998, is known for his work with underprivileged children, and has written extensively on how children experience the world.

Alex Comfort (1920–2000) is best known for his books on sexual technique, but his career ranged through fiction, poetry, anarchist theory, and geriatric psychology.

James H. Cone (b. 1938) is the leading exponent of Black Theology and is Charles A. Briggs Distinguished Professor of Systematic Theology at Union Theological Seminary, New York.

Sir Bernard Crick (b. 1929) is a professor emeritus of politics at the University of London and previously professor of political theory at Sheffield University. As a scholar he is best known for his book *In Defence of Politics* (1972 and later editions) and *George Orwell: A Life* (1982). He was knighted for service to citizenship education from his work chairing the Advisory Group on Citizenship in England, which issued the "Crick Report" in 1998.

Robert A. Dahl (b. 1915) is Sterling Professor of Political Science Emeritus at Yale University.

Dante Alighieri (1265–1321) was an Italian poet best known as the author of the *Divine Comedy* who also contributed to political theory.

Charles Darwin (1809–82) was a famous English naturalist who put forth a number of important theses about evolution.

Dorothy Day (1897–1980) was a leader of the Catholic Worker Movement. She was jailed in 1917 for protesting in front of the White House in favor of women's suffrage.

Milovan Djilas (1911–95) was vice president under Josep Tito when Tito originally came to power in 1945. He was expelled from the party in 1954, losing all his government positions, because of articles he had written criticizing the manner in which communism was developing in Yugoslavia. He was jailed in 1956 for writing about the "New Class" of communist elites that shared privileges and was jailed again from 1962 to 1966 for publishing *Conversations with Stalin*, which was based on his personal experience.

Paul Ehrlich (b. 1932) is Bing Professor of Population Studies, Stanford University, and was one of the first people in the twentieth century to write about the problems of overpopulation.

Dwight David Eisenhower (1890–1969) was the thirty-fourth president of the United States (1953 to 1961). Before becoming president, he was a general in the U.S. Army and one of the leaders of the allied forces in World War II, chief of staff of the U.S. Army (1945–48), and president of Columbia University (1948–53).

Jon Elster (b. 1940) is Robert K. Merton Professor of Social Sciences, Political

Science Department, Columbia University, and is known for his work on rational choice theory.

Friedrich Engels (1820–95) was a friend of and coauthor with Karl Marx.

Amitai Etzioni is University Professor and Director of the Institute of Communitarian Policy Studies at George Washington University.

Louis Farrakhan (originally Louis Eugene Walkott, b. 1933) is the current head of the Nation of Islam.

Shulamith Firestone (b. 1945) is the author of *The Dialectic of Sex* (1970), one of the more radical feminist texts of the period, and a strong advocate of women's reproductive rights.

Henry Ford (1863–1947) established the Ford Motor Company using assembly-line production.

Dave Foreman (b. 1946) is an active environmentalist and was a founder of Earth First! He left Earth First! in 1989 and founded the Wildlands Project, which wants to restrict humanity to specific areas.

Charles Fourier (1772–1837) was a French utopian socialist.

Francis of Assisi (born Giovanni Francesco Bernardone, 1182–1226) was the radical founder of the Franciscan movement and is now recognized in Liberation Theology as an early advocate of the poor.

Michael Freeden (b. 1944) is Professor of Politics and Professorial Fellow, Mansfield College, Oxford University, and is the editor of the *Journal of Political Ideologies*.

Paulo Freire (1921–97) was a Brazilian social theorist best known for his book *The Pedagogy of the Oppressed* (1972) and seen as a theorist of both anarchism and Liberation Theology.

Sigmund Freud (1856–1939) was the Austrian founder of psychoanalysis.

Betty Friedan (b. 1921) is a feminist author and lecturer.

Milton Friedman (b. 1912) won the Nobel Prize in Economics in 1976 for his work on monetary theory. He is the best known conservative economist in the United States and taught economics at the University of Chicago for many years. He is currently Senior Research Fellow, Hoover Institution, Stanford University.

Francis Fukuyama (b. 1952) restarted the "end of ideology" debate in 1989. He is Bernard L. Schwartz Professor of International Political Economy at the Paul H. Nitze School of Advanced International Studies, Johns Hopkins University.

Margaret Fuller (1810–50) was a teacher and writer struggling against the limited roles allowed women during her lifetime.

Mu'ammar Gadafi (al-Qaddafi) (b. 1942) took over the leadership of Libya in 1969. He renamed the country the Libyan Arab Republic and led it under various titles until he renounced all titles in 1979. For many years he provided financial support for various terrorist groups and supported most movements opposed to the West. In the last few years he has begun to establish more positive relations with the West.

Mohandas K. Gandhi (1869–1948) was a leader of the anticolonial movement in India who used nonviolence as a means of bringing about social change. He had been influenced by Henry David Thoreau and influenced Martin Luther King, Jr.

Roger Garaudy (b. 1913) is a French Marxist philosopher who was raised as a Roman Catholic and converted to Islam in 1982. In 1995 he published a book denying the Holocaust and was tried and fined by a French court.

Clifford Geertz (b. 1926) is Professor Emeritus in the School of Social Science at the Institute for Advanced Study, Princeton, New Jersey.

Henry George (1839–97) was an American economic theorist who developed a theory based on land taxation, known as the *single tax,* as a means of redistributing wealth.

Anthony Giddens (b. 1938) is a theorist and advocate of "third way politics."

Charlotte Perkins Gilman (1860–1935) was a feminist writer, lecturer, and activist. She is now best known for her novel *Herland* (1915).

William Godwin (1756–1836) was the earliest British anarchist theorist.

Joseph Goebbels (1897–1945) was Germany's minister for propaganda and national enlightenment under Adolf Hitler.

Emma Goldman (1869–1940) was known as "Red Emma" and was a leading anarchist, lecturer, popularizer of the arts, and agitator for birth control, women's rights, and free speech.

Albert [Arnold] Gore, Jr. (b. 1948) was the forty-fifth vice president of the United States. He served in the U.S. House of Representatives from 1977 to 1985 and was elected to the Senate from Tennessee in 1985, serving until 1993. He lost the 2000 presidential election to George W. Bush, even though he won the popular vote.

André Gorz (b. 1924) is a French social theorist.

Antonio Gramsci (1891–1937) was an Italian social theorist and is considered one of the most original Marxist theorists.

T[homas] H. Green (1836–82) was a professor of philosophy at Oxford University.

Angelina E. Grimké (1805–79) was an abolitionist and women's rights pioneer.

Sarah Moore Grimké (1792–1873) was an abolitionist and women's rights pioneer.

Gustavo Gutiérrez (b. 1928) is one of the founders of Liberation Theology, a Peruvian theologian, and was a professor at the Pontifical University of Peru. He is currently John Cardinal O'Hara Professor of Theology at the University of Notre Dame in the United States.

Jürgen Habermas (b. 1929) is one of the most important contemporary thinkers influenced by Marxism and the Frankfurt School. He is now probably most important as a theorist of deliberative democracy. He is Professor Emeritus of Philosophy, University of Frankfurt.

Jörg Haider (b. 1950) was the leader of the Freedom Party (FPO) of Austria, a right-wing party that became part of the ruling coalition in Austria in 2000. Because of controversy over his stated beliefs, he resigned from the leadership of the party, but he remains a powerful force within the party and the country.

Matt Hale (b. 1971) is the leader of the Creativity Movement, formerly called the World Church of the Creator, a white supremacist church.

Michael Hardt is Associate Professor of Literature and Romance Studies and Director of Graduate Studies at Duke University.

Michael Harrington (1928–89) was cochair of the Democratic Socialists of America and a professor of political science at Queens College of the City University of New York.

Nancy C. M. Hartsock (b. 1943) is a professor of political science and women's studies at the University of Washington in Seattle.

F. A. Hayek (1899–1992) was one of the most important conservative thinkers of the twentieth century. His *The Road to Serfdom* (1944) provided an ethical defense of free markets.

William Least Heat-Moon is the pseudonym of William Trogdon (b. 1939), the author of *Blue Highways* (1982), *PrairyErth* (1991), and *River-horse* (1999). The name is often seen without the hyphen.

Georg Wilhelm Friedrich Hegel (1770–1831) was the most important German philosopher of the nineteenth century.

Ammon Hennacy (1893–1970) was an important American anarchist.

Johann Gottfried von Herder (1744–1803) was a German philosopher, clergyman, and literary critic.

Julia "Butterfly" Hill (b. 1974) sat in a tree she called Luna for 738 days to protest logging. She was inducted into the Ecology Hall of Fame, continues as an environmental and political activist, and founded an organization called Circle of Life.

Adolf Hitler (1889–1945) was founder and leader of the National German Workers' Party, chancellor (1933–45), and head of state (1934–45) of Germany. He was the leading figure of the Nazi movement and is still venerated by Nazis and neo-Nazis everywhere.

Bonnie Honig (b. 1959) is Professor of Political Science at Northwestern University and Senior Research Fellow at the American Bar Foundation in Chicago.

bell hooks is the pseudonym of Gloria Watkins (b. 1952), and as hooks she has written a number of important works of African American feminism.

Dwight N. Hopkins is Professor of Theology at the University of Chicago Divinity School.

Max Horkheimer (1895–1973) was the director of the Institute for Social Research in Frankfurt, Germany, and developed the philosophical basis for critical theory.

Barry Horne (1952–2001) was an animal rights protestor who died while on a hunger strike in a prison in the UK at age 49.

Hubert H. Humphrey (1911–1978) was Democratic Senator from Minnesota from 1949 to 1964 and from 1971 to 1978 and vice president from 1964 to 1968. He was the Democratic nominee for president in 1968.

Ivan Illich (1926–2002) was the Austrian-born cofounder of the Center for Intercultural Documentation (CIDOC) in Cuernavaca, Mexico. He is a radical priest who has written extensively about contemporary society.

Ada Maria Isasi-Diaz (b. 1943) is a former Roman Catholic nun and a political refugee from Cuba and the founder and primary exponent of Mujerista Theology, which addresses the concerns of Latina women.

Thomas Jefferson (1743–1826) was the third president of the United States. Of all the things he accomplished, Jefferson thought his three most important actions were writing the Declaration of Independence and the Virginia Act for Establishing Religious Freedom and founding the University of Virginia.

John Paul II (1920–2005, born as Karol Joseph Wojtyla), the first pope from Poland, was elected pope in 1978.

Lyndon Baines Johnson (1908–73), president from 1963 to 1969, presided over a period of great change in U.S. social policy, particularly the beginnings of the extension of civil rights to African Americans and the war on poverty. He is still best known for his failure to solve the Vietnam crisis.

Theodore Kaczynski (b. 1942) is the Unabomber, who assembled and mailed bombs that injured or killed individuals who worked in the fields of technology and industry. He published a manifesto calling for a return to a less technology-based life and direct action to achieve that goal. He is currently serving time in prison for his actions.

John Maynard Keynes (1883–1946) was an English economist who argued for the use of government spending to stimulate the economy.

Ayatollah Ruhollah Khomeini (1900–1989) was the religious leader of Iran after the Shiite overthrow of the Shah. He was one of the intellectual fathers of Islamic revivalism.

Russell Kirk (1918–94) was an important modern conservative. His *The Conservative Mind* (1953) provided an intellectual basis for modern conservatism. He founded the journals *Modern Age* in 1957 and *University Bookman* in 1960; both served as outlets for conservative writing.

Peter Kropotkin (1842–1921) was born into the Russian aristocracy but became the most important anarchist thinker of all time.

Will Kymlicka is Canada Research Chair in Political Philosophy, Queen's University, Canada, and one of the foremost theorists of multiculturalism.

Ernesto Laclau is a professor of government at the University of Essex in the United Kingdom.

Emma Lazarus (1849–87) was an American poet and essayist best known for her poem "The New Colossus," which appears on a plaque on the Statue of Liberty.

Ursula K. Le Guin (b. 1929) is a major science fiction, fantasy, and children's author whose novel *The Dispossessed* (1974) is a contribution to anarchist theory.

Vladimir Ilyich Lenin (born Vladimir Ilyich Ulyanov, 1870–1924) was the leader of the Russian Revolution of 1917 and ruled the Soviet Union from the revolution to his death.

Aldo Leopold (1886–1949) was the author of *A Sand County Almanac* (1949) and an early environmentalist.

Jean-Marie Le Pen (b. 1928) is the leader of the National Front in France.

Abraham Lincoln (1809–65) was the sixteenth president of the United States.

John Locke (1632–1704) was an important British philosopher and political thinker. His most important works were *Essay Concerning Human Understanding* (1689), and, in political thought, *Two Treatises of Government* (published in 1690 but written earlier). The U.S. Declaration of Independence was based on the *Second Treatise of Government*.

Ned Lud (or Ludd) (fl. 1779) provided the name for the Luddites. He broke up machinery (stocking frames) around 1799 because he believed the machines would take over his job. Possibly a mythical figure.

Georg Lukács (1885–1971) was a Hungarian philosopher and literary critic whose theoretical work, particularly *Geschichte und Klassenbewusstsein* (*History and Class Consciousness,* 1923) led to a revival of Marxist thought.

Rosa Luxemburg (1870–1919) was a Polish Marxist revolutionary who opposed both Lenin's centralism and Bernstein's gradualism.

Jean-François Lyotard (1924–98) was a French philosopher best known for his exposition of postmodernism.

Wangari Maathai (b. 1940) won the Nobel Peace Prize in 2004. She founded the Green Belt Movement, a grassroots development organization that mobilized poor women to plant over 30 million trees, and provides education, family planning, and nutrition. She is the first woman from Africa to receive the Nobel Peace Prize.

Catharine A. MacKinnon (b. 1946) is Professor of Law, University of Michigan, and the most important feminist legal theorist.

James Madison (1751–1836) was secretary of state (1801–09) during the presidency of Thomas Jefferson and then the fourth president of the United States (1809–17). Madison is now mostly remembered as one of the authors of *The Federalist Papers* (1787–88) and as a major contributor to the drafting of the U.S. Constitution.

Errico Malatesta (1850–1932) was a leading Italian anarchist theorist.

Malcolm X (originally Malcolm Little, 1925–65) was a leader of the Nation of Islam, but split from it to form the Organization of Afro-American Unity before his assassination.

Nelson Rolhlahla Mandela (b. 1918) was the symbol of the campaign by the African National Congress (ANC) against apartheid or racial separation in South Africa. Imprisoned from 1964 to 1990, on his release he was elected president of the ANC and then served as president of South Africa from 1994 to 1999.

Karl Mannheim (1893–1947) was a Hungarian-born sociologist active in Germany until he fled the Nazis in 1933. He is best known as the major theorist of the sociology of knowledge.

Mao Zedong (1893–1976) was the longtime leader of the People's Republic of China.

Subcomandante Marcos is the name used by the best-known leader of the Zapatista movement. He has recently been tentatively identified as Rafael Sebastián Guillén Vicente.

Herbert Marcuse (1898–1979) was a member of the Frankfurt School who stayed in the United States after the school returned to Germany following World War II. He was a major influence on the New Left.

Karl Marx (1818–83) was the founder of communism.

Abu al-A'la al-Mawdudi (1903–79) of Pakistan was one of the intellectual founders of Islamic revivalism.

George McKay (b. 1950) is professor of cultural studies at the University of Central Lancashire, England.

Timothy McVeigh (1968–2001) was executed for bombing the Alfred P. Murrah Federal Office Building in Oklahoma City.

Lester Milbrath (b. 1925) is Professor Emeritus of Political Science and Sociology, State University of New York–Buffalo. Formerly he was the Director of the Research Program in Environment and Society at Buffalo.

Angela Miles (b. 1946) is Professor in the Department of Adult Education and Counseling Psychology at the Ontario Institute for Studies in Education in Toronto and Associate Director of the Transformative Learning Centre.

John Stuart Mill (1806–73) was the most influential philosopher in the English-speaking world in the nineteenth century. He is best known today for his essay *On Liberty* (1859).

David Miller (b. 1946) is Official Fellow of Politics at Nuffield College, Oxford University, England, and an important political theorist.

Warith Deen Mohammad (b. 1933 as Wallace Dean Muhammad) became the leader of the Nation of Islam after the death of his father Elijah Muhammad. But he rejected his father's racial message, renamed the organization the American Muslim Mission, and took it into the mainstream of Islam.

Charles de Secondat de La Brède et de Montesquieu (known as Montesquieu) (1689–1755) was a French political thinker whose book *De l'esprit des lois (The Spirit of the Laws)* (1748) influenced the writers of the U.S. Constitution, particularly his advocacy of a separation of powers.

Margaret Moore (b. 1960) is an associate professor of political science at the University of Waterloo in Canada and author of *The Ethics of Nationalism*.

J[ohn] P[ierpont] Morgan (1837–1913) was an American banker and financier.

William Morris (1834–96) was the leader of the British arts and crafts movement

whom some label as an anarchist theorist. He considered himself a Marxist.

Johann Most (1846–1906) was a German immigrant to the United States who advocated "propaganda by the deed" and published bomb-making manuals.

Chantal Mouffe is Quinton Hogg Senior Research Fellow at the Centre for the Study of Democracy at the University of Westminster (UK).

Muhammad (570–632) was the founder of Islam.

Elijah Muhammad (originally Elijah Poole, 1897–1975) was the spiritual leader of the Nation of Islam.

John Muir (1838-1914) was born in Scotland but spent his life in the United States as a naturalist and advocate for the preservation of the wilderness. In particular, he was instrumental in getting Congress to pass the bill that established a national park to protect the Yosemite Valley. He was one of the founders and the first president of the Sierra Club.

Benito Mussolini (1883–1945) was the founder of the fascist movement and head of the Fascist Party in Italy.

Ralph Nader (b. 1934) was a leader for automobile safety and on various environmental and safety issues before becoming the presidential candidate of the Green Party in the 2000 U.S. election. He ran as an independent candidate in the 2004 presidential election.

Arne Naess (b. 1912) is a Norwegian philosopher who coined the term *Deep Ecology*.

Gamal Abdel Nasser (1918–70) was the leader of the Egyptian revolution and head of the country for many years.

Sergei Nechaev (1847–82) was an advocate of terrorism and the inspiration for the insane revolutionary in Fyodor Dostoevsky's *The Possessed* (1871).

Antonio Negri (b. 1933) was a professor of political science at the University of Padua. He was arrested in connection with terrorist activities in Italy in the seventies, spent some years in exile in France, and is currently serving his sentence in Rome. Many believe that his arrest and conviction were without basis.

Jawaharlal Nehru (1889–1964) was a leader of the anticolonial movement in India and prime minister of India from 1947 to 1964.

A. S. Neill (1883–1973) was a pioneering educator who founded a school, Summerhill School, based on democratic ideals.

Richard Milhous Nixon (1913–94) was president of the United States from 1969 to 1974 and is the only president who has been forced to resign from office to avoid impeachment. He presided over the largest expansion of social welfare programs in U.S. history, ended the war in Vietnam, and reestablished political relations with the People's Republic of China.

Kwame Nkrumah (1909–72) was the leader of Ghana from 1957, when it gained independence, to 1966.

Robert Nozick (1938–2002) was a professor of philosophy at Harvard University and author of *Anarchy, State, and Utopia* (1974), the best exposition of anarcho-capitalism.

U Nu (1907–95) was a leader of Burmese independence, the first prime minister of Burma (1948–62), and, as U Thant, secretary general of the United Nations from 1961 to 1971.

Julius K. Nyerere (1922–99) was the first president of Tanganyika and then of Tanzania.

Susan Moller Okin (1947–2004) was Martha Sutton Weeks Professor of Ethics in Society in the Department of Political Science at Stanford University. At the time of her death she was the Marta S. Horner Distinguished Visiting Professor at the Radcliffe Institute for Advanced Study.

Robert Owen (1771–1858) was a British utopian socialist who founded the New Harmony community in Indiana.

Robert C. Paehlke (b. 1941) is Professor and Chair, Environmental and Resource Studies Program, Trent University, Canada.

Thomas Paine (1737–1809) was a political agitator, revolutionist, and political theorist.

Ian Richard Kyle Paisley (b. 1926) is the Moderator of the Free Presbyterian Church in Northern Ireland and founder and leader of the Democratic Unionist Party, the largest party in Northern Ireland that favors continued union with Great Britain.

Olof Palme (1927–86) was a Swedish leader of European democratic socialists.

Christobel Pankhurst (1880–1958) was a daughter of Emmeline Pankhurst and active in the British suffrage movement.

Emmeline Pankhurst (1858–1928) was a leader of the British suffrage movement.

Sylvia Pankhurst (1882–1960) was a leader of the British suffrage movement.

Anton Pannekoek (1873–1960) was the Dutch founder of Council Communism.

William L[uther] Pierce (1933–2002) was the leader of the National Alliance.

Augusto Pinochet (b. 1915) was head of the military government that ruled Chile from 1973 to 1990. In power he suppressed the opposition, leaving at least 3,000 Chileans dead. He is also credited with reviving the Chilean economy.

Plato (427?–347 B.C.) was the founder of social philosophy in the West.

Pierre-Joseph Proudhon (1809–65) was a leading French anarchist theorist.

Vladimir Putin (b. 1952) is the president of the Russian Federation. He was a colonel in the KGB (the Soviet equivalent of the CIA) until 1990. In 1999 Boris Yeltsin (b. 1931) appointed him prime minister, and later that year Yeltsin named Putin acting president when he stepped down. Putin was elected president in 2000.

Robert D. Putnam is the Peter and Isabel Malkin Professor of Public Policy at Harvard University and the author of *Bowling Alone: The Collapse and Revival of American Community* (2000).

Sayyid Qutb (1906–66) was an Egyptian Sunni Muslim leader and one of the intellectual founders of Islamic revivalism. He was jailed from 1954 to 1964 and executed for his opposition to Egypt's leaders.

Thomas Rainsborough (1610–1648) was one of the leaders of the army who sided with the Levellers in the English Civil War.

Tariq Ramadan (b. 1962) is a philosopher who advocates anchoring Islamic principles in the culture of western Europe. He is Professor of Philosophy, College of Geneva, Switzerland, and Professor of Islamic Studies, University of Fribourg. He was granted a visa to teach at Notre Dame University in Indiana, but his visa was revoked at the last minute by the Department of Homeland Security.

Ayn Rand (1905–82) was a novelist, lecturer, and essayist who influenced the growth of libertarianism and minimalism in the United States.

John Rawls (1921–2002) was a professor of philosophy at Harvard University and has been the major liberal theorist of the twentieth century.

Élisée Réclus (1830–1905) was a Belgian geographer and an anarchist theorist.

Ernest Renan (1823–92) was a French philologist and historian.

Rudolf Rocker (1873–1958) was an anarchist theorist who was born in Germany and lived and wrote mostly in the United Kingdom and the United States.

George Lincoln Rockwell (1918–67) was the leader of the American Nazi Party until his assassination.

John Roemer is the Elizabeth S. and A. Varick Stout Professor of Political Science and Economics at Yale University.

Murray Rothbard (1926–95) was a leading American anarcho-capitalist.

Jean-Jacques Rousseau (1712–78) is the best-known French political philosopher.

Claude-Henri Saint-Simon (1760–1825) was a French utopian socialist.

Margaret Sanger (1883–1966) was an early advocate of birth control and women's rights.

Jean-Paul Sartre (1905–80) was a French novelist and philosopher.

Albert Sauvy (1898–1990) was a French demographer who coined the term *Third World*.

E[rnst] F[riedrich] Schumacher (1911–1977) believed in and advanced the idea of sustainable economics, which incorporates theories of nonviolence, intermediate technology, and economies of scale.

Sarah Scott (1723–95) was a British writer now considered an early feminist.

Amartya Sen (b. 1933) is Lamont University Professor, Harvard University, and Adjunct Professor of Population and International Health, Harvard University, and a Fellow of Trinity College, Cambridge University. He won the Nobel Prize in Economics in 1998.

Léopold Sédar Senghor (1906–2001) was a leader of the anticolonial movement in Senegal and the leader of the country after independence, and became known as a significant poet in French.

George Sessions (b. 1938) is one of the primary theorists of Deep Ecology. He is the former Chair of the Philosophy Department and Professor of Philosophy at Sierra College, Rocklin, California.

Luíz Ignácio Lula da Silva (b. 1945) was elected president of Brazil in 2002.

Peter Singer (b. 1946) is the Ira W. DeCamp Professor of Bioethics at the University Center for Human Values, Princeton University. He is the author of *Animal Liberation: A New Ethics for Our Treatment of Animals* (1975) and is credited with beginning the modern animal rights movement.

Adam Smith (1723–90) is best known as the author of T*he Wealth of Nations* (*An Inquiry into the Nature and Causes of the Wealth of Nations* [1776]).

Benjamin Nathaniel Smith (1978–99) was a member of the World Church of the Creator who, on July 3 and 4, 1999, in racially motivated attacks, killed two people, wounded eight people, and shot at and missed nine others before killing himself.

Georges Sorel (1847–1922) was a French journalist and political theorist.

Herbert Spencer (1820–1903) was an English philosopher and the major proponent of social Darwinism.

Lysander Spooner (1808–87) was a lawyer and abolitionist and an early American anarcho-capitalist.

Joseph Stalin (born Iosif Vissarionovich Dzhugashvili, 1879–1953) was the leader of the Soviet Union after Lenin.

Elizabeth Cady Stanton (1815–1902) was one of the founders of the first women's rights conventions in Seneca Falls, New York, in 1848 and a leader of the nineteenth-century women's rights movement.

Max Stirner (pseud. of Johann Kasper Schmidt, 1806–56) was the founder of individualist anarchism.

Charles Taylor (b. 1931) is Board of Trustees Professor of Law and Philosophy at Northwestern University and Professor Emeritus of Political Science and Philosophy at McGill University. He was formerly Chicele Professor of Moral Philosophy at Oxford University.

Harriet Taylor (1808–58) wrote on women's rights and was the wife of John Stuart Mill, whom she influenced to write on the subject.

William Thompson (1775–1833) wrote on socialism and women's rights, the latter material in collaboration with Anna Doyle Wheeler.

Henry David Thoreau (1817–62) was a naturalist, writer, and advocate of civil disobedience.

James Tobin (1918–2002) won the Nobel Prize in Economics in 1981. He proposed a worldwide tax on foreign exchange trading and bond trading that became known as the "Tobin Tax."

Leo Tolstoi (1828–1910) was a famous Russian novelist who is also known as an anarchist theorist.

Camilo Torres (1929–66) was a priest who joined the National Liberation Army (ELN) of Columbia and died in combat.

Benjamin R. Tucker (1854–1939) was one of the most important American anarchist theorists.

Sojourner Truth (b. Isabella Baumfree 1797–1883) was born a slave and became a noted lecturer and abolitionist.

Unabomber; *see* Theodore Kaczynski.

Tabare Vazquez (b. 1940) was elected president of Uruguay in 2004.

Wilhelm Richard Wagner (1813–83) is best known for his operas expressing Teutonic mythology.

Muhammad bin Abd al-Wahab (1703–1791) was the founder of the Wahabist sect of Islam, whose descendants unified the Saudi kingdom. He encouraged people to abandon polytheism and worship Allah alone.

Alice Walker (b. 1944) is an African American author, best known for her novel *The Color Purple* (1982).

Nicolas Walter (1934–99) was a major British anarchist theorist.

Colin Ward (b. 1924) was one of the editors of the anarchist weekly *Freedom* from 1947 to 1960. He founded *Anarchy* and edited it from 1961 to 1970. An architect, teacher, lecturer, and freelance writer, Ward significantly advanced anarchist theory in the second half of the twentieth century.

Josiah Warren (1798?–1874) was an early American anarchist theorist.

Anna Doyle Wheeler (1785–1848) was an early English socialist feminist and collaborated with William Thompson on many projects, but particularly on *Appeal of One Half of the Human Race, Women, Against the Pretensions of the Other Half, Men* [1825]).

Mary Wollstonecraft (1759–97) was one of the earliest feminist theorists.

George Woodcock (1912–95) was a British anarchist theorist who settled in Canada.

Frances Wright (1795–1852) was a lecturer and writer concerned with women's rights, slavery, and the plight of workers.

Index